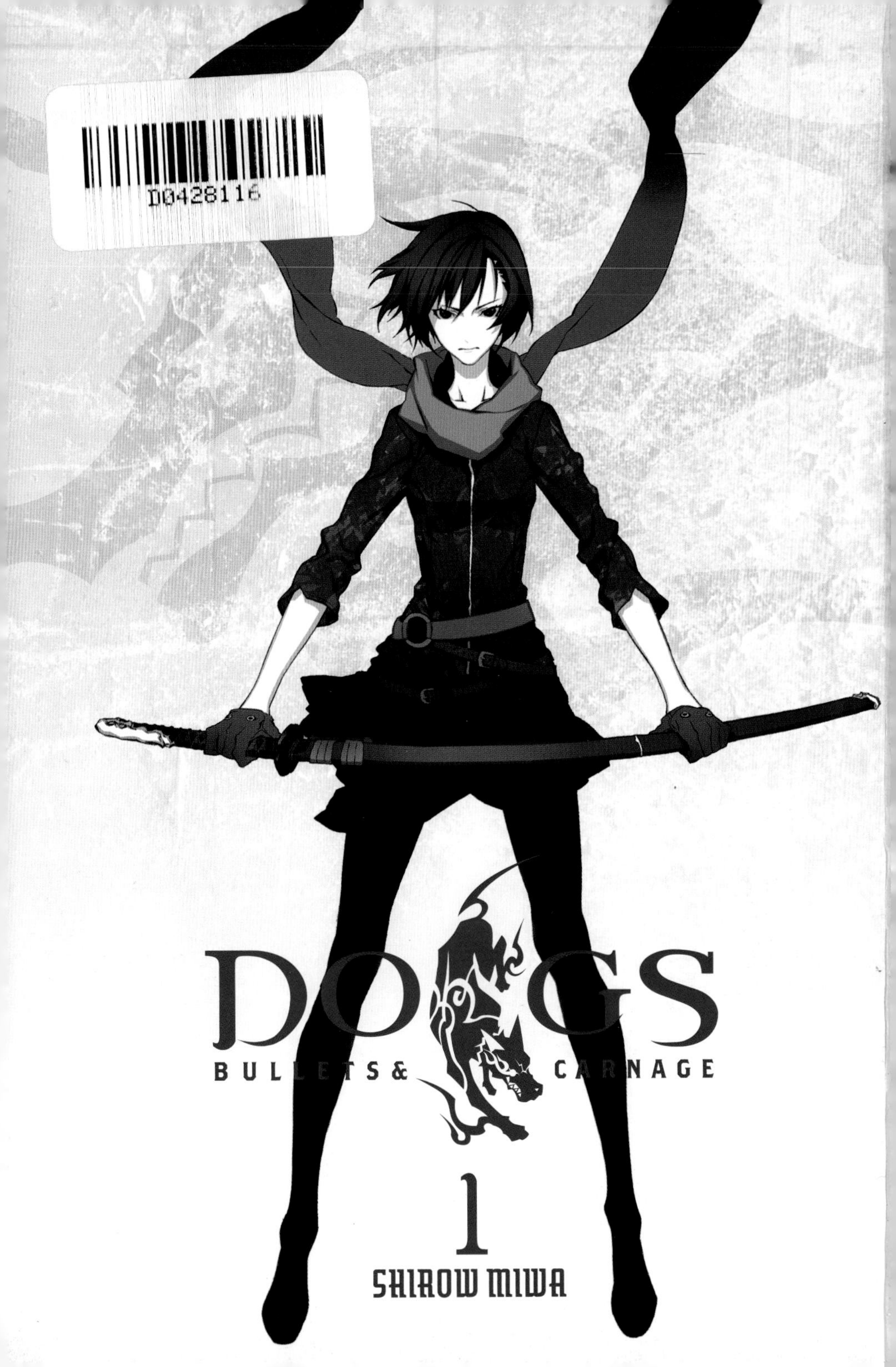

DOGS
BULLETS & CARNAGE

1

SHIROW MIWA

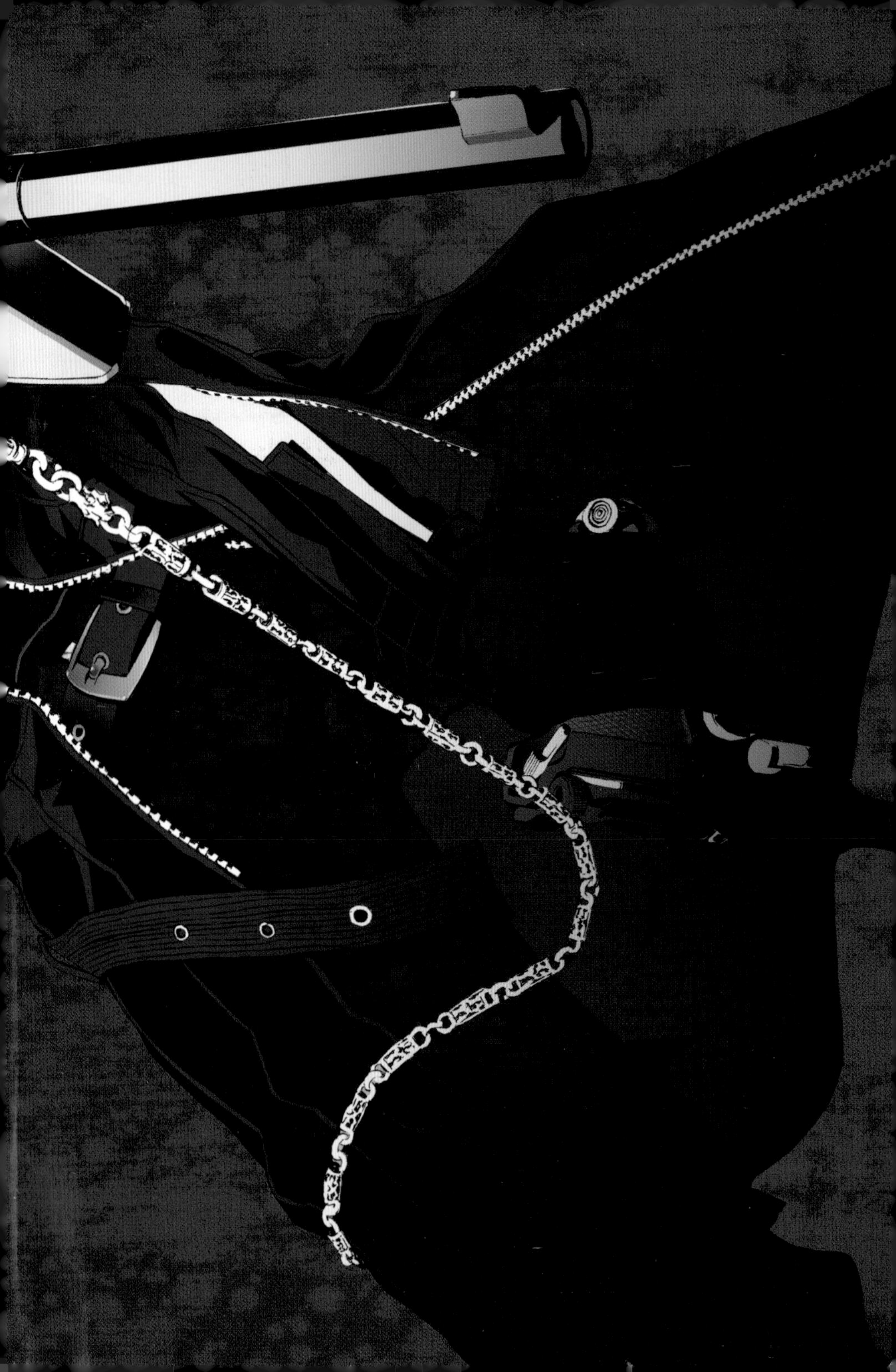

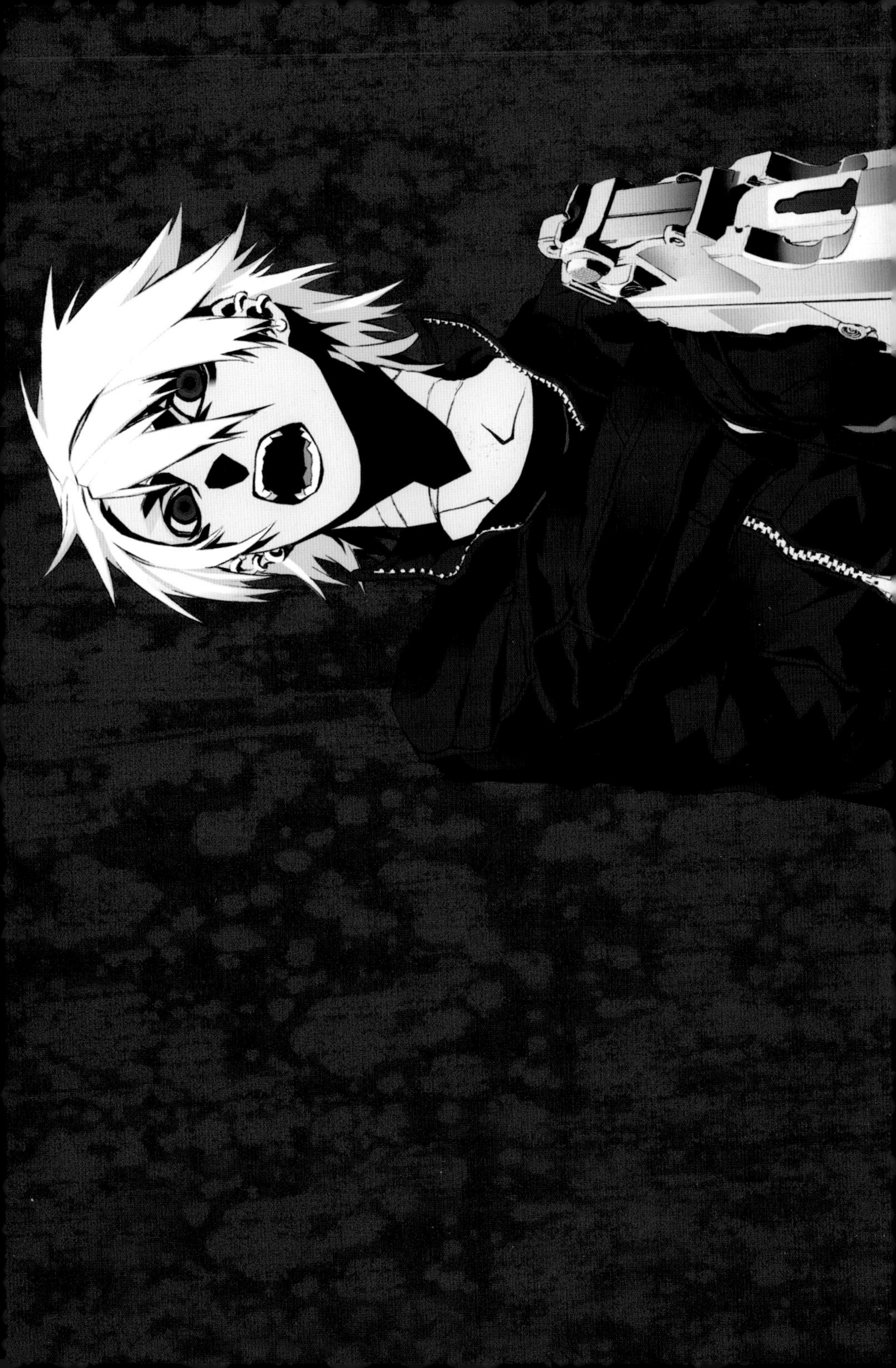

DOGS
BULLETS & CARNAGE

CONTENTS 1

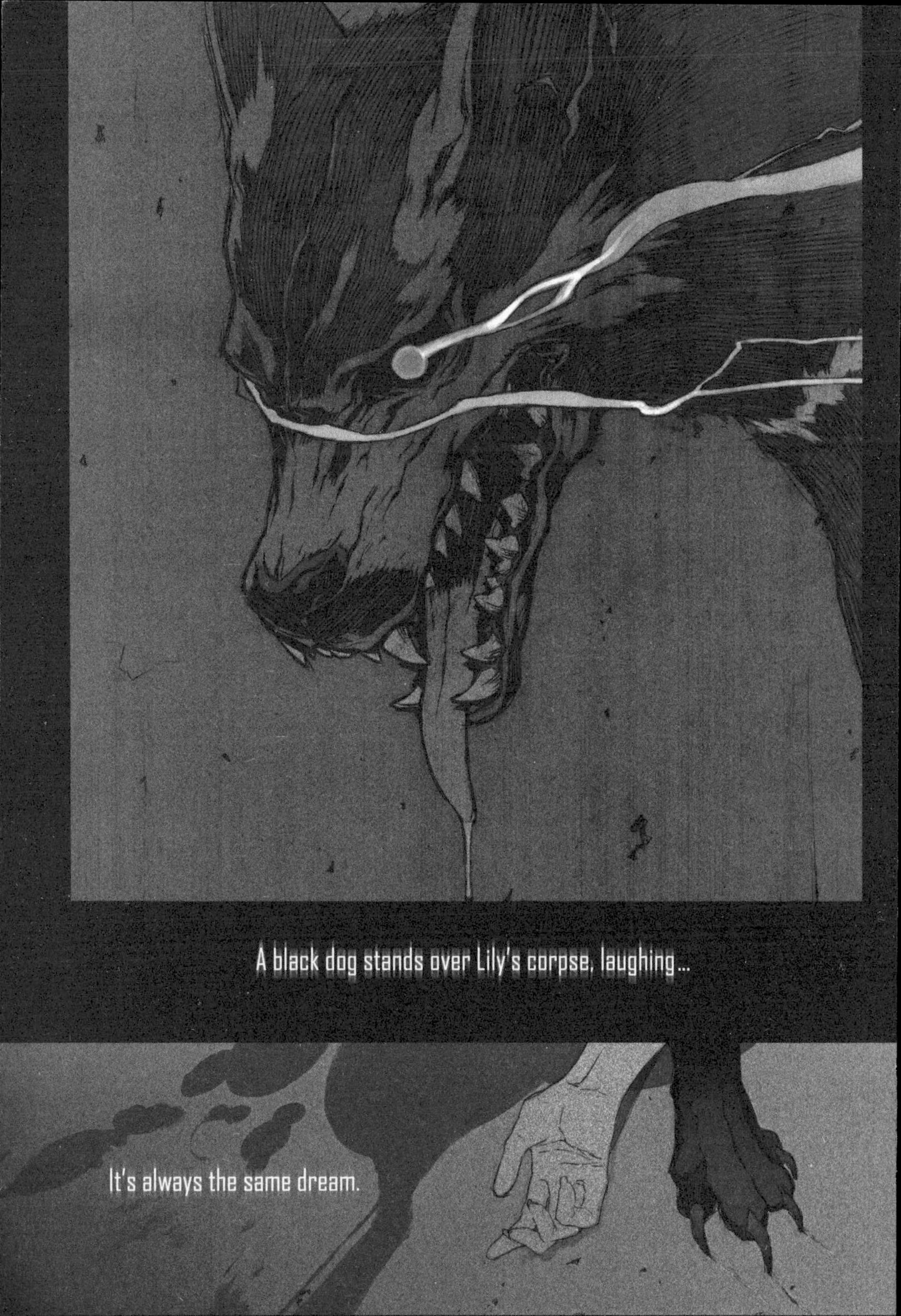
A black dog stands over Lily's corpse, laughing...
It's always the same dream.

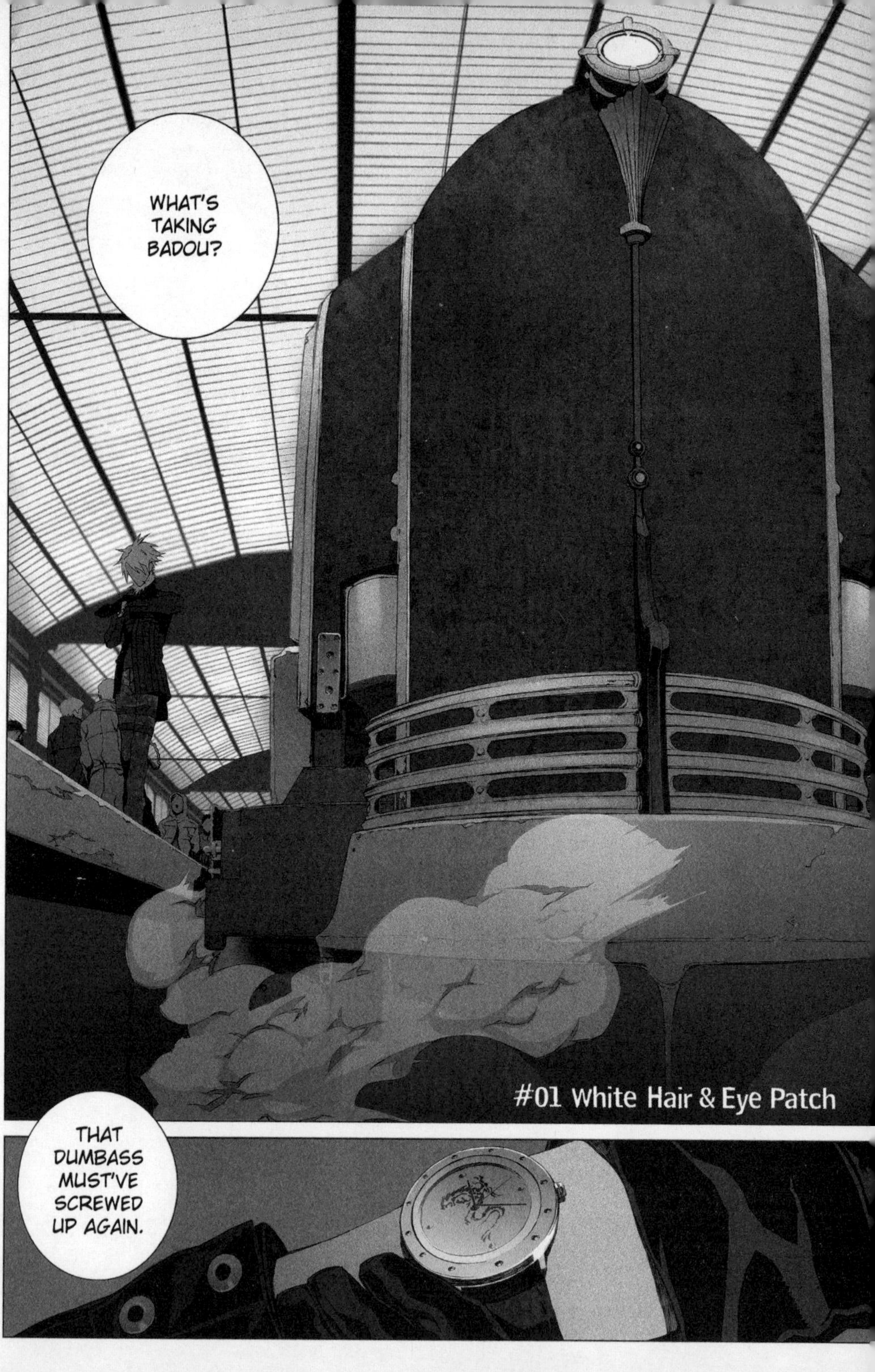
WHAT'S TAKING BADOU?
#01 White Hair & Eye Patch
THAT DUMBASS MUST'VE SCREWED UP AGAIN.

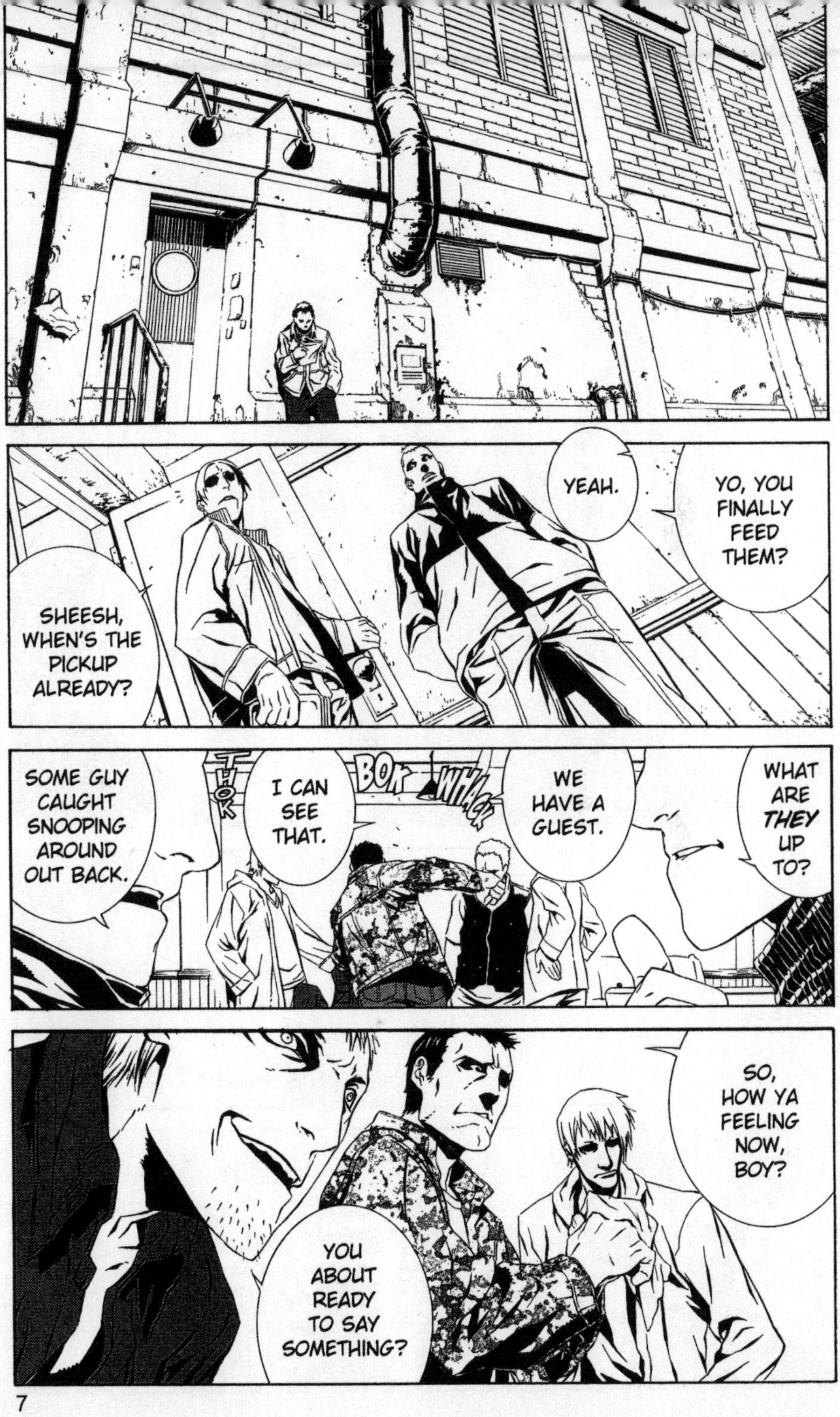
YO, YOU FINALLY FEED THEM?
YEAH.
SHEESH, WHEN'S THE PICKUP ALREADY?
WHAT ARE *THEY* UP TO?
WE HAVE A GUEST.
WHACK
BOK
THOK
I CAN SEE THAT.
SOME GUY CAUGHT SNOOPING AROUND OUT BACK.
SO, HOW YA FEELING NOW, BOY?
YOU ABOUT READY TO SAY SOMETHING?

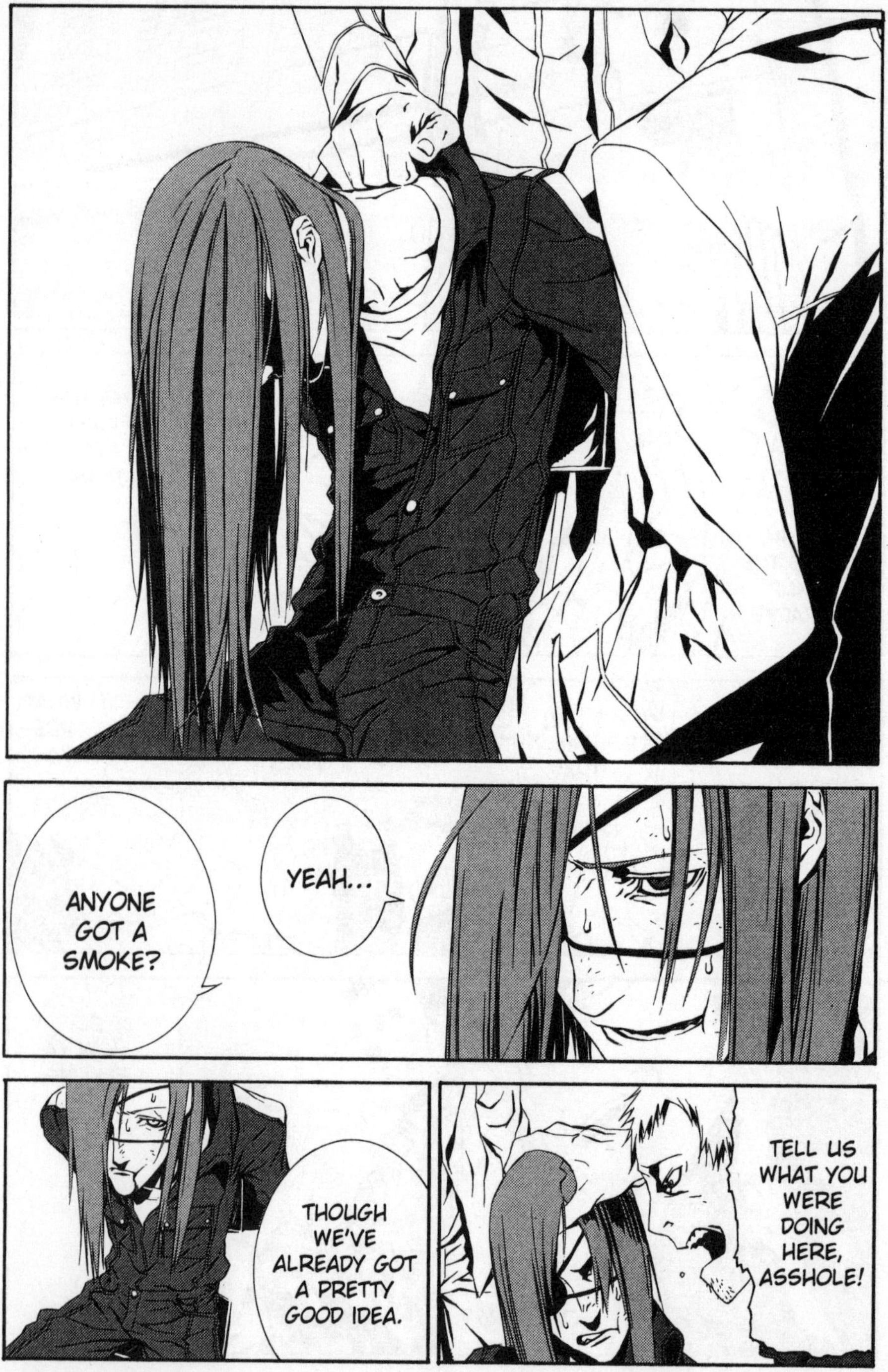
YEAH...
ANYONE GOT A SMOKE?
TELL US WHAT YOU WERE DOING HERE, ASSHOLE!
THOUGH WE'VE ALREADY GOT A PRETTY GOOD IDEA.

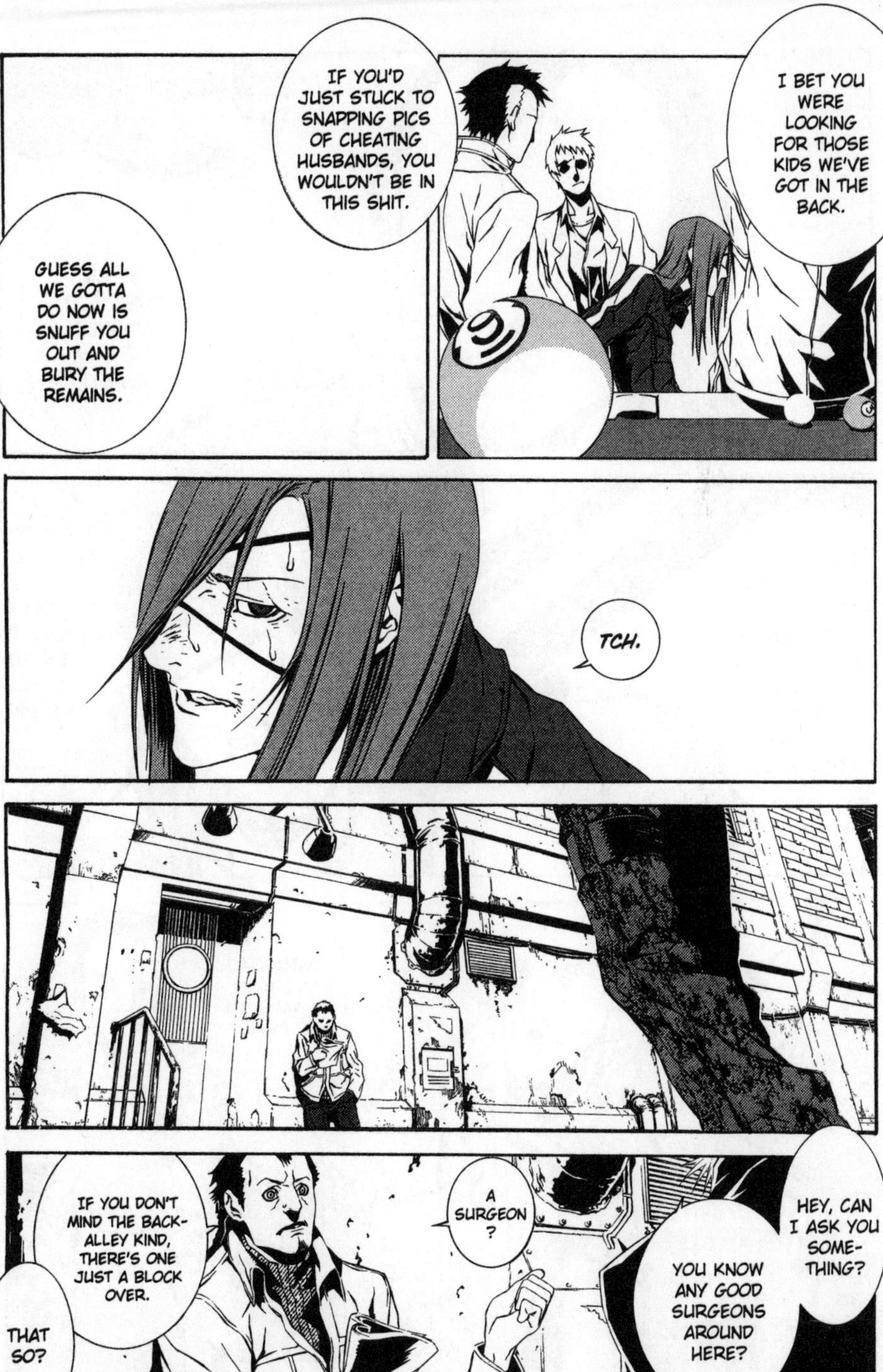
I BET YOU WERE LOOKING FOR THOSE KIDS WE'VE GOT IN THE BACK.
IF YOU'D JUST STUCK TO SNAPPING PICS OF CHEATING HUSBANDS, YOU WOULDN'T BE IN THIS SHIT.
GUESS ALL WE GOTTA DO NOW IS SNUFF YOU OUT AND BURY THE REMAINS.
TCH.
HEY, CAN I ASK YOU SOME-THING?
YOU KNOW ANY GOOD SURGEONS AROUND HERE?
A SURGEON?
IF YOU DON'T MIND THE BACK-ALLEY KIND, THERE'S ONE JUST A BLOCK OVER.
THAT SO?

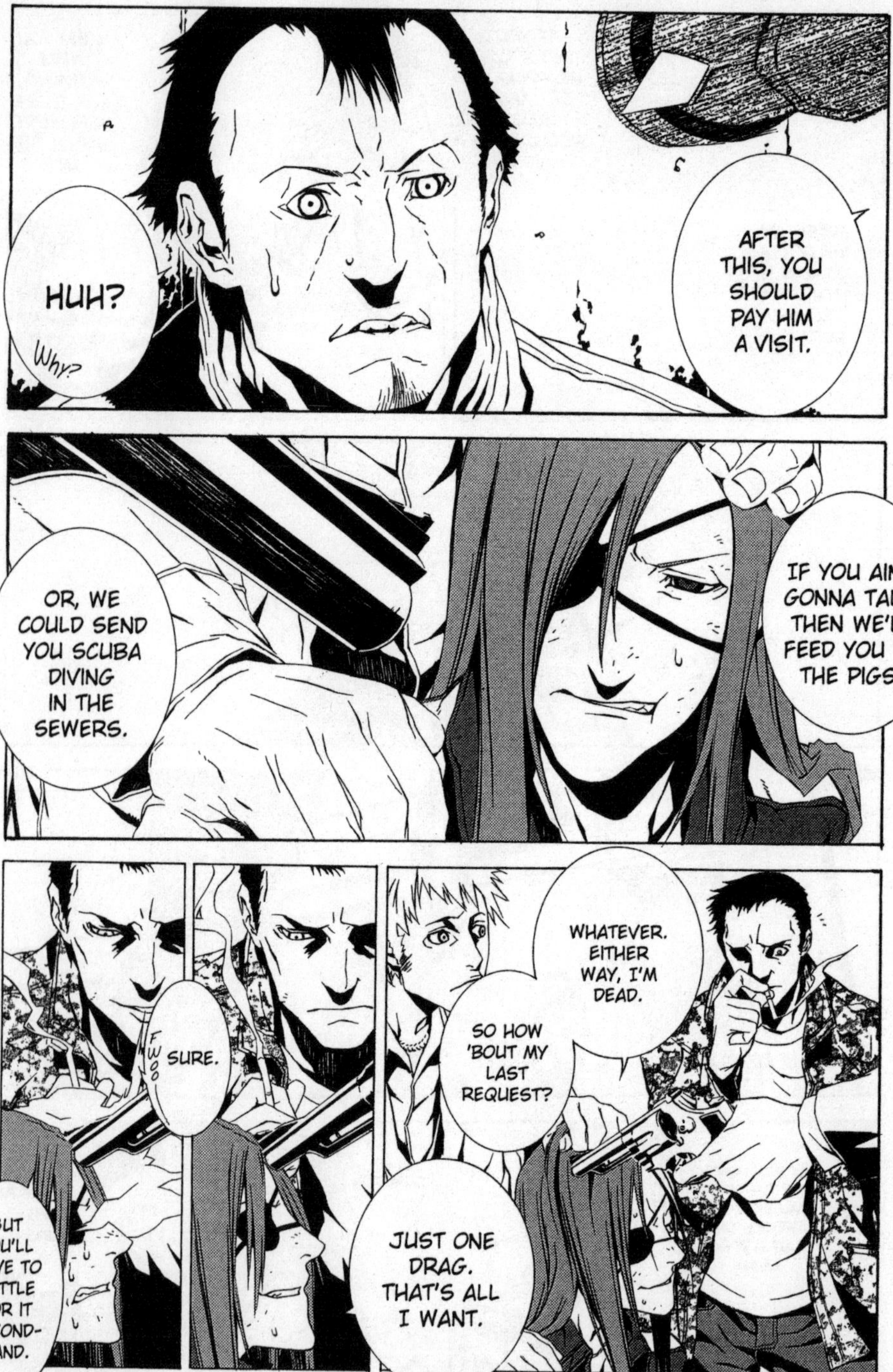
AFTER THIS, YOU SHOULD PAY HIM A VISIT.
HUH?
Why?
IF YOU AIN'T GONNA TALK, THEN WE'LL FEED YOU TO THE PIGS.
OR, WE COULD SEND YOU SCUBA DIVING IN THE SEWERS.
WHATEVER. EITHER WAY, I'M DEAD.
SO HOW 'BOUT MY LAST REQUEST?
JUST ONE DRAG. THAT'S ALL I WANT.
FWOO
SURE.
BUT YOU'LL HAVE TO SETTLE FOR IT SECOND-HAND.

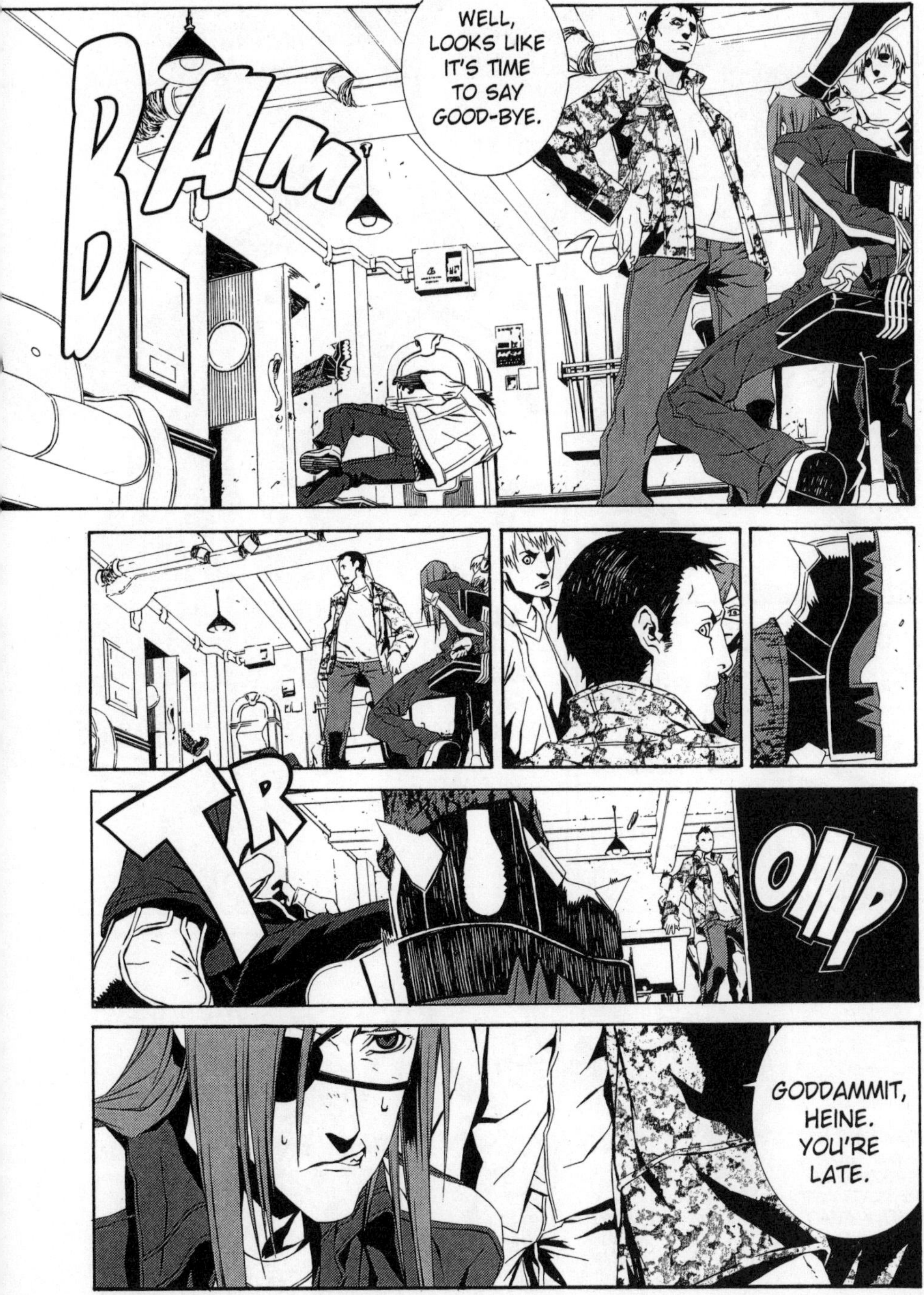
WELL, LOOKS LIKE IT'S TIME TO SAY GOOD-BYE.
BAM
TR
OMP
GODDAMMIT, HEINE. YOU'RE LATE.

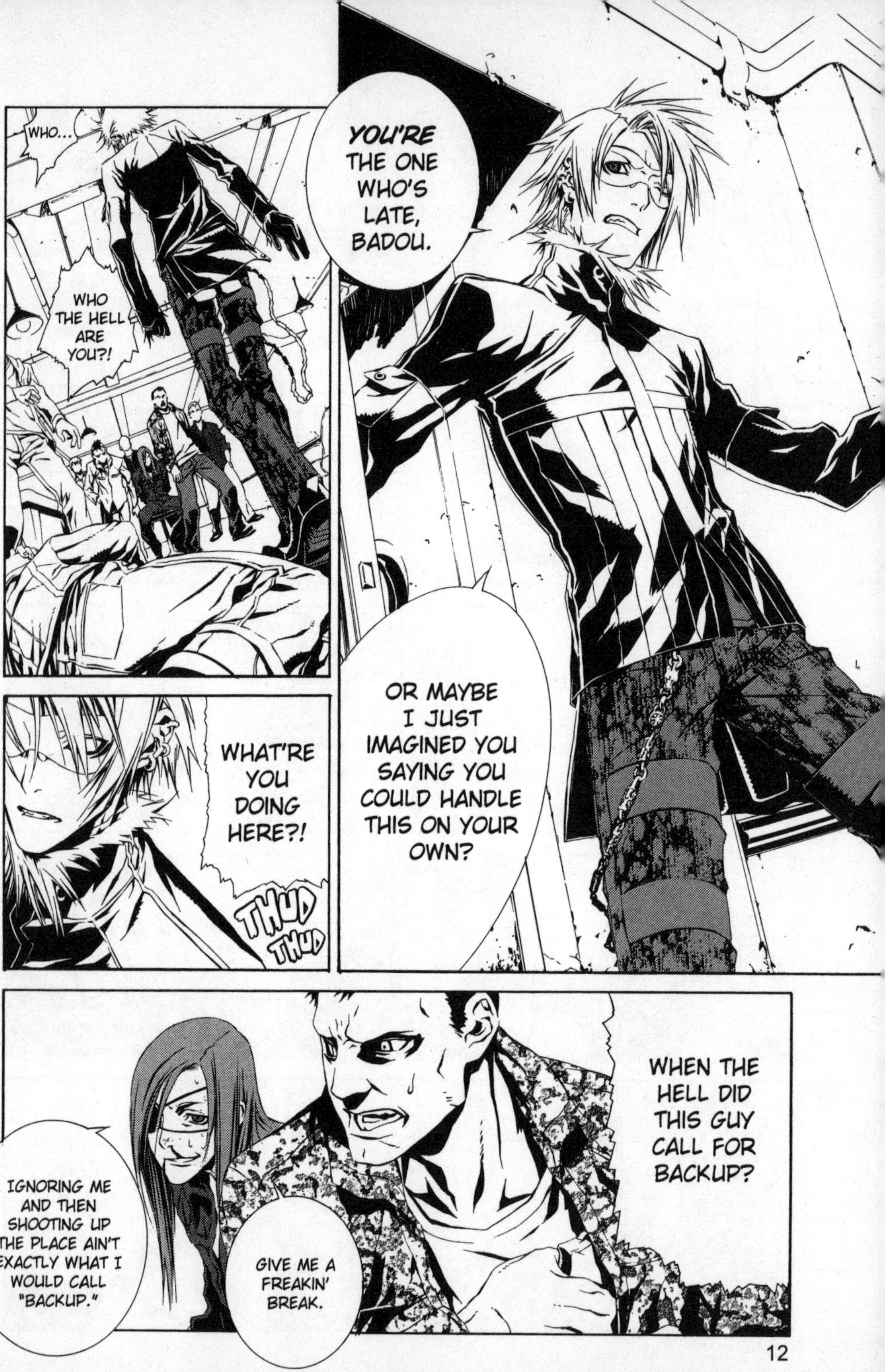
YOU'RE THE ONE WHO'S LATE, BADOU.
OR MAYBE I JUST IMAGINED YOU SAYING YOU COULD HANDLE THIS ON YOUR OWN?
WHO...
WHO THE HELL ARE YOU?!
WHAT'RE YOU DOING HERE?!
THUD THUD
WHEN THE HELL DID THIS GUY CALL FOR BACKUP?
GIVE ME A FREAKIN' BREAK.
IGNORING ME AND THEN SHOOTING UP THE PLACE AIN'T EXACTLY WHAT I WOULD CALL "BACKUP."

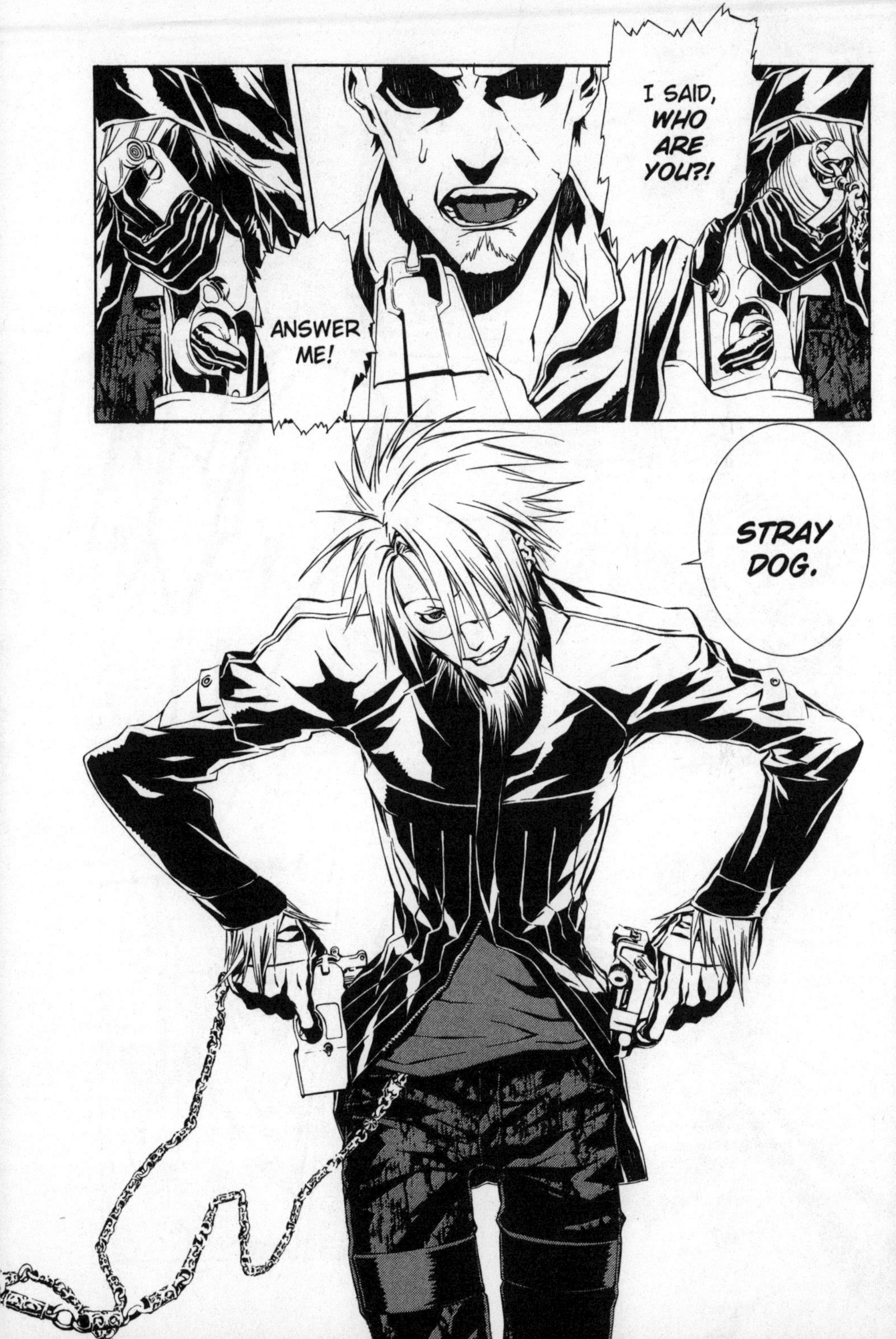
I SAID, WHO ARE YOU?!
ANSWER ME!
STRAY DOG.

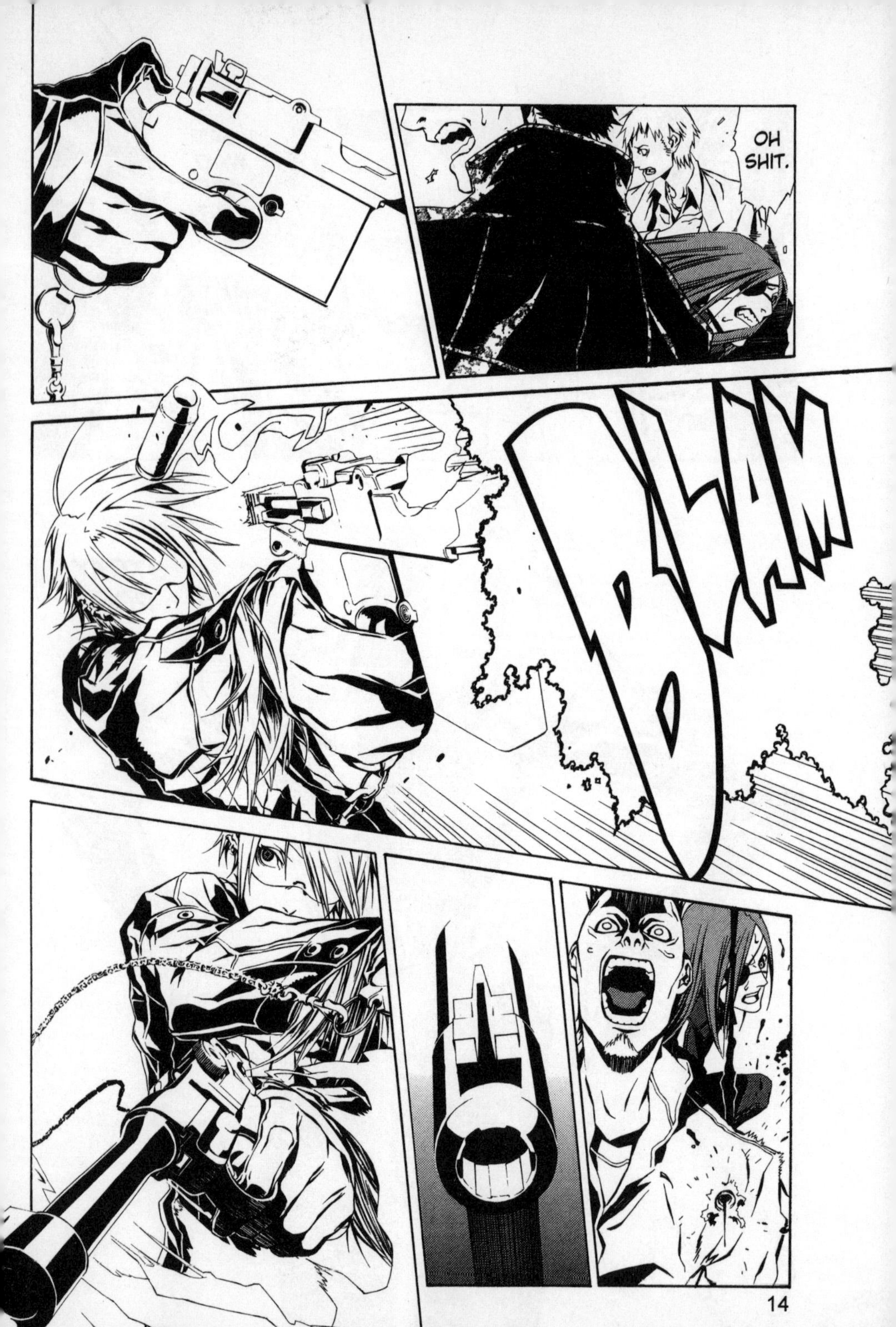
OH SHIT.
BLAM

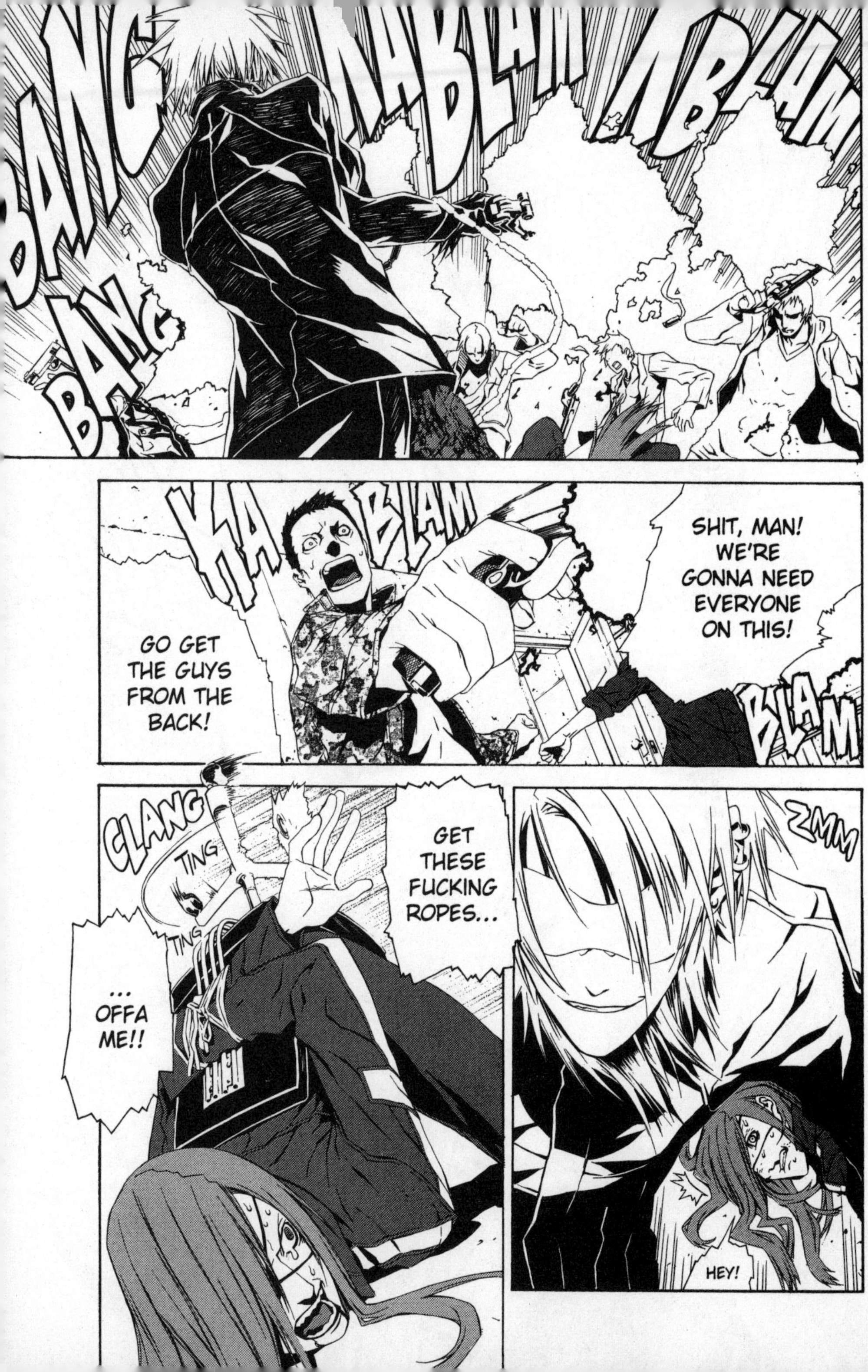
KABLAM
KABLAM
BANG
BANG
SHIT, MAN! WE'RE GONNA NEED EVERYONE ON THIS!
BLAM
KABLAM
GO GET THE GUYS FROM THE BACK!
ZMM
HEY!
GET THESE FUCKING ROPES...
CLANG
TING
TING
... OFFA ME!!

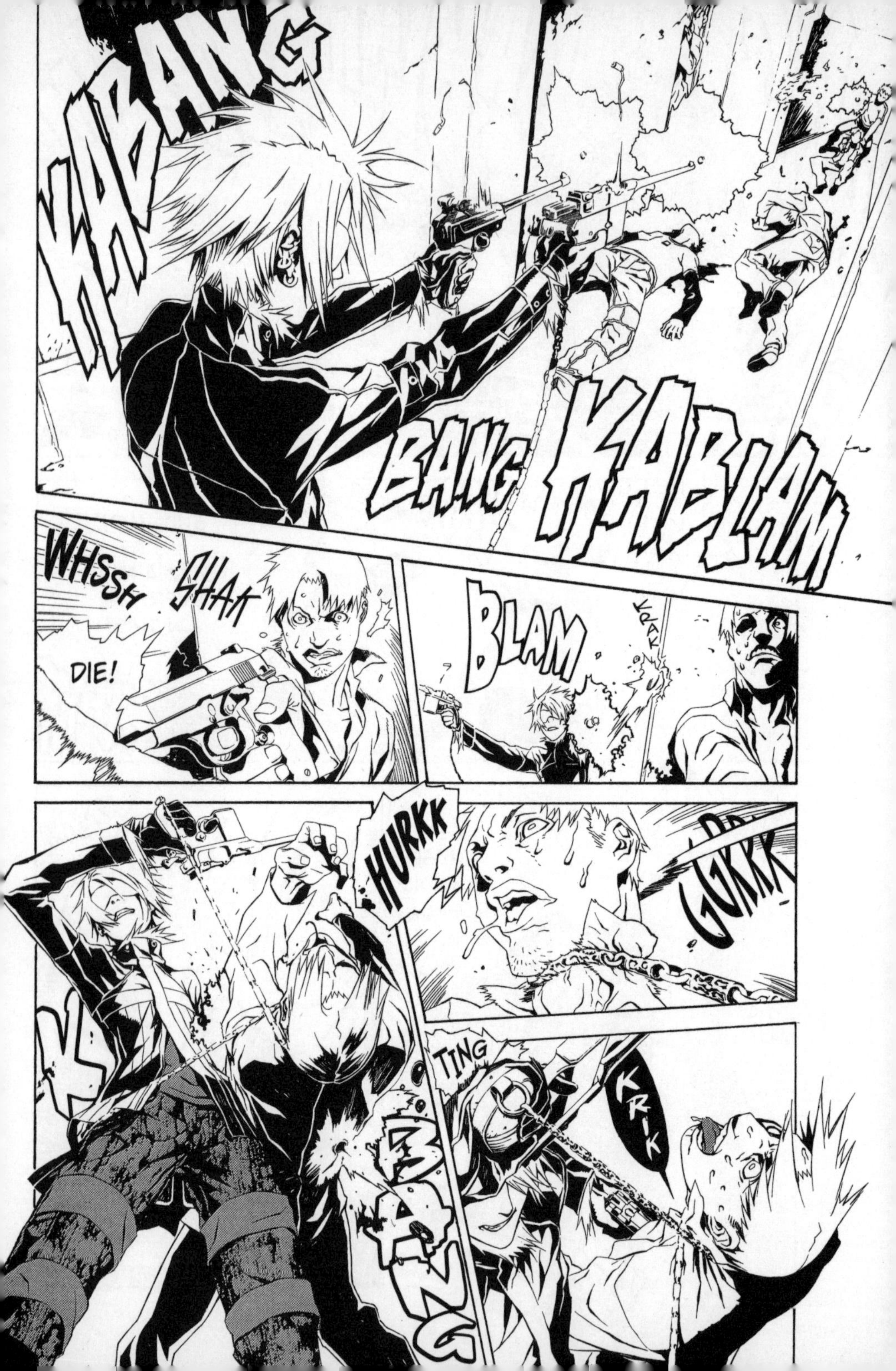
KABANG
BANG
KABLAM
BLAM
KRAK
SHAK
WHSSH
DIE!
GRKK
HURKK
TING
KRIK
BANG

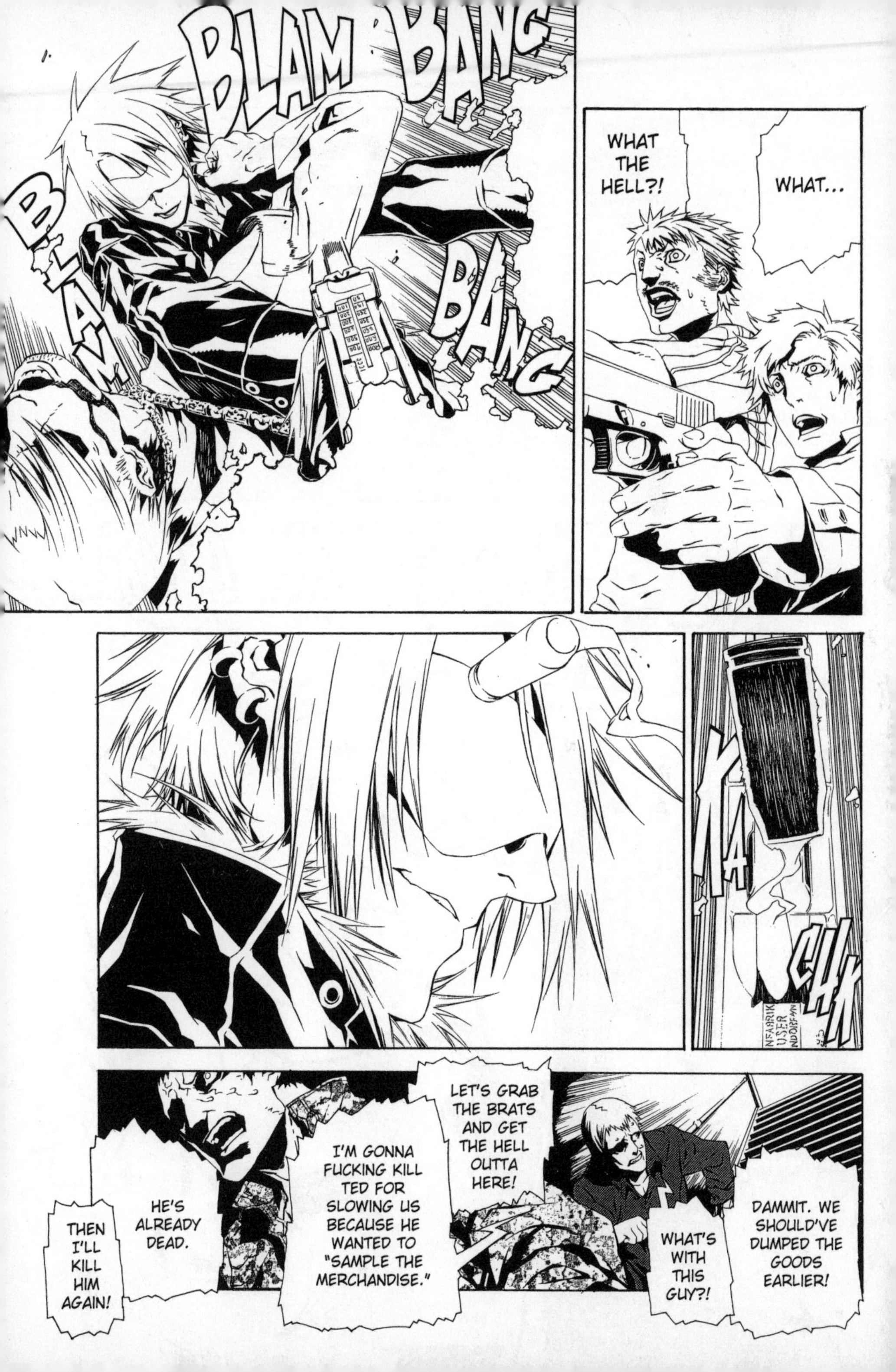

WHAT...
WHAT THE HELL?!
BANG
BLAM
BANG
BLAM
KA
CHK
DAMMIT. WE SHOULD'VE DUMPED THE GOODS EARLIER!
WHAT'S WITH THIS GUY?!
LET'S GRAB THE BRATS AND GET THE HELL OUTTA HERE!
I'M GONNA FUCKING KILL TED FOR SLOWING US BECAUSE HE WANTED TO "SAMPLE THE MERCHANDISE."
HE'S ALREADY DEAD.
THEN I'LL KILL HIM AGAIN!

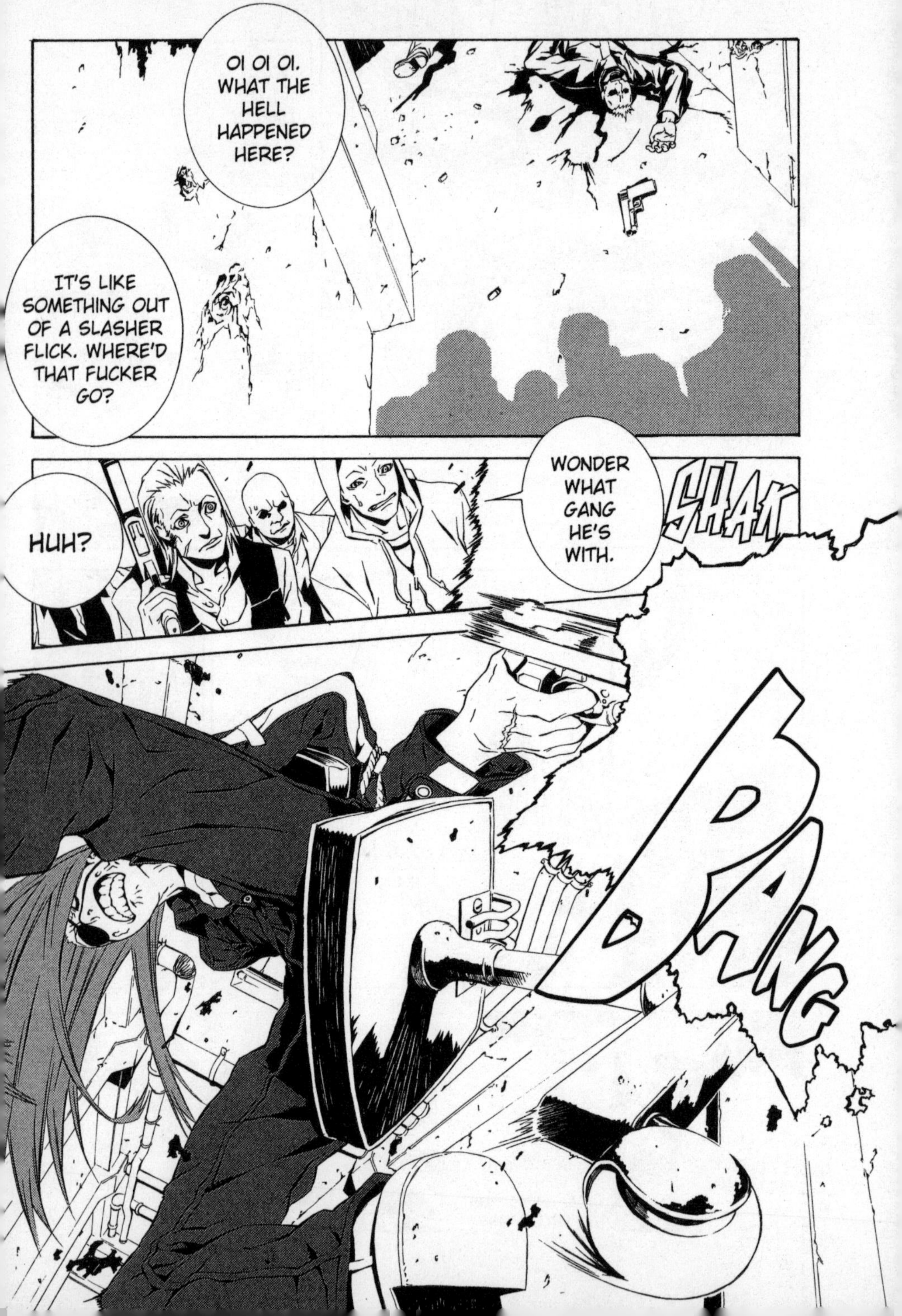
OI OI OI. WHAT THE HELL HAPPENED HERE?
IT'S LIKE SOMETHING OUT OF A SLASHER FLICK. WHERE'D THAT FUCKER GO?
WONDER WHAT GANG HE'S WITH.
SHAK
HUH?
BANG

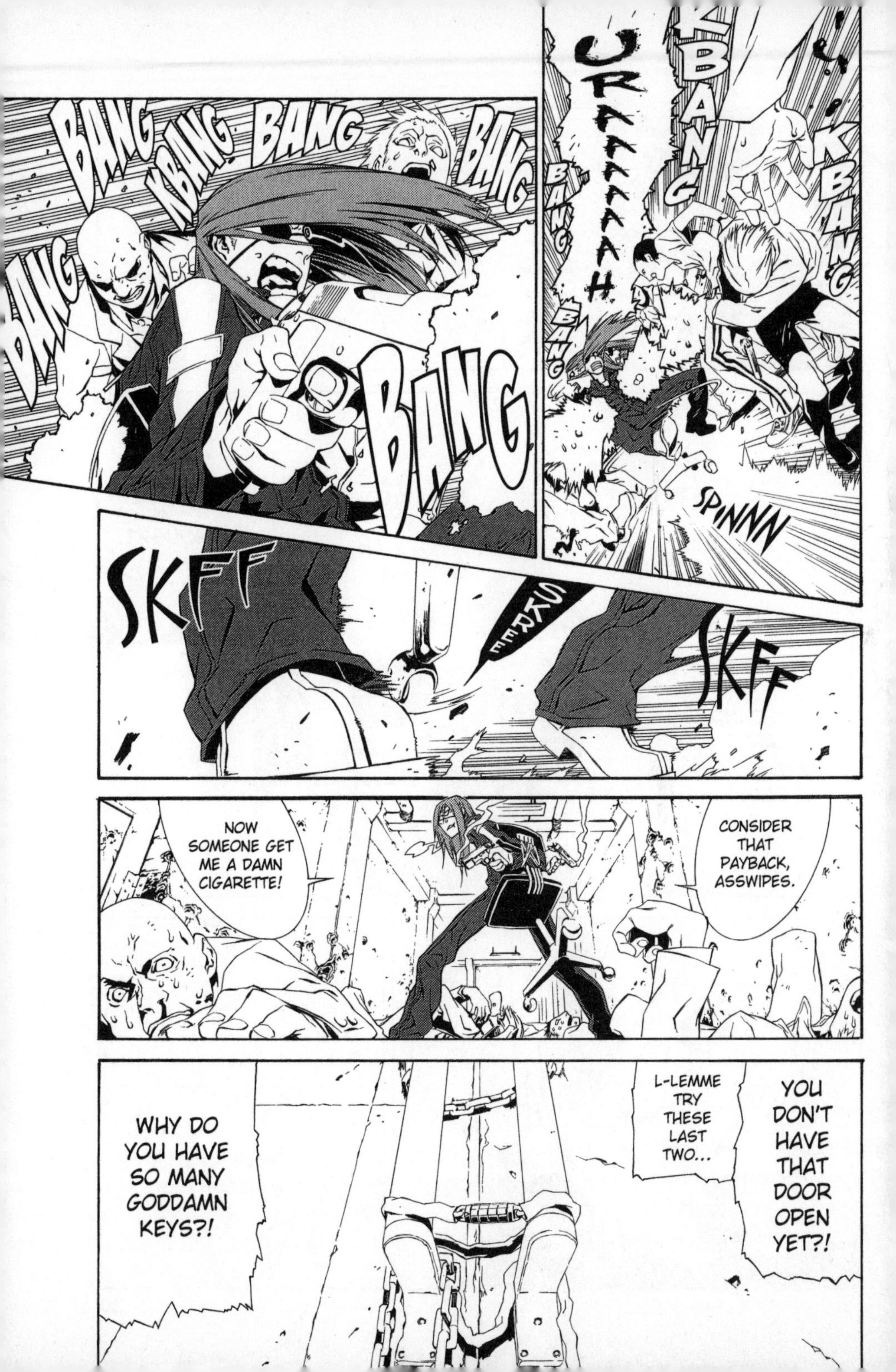

KBANG
URAFFFFAAH
KBANG
BANG
BANG
SPINNN
BANG
BANG
KBANG
BANG
BANG
BANG
SKFF
SKREE
SKFF
CONSIDER THAT PAYBACK, ASSWIPES.
NOW SOMEONE GET ME A DAMN CIGARETTE!
YOU DON'T HAVE THAT DOOR OPEN YET?!
L-LEMME TRY THESE LAST TWO...
WHY DO YOU HAVE SO MANY GODDAMN KEYS?!

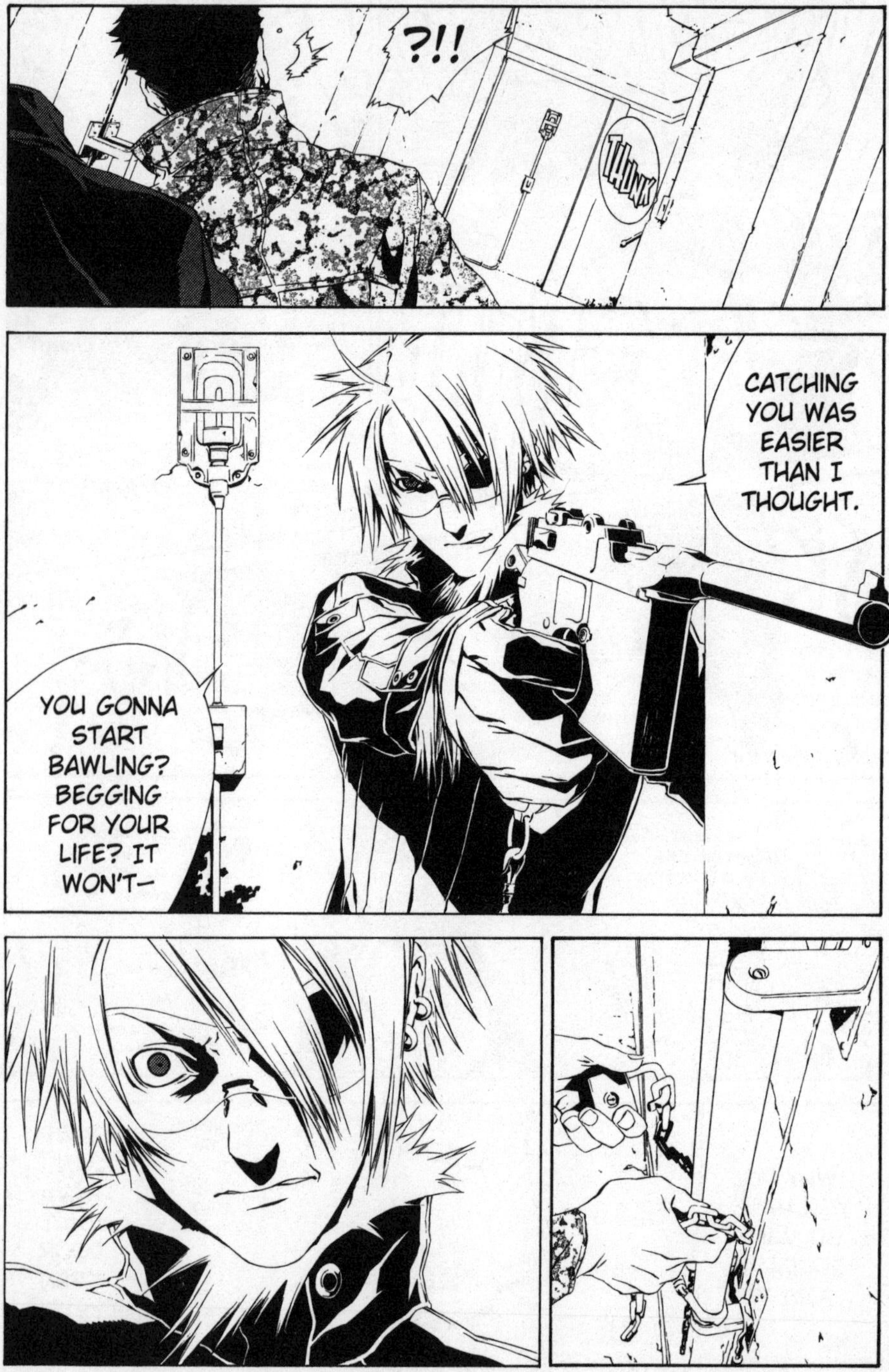
?!!
THINK
CATCHING YOU WAS EASIER THAN I THOUGHT.
YOU GONNA START BAWLING? BEGGING FOR YOUR LIFE? IT WON'T–

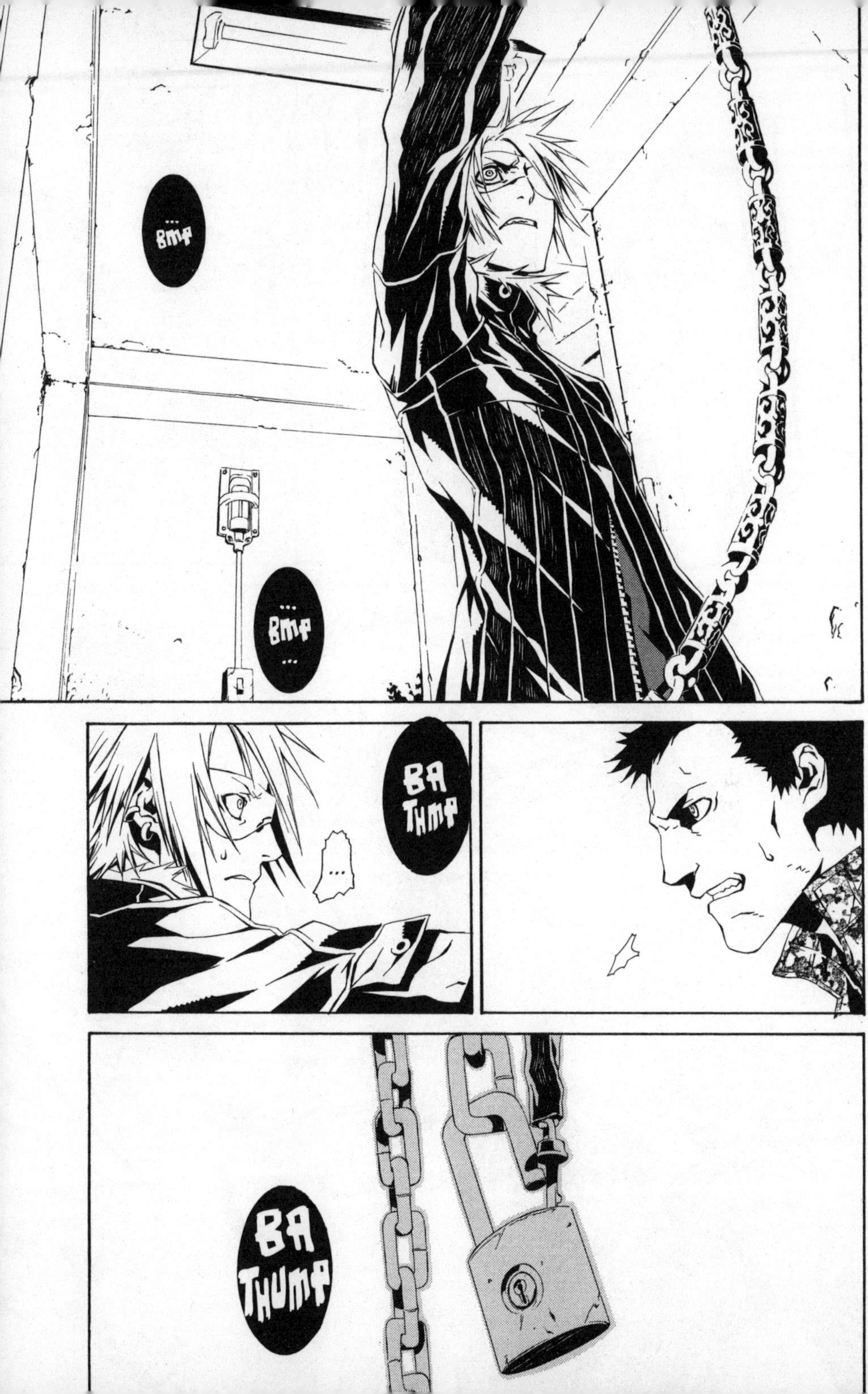
...
BMP
...
BMP
...
BA THUMP
...
BA THUMP

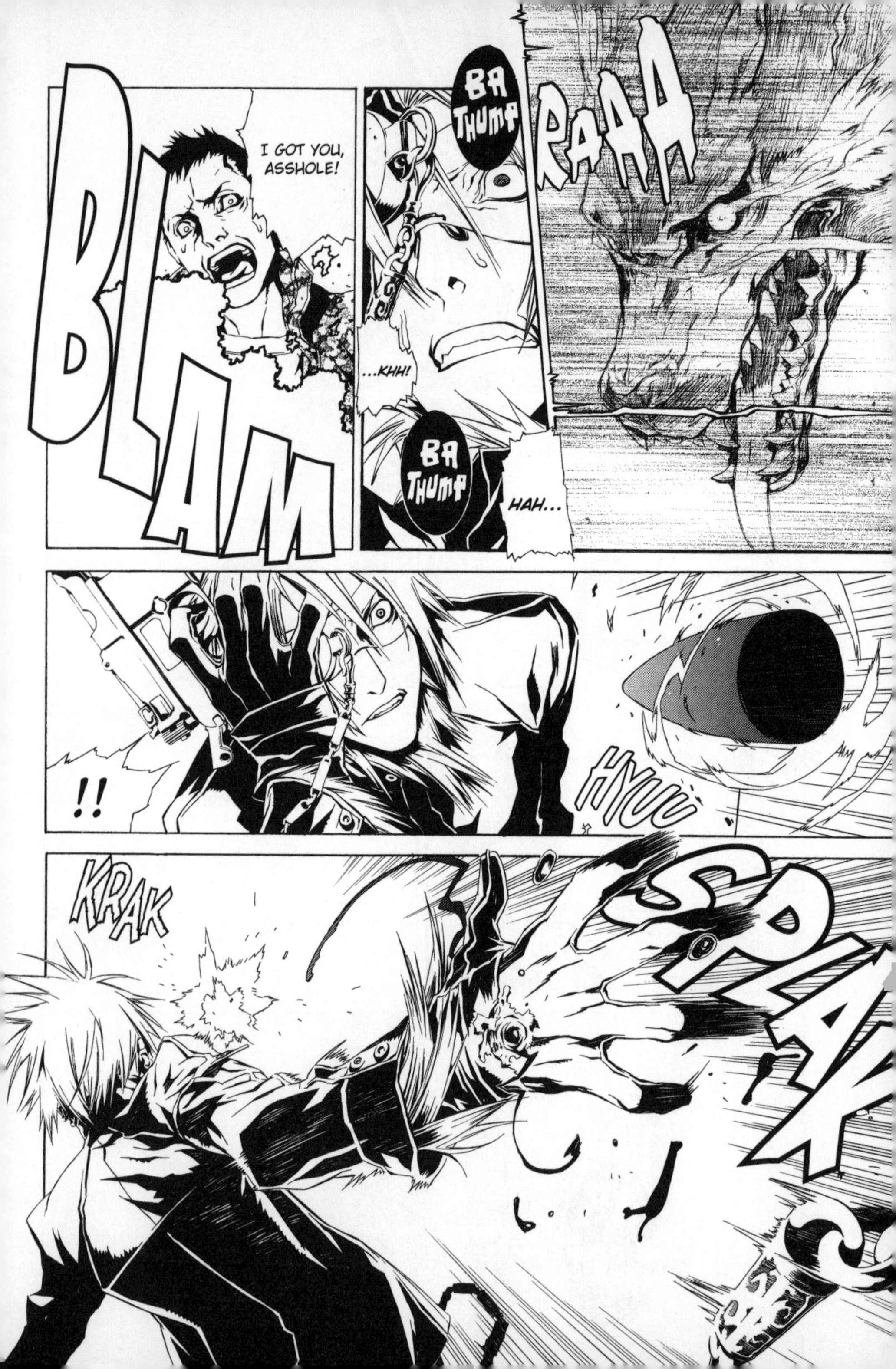
RAAA
BA THUMP
...KHH!
BA THUMP
HAH...
I GOT YOU, ASSHOLE!
BLAM
HYUU
!!
SPLAK
KRAK

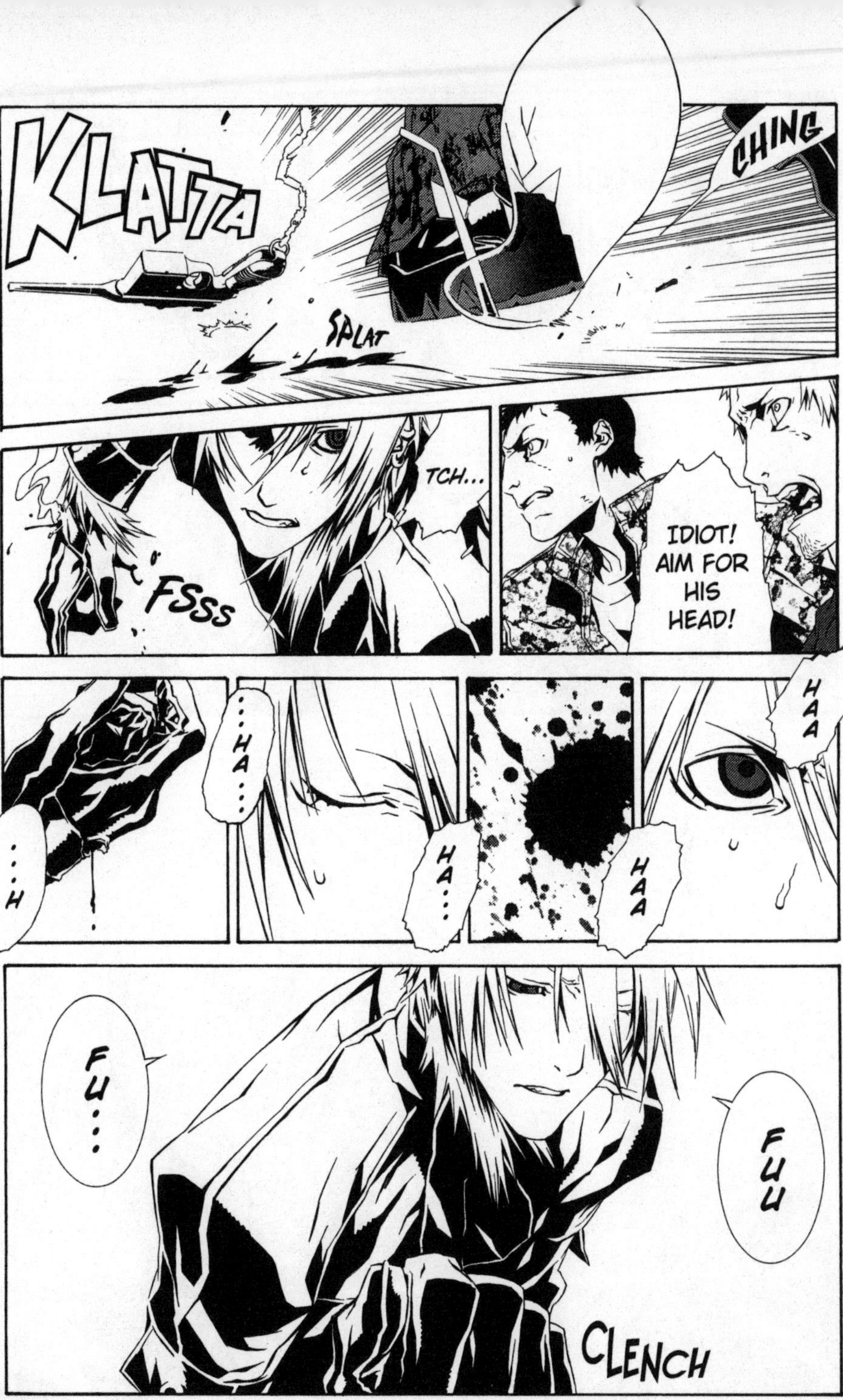
CHING
KLATTA
SPLAT
IDIOT! AIM FOR HIS HEAD!
TCH...
FSSS
HAA
HAA
HA...
...HA...
...H
FUU
FU...
CLENCH

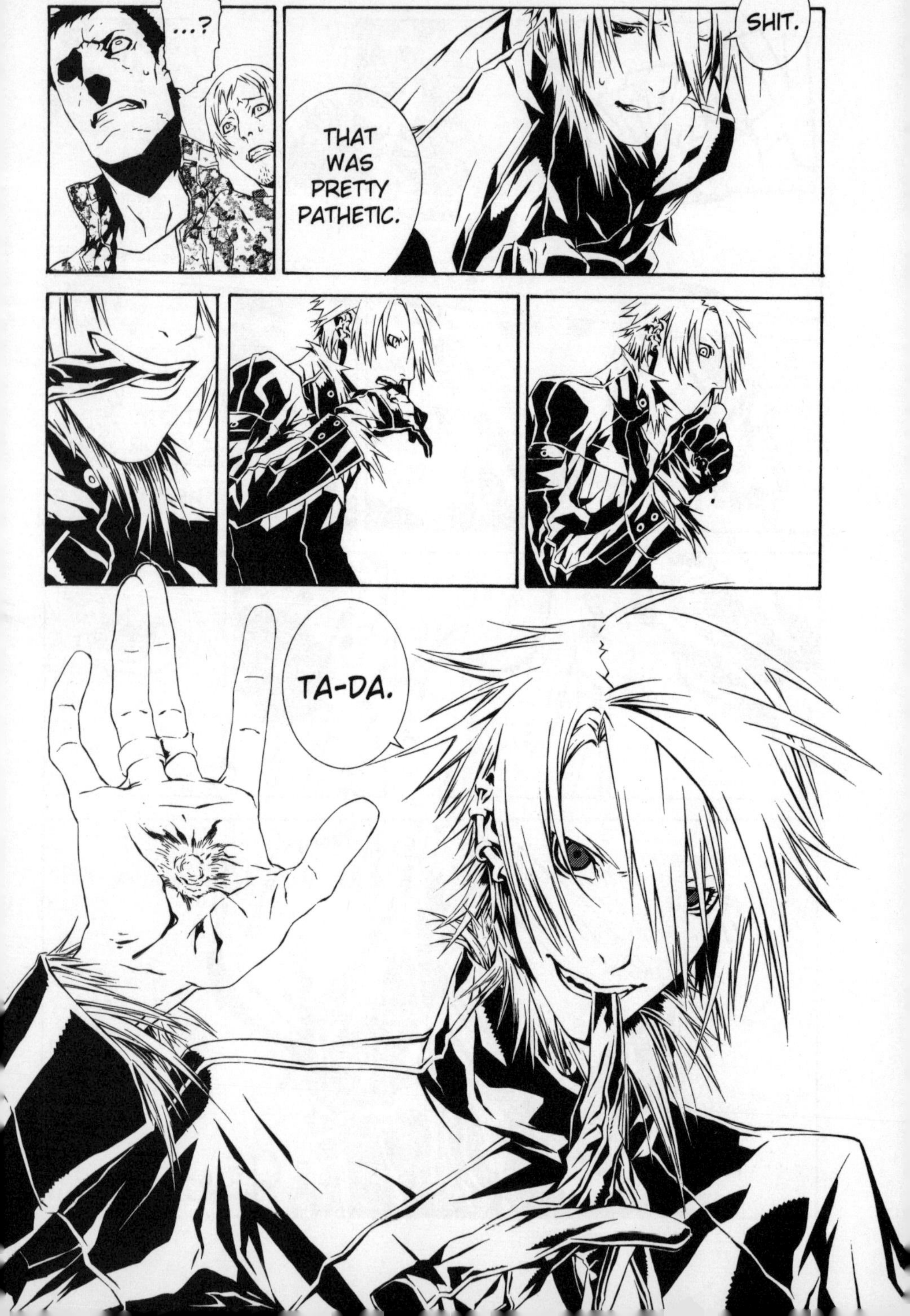
SHIT.
THAT WAS PRETTY PATHETIC.
...?
TA-DA.

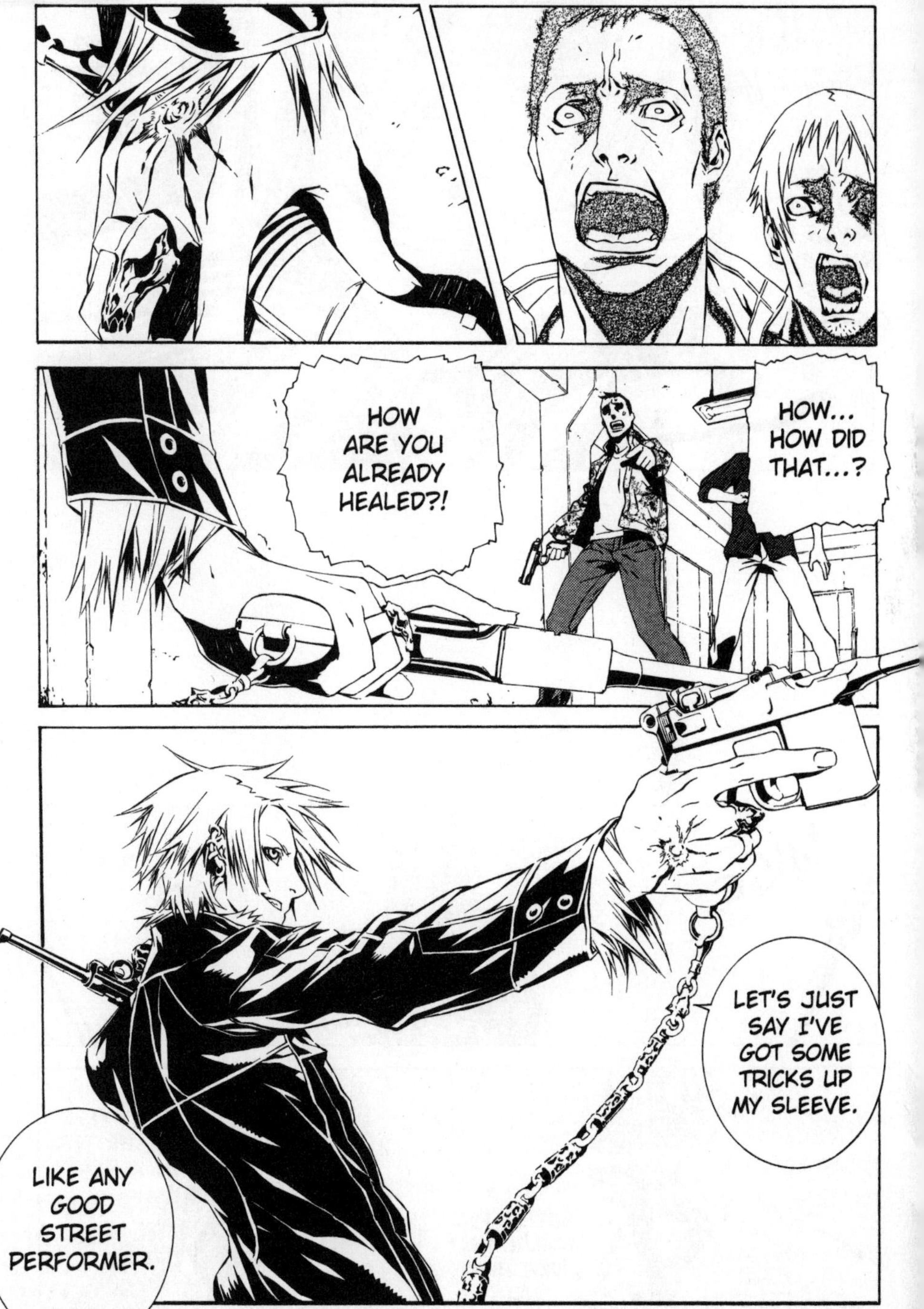
HOW... HOW DID THAT...?
HOW ARE YOU ALREADY HEALED?!
LET'S JUST SAY I'VE GOT SOME TRICKS UP MY SLEEVE.
LIKE ANY GOOD STREET PERFORMER.

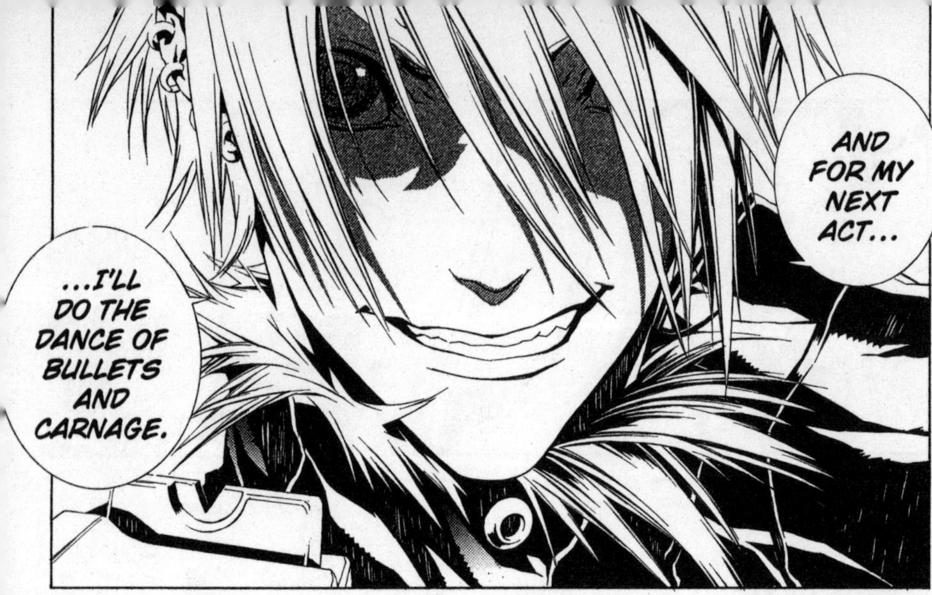
AND FOR MY NEXT ACT...
...I'LL DO THE DANCE OF BULLETS AND CARNAGE.

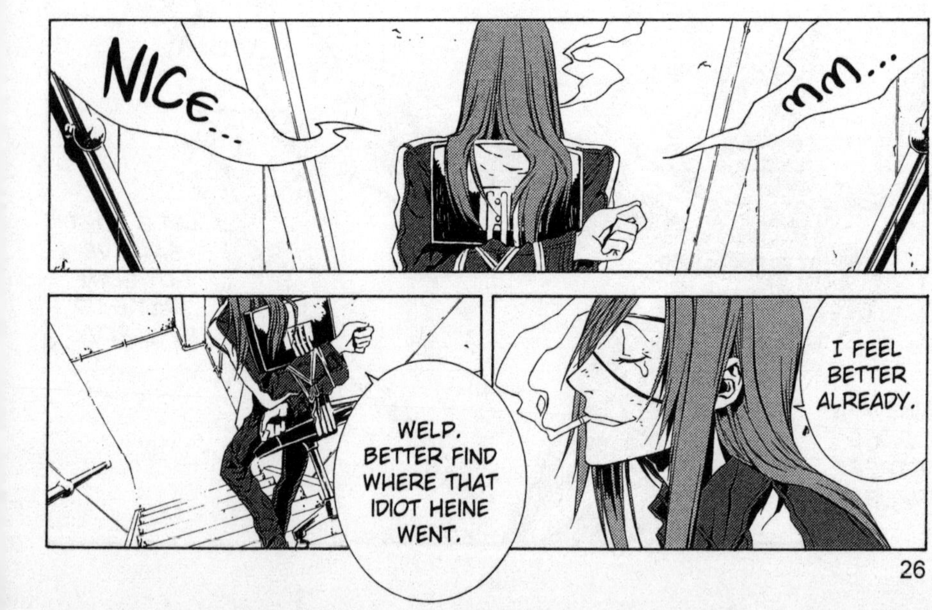
MM...
NICE...
I FEEL BETTER ALREADY.
WELP. BETTER FIND WHERE THAT IDIOT HEINE WENT.

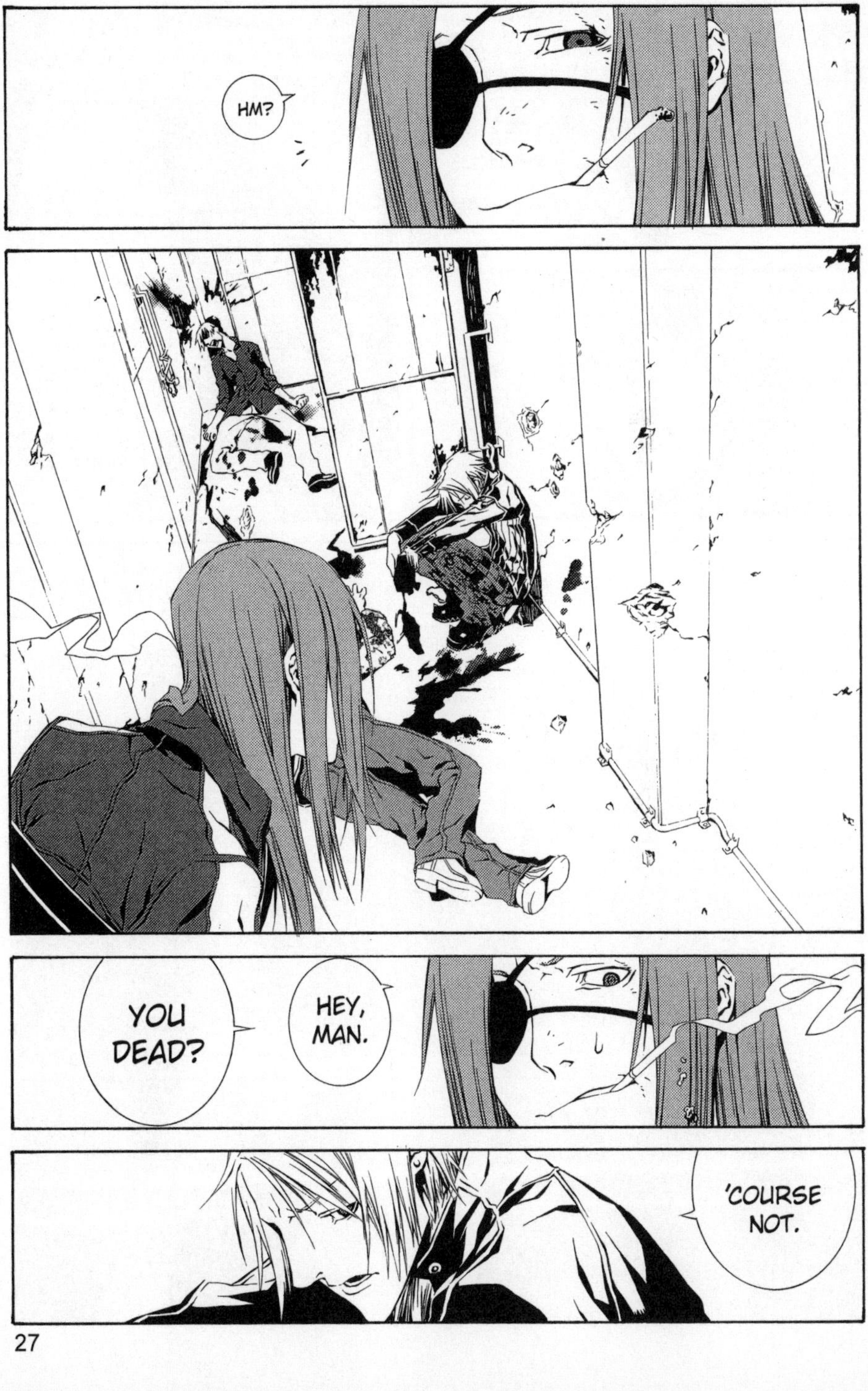
HM?
HEY, MAN.
YOU DEAD?
'COURSE NOT.

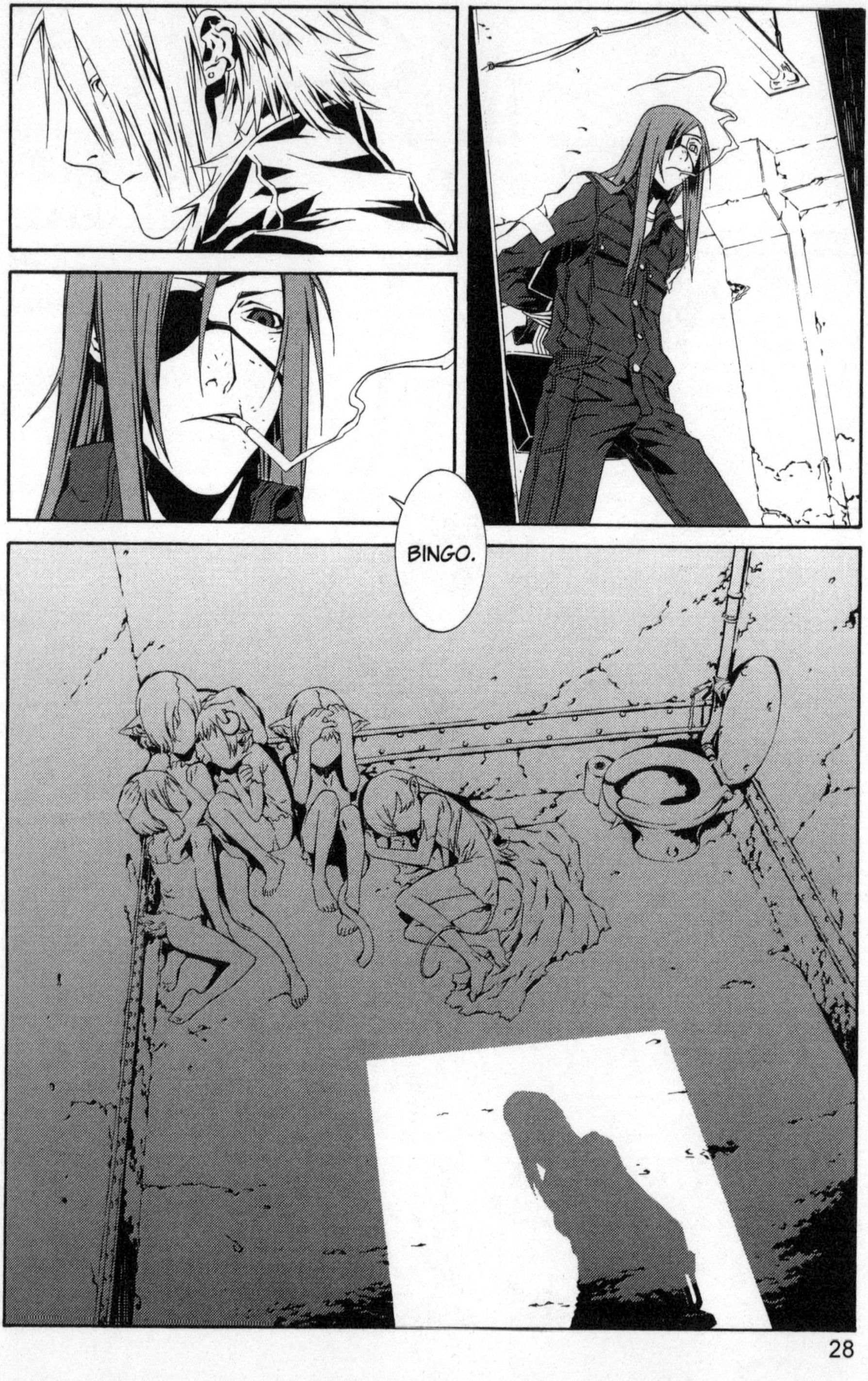
BINGO.

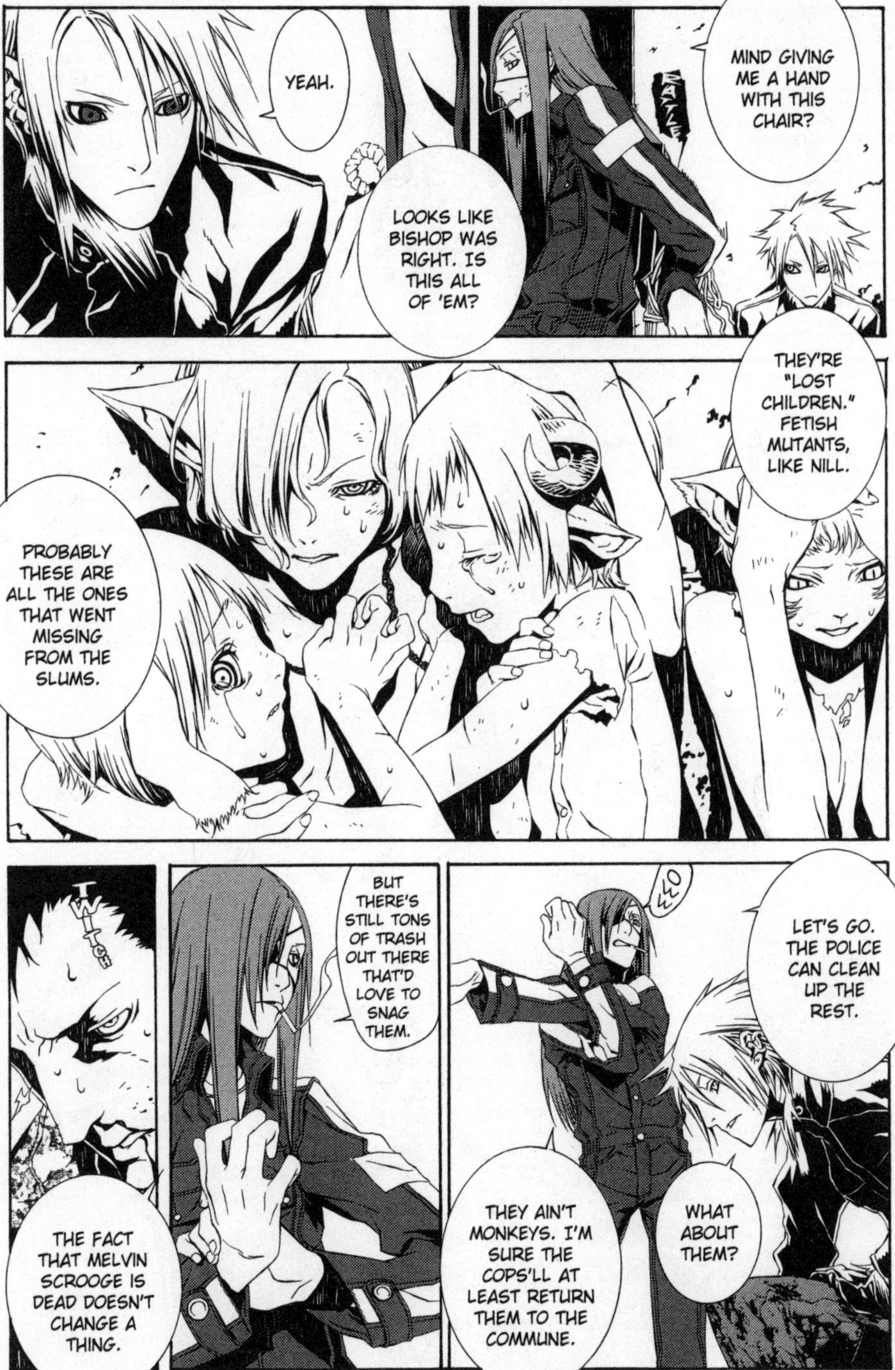
MIND GIVING ME A HAND WITH THIS CHAIR?
LOOKS LIKE BISHOP WAS RIGHT. IS THIS ALL OF 'EM?
YEAH.
THEY'RE "LOST CHILDREN." FETISH MUTANTS, LIKE NILL.
PROBABLY THESE ARE ALL THE ONES THAT WENT MISSING FROM THE SLUMS.
LET'S GO. THE POLICE CAN CLEAN UP THE REST.
WHAT ABOUT THEM?
THEY AIN'T MONKEYS. I'M SURE THE COPS'LL AT LEAST RETURN THEM TO THE COMMUNE.
BUT THERE'S STILL TONS OF TRASH OUT THERE THAT'D LOVE TO SNAG THEM.
TWITCH
THE FACT THAT MELVIN SCROOGE IS DEAD DOESN'T CHANGE A THING.

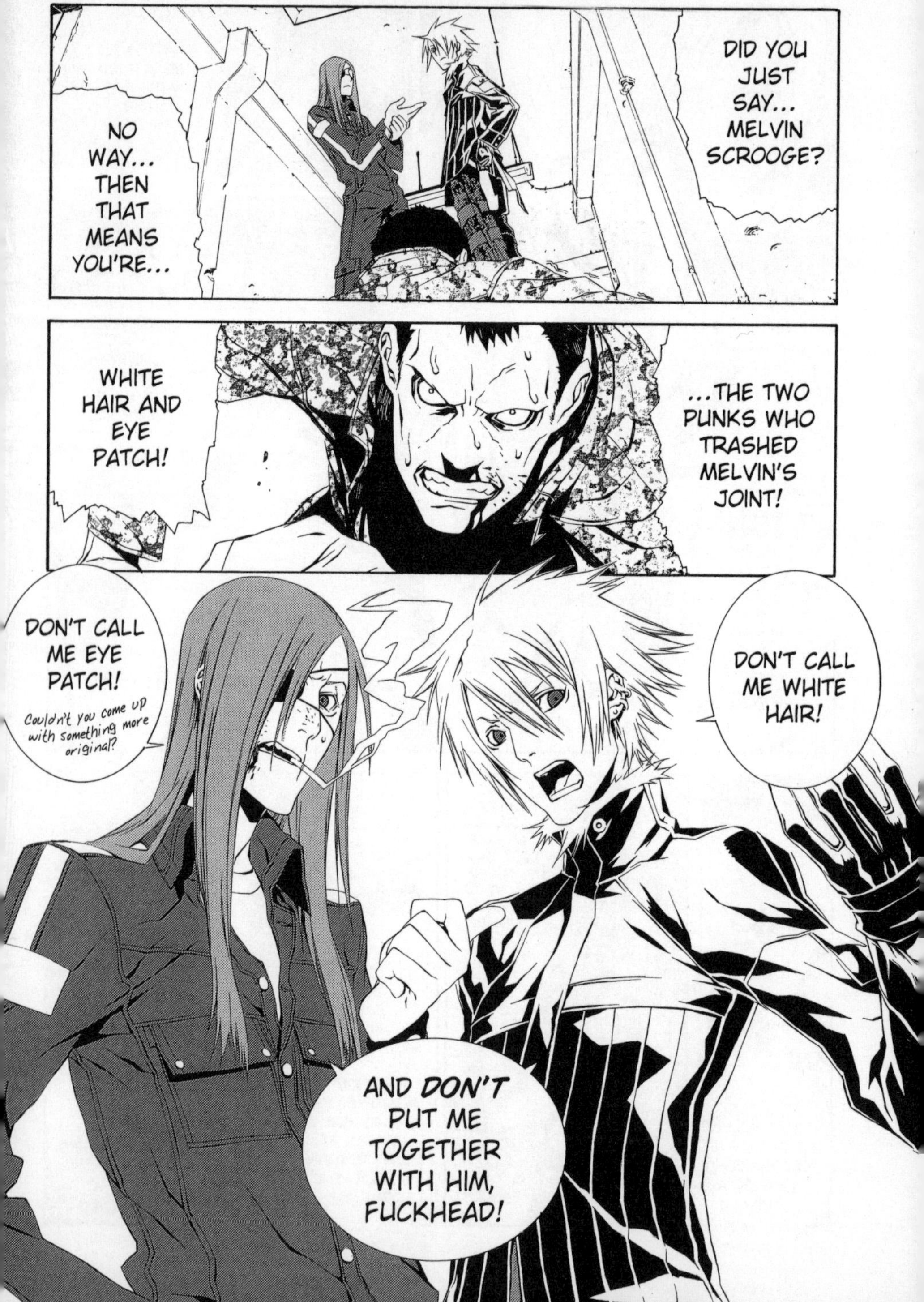
DID YOU JUST SAY... MELVIN SCROOGE?
NO WAY... THEN THAT MEANS YOU'RE...
...THE TWO PUNKS WHO TRASHED MELVIN'S JOINT!
WHITE HAIR AND EYE PATCH!
DON'T CALL ME WHITE HAIR!
DON'T CALL ME EYE PATCH!
Couldn't you come up with something more original?
AND *DON'T* PUT ME TOGETHER WITH HIM, FUCKHEAD!

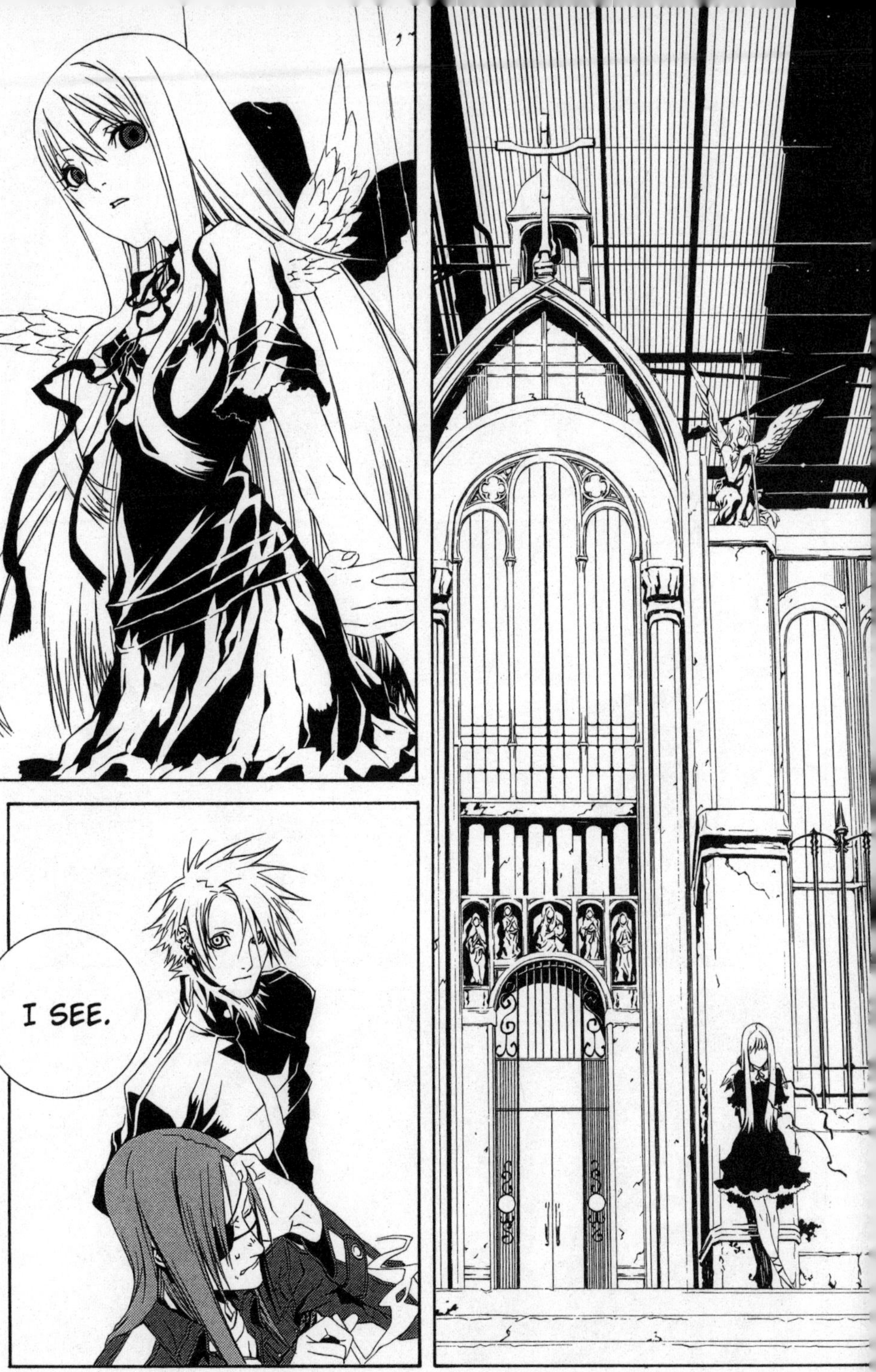
I SEE.

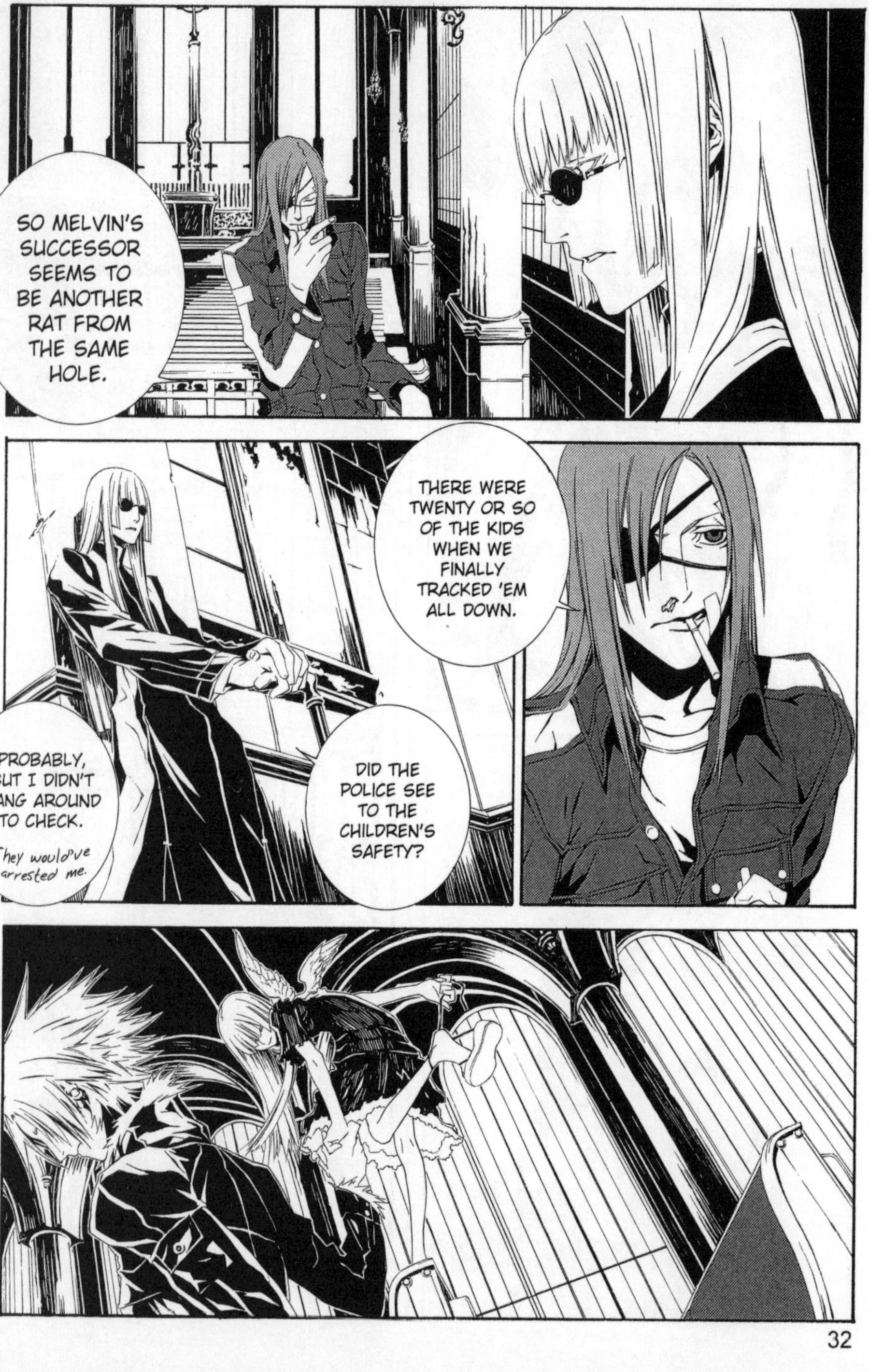
SO MELVIN'S SUCCESSOR SEEMS TO BE ANOTHER RAT FROM THE SAME HOLE.
THERE WERE TWENTY OR SO OF THE KIDS WHEN WE FINALLY TRACKED 'EM ALL DOWN.
DID THE POLICE SEE TO THE CHILDREN'S SAFETY?
PROBABLY, BUT I DIDN'T HANG AROUND TO CHECK.
They would've arrested me.

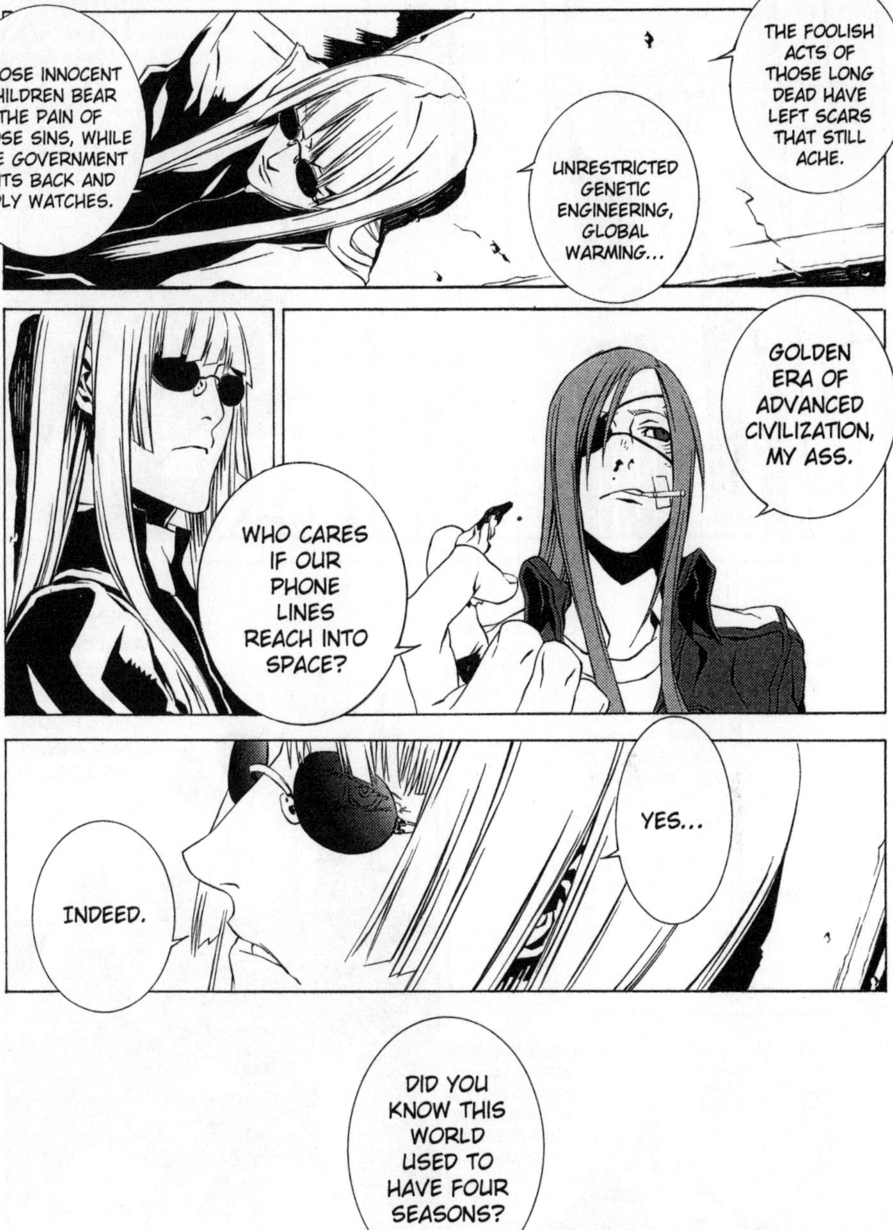
THE FOOLISH ACTS OF THOSE LONG DEAD HAVE LEFT SCARS THAT STILL ACHE.
UNRESTRICTED GENETIC ENGINEERING, GLOBAL WARMING...
THOSE INNOCENT CHILDREN BEAR THE PAIN OF THOSE SINS, WHILE THE GOVERNMENT SITS BACK AND IDLY WATCHES.
GOLDEN ERA OF ADVANCED CIVILIZATION, MY ASS.
WHO CARES IF OUR PHONE LINES REACH INTO SPACE?
YES...
INDEED.
DID YOU KNOW THIS WORLD USED TO HAVE FOUR SEASONS?

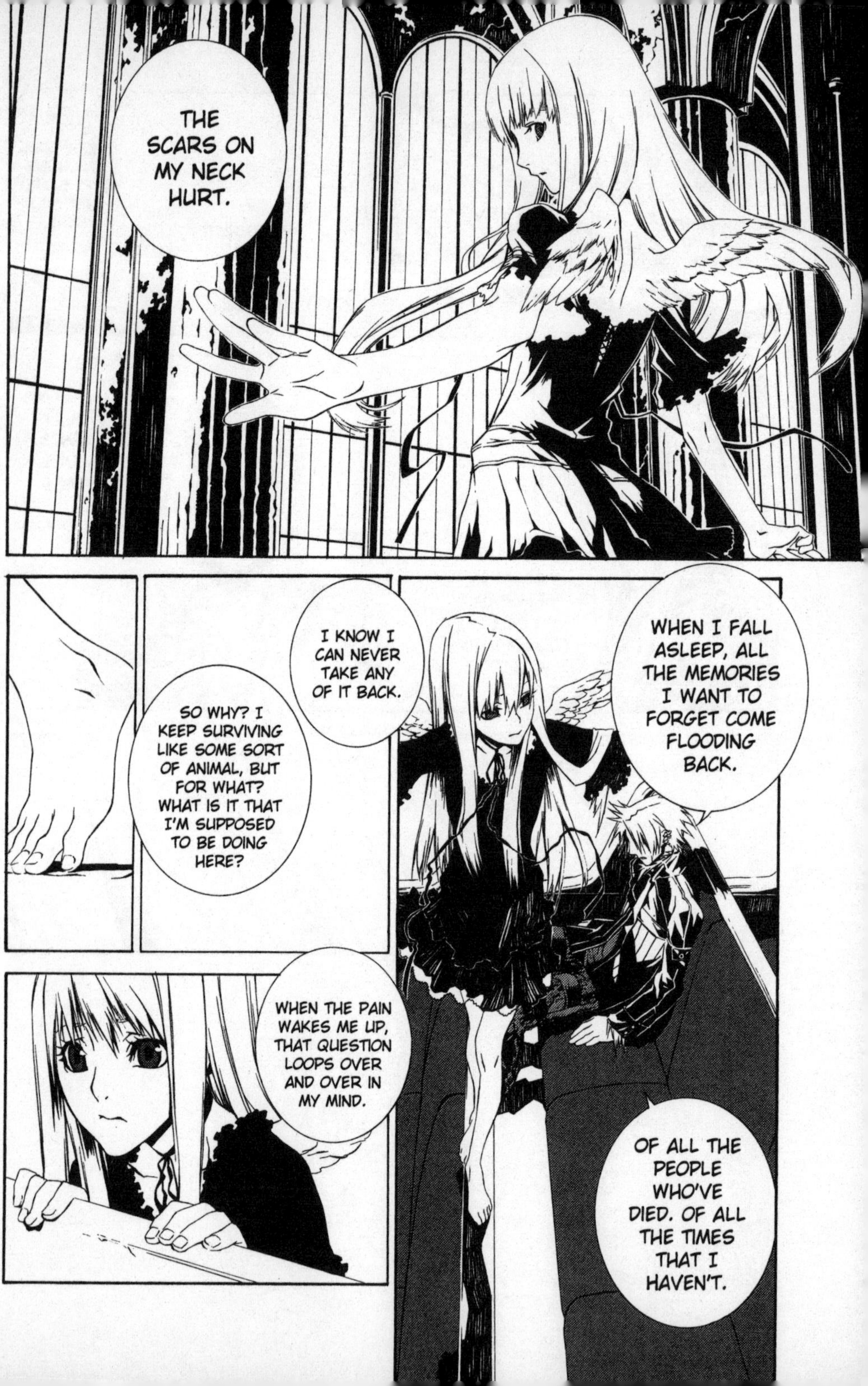
THE SCARS ON MY NECK HURT.
WHEN I FALL ASLEEP, ALL THE MEMORIES I WANT TO FORGET COME FLOODING BACK.
OF ALL THE PEOPLE WHO'VE DIED. OF ALL THE TIMES THAT I HAVEN'T.
I KNOW I CAN NEVER TAKE ANY OF IT BACK.
SO WHY? I KEEP SURVIVING LIKE SOME SORT OF ANIMAL, BUT FOR WHAT? WHAT IS IT THAT I'M SUPPOSED TO BE DOING HERE?
WHEN THE PAIN WAKES ME UP, THAT QUESTION LOOPS OVER AND OVER IN MY MIND.

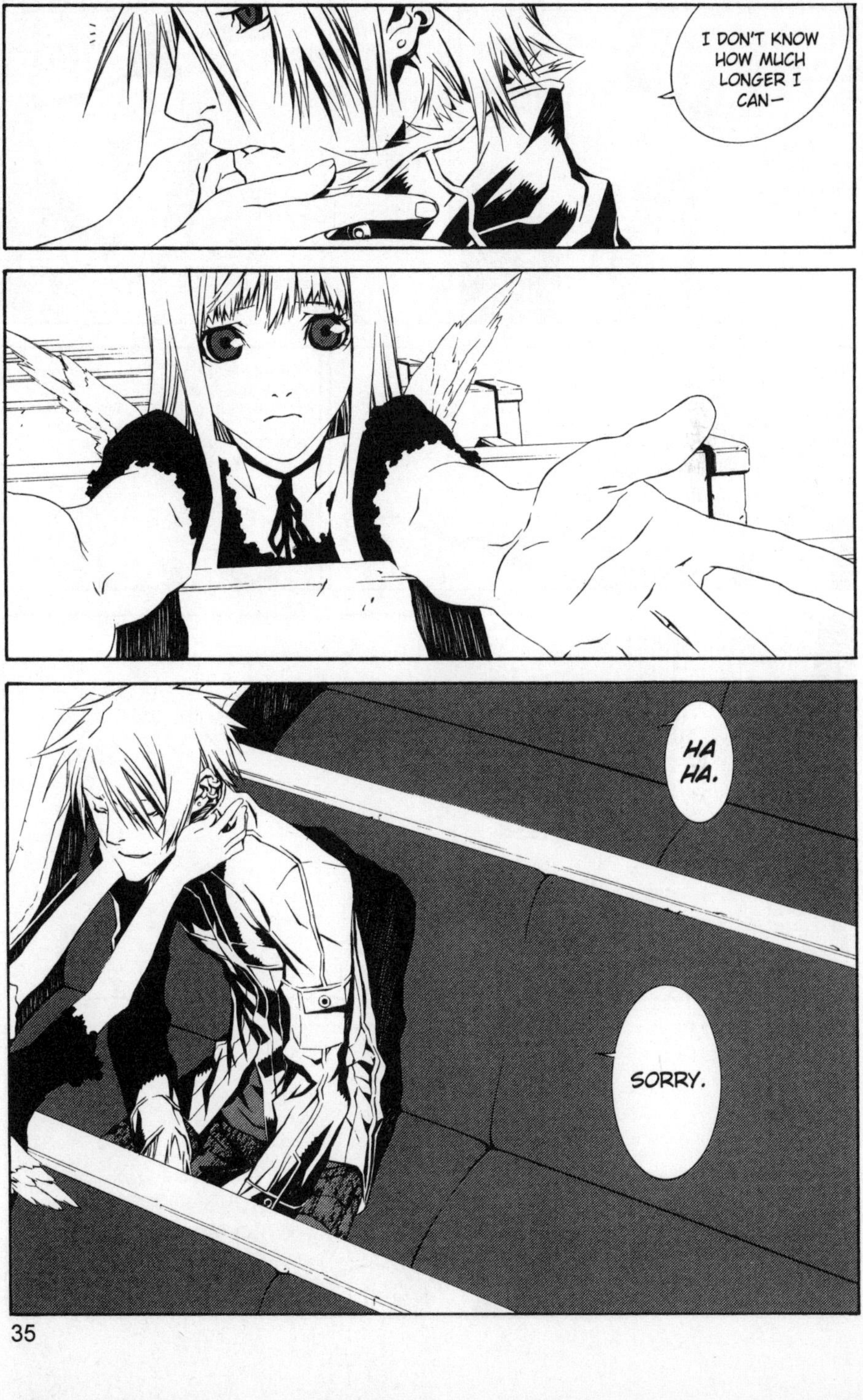
I DON'T KNOW HOW MUCH LONGER I CAN—
HA HA.
SORRY.

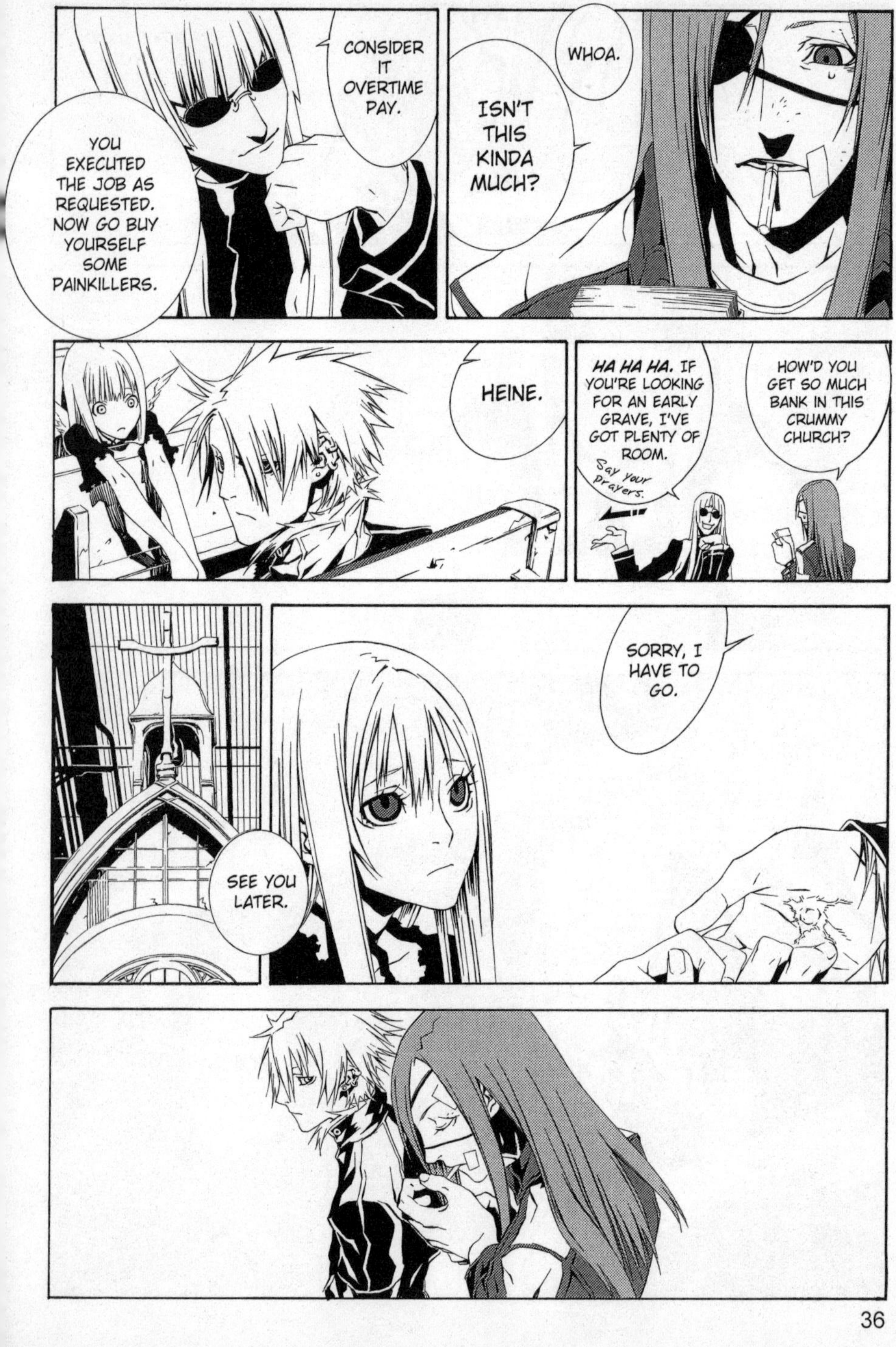
WHOA.
ISN'T THIS KINDA MUCH?
CONSIDER IT OVERTIME PAY.
YOU EXECUTED THE JOB AS REQUESTED. NOW GO BUY YOURSELF SOME PAINKILLERS.
HOW'D YOU GET SO MUCH BANK IN THIS CRUMMY CHURCH?
HA HA HA. IF YOU'RE LOOKING FOR AN EARLY GRAVE, I'VE GOT PLENTY OF ROOM.
Say your prayers.
HEINE.
SORRY, I HAVE TO GO.
SEE YOU LATER.

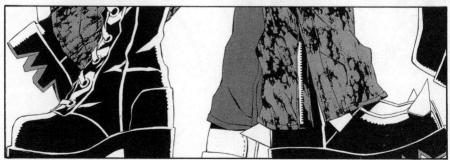

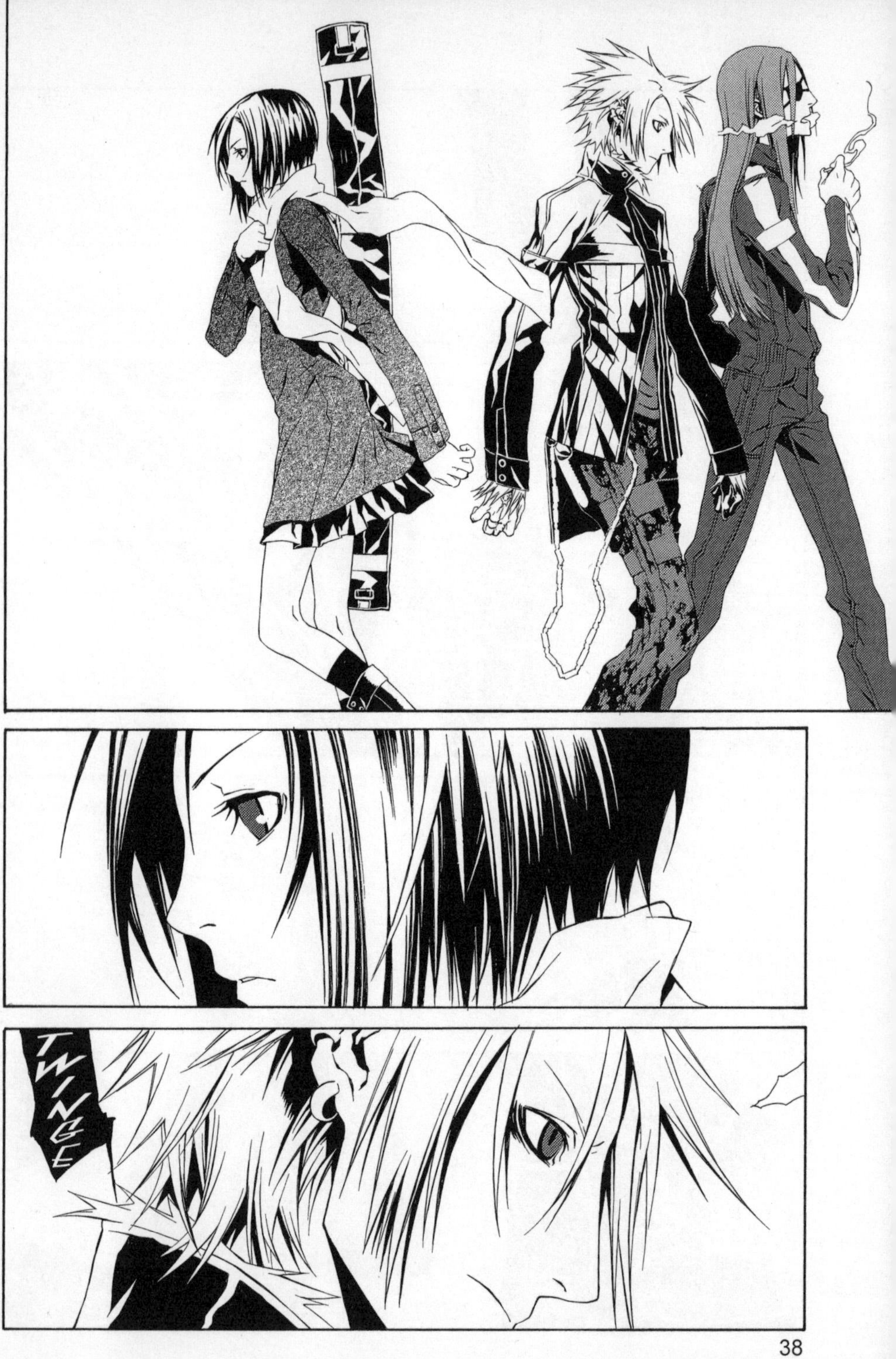
TWINGE

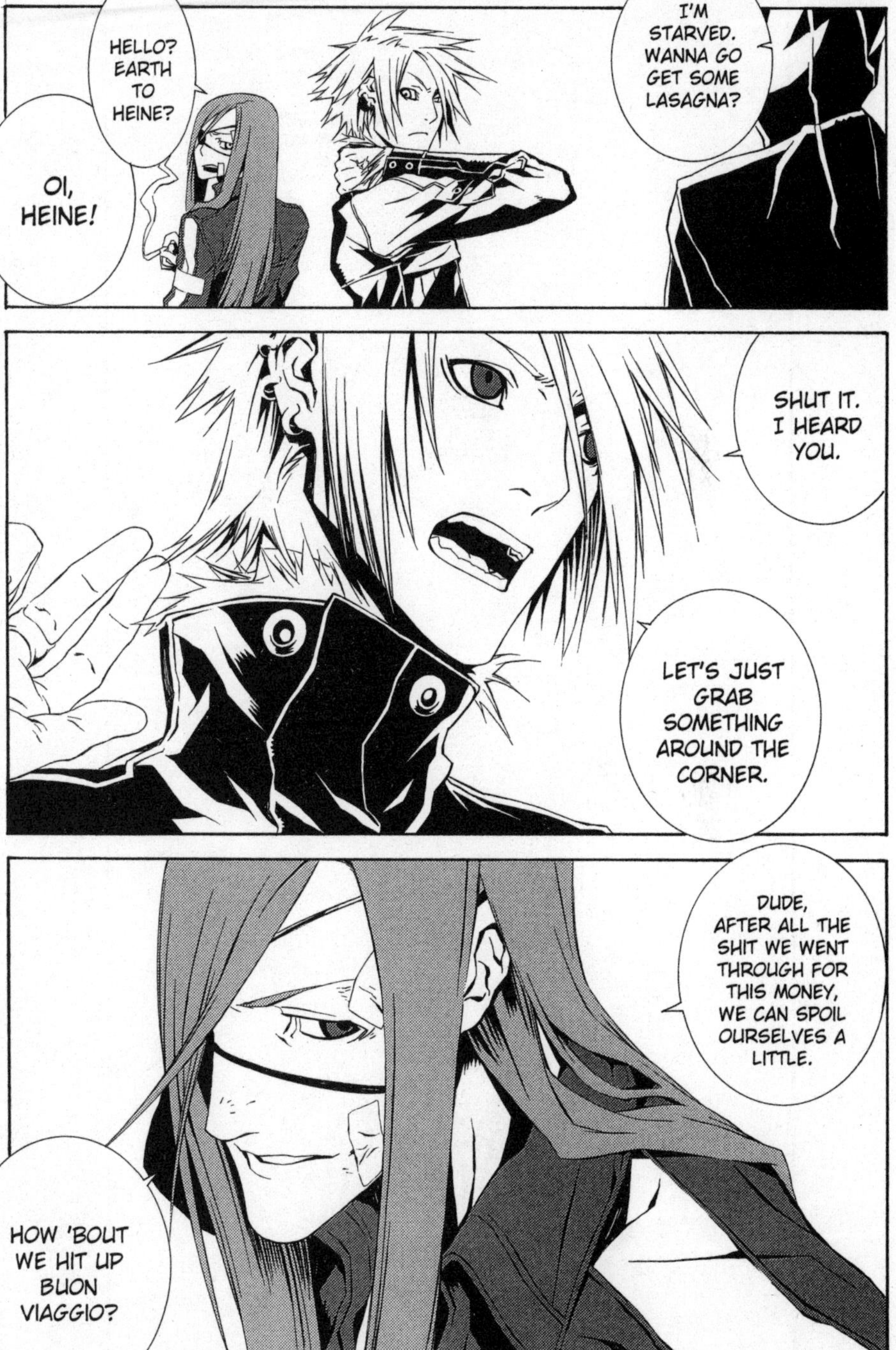
I'M STARVED. WANNA GO GET SOME LASAGNA?
HELLO? EARTH TO HEINE?
OI, HEINE!
SHUT IT. I HEARD YOU.
LET'S JUST GRAB SOMETHING AROUND THE CORNER.
DUDE, AFTER ALL THE SHIT WE WENT THROUGH FOR THIS MONEY, WE CAN SPOIL OURSELVES A LITTLE.
HOW 'BOUT WE HIT UP BUON VIAGGIO?

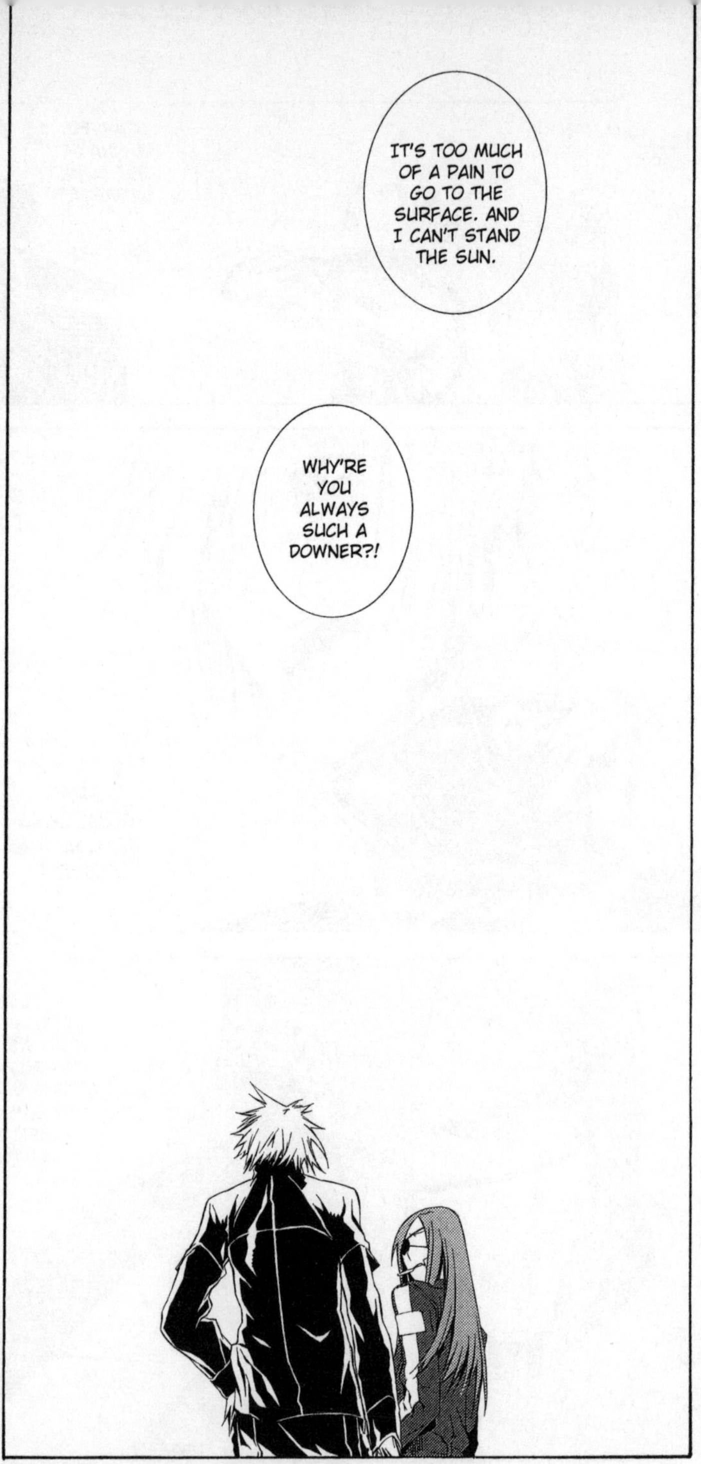
IT'S TOO MUCH OF A PAIN TO GO TO THE SURFACE. AND I CAN'T STAND THE SUN.
WHY'RE YOU ALWAYS SUCH A DOWNER?!

#02 Maiden & Eisen

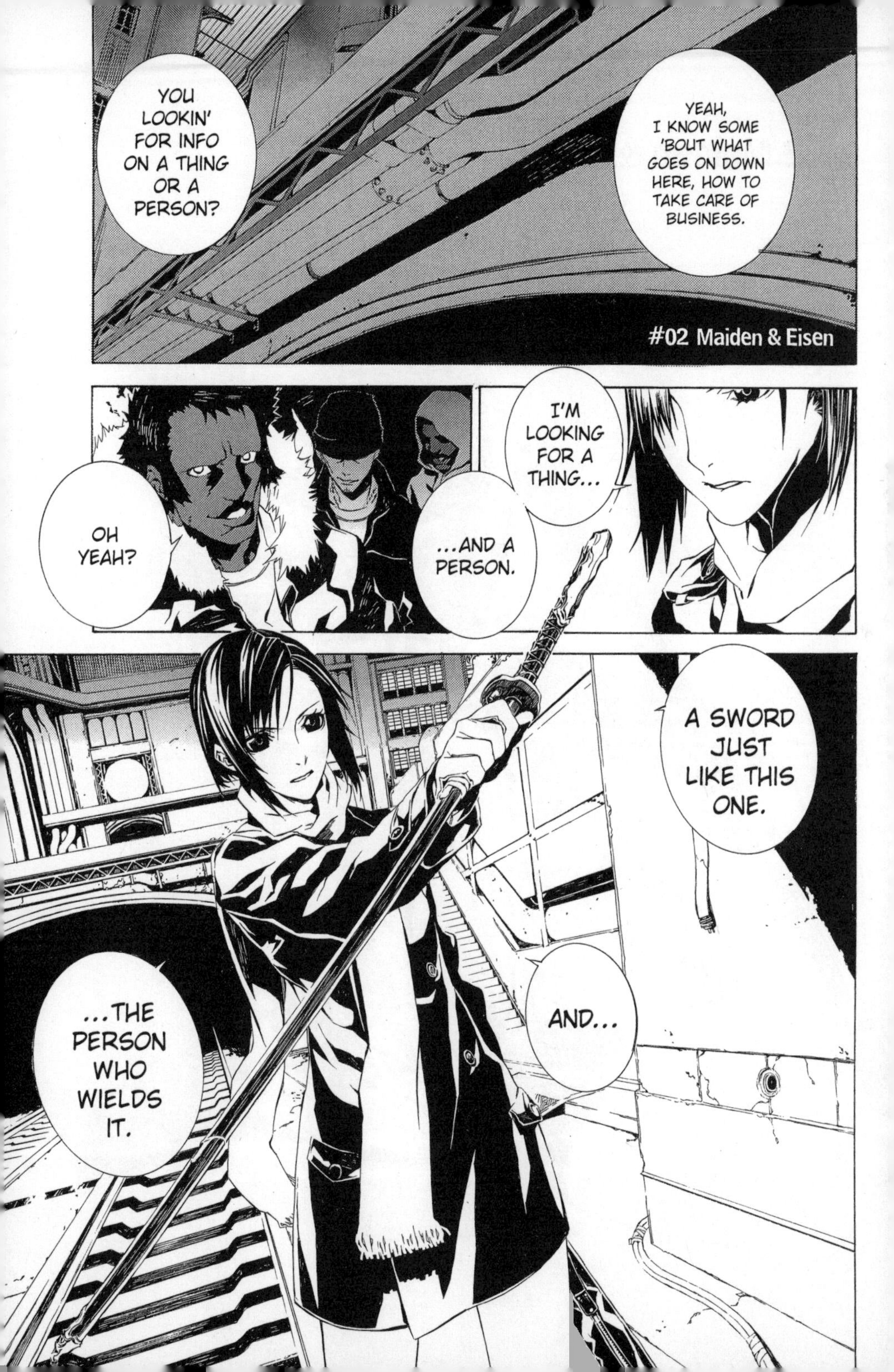
YEAH, I KNOW SOME 'BOUT WHAT GOES ON DOWN HERE, HOW TO TAKE CARE OF BUSINESS.
YOU LOOKIN' FOR INFO ON A THING OR A PERSON?
I'M LOOKING FOR A THING...
...AND A PERSON.
OH YEAH?
A SWORD JUST LIKE THIS ONE.
AND...
...THE PERSON WHO WIELDS IT.

#02 Maiden & Eisen

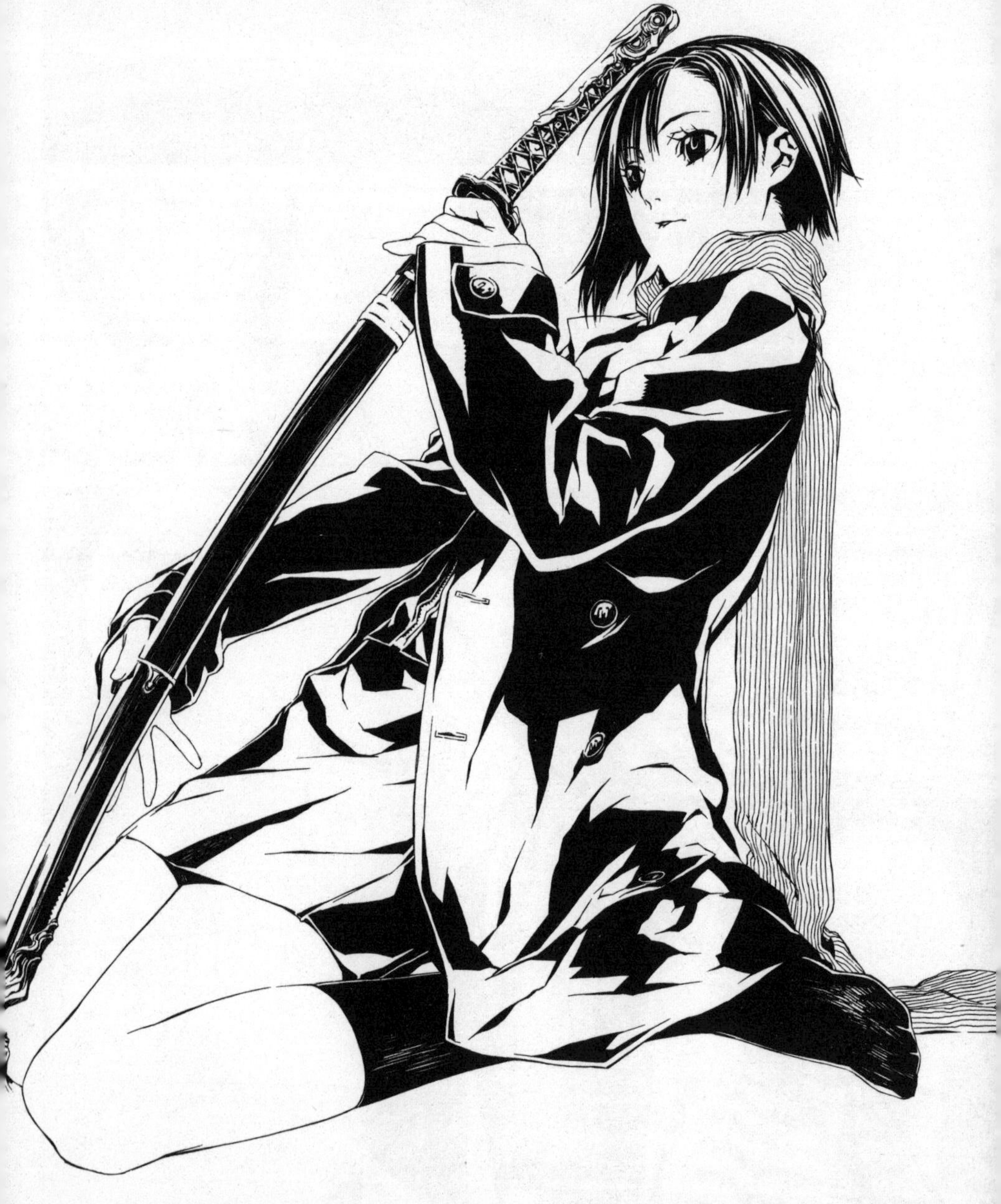

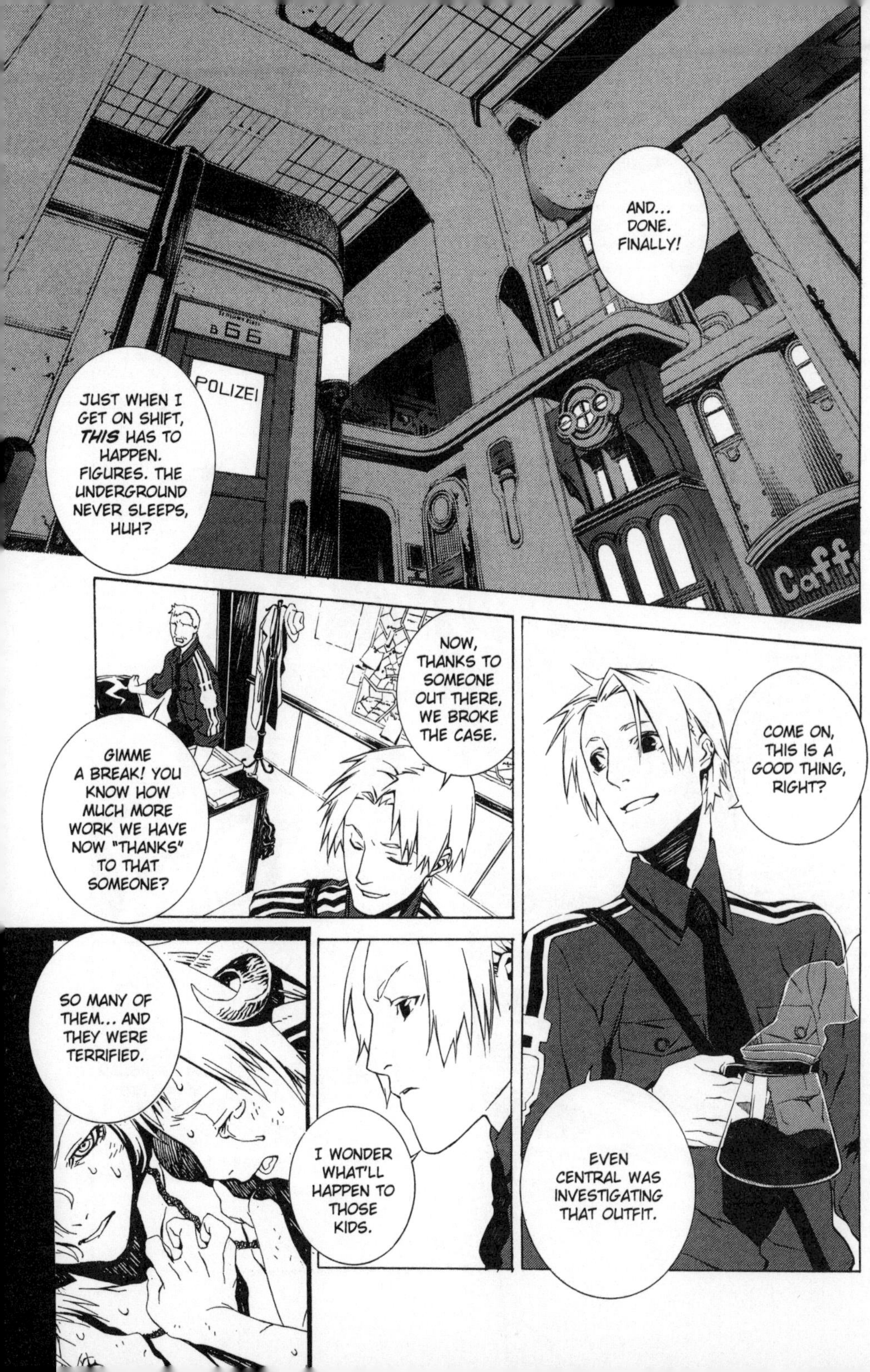
AND... DONE. FINALLY!
POLIZEI
JUST WHEN I GET ON SHIFT, ***THIS*** HAS TO HAPPEN. FIGURES. THE UNDERGROUND NEVER SLEEPS, HUH?
COME ON, THIS IS A GOOD THING, RIGHT?
EVEN CENTRAL WAS INVESTIGATING THAT OUTFIT.
NOW, THANKS TO SOMEONE OUT THERE, WE BROKE THE CASE.
GIMME A BREAK! YOU KNOW HOW MUCH MORE WORK WE HAVE NOW "THANKS" TO THAT SOMEONE?
I WONDER WHAT'LL HAPPEN TO THOSE KIDS.
SO MANY OF THEM... AND THEY WERE TERRIFIED.

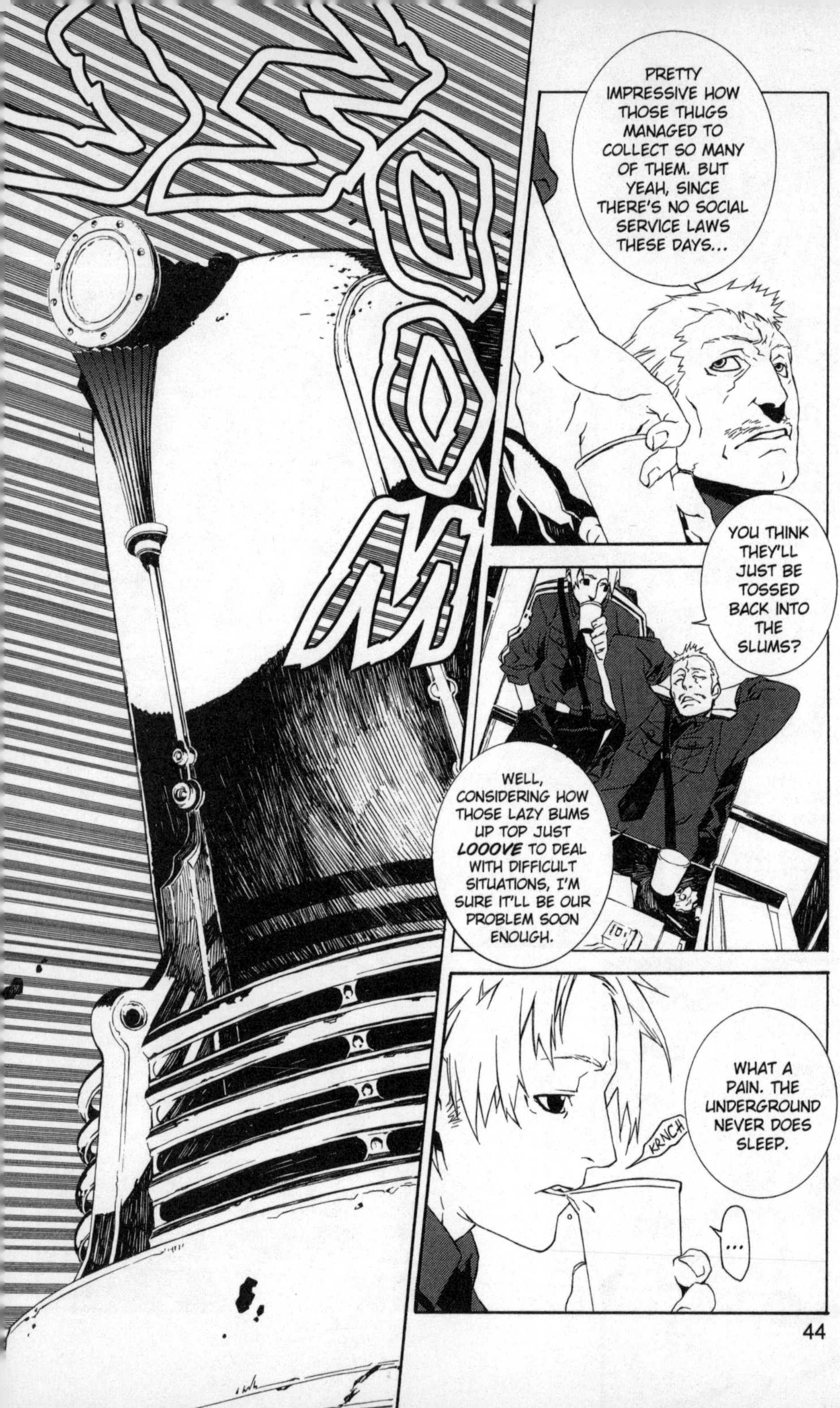
PRETTY IMPRESSIVE HOW THOSE THUGS MANAGED TO COLLECT SO MANY OF THEM. BUT YEAH, SINCE THERE'S NO SOCIAL SERVICE LAWS THESE DAYS...
YOU THINK THEY'LL JUST BE TOSSED BACK INTO THE SLUMS?
WELL, CONSIDERING HOW THOSE LAZY BUMS UP TOP JUST *LOOOVE* TO DEAL WITH DIFFICULT SITUATIONS, I'M SURE IT'LL BE OUR PROBLEM SOON ENOUGH.
WHAT A PAIN. THE UNDERGROUND NEVER DOES SLEEP.
KRNCH
...

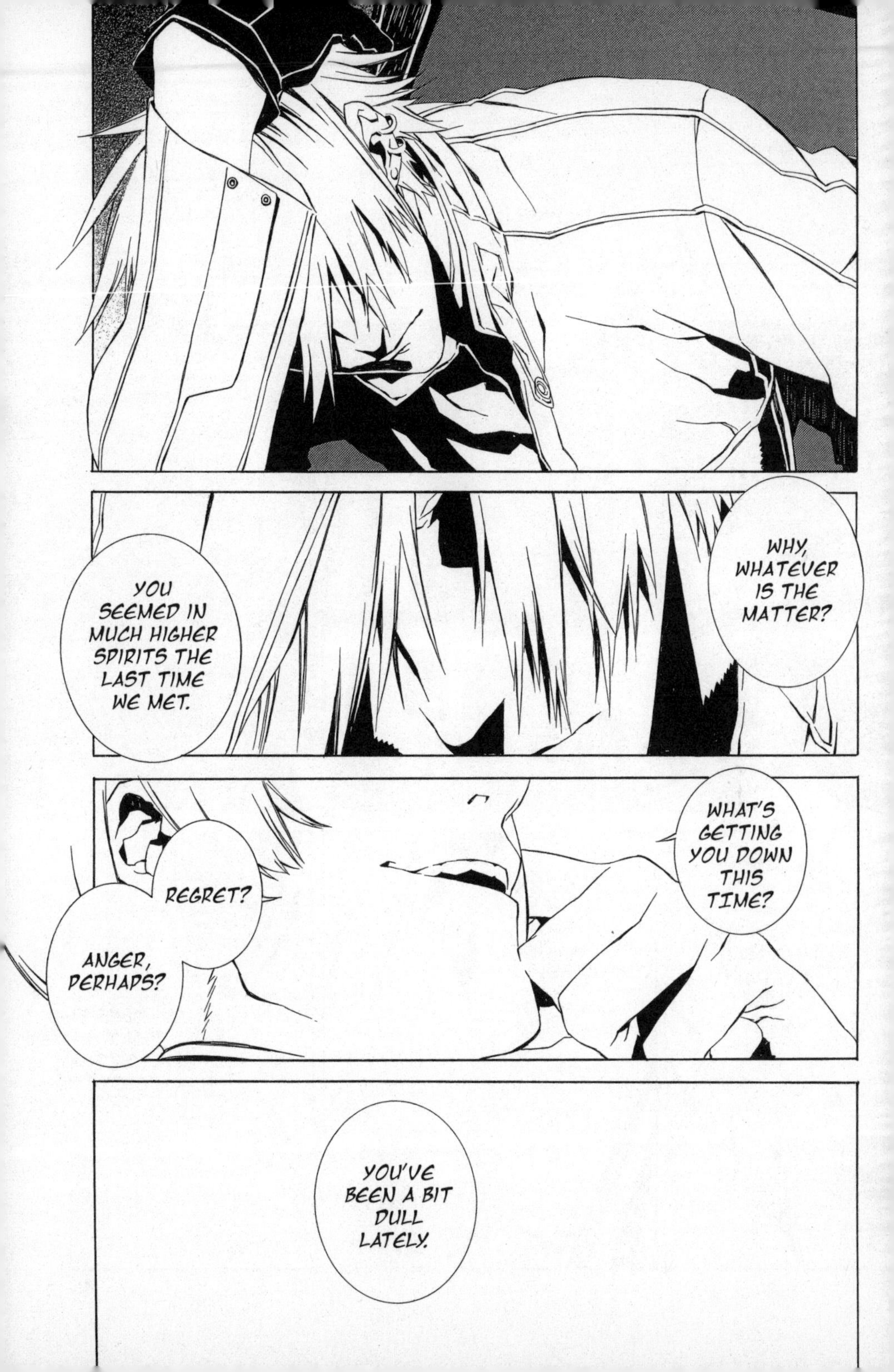
WHY, WHATEVER IS THE MATTER?
YOU SEEMED IN MUCH HIGHER SPIRITS THE LAST TIME WE MET.
WHAT'S GETTING YOU DOWN THIS TIME?
REGRET?
ANGER, PERHAPS?
YOU'VE BEEN A BIT DULL LATELY.

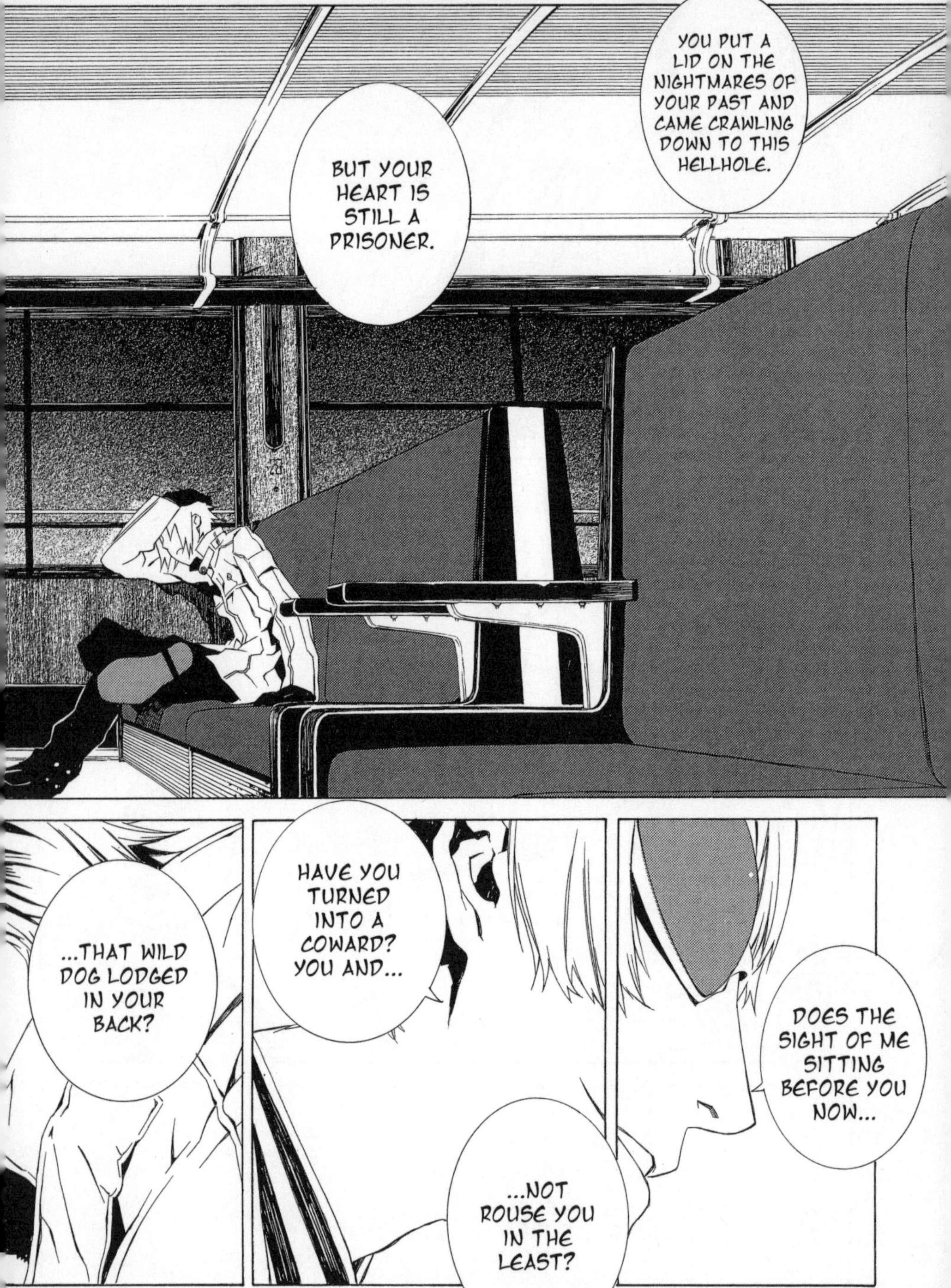
YOU PUT A LID ON THE NIGHTMARES OF YOUR PAST AND CAME CRAWLING DOWN TO THIS HELLHOLE.
BUT YOUR HEART IS STILL A PRISONER.
DOES THE SIGHT OF ME SITTING BEFORE YOU NOW...
...NOT ROUSE YOU IN THE LEAST?
HAVE YOU TURNED INTO A COWARD? YOU AND...
...THAT WILD DOG LODGED IN YOUR BACK?

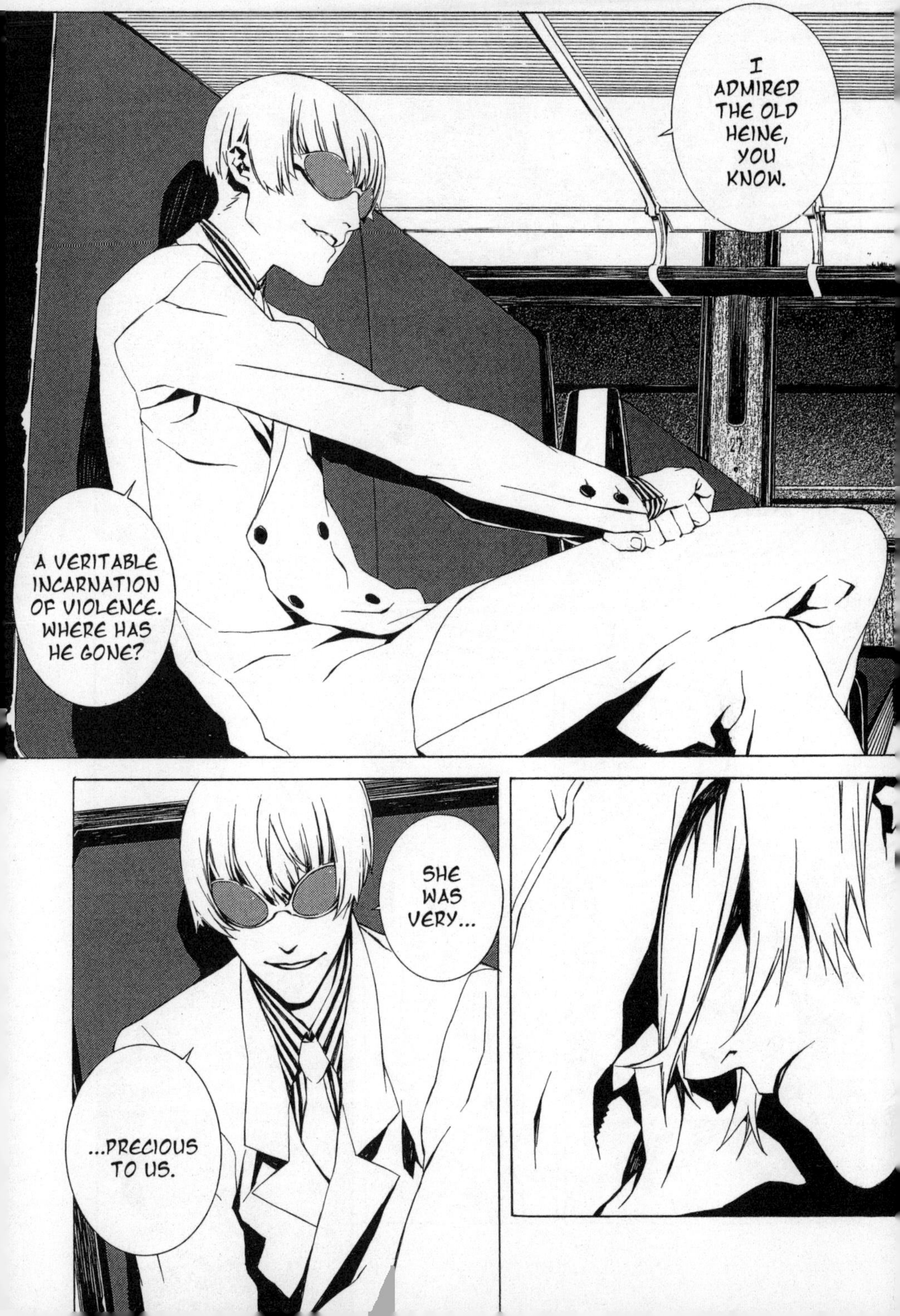
I ADMIRED THE OLD HEINE, YOU KNOW.
A VERITABLE INCARNATION OF VIOLENCE. WHERE HAS HE GONE?
SHE WAS VERY...
...PRECIOUS TO US.

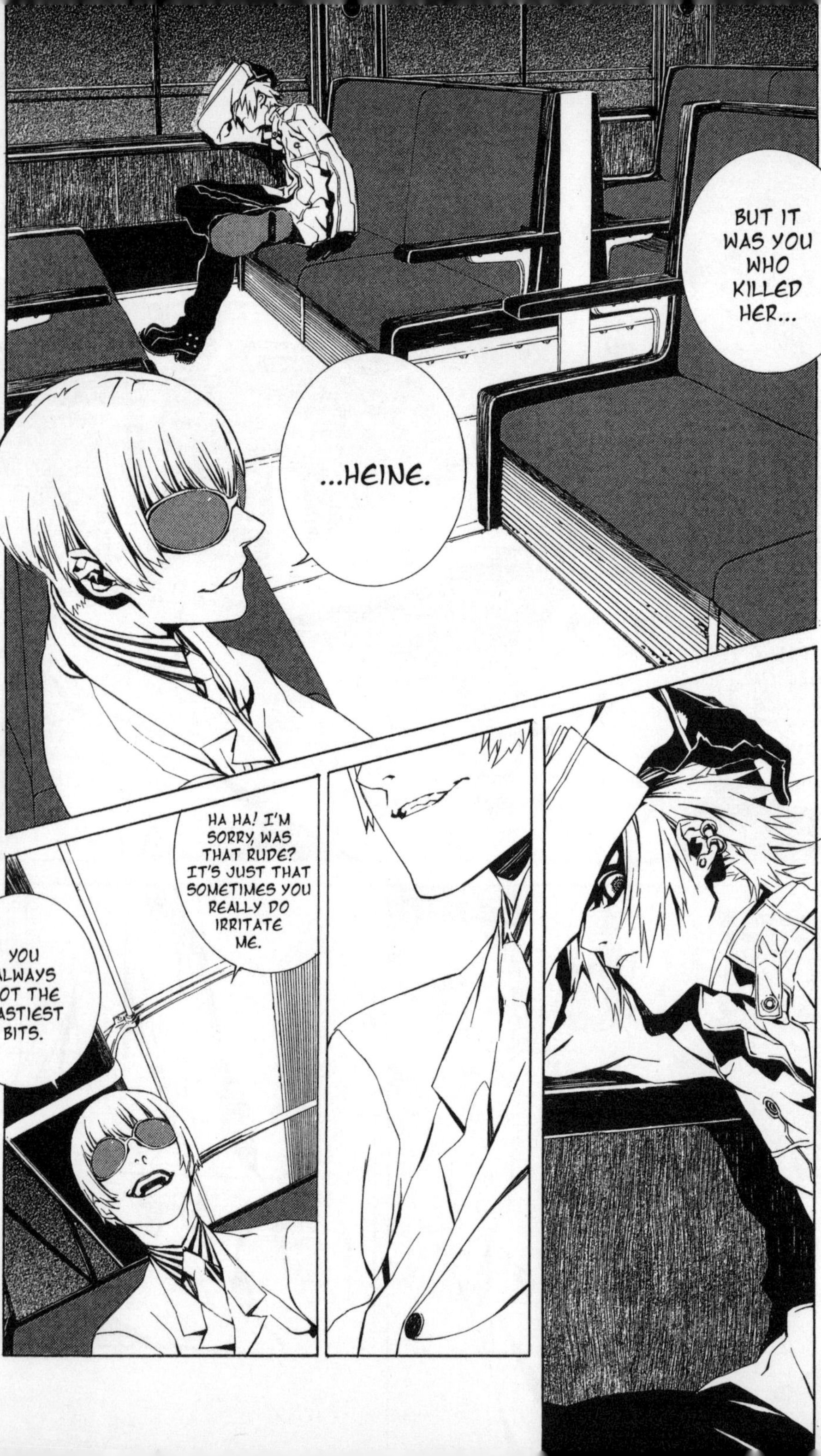
BUT IT WAS YOU WHO KILLED HER...
...HEINE.
HA HA! I'M SORRY, WAS THAT RUDE? IT'S JUST THAT SOMETIMES YOU REALLY DO IRRITATE ME.
YOU ALWAYS GOT THE TASTIEST BITS.

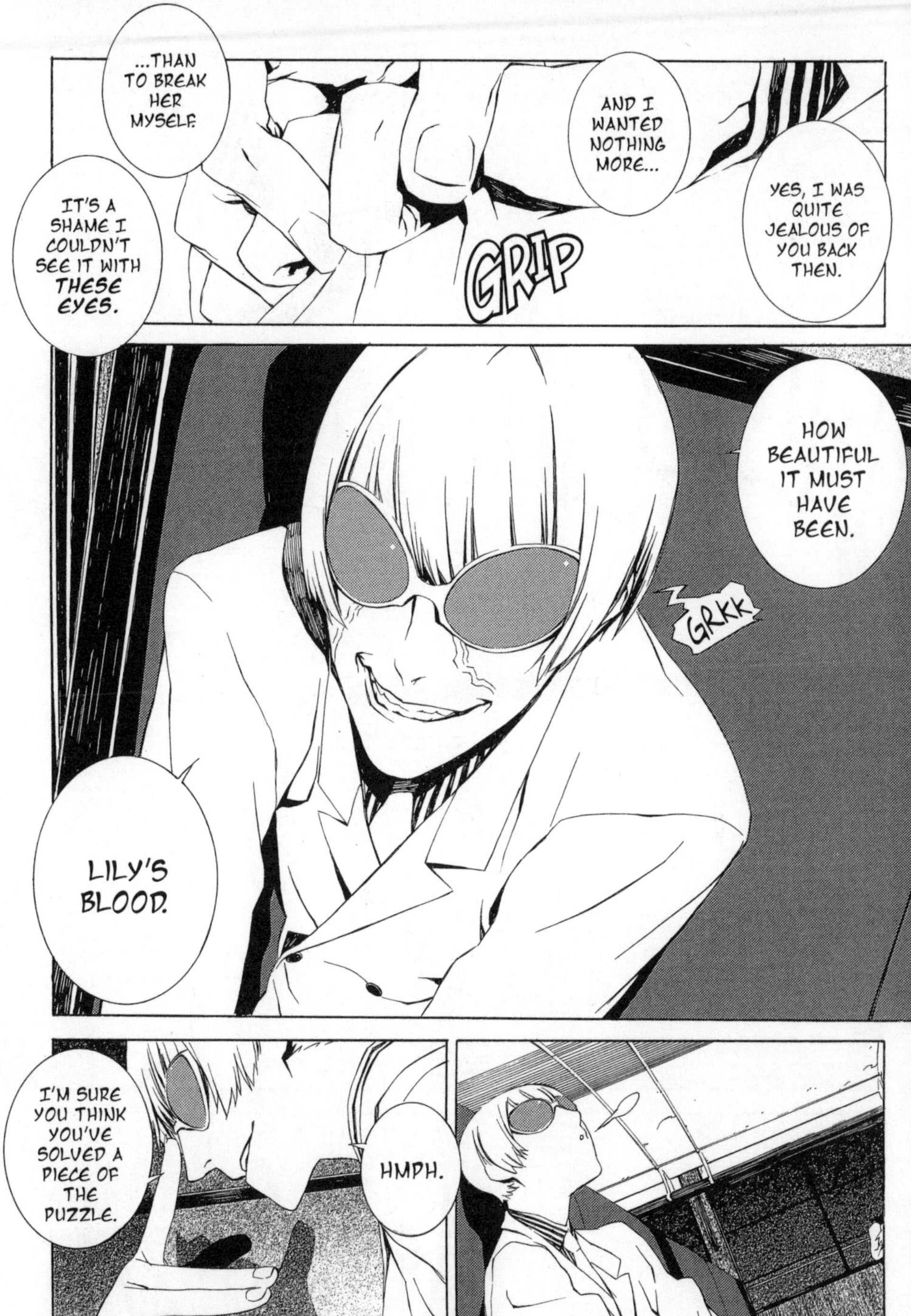
YES, I WAS QUITE JEALOUS OF YOU BACK THEN.
AND I WANTED NOTHING MORE...
...THAN TO BREAK HER MYSELF.
GRIP
IT'S A SHAME I COULDN'T SEE IT WITH THESE EYES.
HOW BEAUTIFUL IT MUST HAVE BEEN.
GRKK
LILY'S BLOOD.
HMPH.
I'M SURE YOU THINK YOU'VE SOLVED A PIECE OF THE PUZZLE.

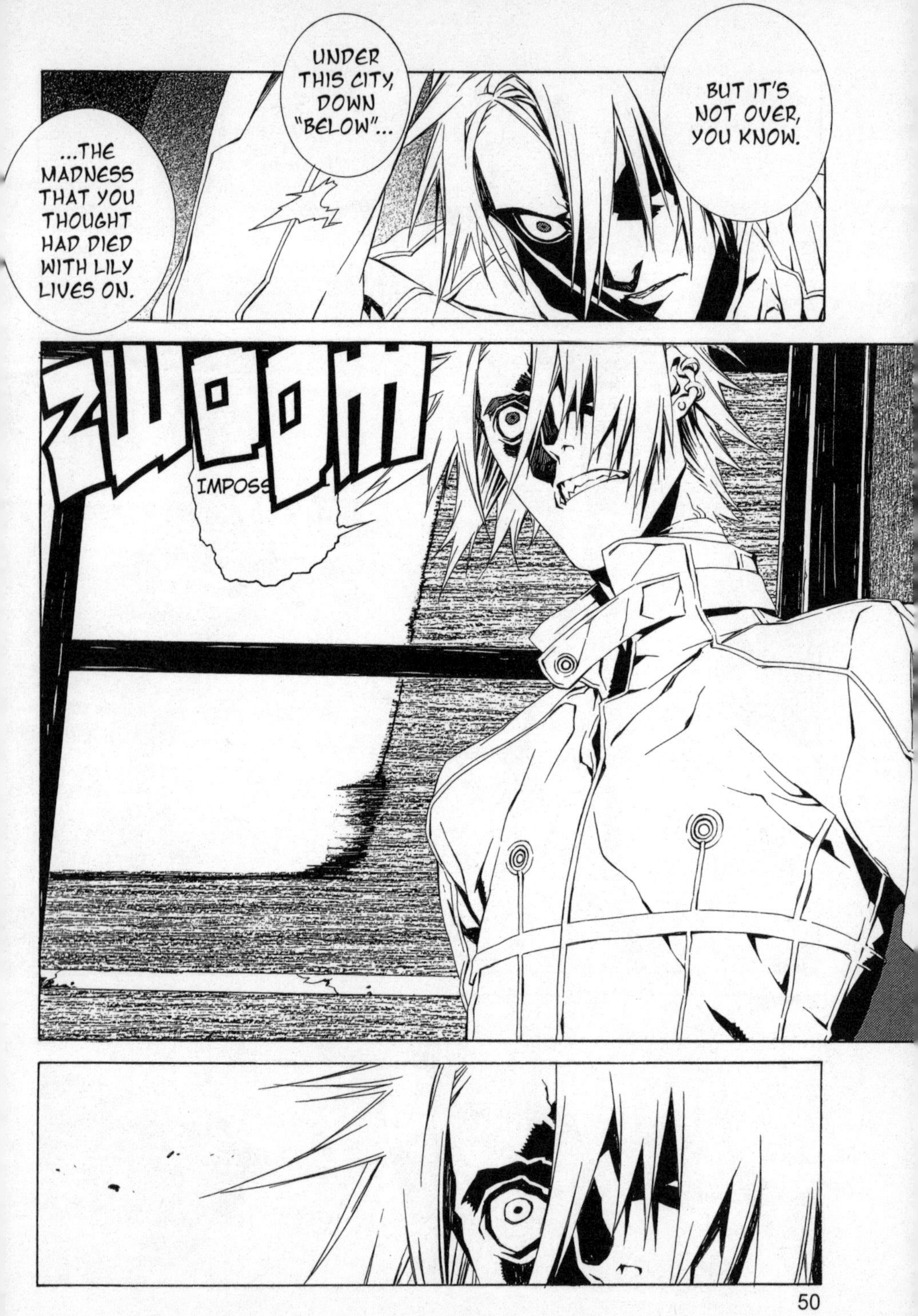
BUT IT'S NOT OVER, YOU KNOW.
UNDER THIS CITY, DOWN "BELOW"...
...THE MADNESS THAT YOU THOUGHT HAD DIED WITH LILY LIVES ON.
ZUOOM
IMPOSS

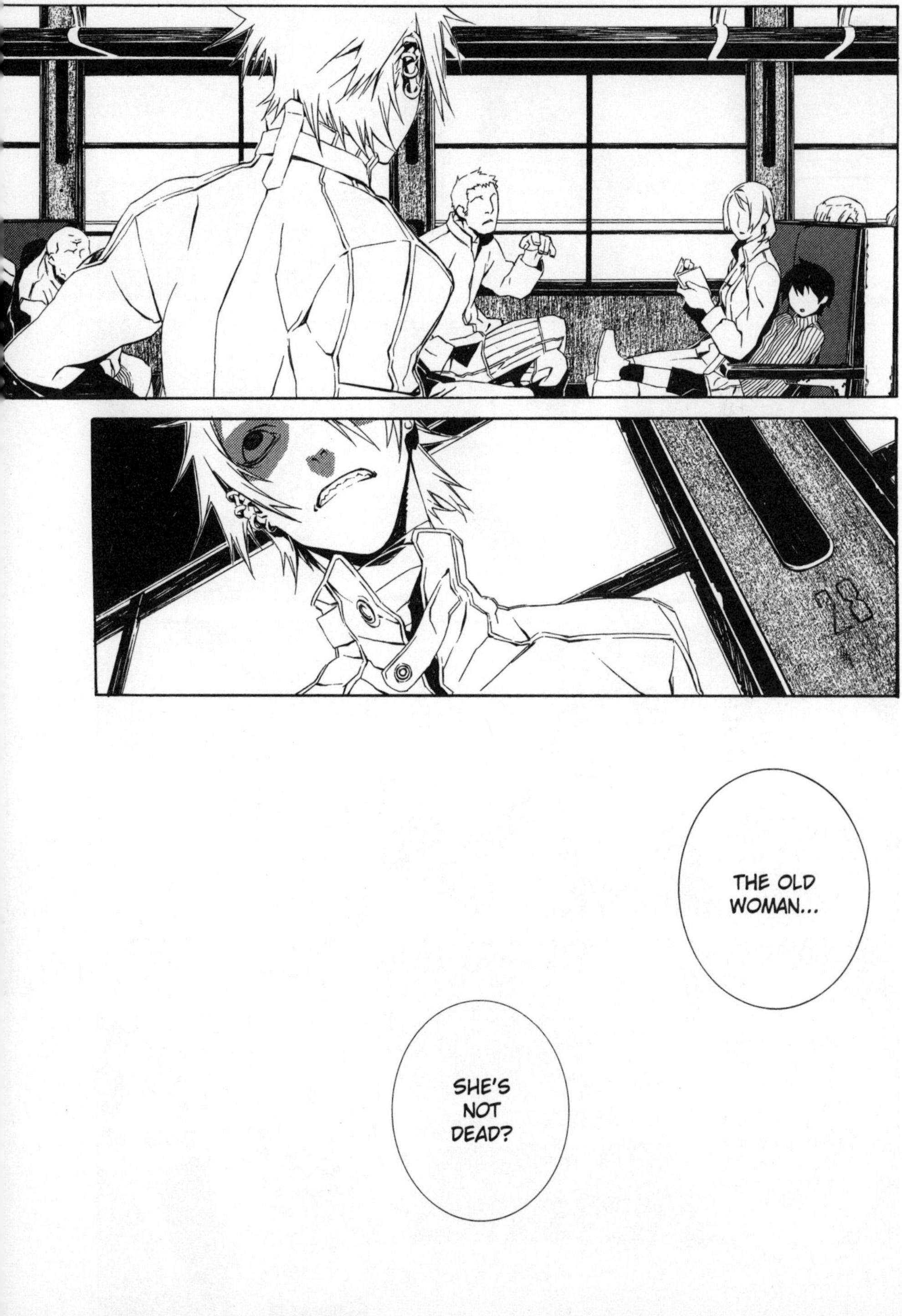
THE OLD WOMAN...
SHE'S NOT DEAD?

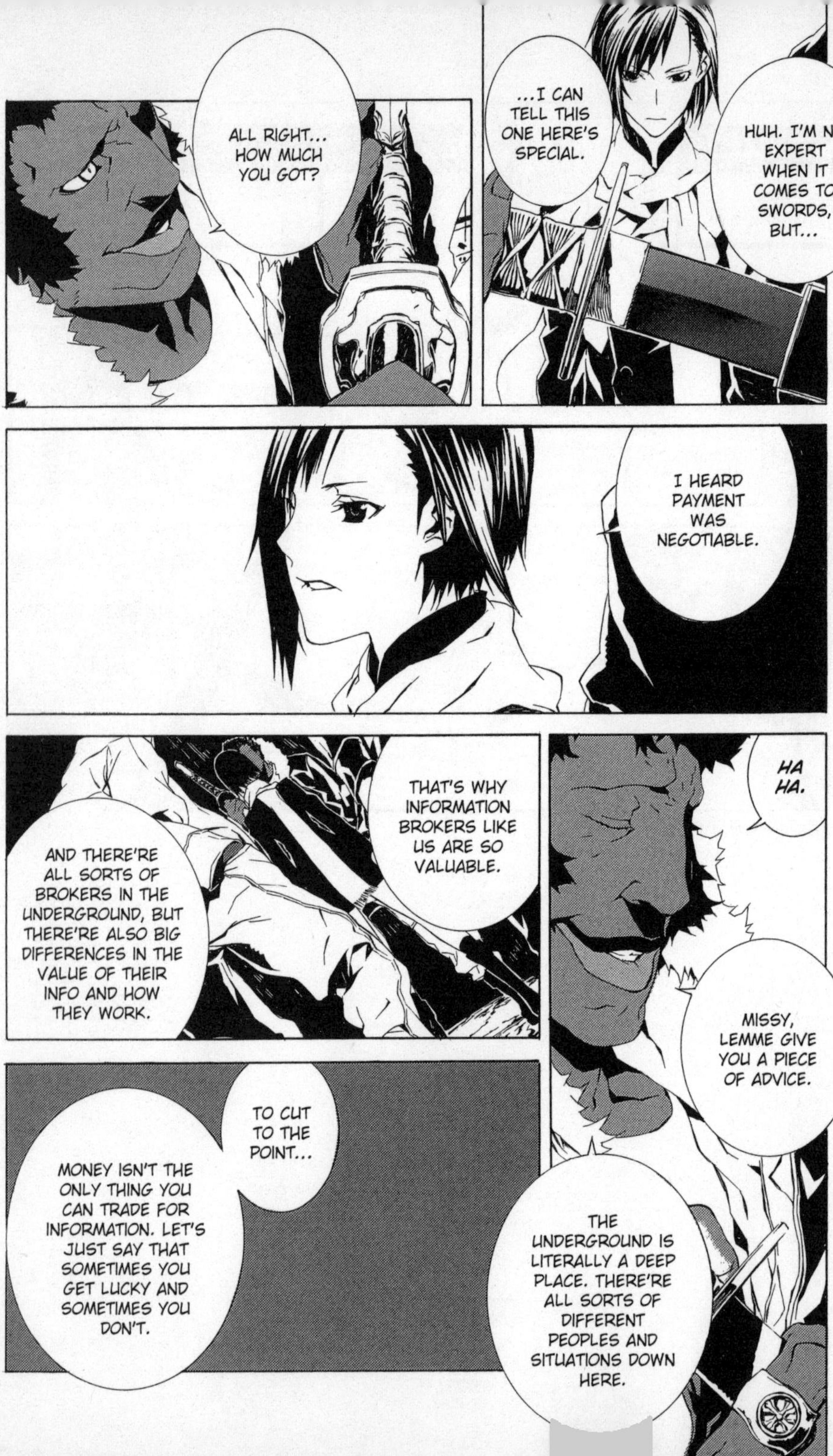
HUH. I'M NO EXPERT WHEN IT COMES TO SWORDS, BUT...
...I CAN TELL THIS ONE HERE'S SPECIAL.
ALL RIGHT... HOW MUCH YOU GOT?
I HEARD PAYMENT WAS NEGOTIABLE.
HA HA.
MISSY, LEMME GIVE YOU A PIECE OF ADVICE.
THE UNDERGROUND IS LITERALLY A DEEP PLACE. THERE'RE ALL SORTS OF DIFFERENT PEOPLES AND SITUATIONS DOWN HERE.
THAT'S WHY INFORMATION BROKERS LIKE US ARE SO VALUABLE.
AND THERE'RE ALL SORTS OF BROKERS IN THE UNDERGROUND, BUT THERE'RE ALSO BIG DIFFERENCES IN THE VALUE OF THEIR INFO AND HOW THEY WORK.
TO CUT TO THE POINT...
MONEY ISN'T THE ONLY THING YOU CAN TRADE FOR INFORMATION. LET'S JUST SAY THAT SOMETIMES YOU GET LUCKY AND SOMETIMES YOU DON'T.

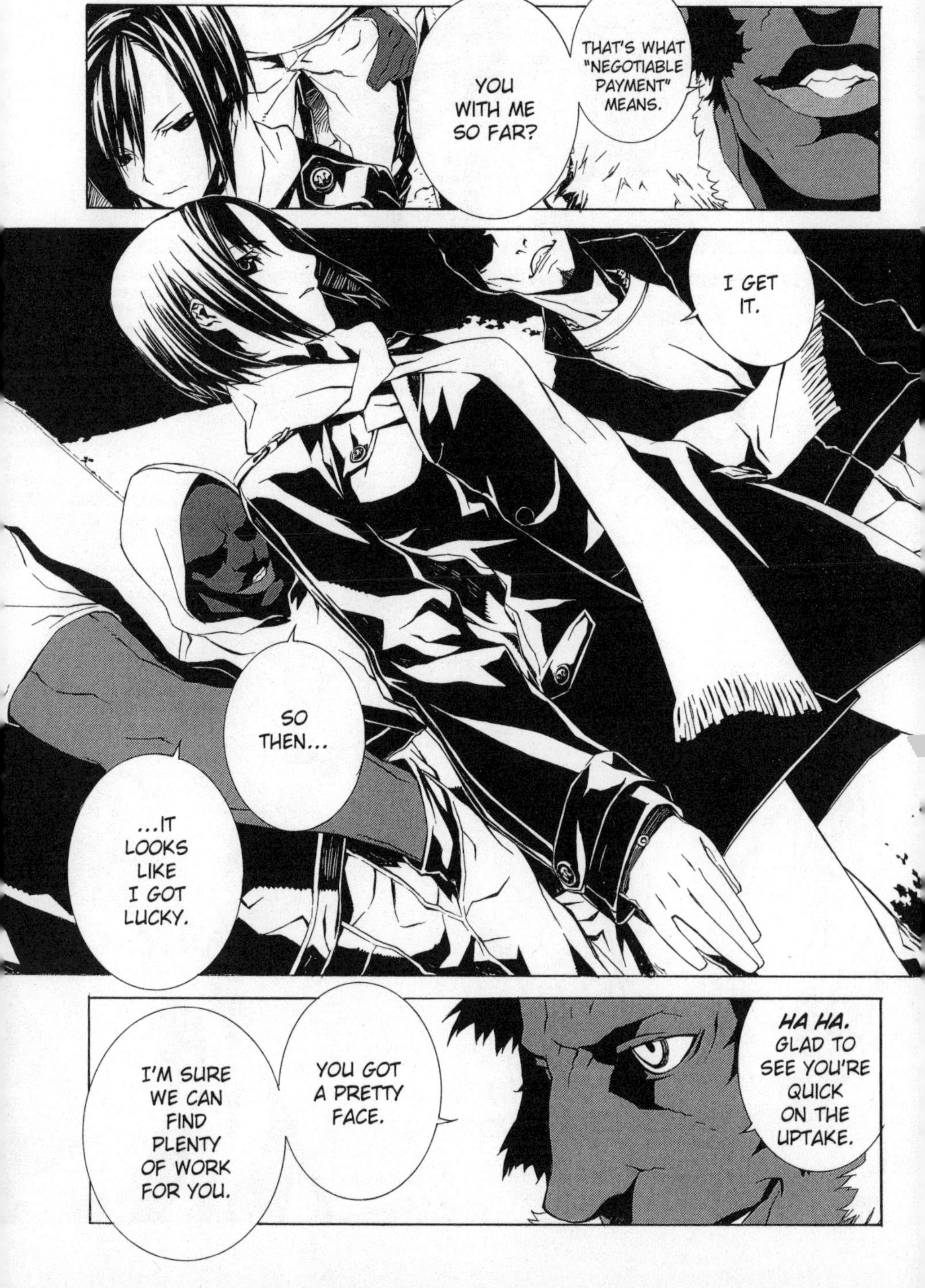
THAT'S WHAT "NEGOTIABLE PAYMENT" MEANS.
YOU WITH ME SO FAR?
I GET IT.
SO THEN...
...IT LOOKS LIKE I GOT LUCKY.
HA HA. GLAD TO SEE YOU'RE QUICK ON THE UPTAKE.
YOU GOT A PRETTY FACE.
I'M SURE WE CAN FIND PLENTY OF WORK FOR YOU.

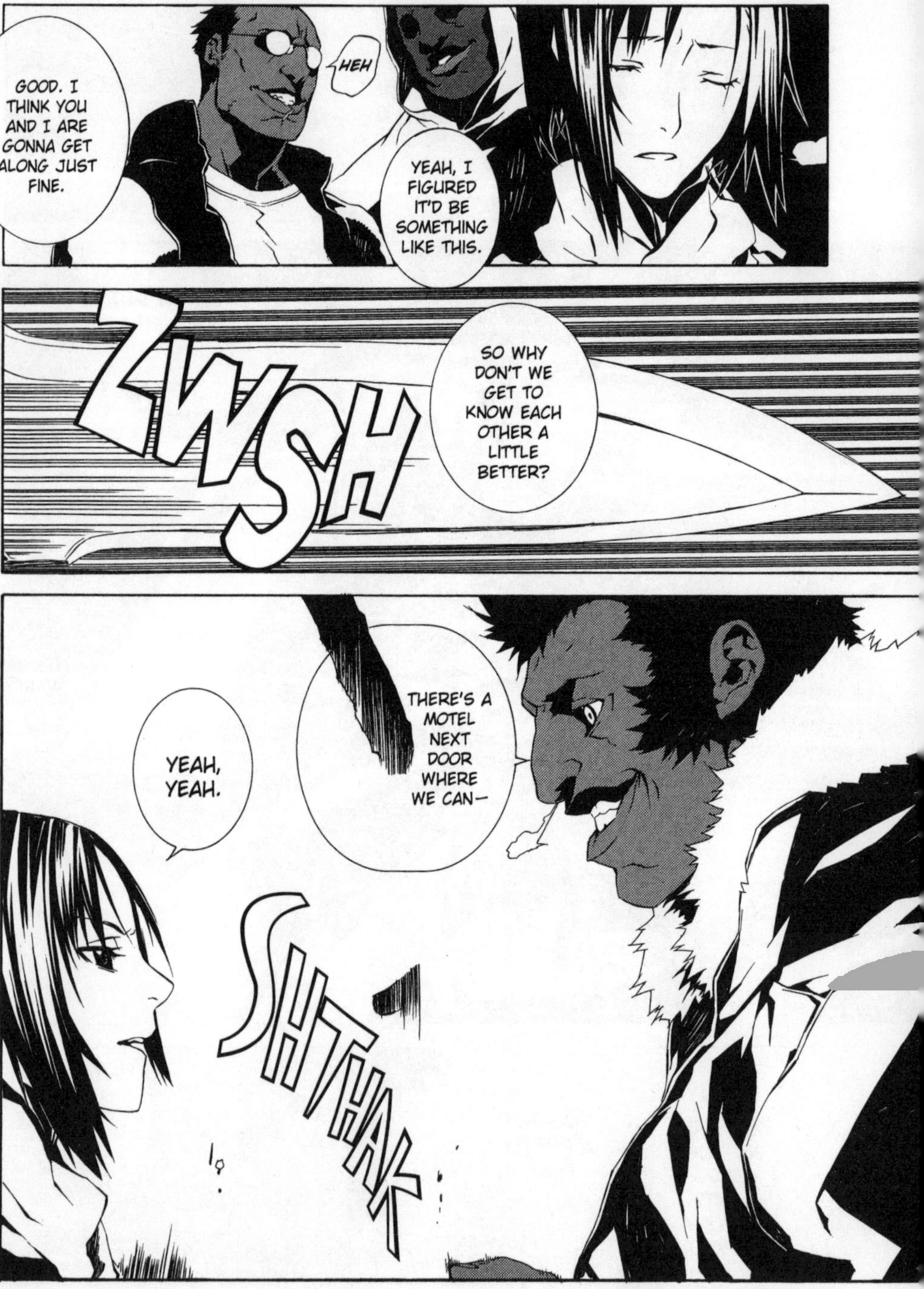
YEAH, I FIGURED IT'D BE SOMETHING LIKE THIS.
HEH
GOOD. I THINK YOU AND I ARE GONNA GET ALONG JUST FINE.
SO WHY DON'T WE GET TO KNOW EACH OTHER A LITTLE BETTER?
ZWSH
THERE'S A MOTEL NEXT DOOR WHERE WE CAN—
YEAH, YEAH.
SHTHAK

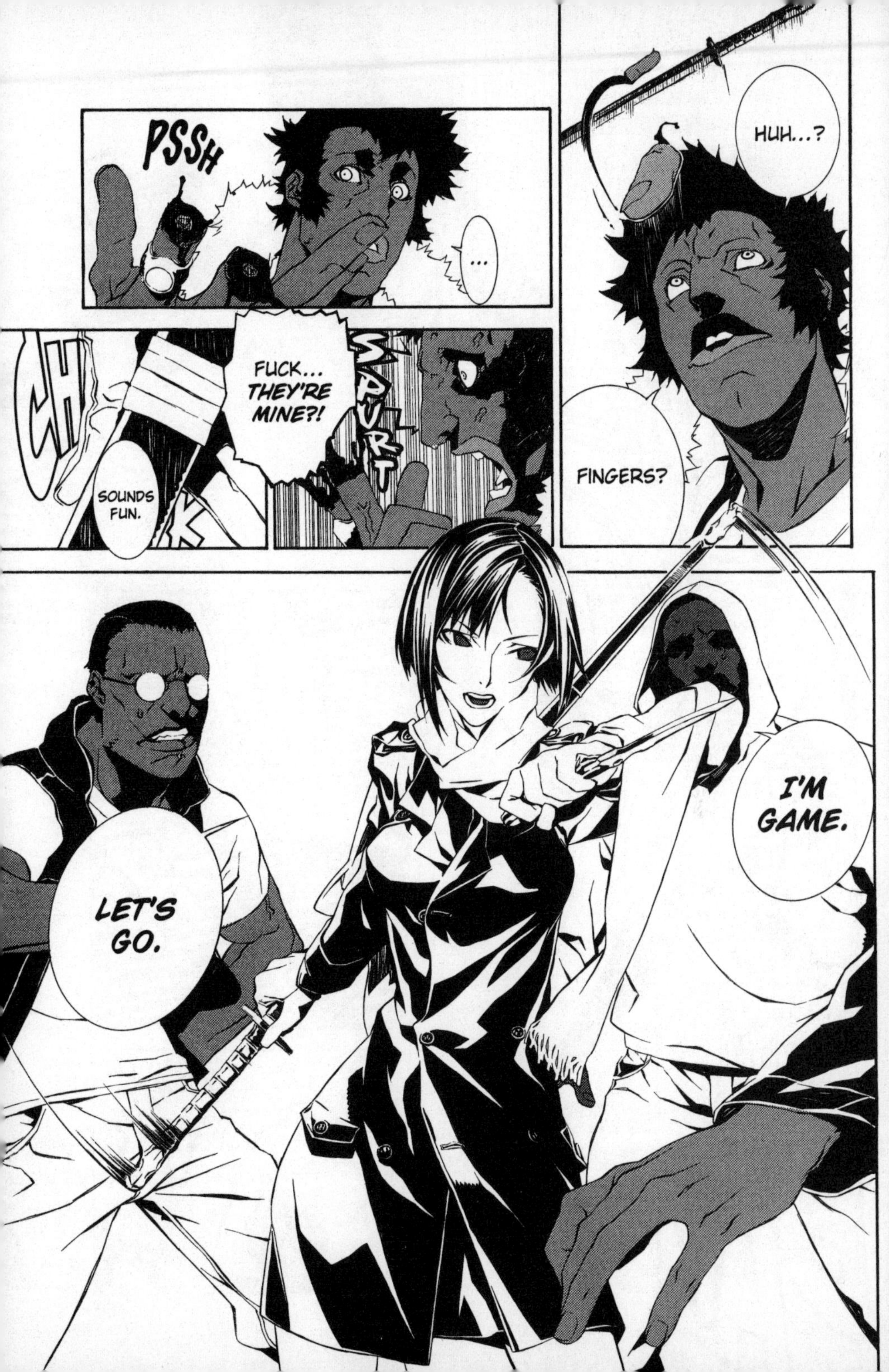
HUH...?
FINGERS?
PSSH
...
SPURT
FUCK... THEY'RE MINE?!
CHK
SOUNDS FUN.
I'M GAME.
LET'S GO.

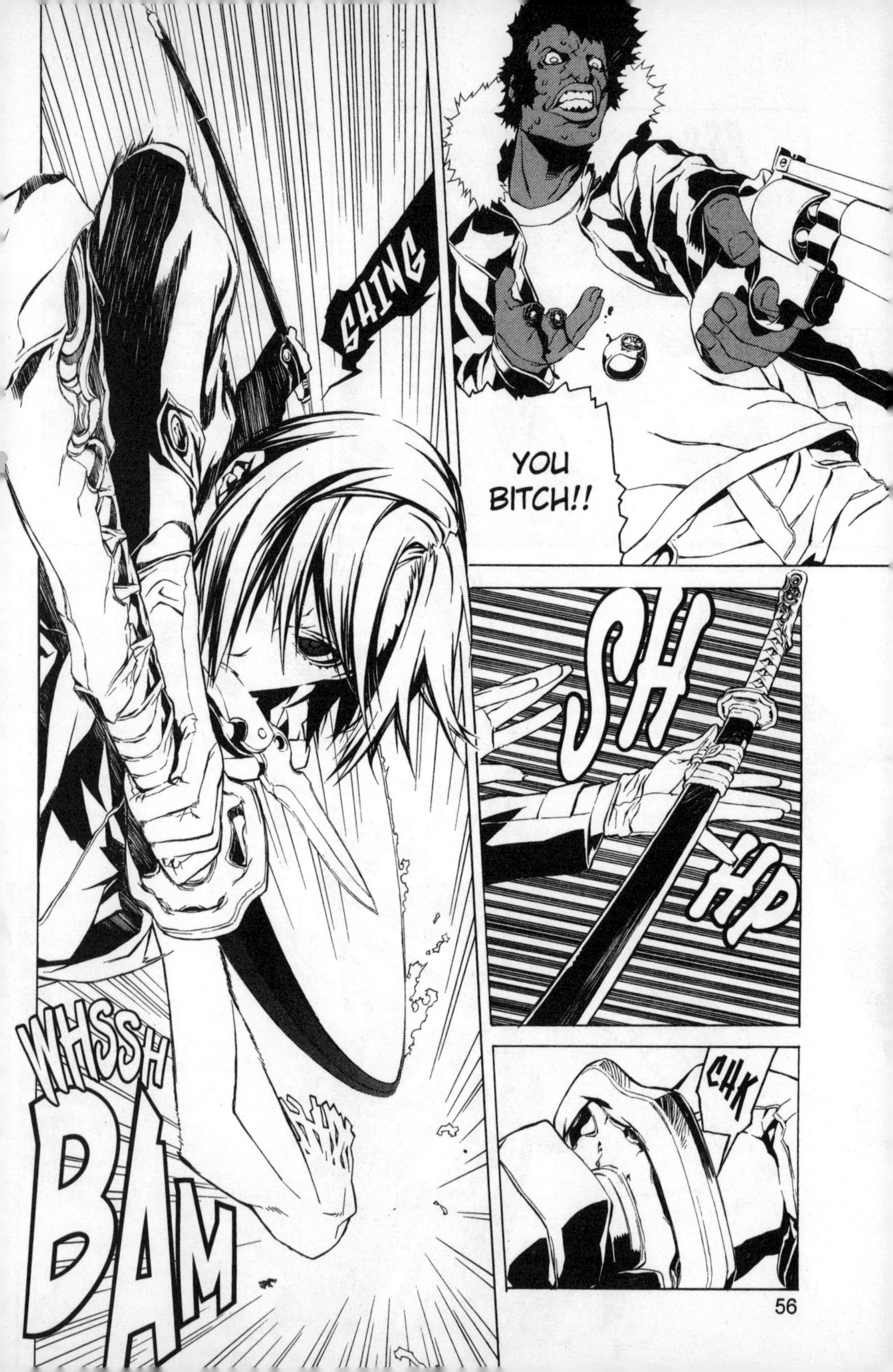
SHING
YOU BITCH!!
SH
HP
CHK
WHSSH
BAM

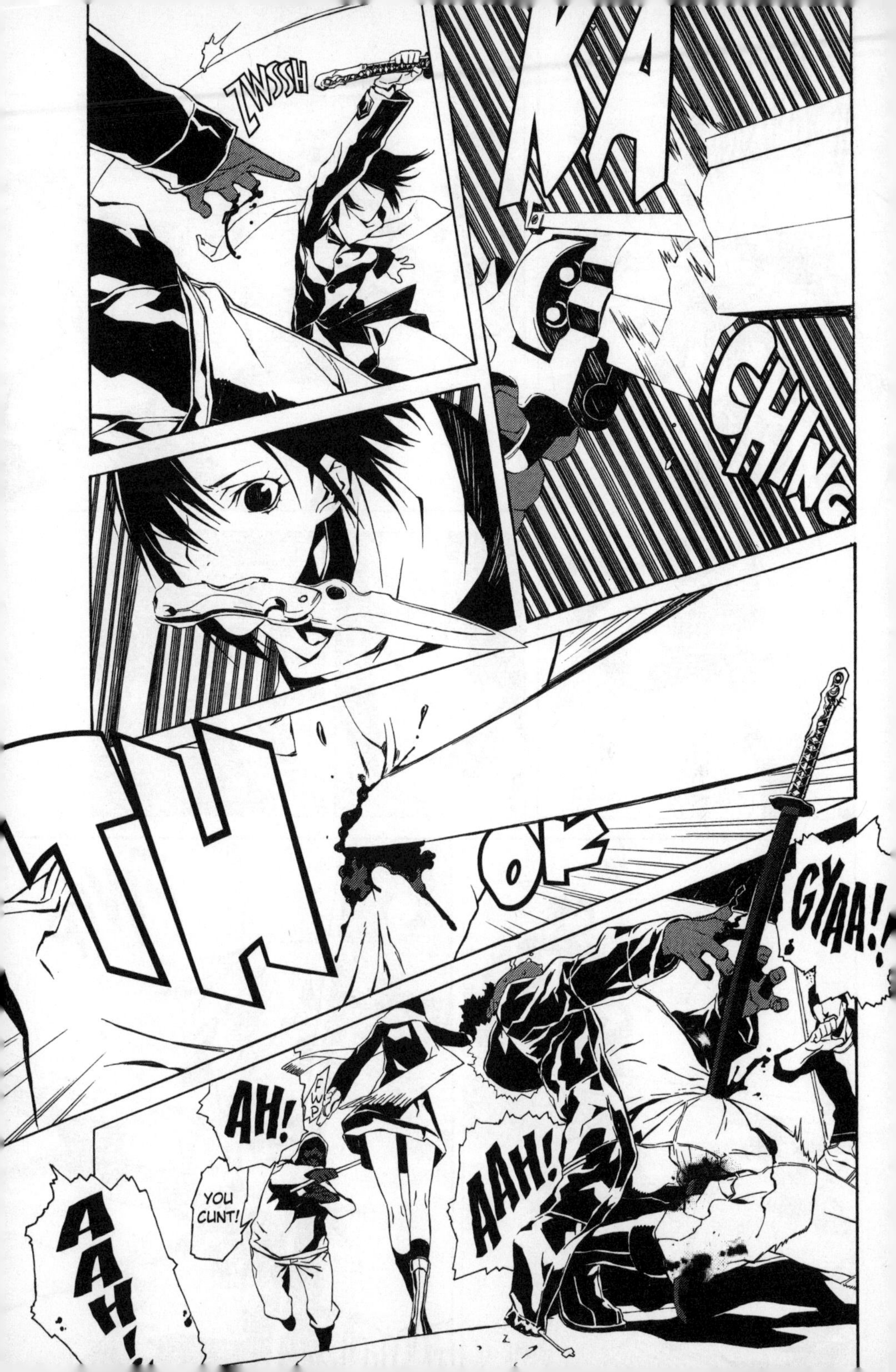

KA
CHING
ZWSSH
THOK
GYAA!!
AAH!
AH!
FWP
YOU CUNT!
AAH!

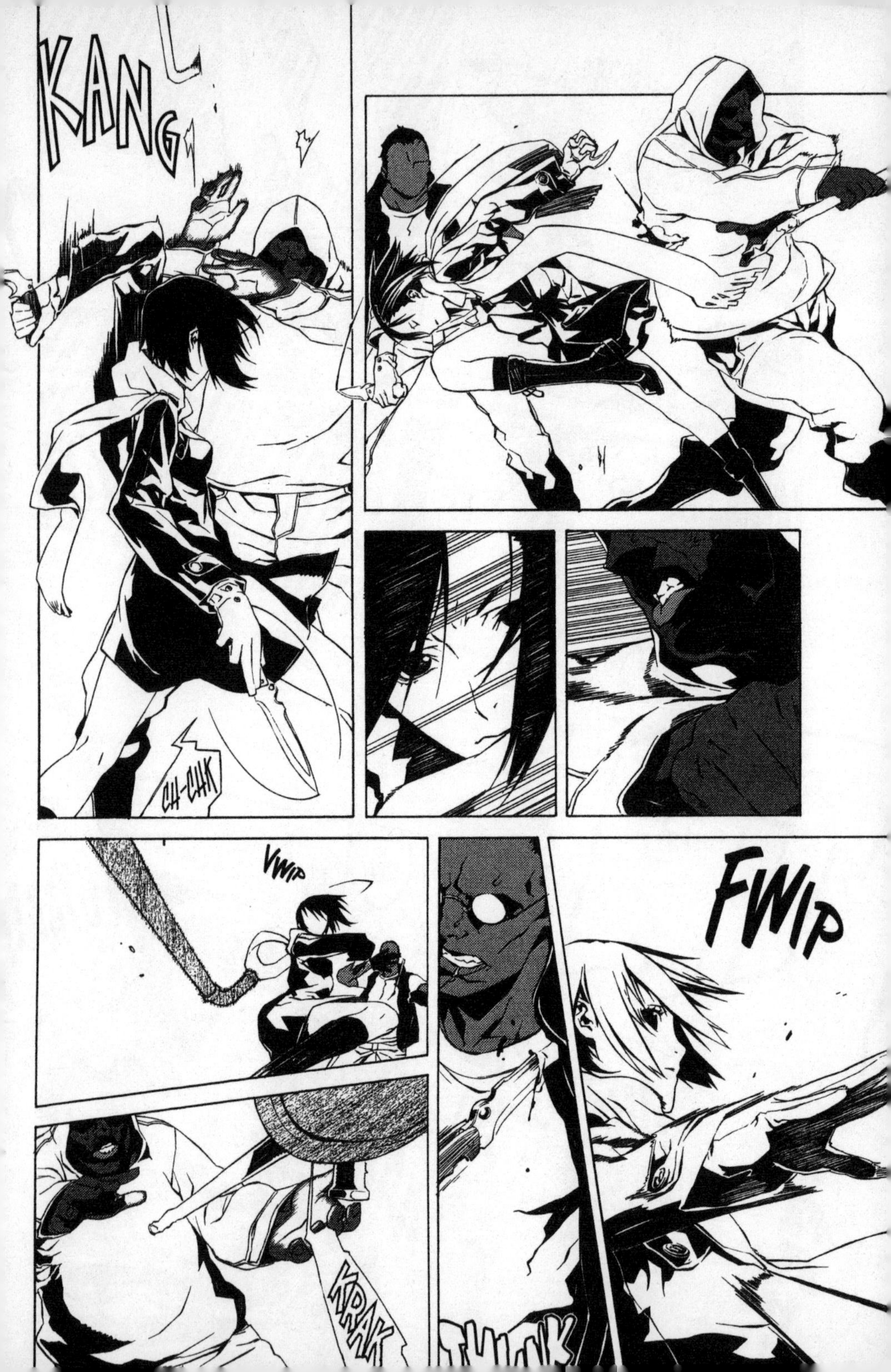
KANG
CH-CHK
FWIP
THUNK
VWIP
KRAK

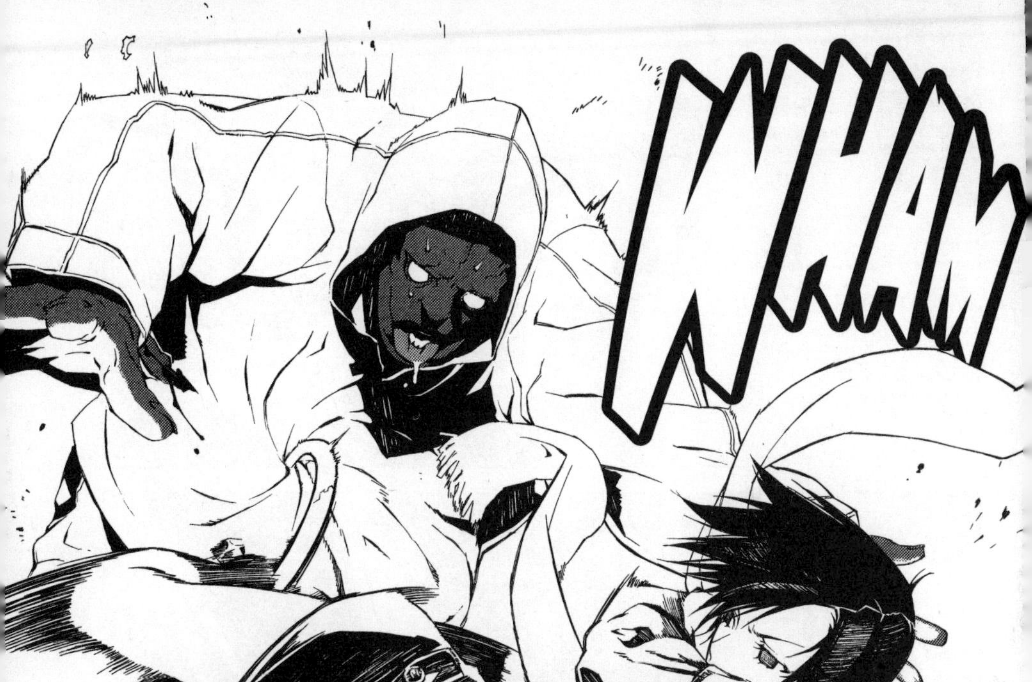
WHAM

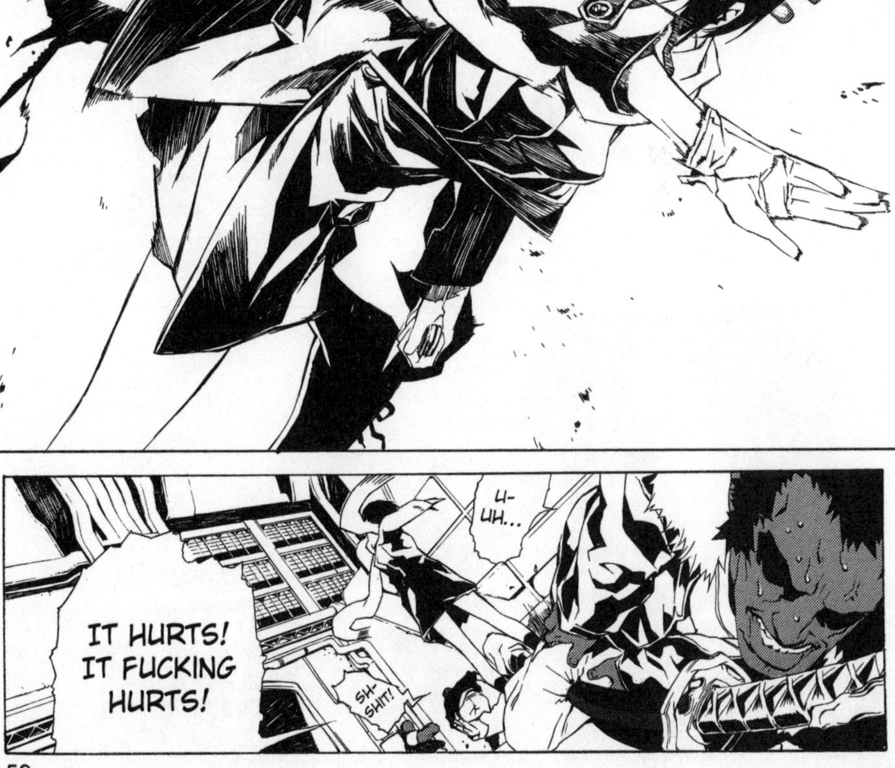
U-
UH...
IT HURTS!
IT FUCKING
HURTS!
SH-
SHIT!

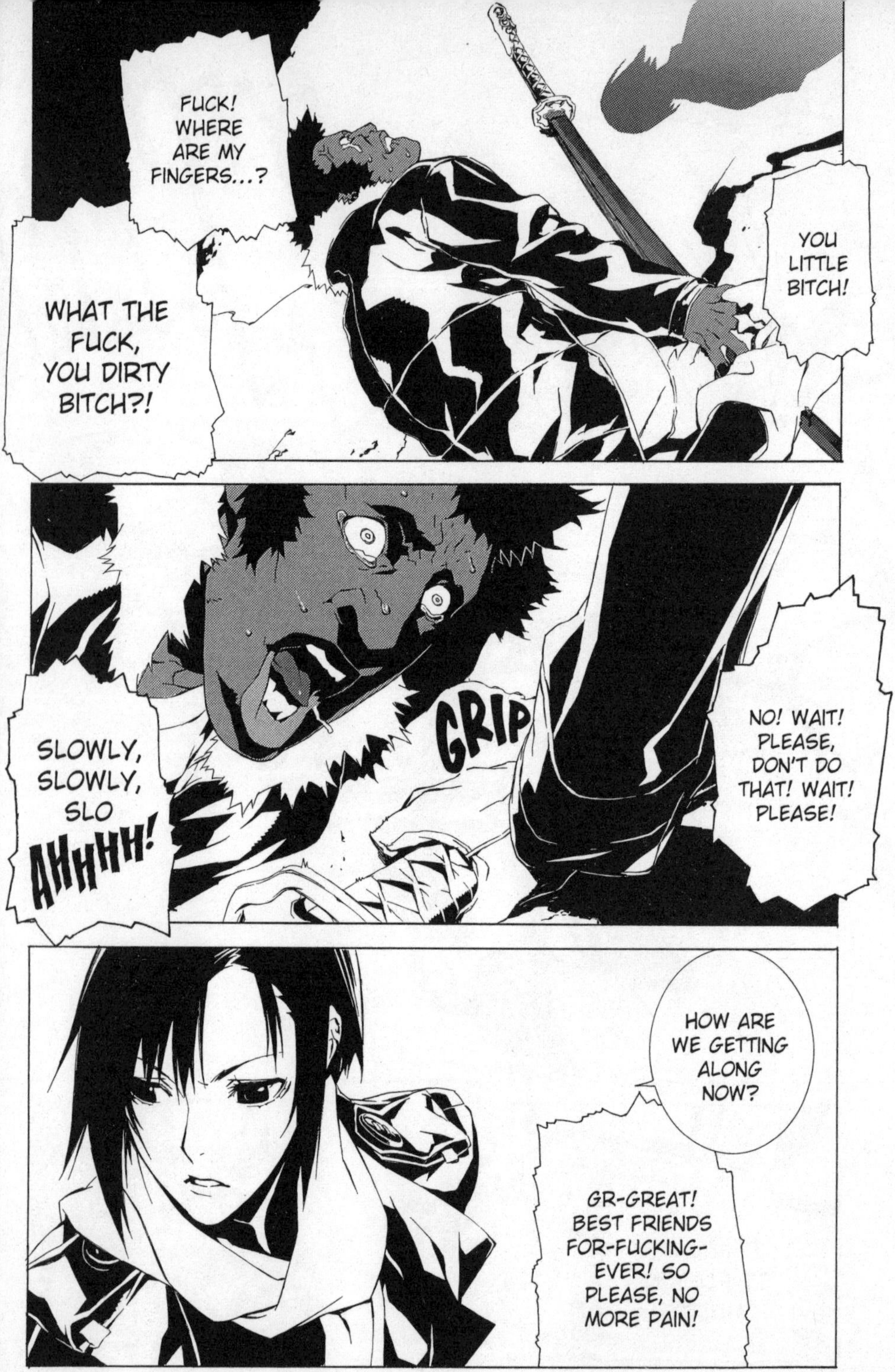
YOU LITTLE BITCH!
FUCK! WHERE ARE MY FINGERS...?
WHAT THE FUCK, YOU DIRTY BITCH?!
NO! WAIT! PLEASE, DON'T DO THAT! WAIT! PLEASE!
GRIP
SLOWLY, SLOWLY, SLO AHHHH!
HOW ARE WE GETTING ALONG NOW?
GR-GREAT! BEST FRIENDS FOR-FUCKING-EVER! SO PLEASE, NO MORE PAIN!

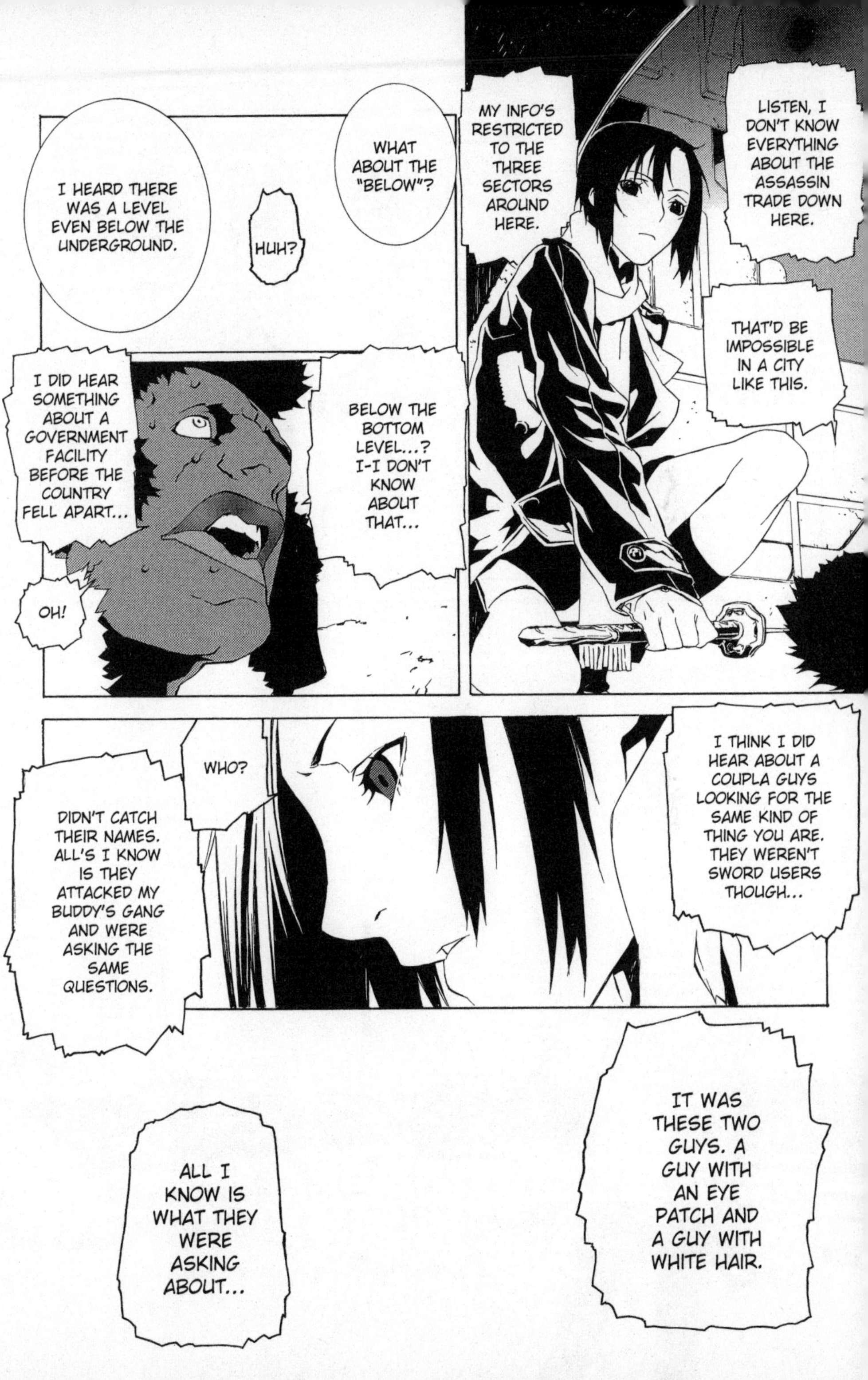
LISTEN, I DON'T KNOW EVERYTHING ABOUT THE ASSASSIN TRADE DOWN HERE.
THAT'D BE IMPOSSIBLE IN A CITY LIKE THIS.
MY INFO'S RESTRICTED TO THE THREE SECTORS AROUND HERE.
WHAT ABOUT THE "BELOW"?
HUH?
I HEARD THERE WAS A LEVEL EVEN BELOW THE UNDERGROUND.
BELOW THE BOTTOM LEVEL...? I-I DON'T KNOW ABOUT THAT...
OH!
I DID HEAR SOMETHING ABOUT A GOVERNMENT FACILITY BEFORE THE COUNTRY FELL APART...
I THINK I DID HEAR ABOUT A COUPLA GUYS LOOKING FOR THE SAME KIND OF THING YOU ARE. THEY WEREN'T SWORD USERS THOUGH...
WHO?
DIDN'T CATCH THEIR NAMES. ALL'S I KNOW IS THEY ATTACKED MY BUDDY'S GANG AND WERE ASKING THE SAME QUESTIONS.
IT WAS THESE TWO GUYS. A GUY WITH AN EYE PATCH AND A GUY WITH WHITE HAIR.
ALL I KNOW IS WHAT THEY WERE ASKING ABOUT...

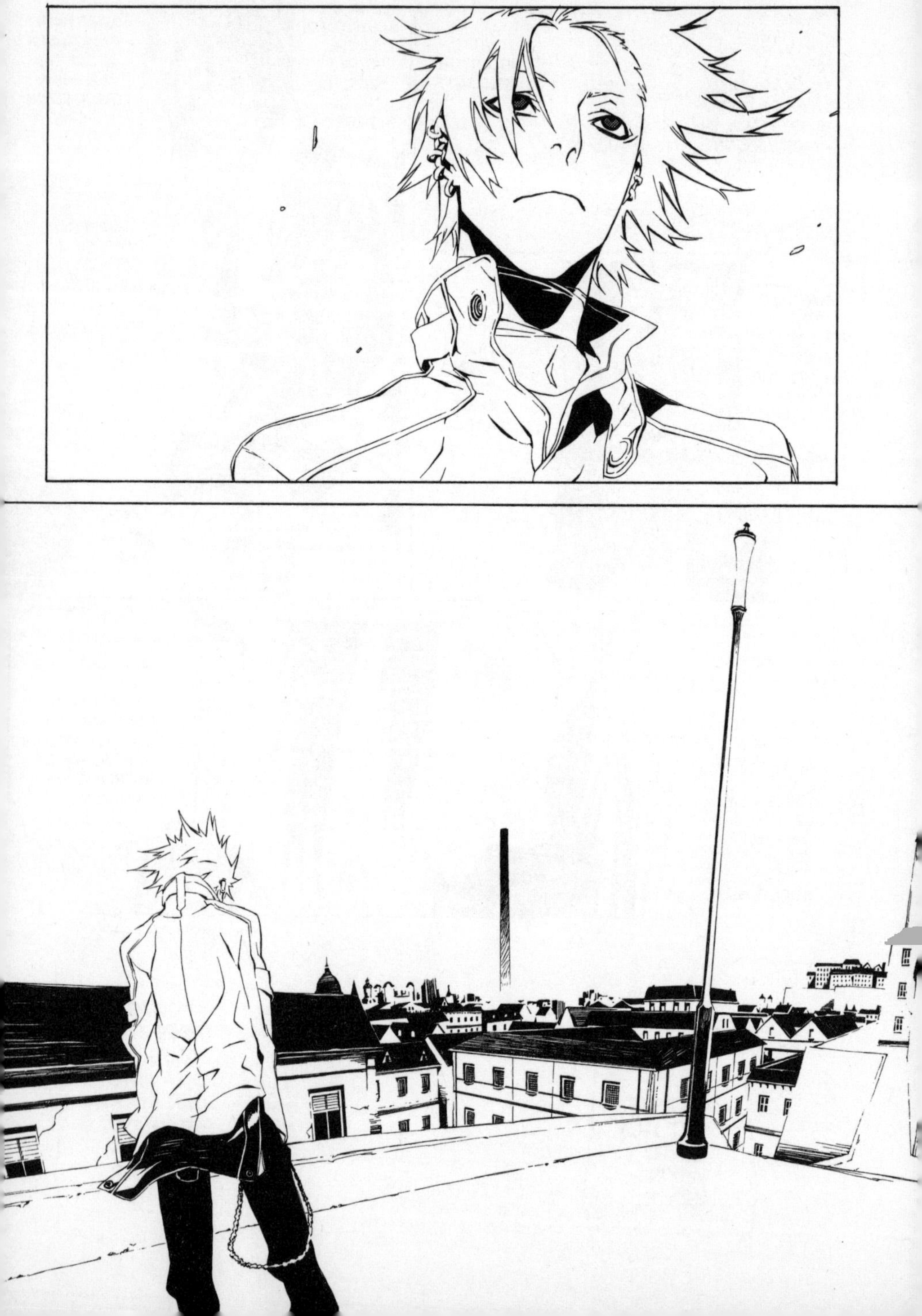

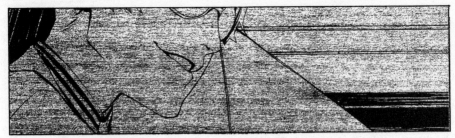

SO IT'S NOT OVER...

LILY...

HEINE!

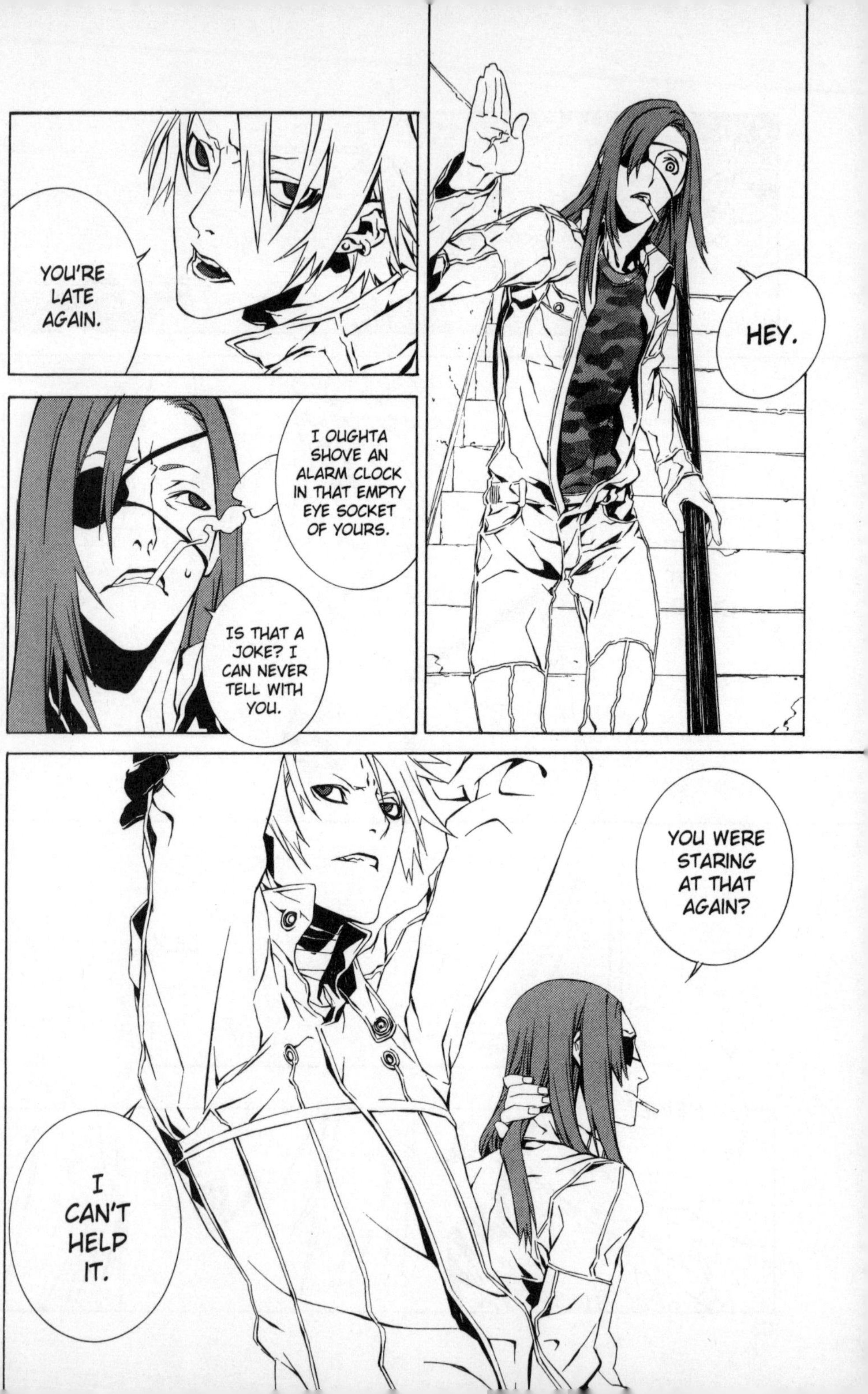
HEY.
YOU'RE LATE AGAIN.
I OUGHTA SHOVE AN ALARM CLOCK IN THAT EMPTY EYE SOCKET OF YOURS.
IS THAT A JOKE? I CAN NEVER TELL WITH YOU.
YOU WERE STARING AT THAT AGAIN?
I CAN'T HELP IT.

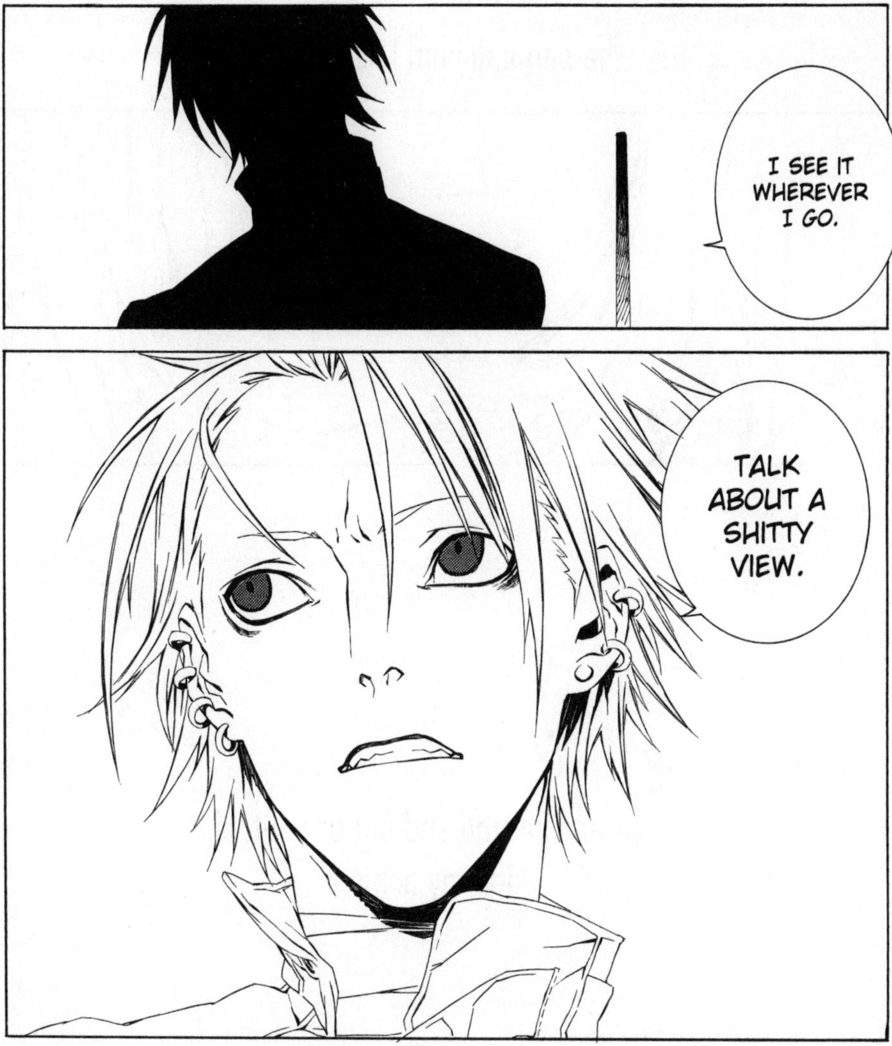
I SEE IT WHEREVER I GO.
TALK ABOUT A SHITTY VIEW.

I remembered that dream...

The same dream I keep having.

Of me, crazed and out of control,
and my arms...

punching right through you.

#03 Wounded & Flawless

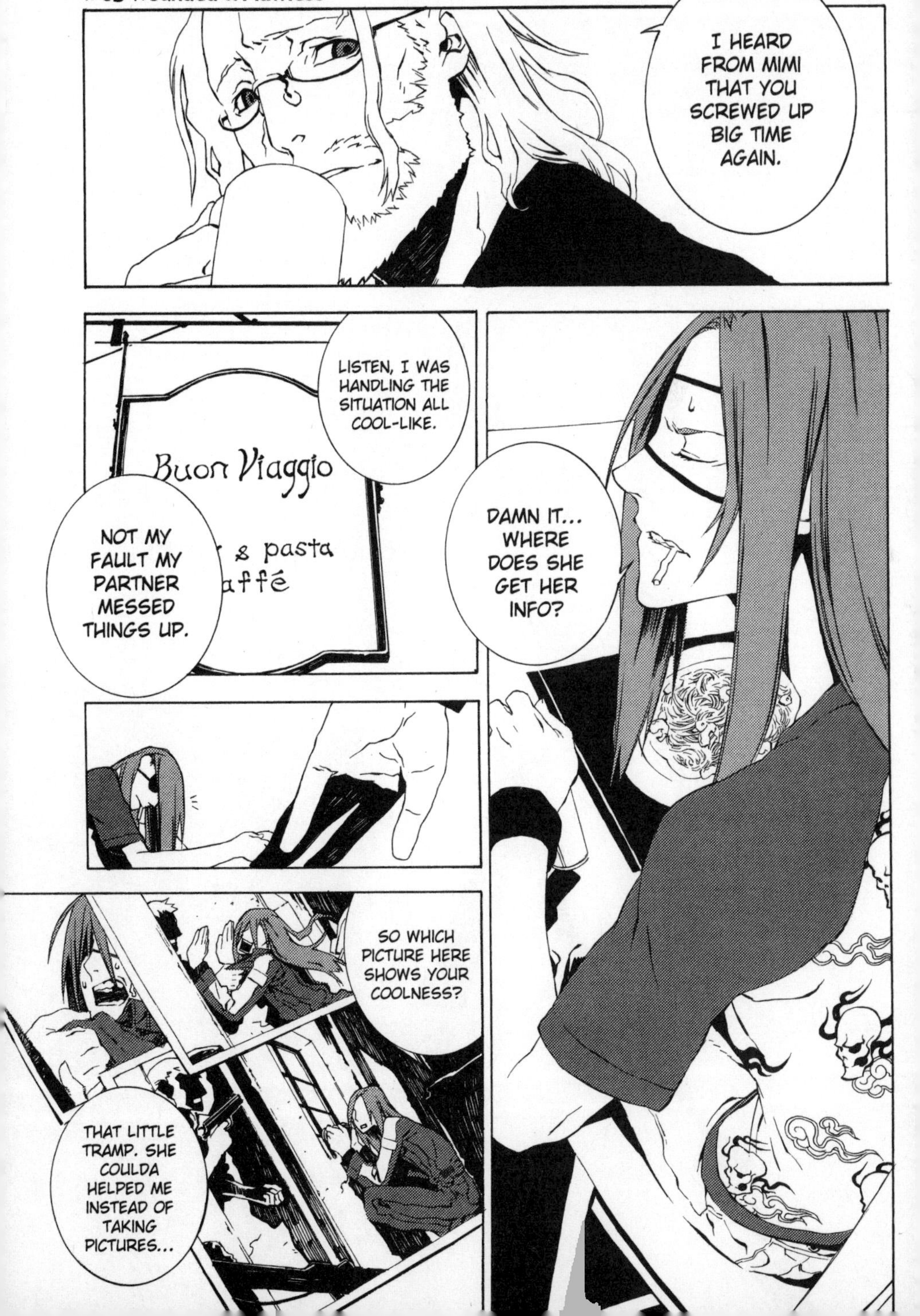
I HEARD FROM MIMI THAT YOU SCREWED UP BIG TIME AGAIN.
DAMN IT... WHERE DOES SHE GET HER INFO?
Buon Viaggio
& pasta
LISTEN, I WAS HANDLING THE SITUATION ALL COOL-LIKE.
NOT MY FAULT MY PARTNER MESSED THINGS UP.
SO WHICH PICTURE HERE SHOWS YOUR COOLNESS?
THAT LITTLE TRAMP. SHE COULDA HELPED ME INSTEAD OF TAKING PICTURES...

#03 Wounded & Flawless

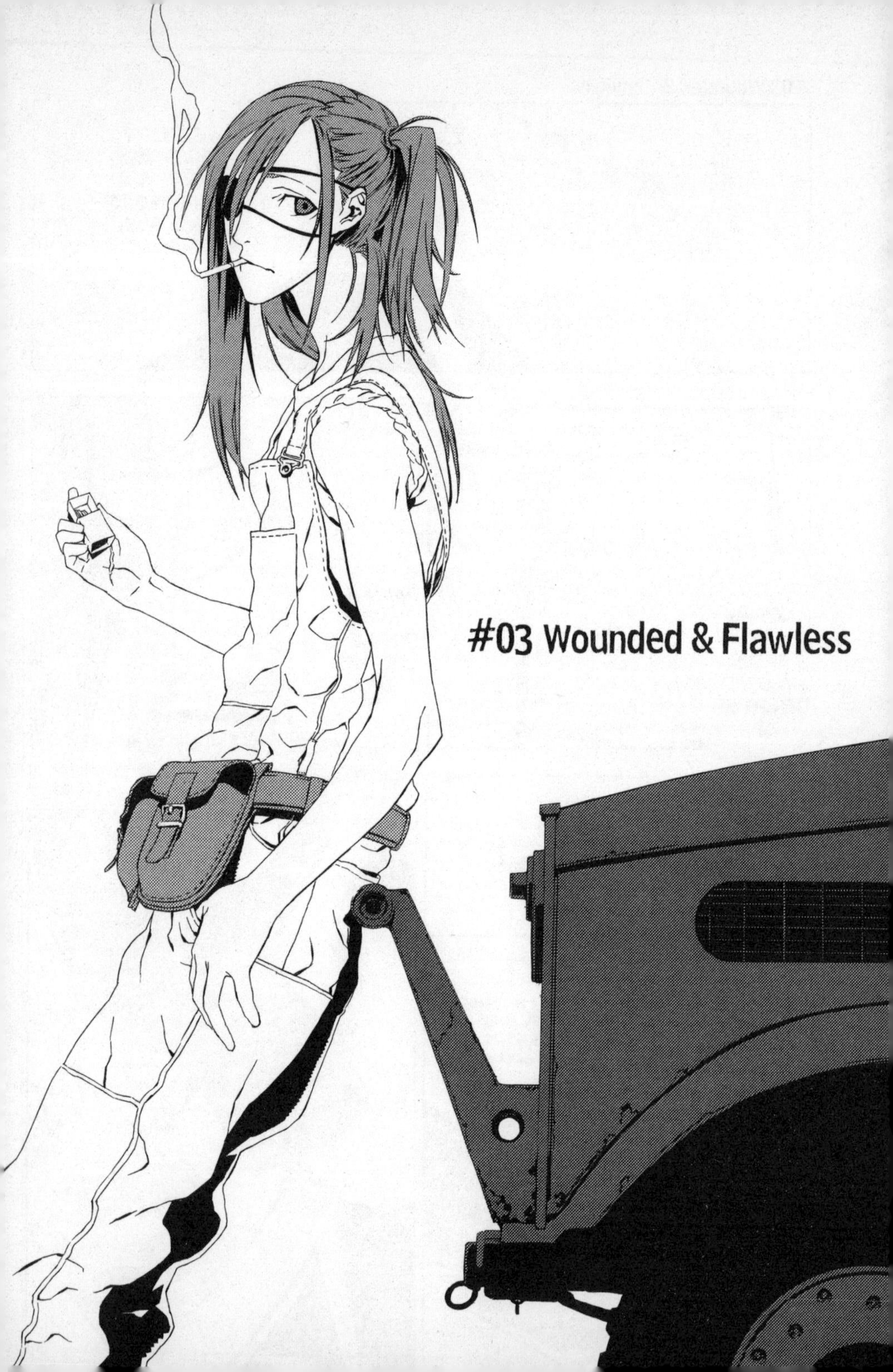

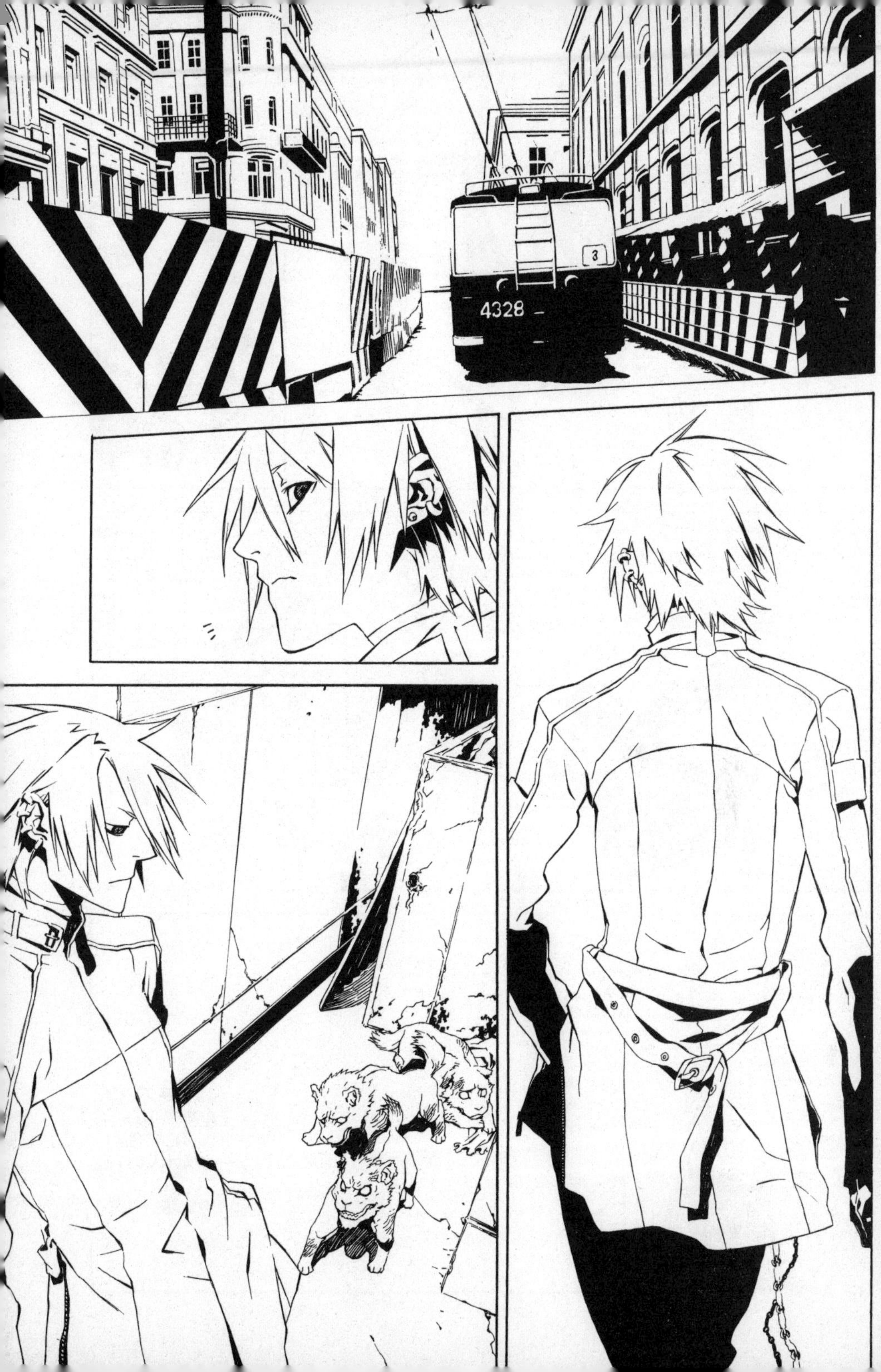
3
4328

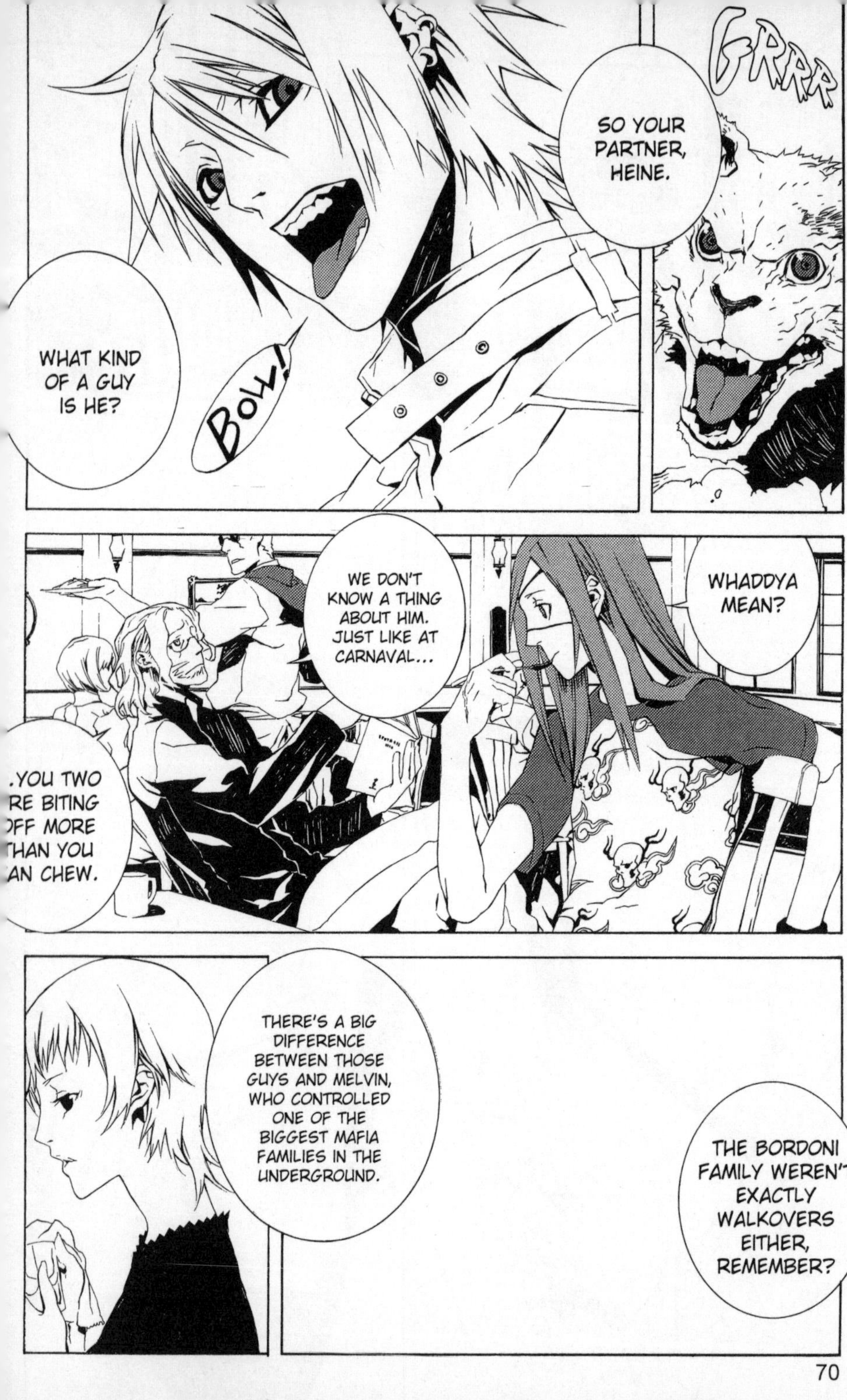
GRRR
SO YOUR PARTNER, HEINE.
BOLL!
WHAT KIND OF A GUY IS HE?
WHADDYA MEAN?
WE DON'T KNOW A THING ABOUT HIM. JUST LIKE AT CARNAVAL...
.YOU TWO RE BITING FF MORE THAN YOU AN CHEW.
THE BORDONI FAMILY WEREN'T EXACTLY WALKOVERS EITHER, REMEMBER?
THERE'S A BIG DIFFERENCE BETWEEN THOSE GUYS AND MELVIN, WHO CONTROLLED ONE OF THE BIGGEST MAFIA FAMILIES IN THE UNDERGROUND.

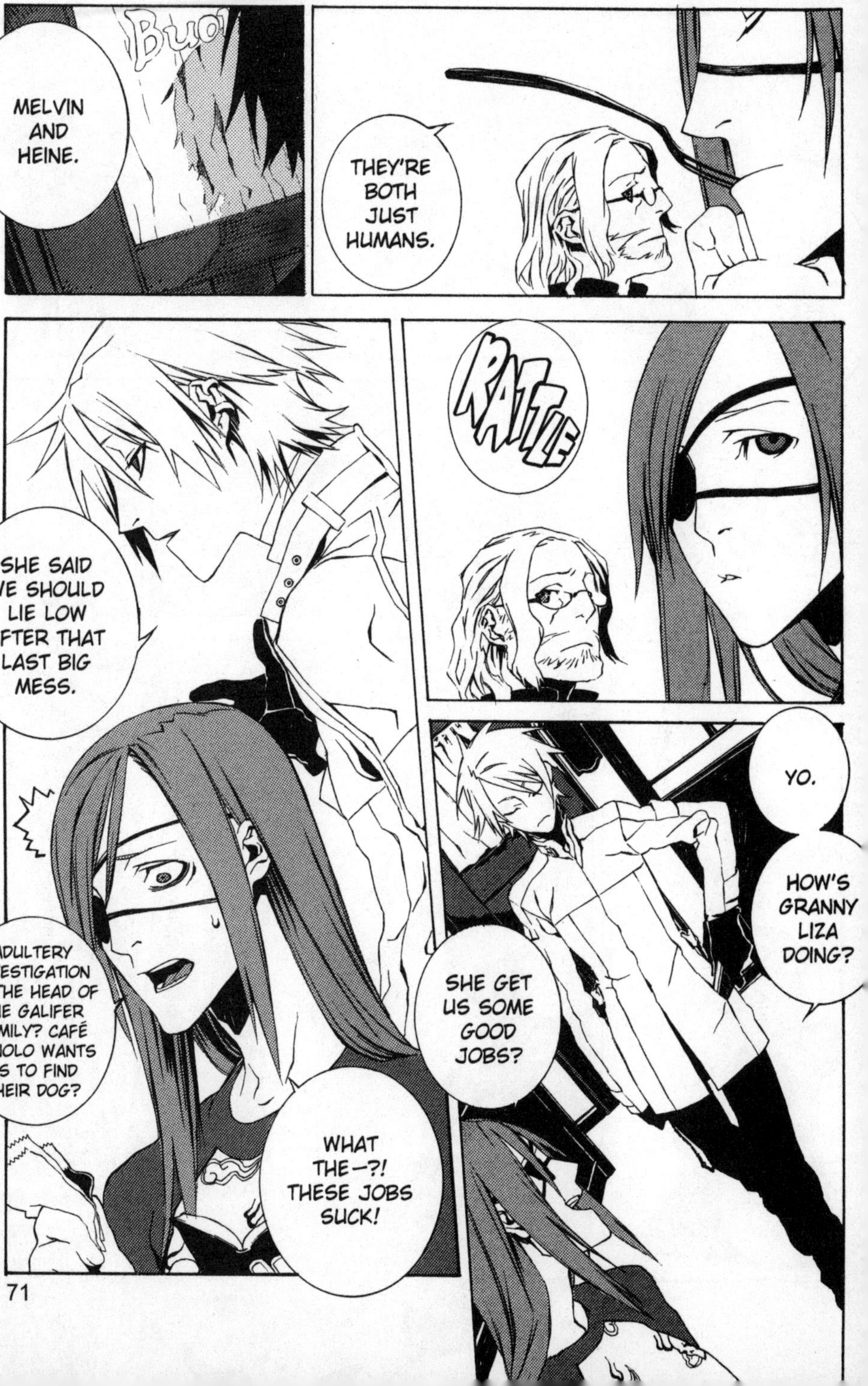
THEY'RE BOTH JUST HUMANS.
Buo
MELVIN AND HEINE.
RATTLE
YO.
HOW'S GRANNY LIZA DOING?
SHE GET US SOME GOOD JOBS?
SHE SAID WE SHOULD LIE LOW AFTER THAT LAST BIG MESS.
ADULTERY INVESTIGATION OF THE HEAD OF THE GALIFER FAMILY? CAFÉ MANOLO WANTS US TO FIND THEIR DOG?
WHAT THE—?! THESE JOBS SUCK!

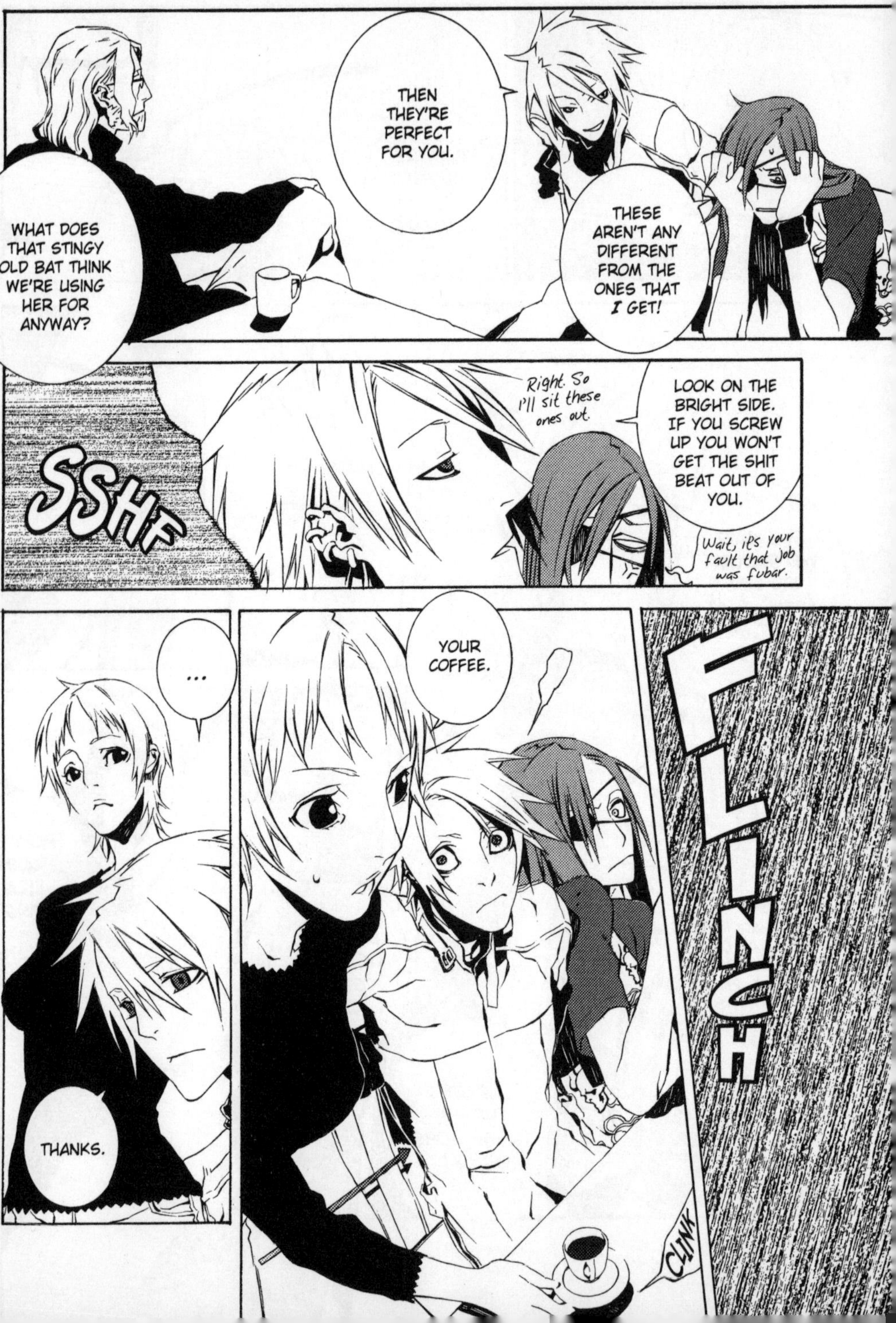
THESE AREN'T ANY DIFFERENT FROM THE ONES THAT I GET!
THEN THEY'RE PERFECT FOR YOU.
WHAT DOES THAT STINGY OLD BAT THINK WE'RE USING HER FOR ANYWAY?
LOOK ON THE BRIGHT SIDE. IF YOU SCREW UP YOU WON'T GET THE SHIT BEAT OUT OF YOU.
Right. So I'll sit these ones out.
Wait, it's your fault that job was fubar.
SSHF
FLINCH
YOUR COFFEE.
CLINK
...
THANKS.

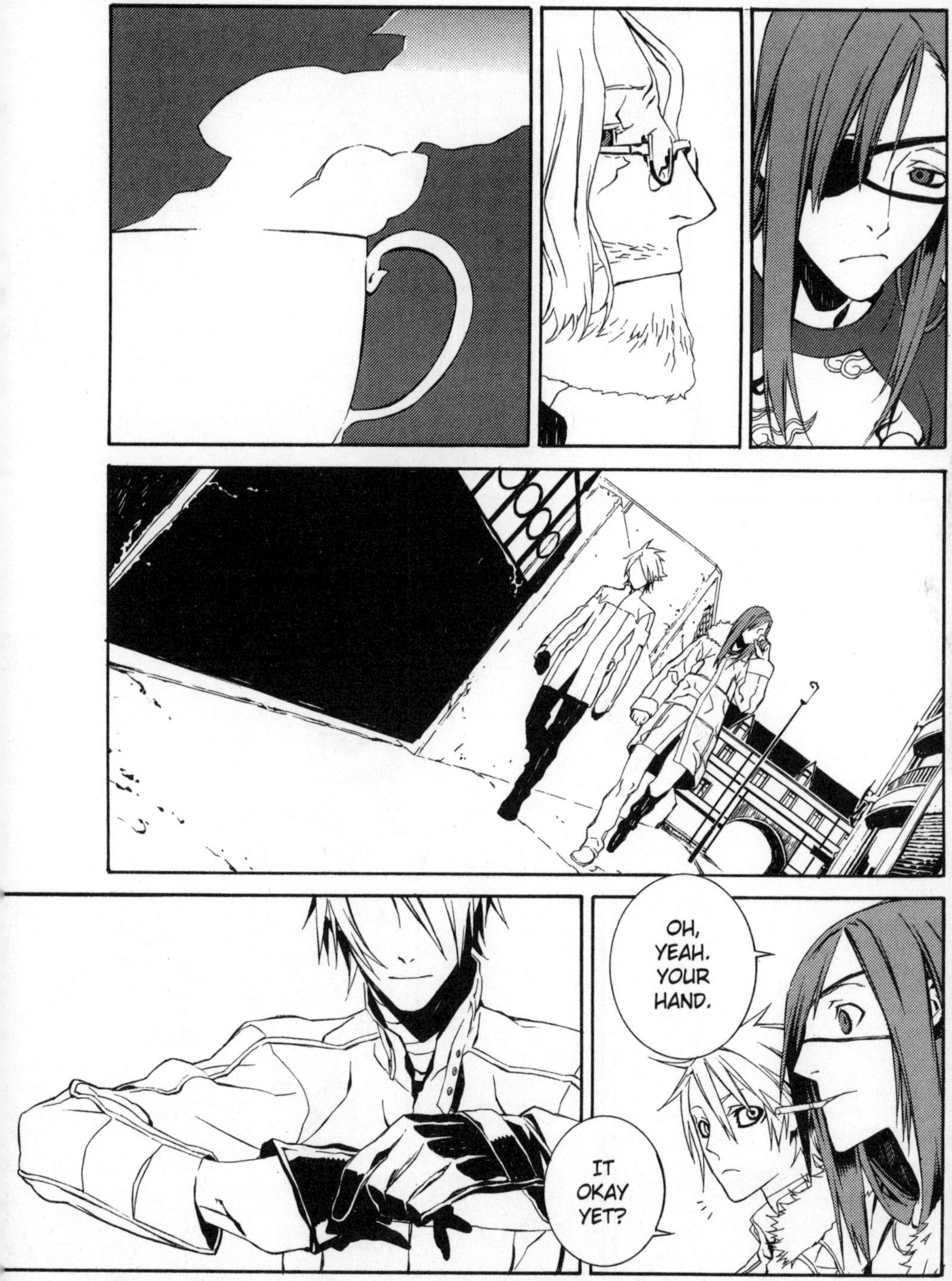
OH, YEAH. YOUR HAND.
IT OKAY YET?

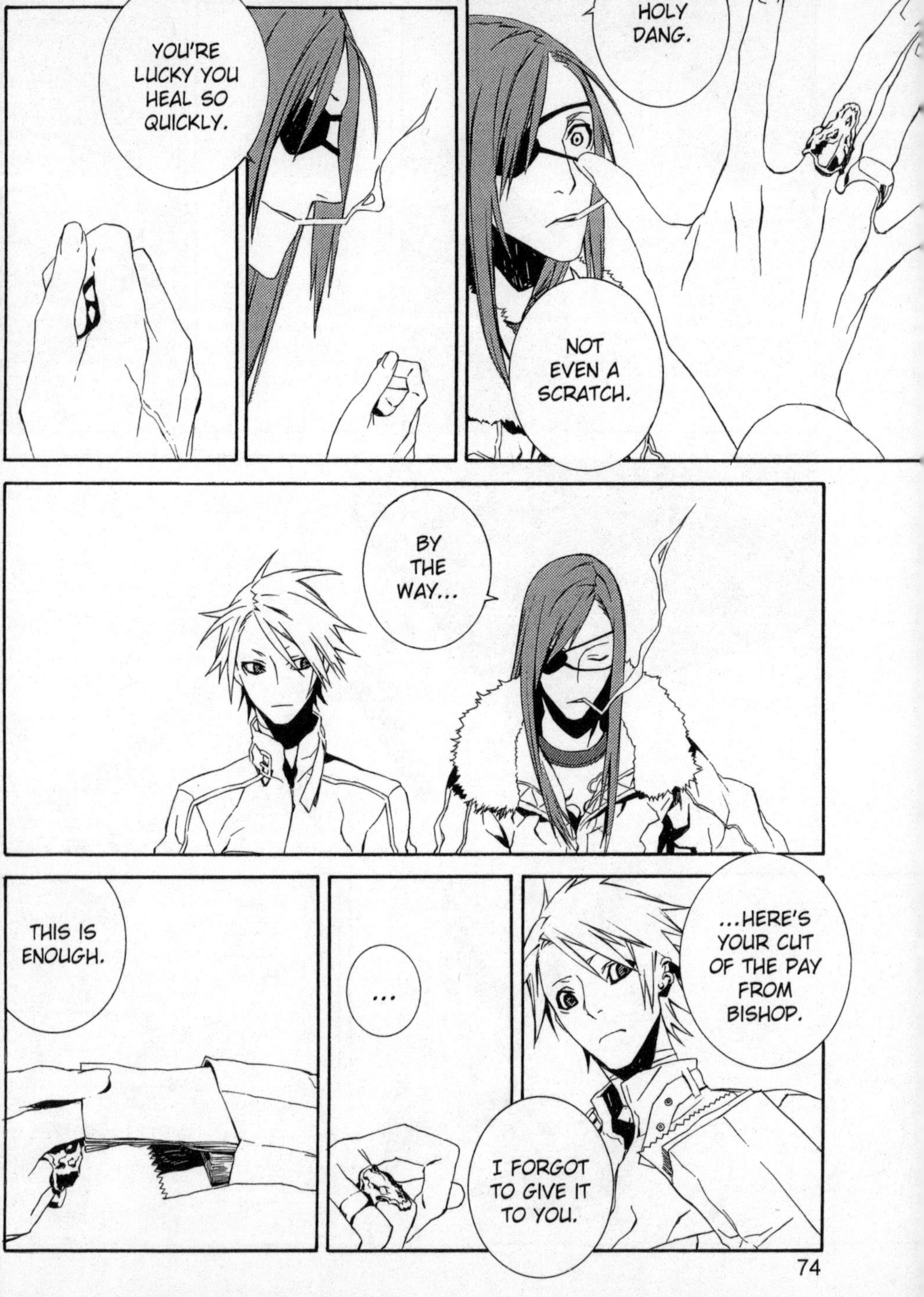
HOLY DANG.
NOT EVEN A SCRATCH.
YOU'RE LUCKY YOU HEAL SO QUICKLY.
BY THE WAY...
...HERE'S YOUR CUT OF THE PAY FROM BISHOP.
I FORGOT TO GIVE IT TO YOU.
...
THIS IS ENOUGH.

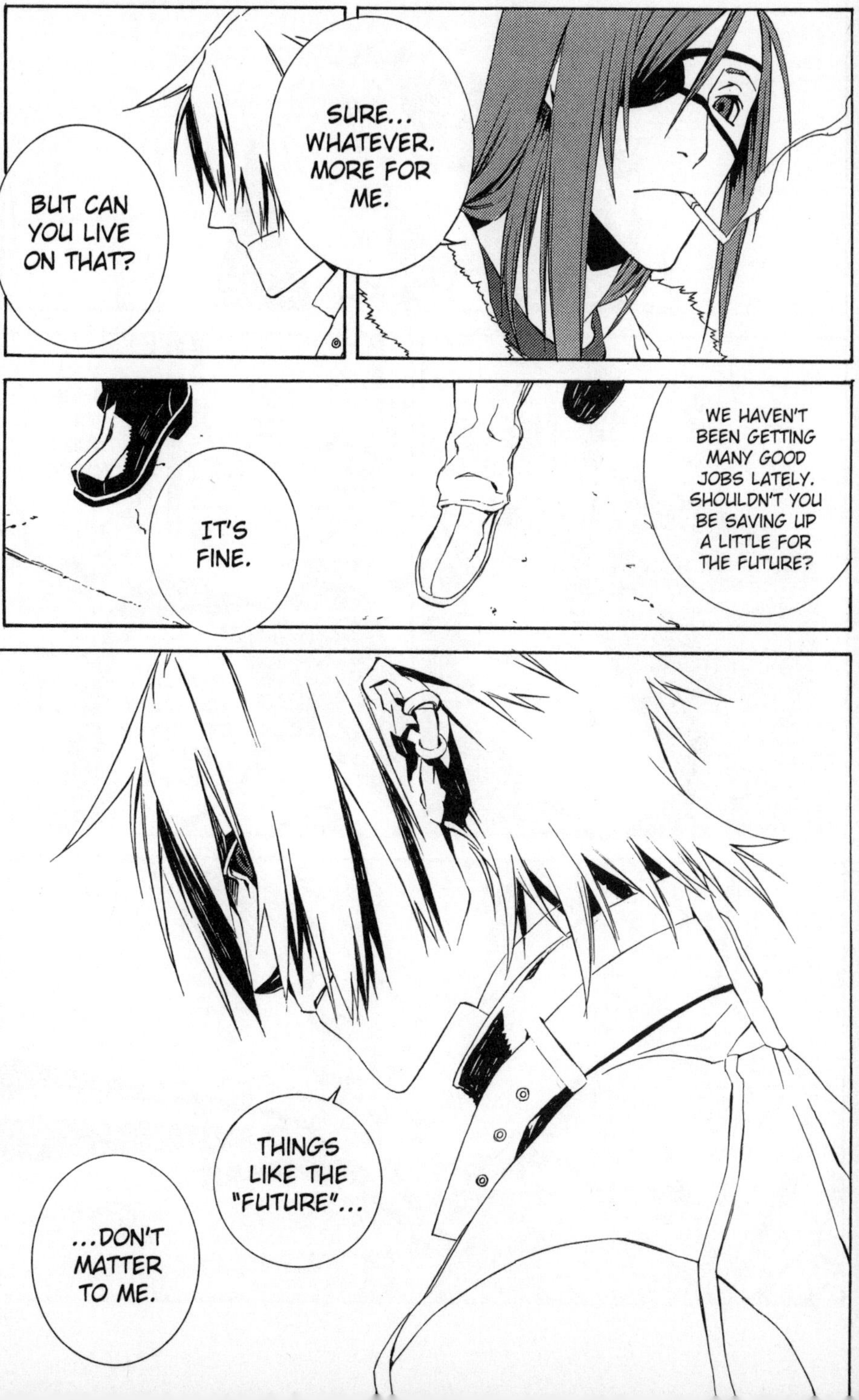
SURE... WHATEVER. MORE FOR ME.
BUT CAN YOU LIVE ON THAT?
WE HAVEN'T BEEN GETTING MANY GOOD JOBS LATELY. SHOULDN'T YOU BE SAVING UP A LITTLE FOR THE FUTURE?
IT'S FINE.
THINGS LIKE THE "FUTURE"...
...DON'T MATTER TO ME.

...

YOU SURE ARE QUIET TODAY.

NOT REALLY... YOU KNOW I'VE NEVER BEEN A TALKER.

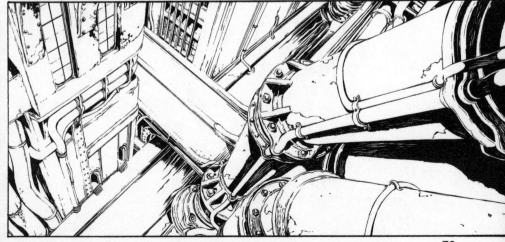

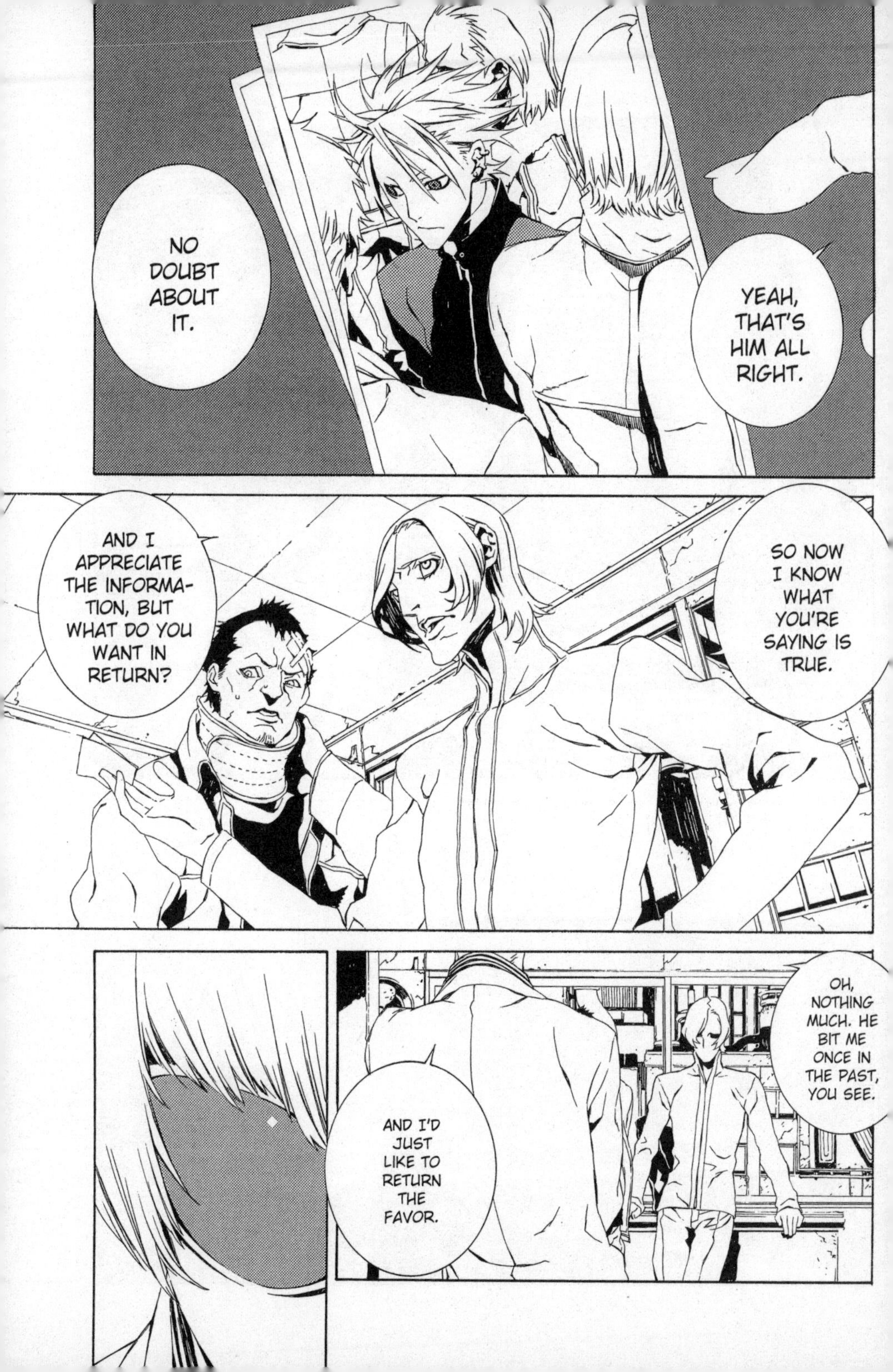
YEAH, THAT'S HIM ALL RIGHT.
NO DOUBT ABOUT IT.
SO NOW I KNOW WHAT YOU'RE SAYING IS TRUE.
AND I APPRECIATE THE INFORMATION, BUT WHAT DO YOU WANT IN RETURN?
OH, NOTHING MUCH. HE BIT ME ONCE IN THE PAST, YOU SEE.
AND I'D JUST LIKE TO RETURN THE FAVOR.

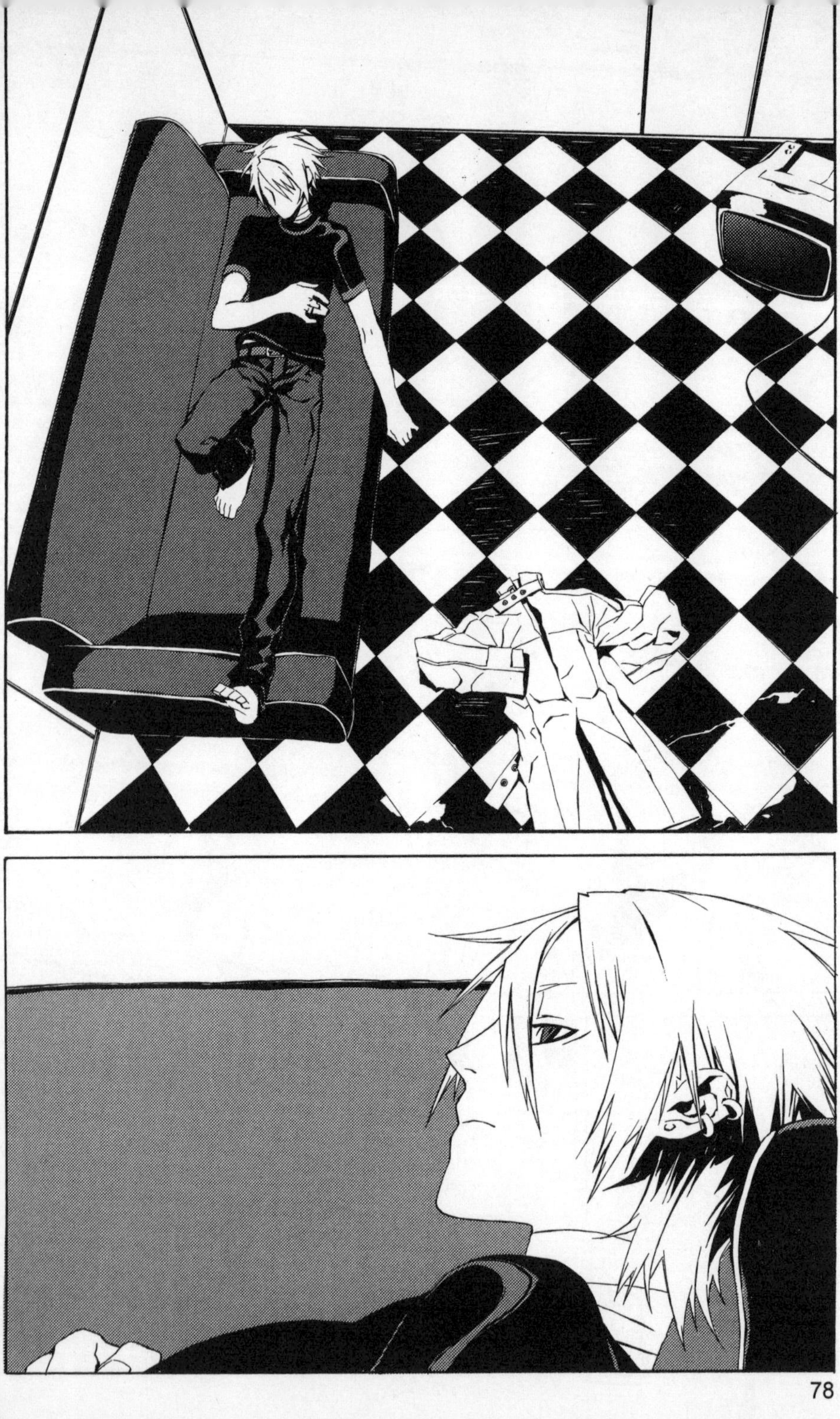

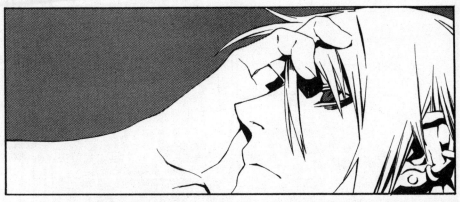

SHIT.

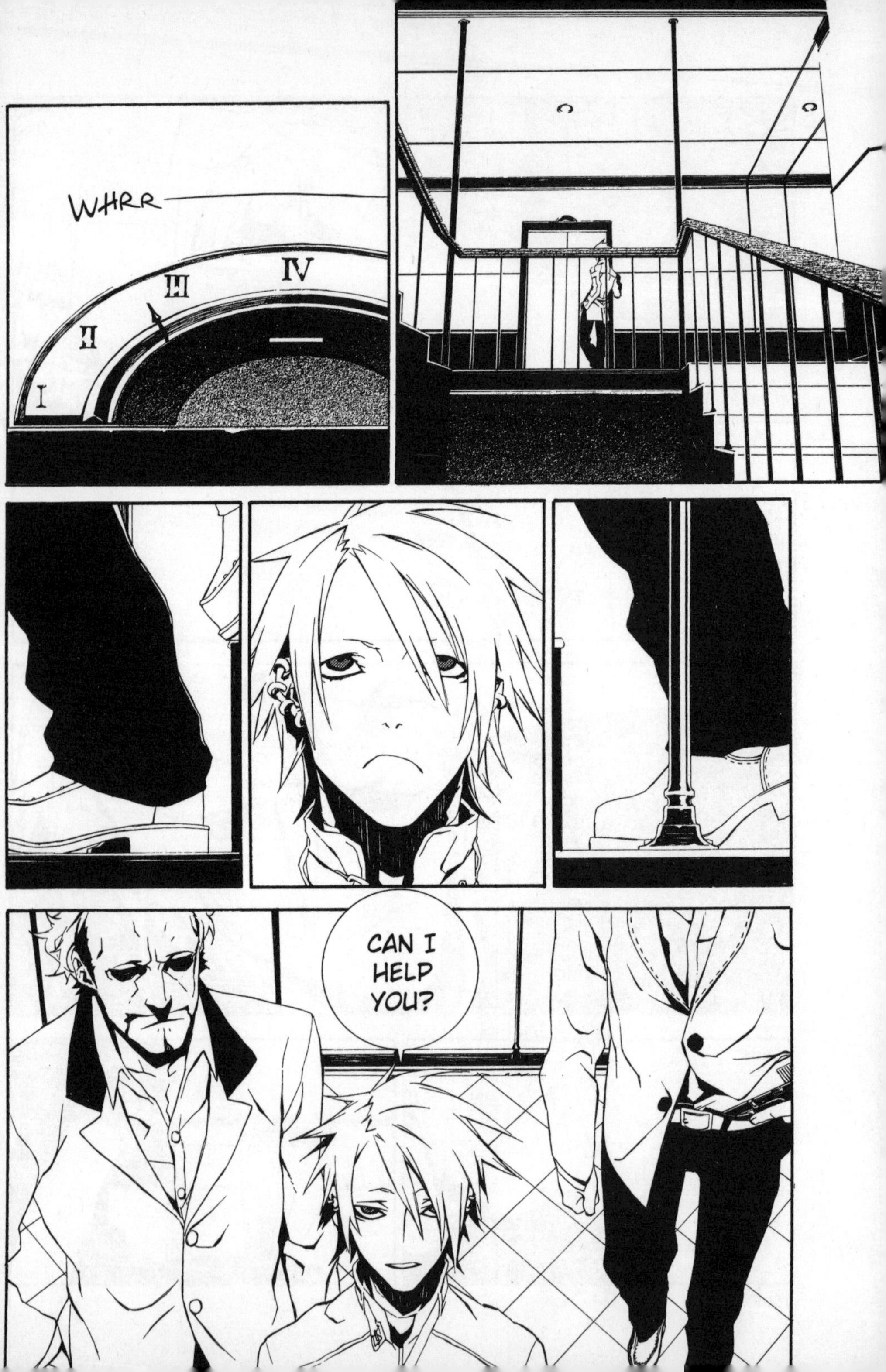
WHRR
CAN I HELP YOU?

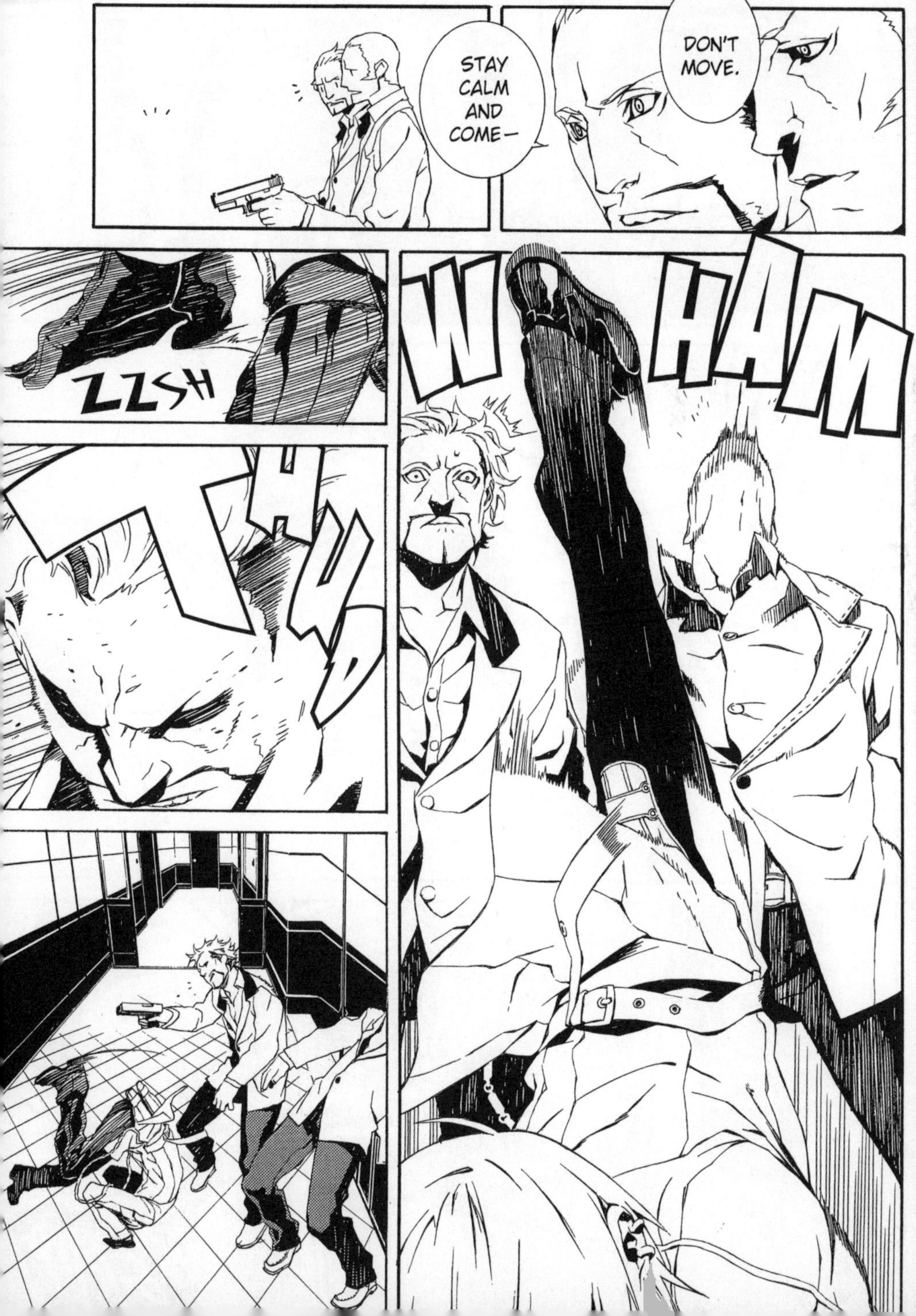
DON'T MOVE.
STAY CALM AND COME—
WHAM
ZZSH
THUD

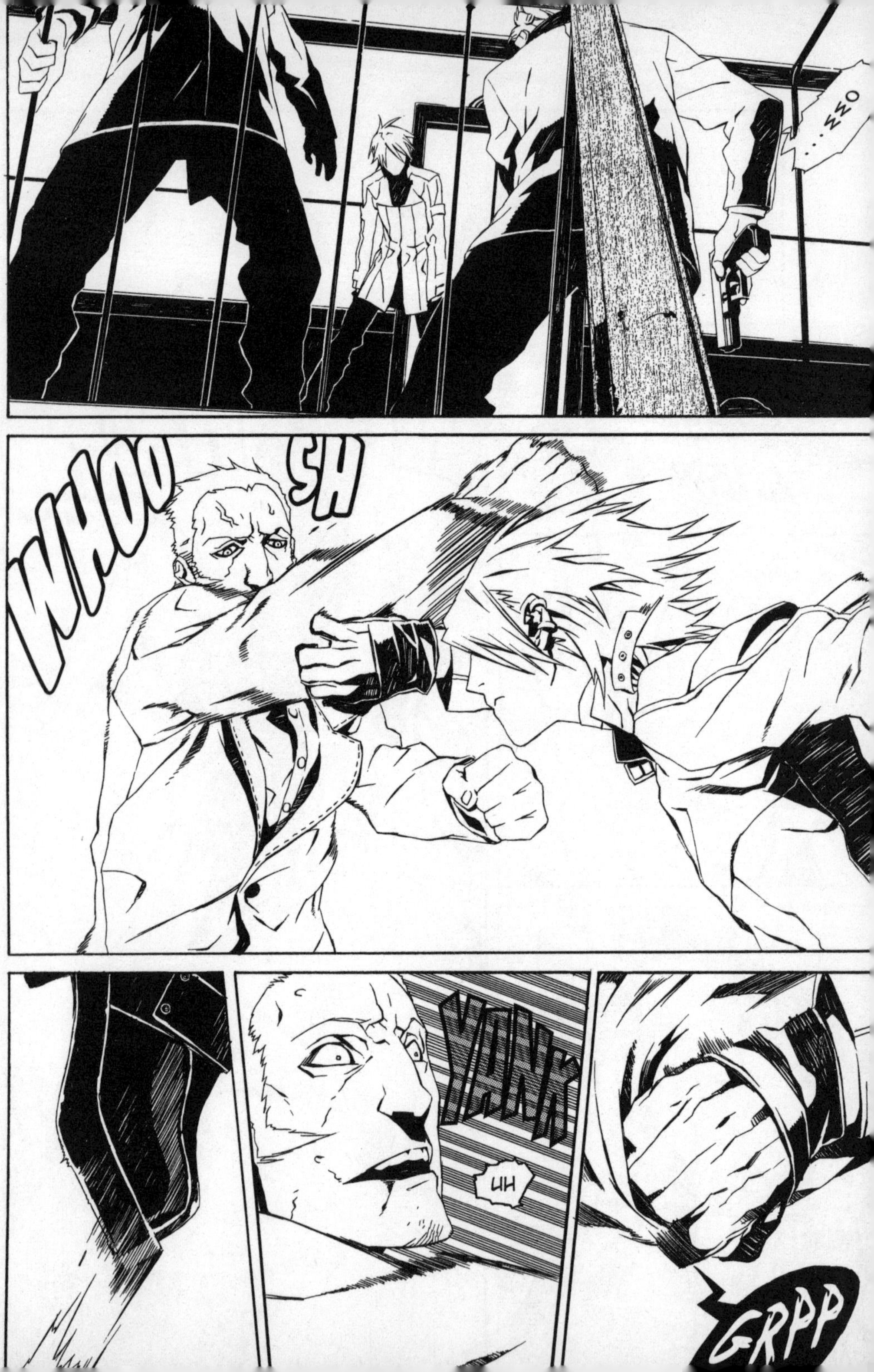
OWW...
WHOOSH
YANK
UH
GRPP

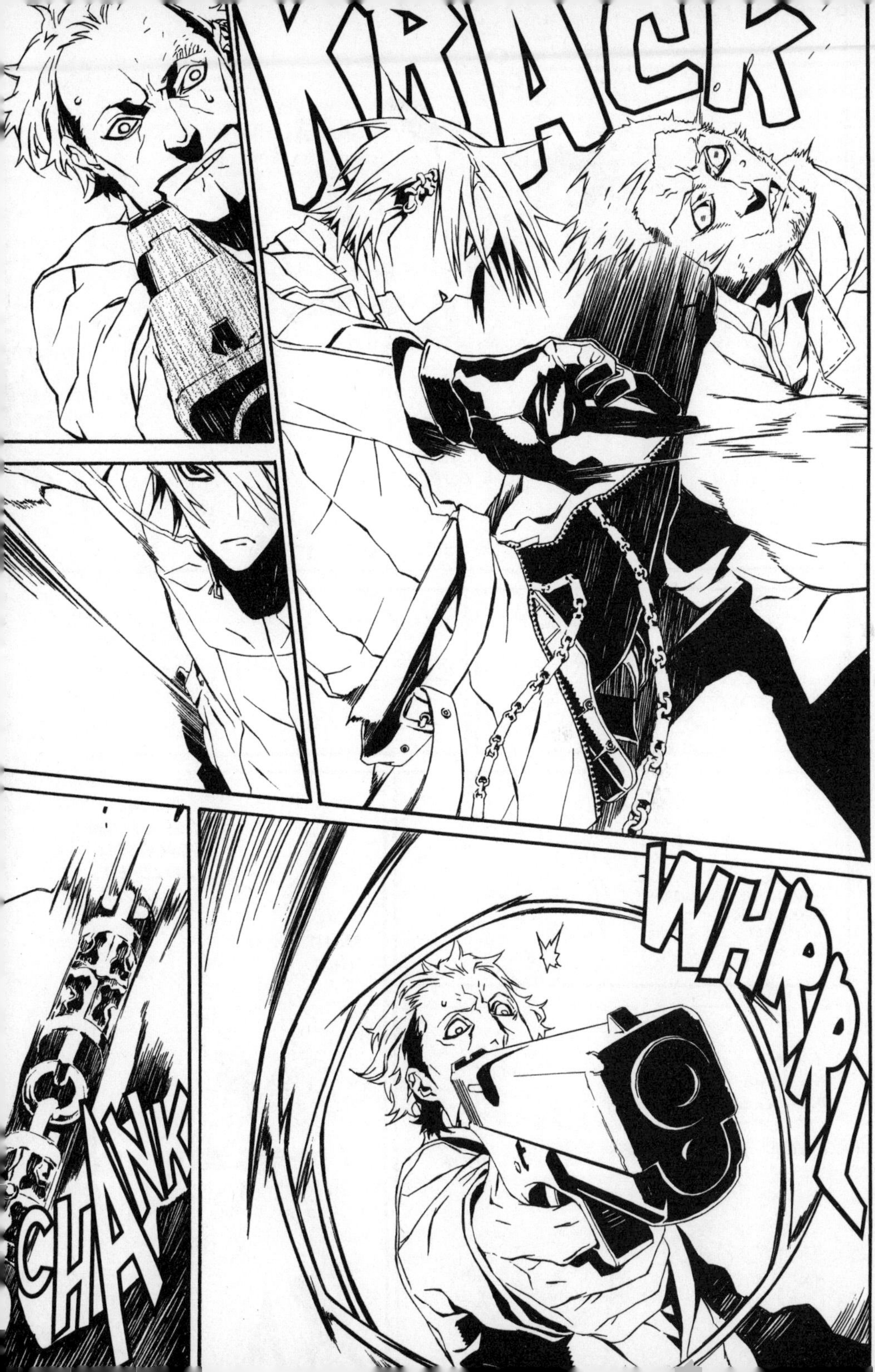
KRACK
WHRRL
CHANK

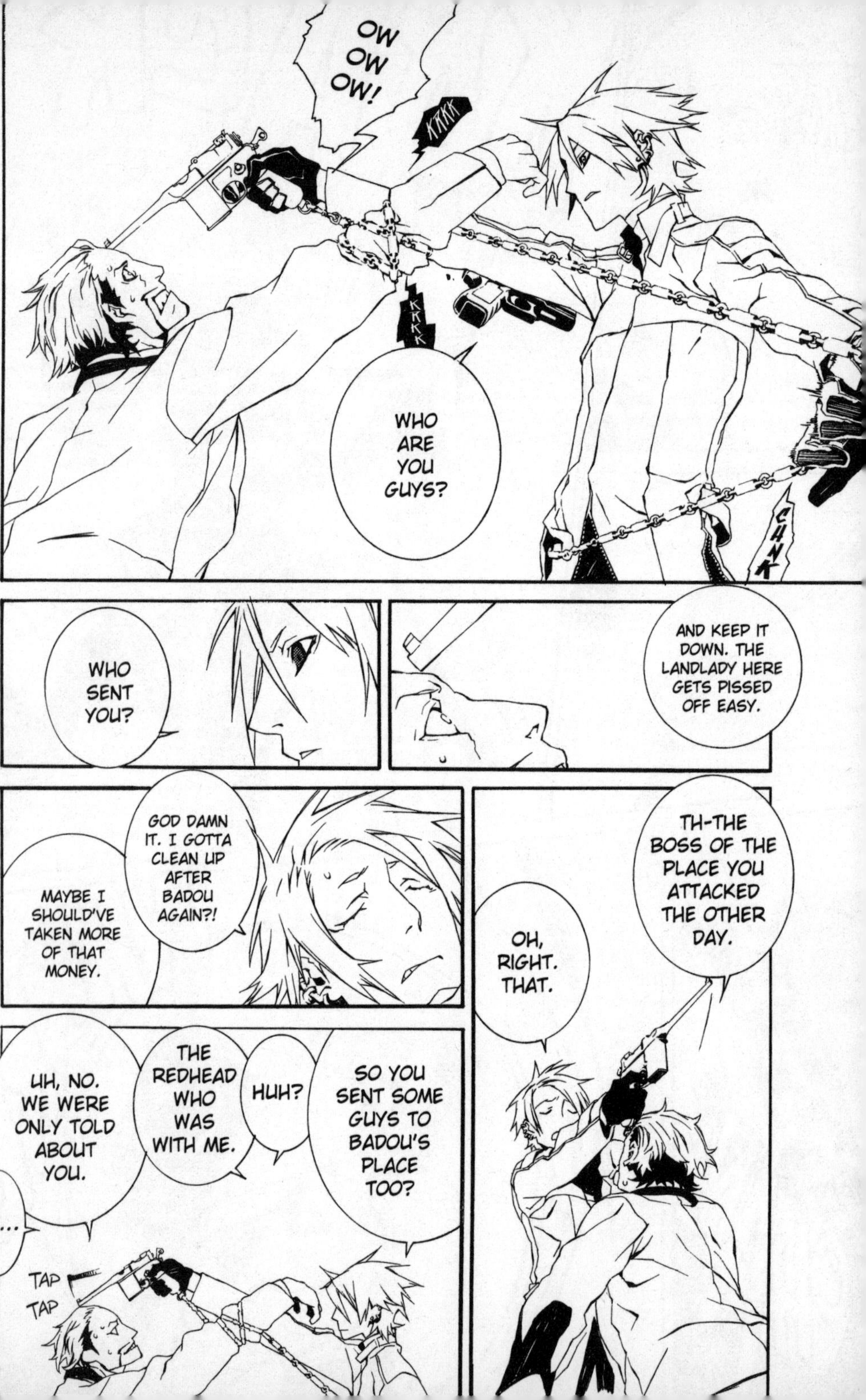
OW OW OW!
KRKK
KRKK
WHO ARE YOU GUYS?
CHNK
AND KEEP IT DOWN. THE LANDLADY HERE GETS PISSED OFF EASY.
WHO SENT YOU?
TH-THE BOSS OF THE PLACE YOU ATTACKED THE OTHER DAY.
OH, RIGHT. THAT.
GOD DAMN IT. I GOTTA CLEAN UP AFTER BADOU AGAIN?!
MAYBE I SHOULD'VE TAKEN MORE OF THAT MONEY.
SO YOU SENT SOME GUYS TO BADOU'S PLACE TOO?
HUH?
THE REDHEAD WHO WAS WITH ME.
UH, NO. WE WERE ONLY TOLD ABOUT YOU.
OH...
TAP TAP

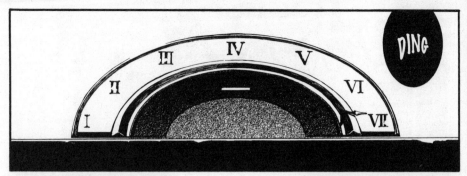

DING
GOT NO CHOICE, I GUESS.
WHRR
I BETTER GO WARN HIM.
DING

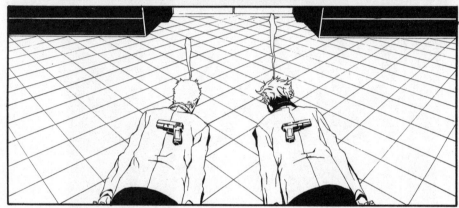

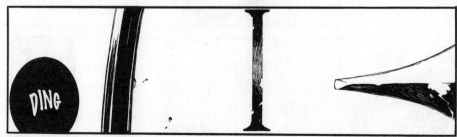

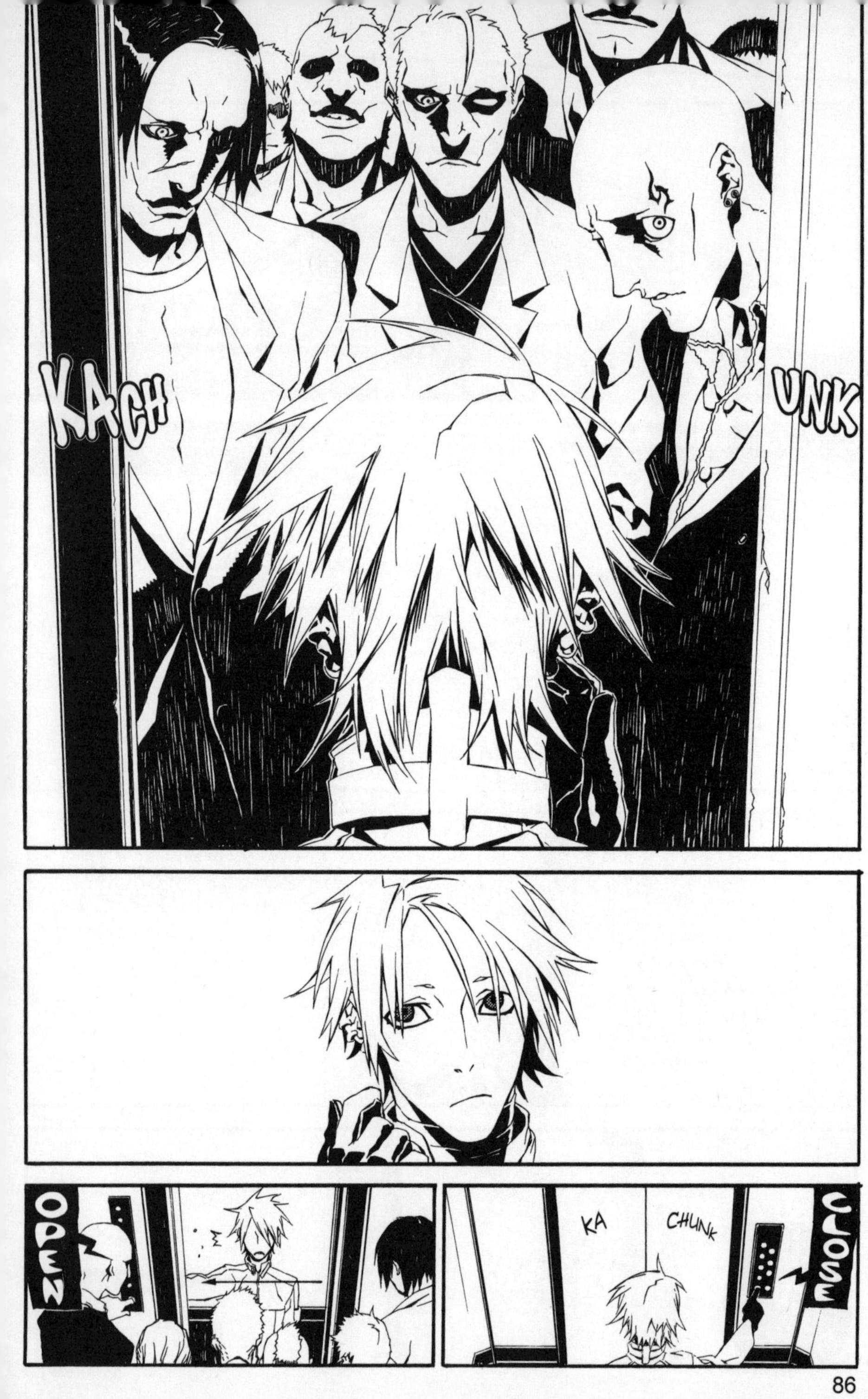
KACH
UNK
CLOSE
KA
CHUNK
OPEN

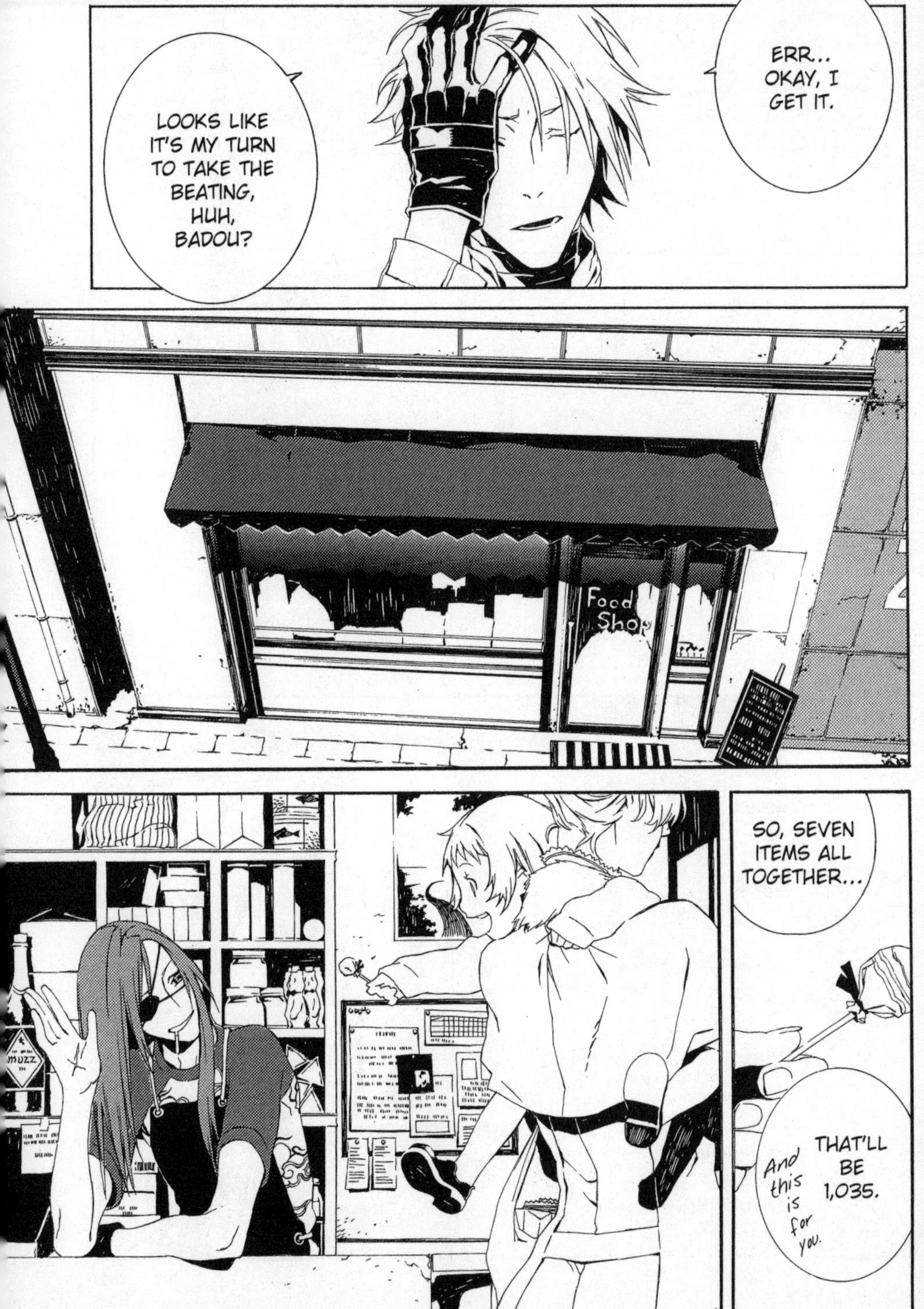
ERR... OKAY, I GET IT.
LOOKS LIKE IT'S MY TURN TO TAKE THE BEATING, HUH, BADOU?
Food Shop
SO, SEVEN ITEMS ALL TOGETHER...
THAT'LL BE 1,035.
And this is for you.

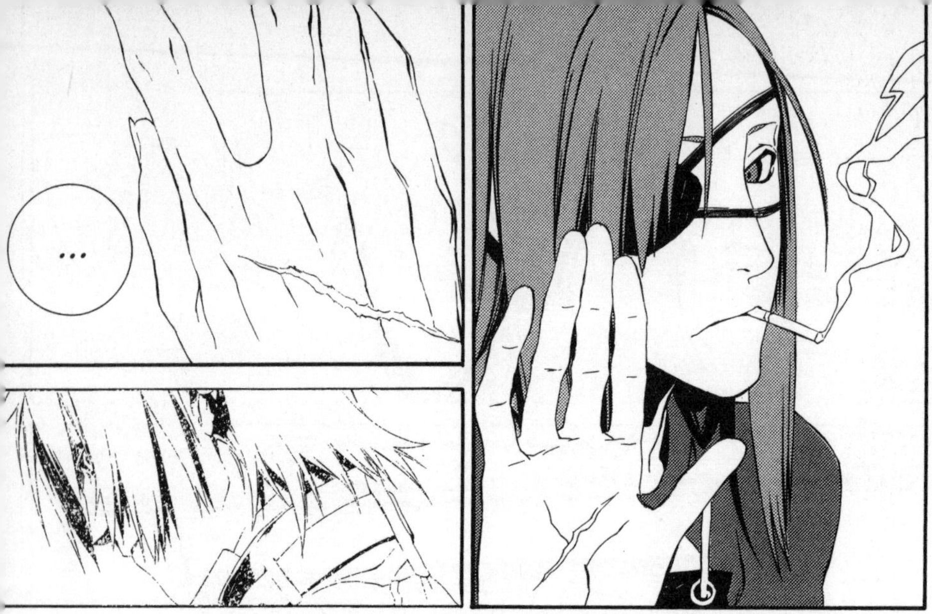
...

"We don't know a thing about him."

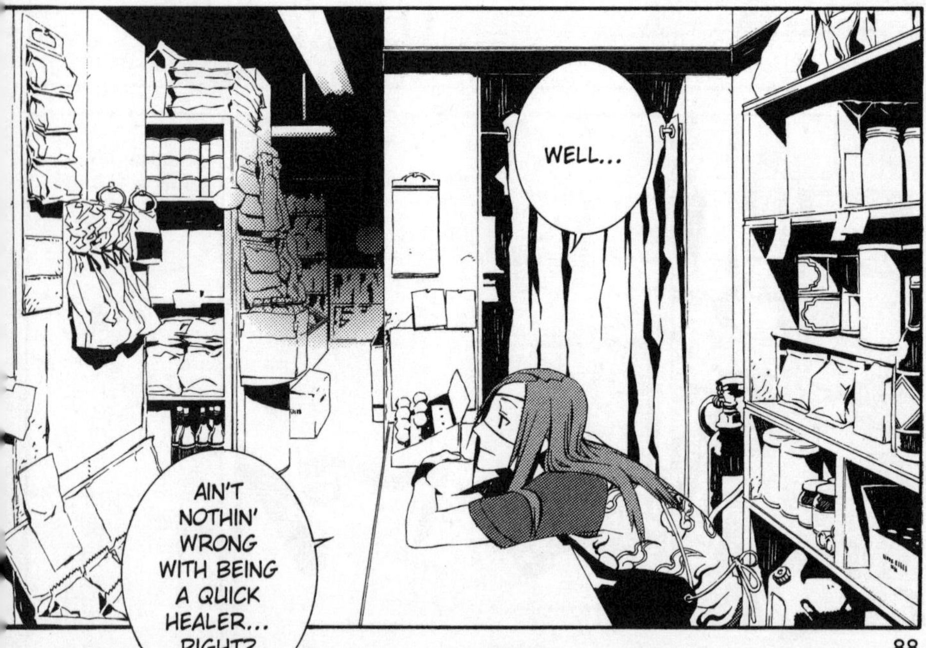
WELL...
AIN'T NOTHIN' WRONG WITH BEING A QUICK HEALER... RIGHT?

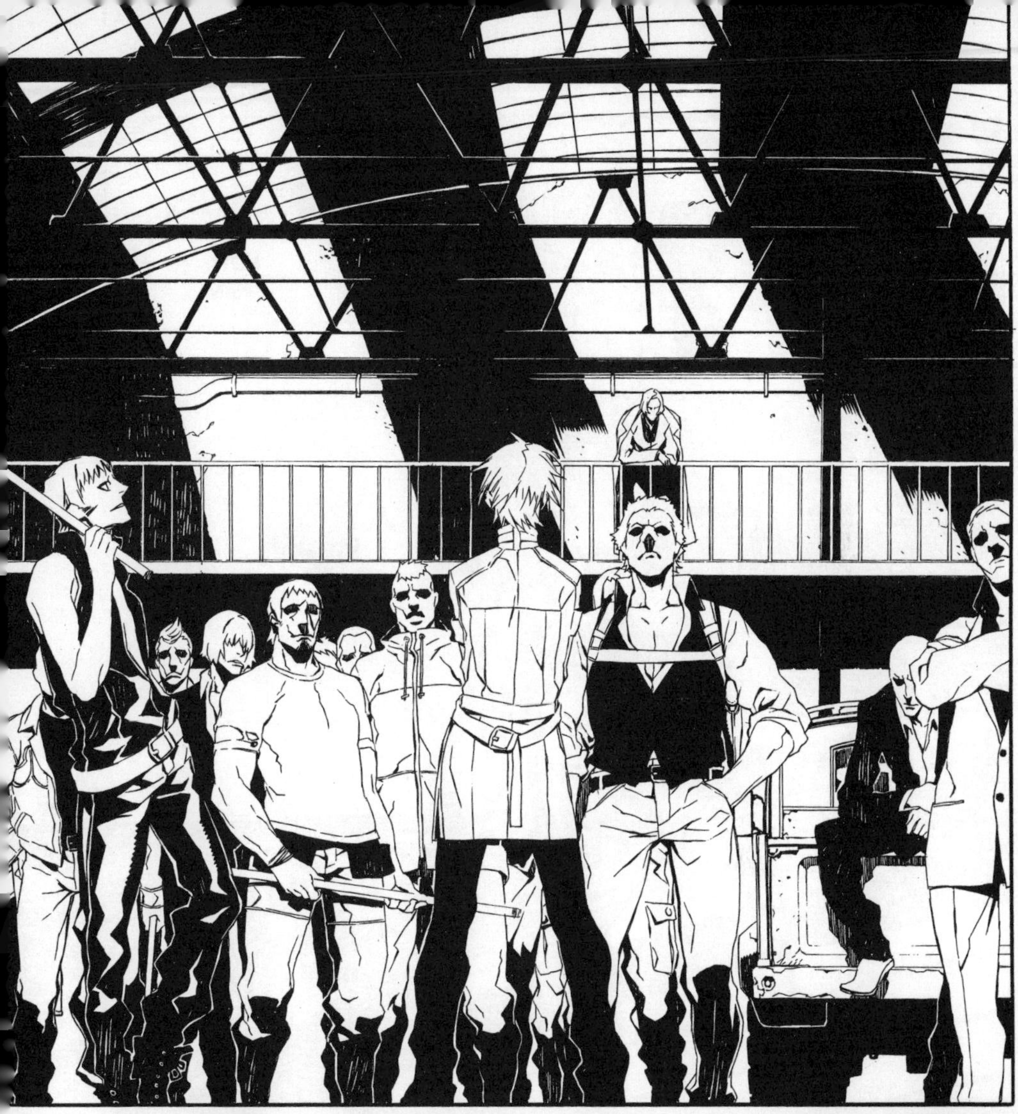

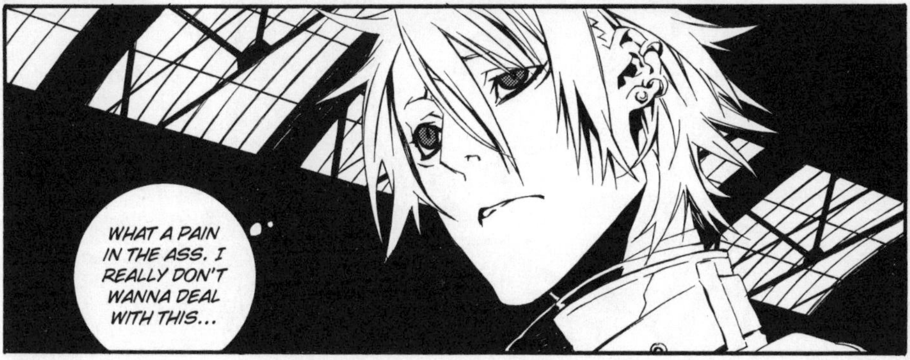
WHAT A PAIN IN THE ASS. I REALLY DON'T WANNA DEAL WITH THIS...

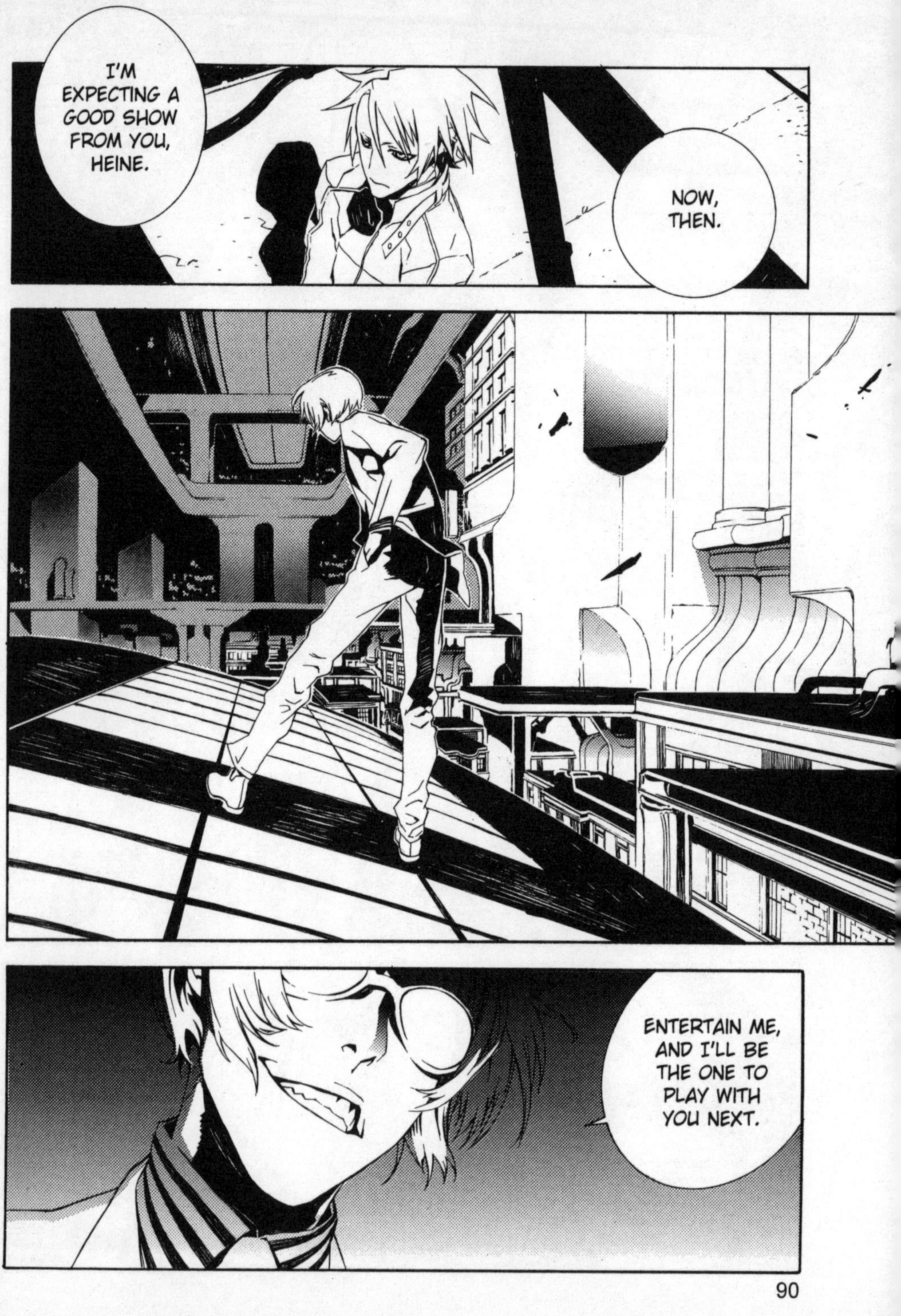
NOW, THEN.
I'M EXPECTING A GOOD SHOW FROM YOU, HEINE.
ENTERTAIN ME, AND I'LL BE THE ONE TO PLAY WITH YOU NEXT.

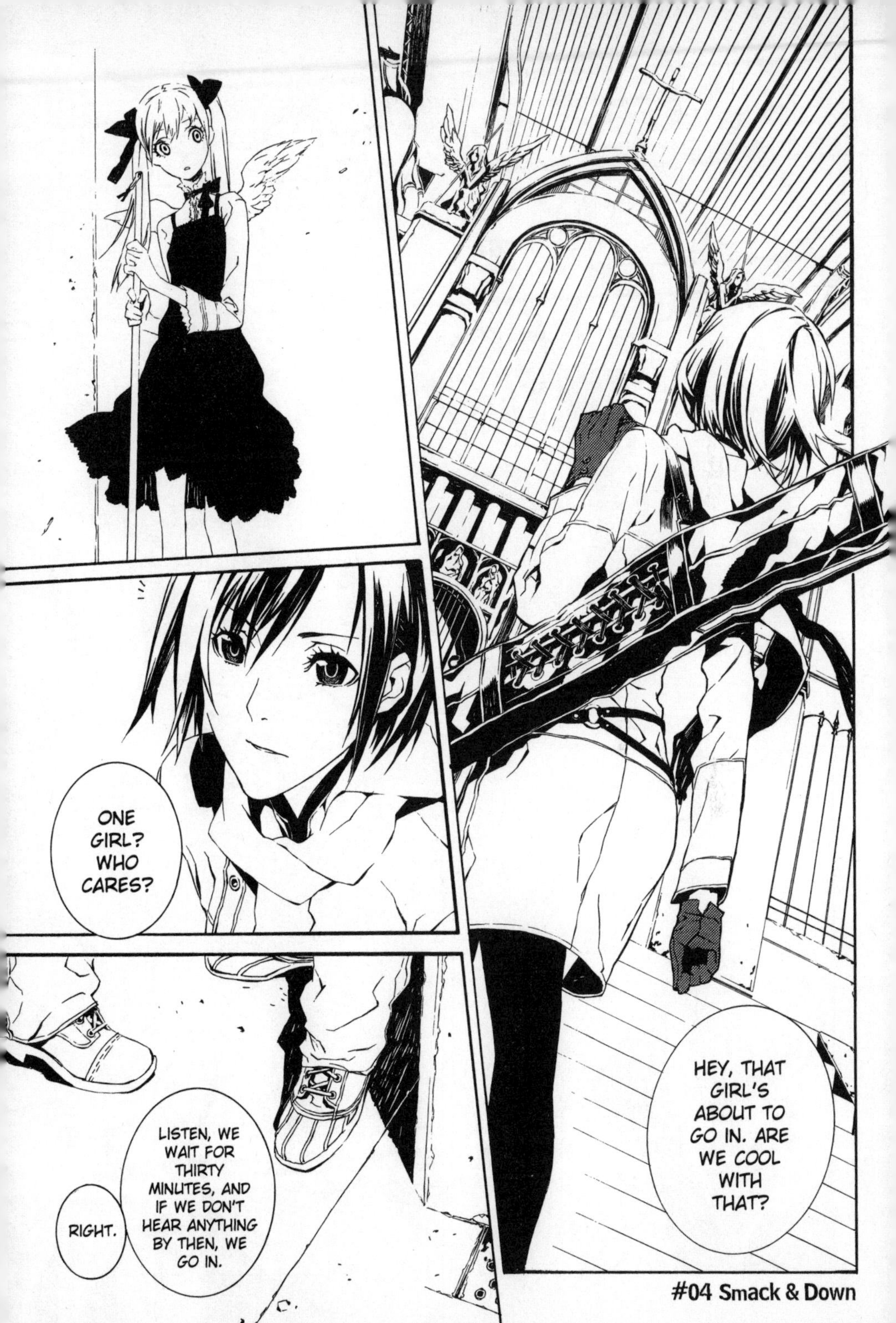
HEY, THAT GIRL'S ABOUT TO GO IN. ARE WE COOL WITH THAT?
ONE GIRL? WHO CARES?
LISTEN, WE WAIT FOR THIRTY MINUTES, AND IF WE DON'T HEAR ANYTHING BY THEN, WE GO IN.
RIGHT.

#04 Smack & Down

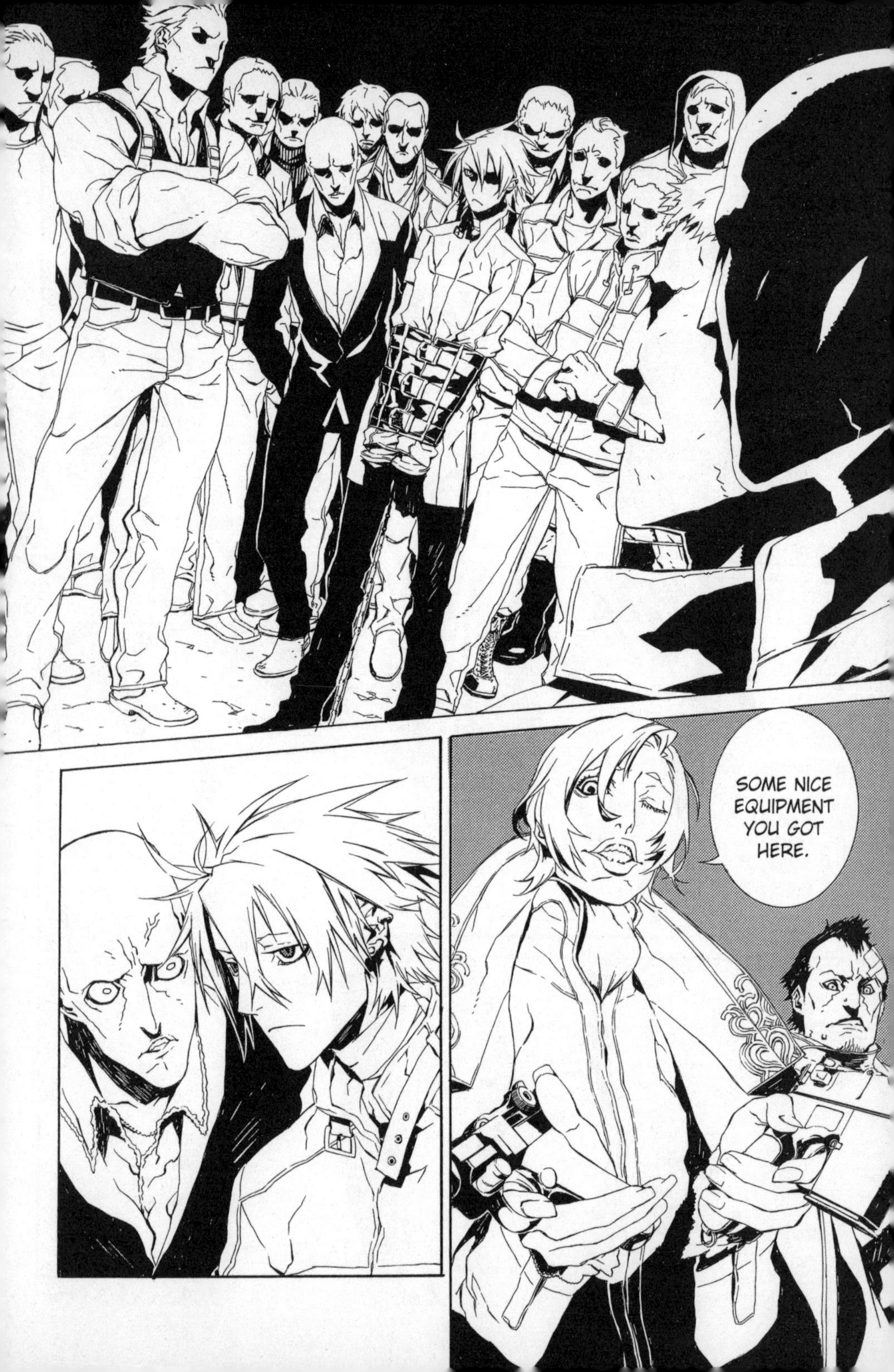
SOME NICE EQUIPMENT YOU GOT HERE.

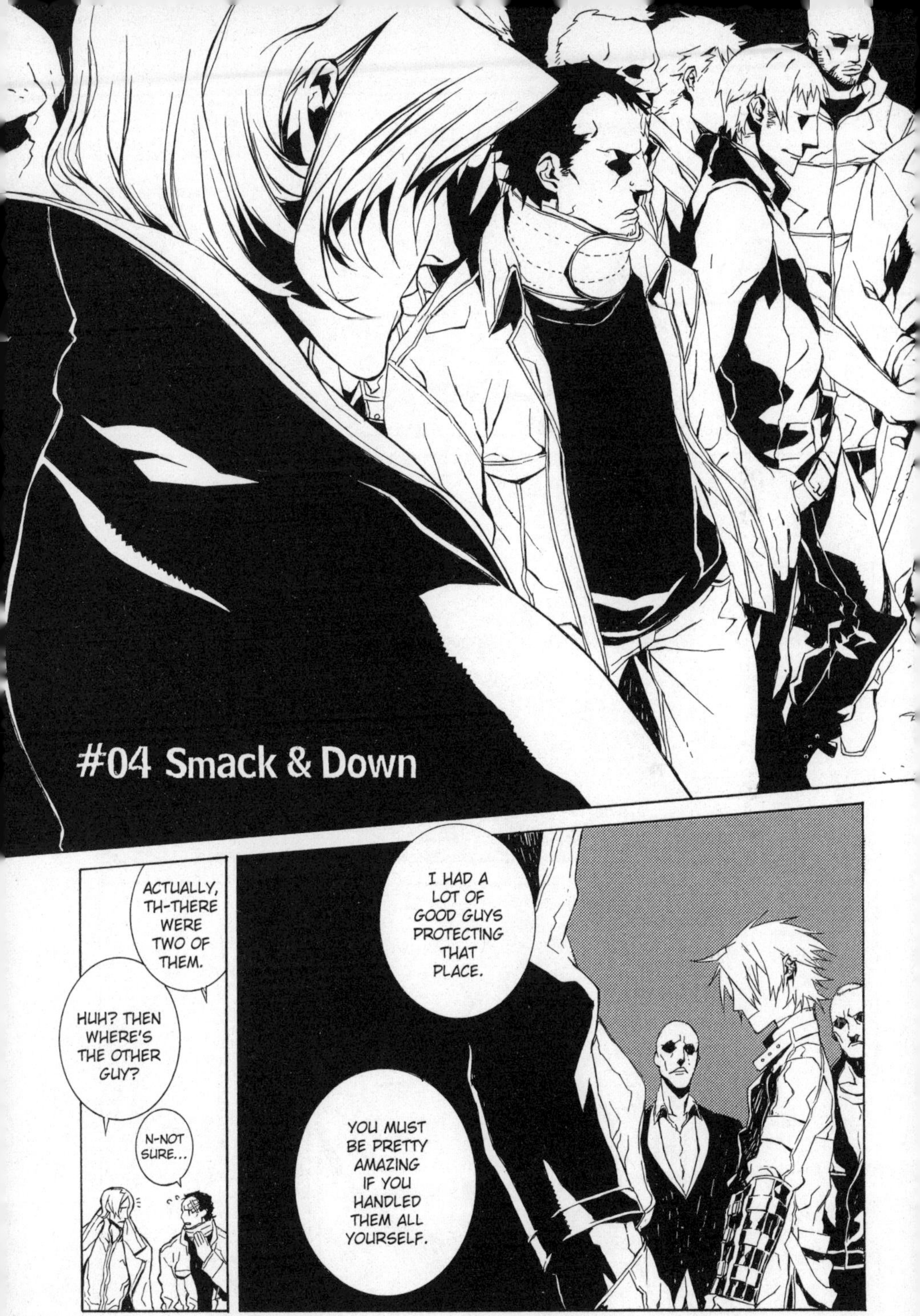
#04 Smack & Down
I HAD A LOT OF GOOD GUYS PROTECTING THAT PLACE.
YOU MUST BE PRETTY AMAZING IF YOU HANDLED THEM ALL YOURSELF.
ACTUALLY, TH-THERE WERE TWO OF THEM.
HUH? THEN WHERE'S THE OTHER GUY?
N-NOT SURE...

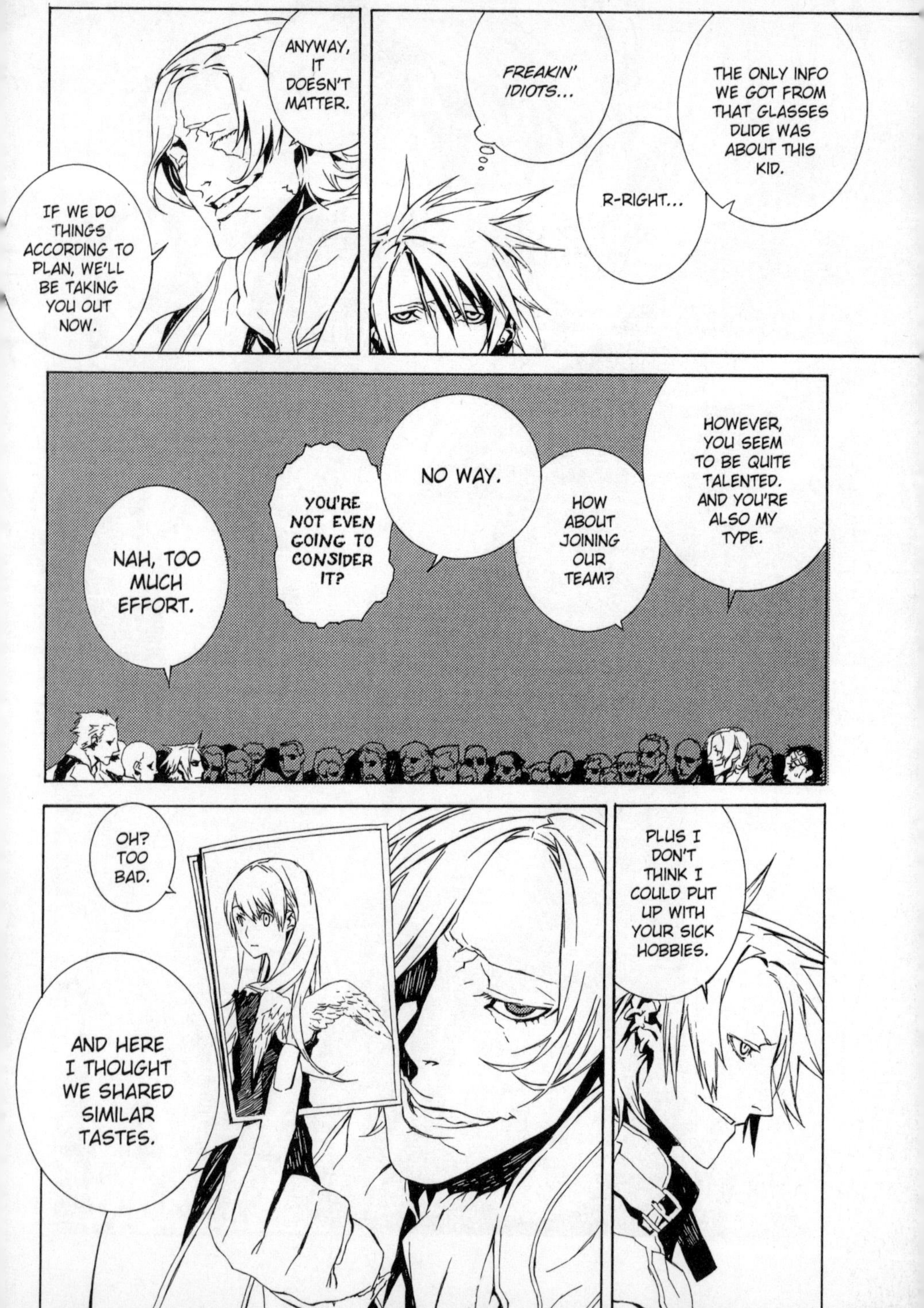
THE ONLY INFO WE GOT FROM THAT GLASSES DUDE WAS ABOUT THIS KID.
R-RIGHT...
FREAKIN' IDIOTS...
ANYWAY, IT DOESN'T MATTER.
IF WE DO THINGS ACCORDING TO PLAN, WE'LL BE TAKING YOU OUT NOW.
HOWEVER, YOU SEEM TO BE QUITE TALENTED. AND YOU'RE ALSO MY TYPE.
HOW ABOUT JOINING OUR TEAM?
NO WAY.
YOU'RE NOT EVEN GOING TO CONSIDER IT?
NAH, TOO MUCH EFFORT.
PLUS I DON'T THINK I COULD PUT UP WITH YOUR SICK HOBBIES.
OH? TOO BAD.
AND HERE I THOUGHT WE SHARED SIMILAR TASTES.

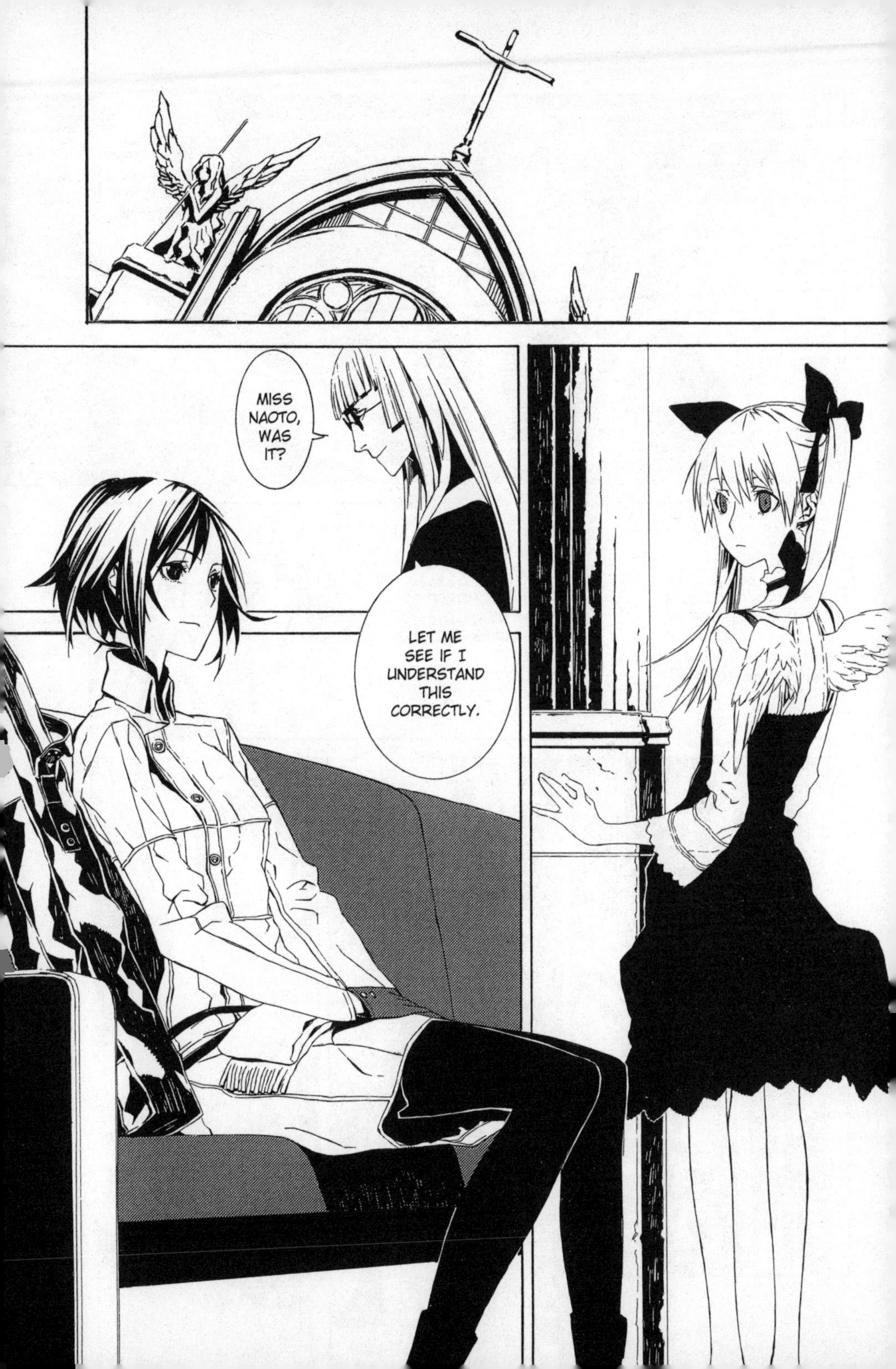
MISS NAOTO, WAS IT?
LET ME SEE IF I UNDERSTAND THIS CORRECTLY.

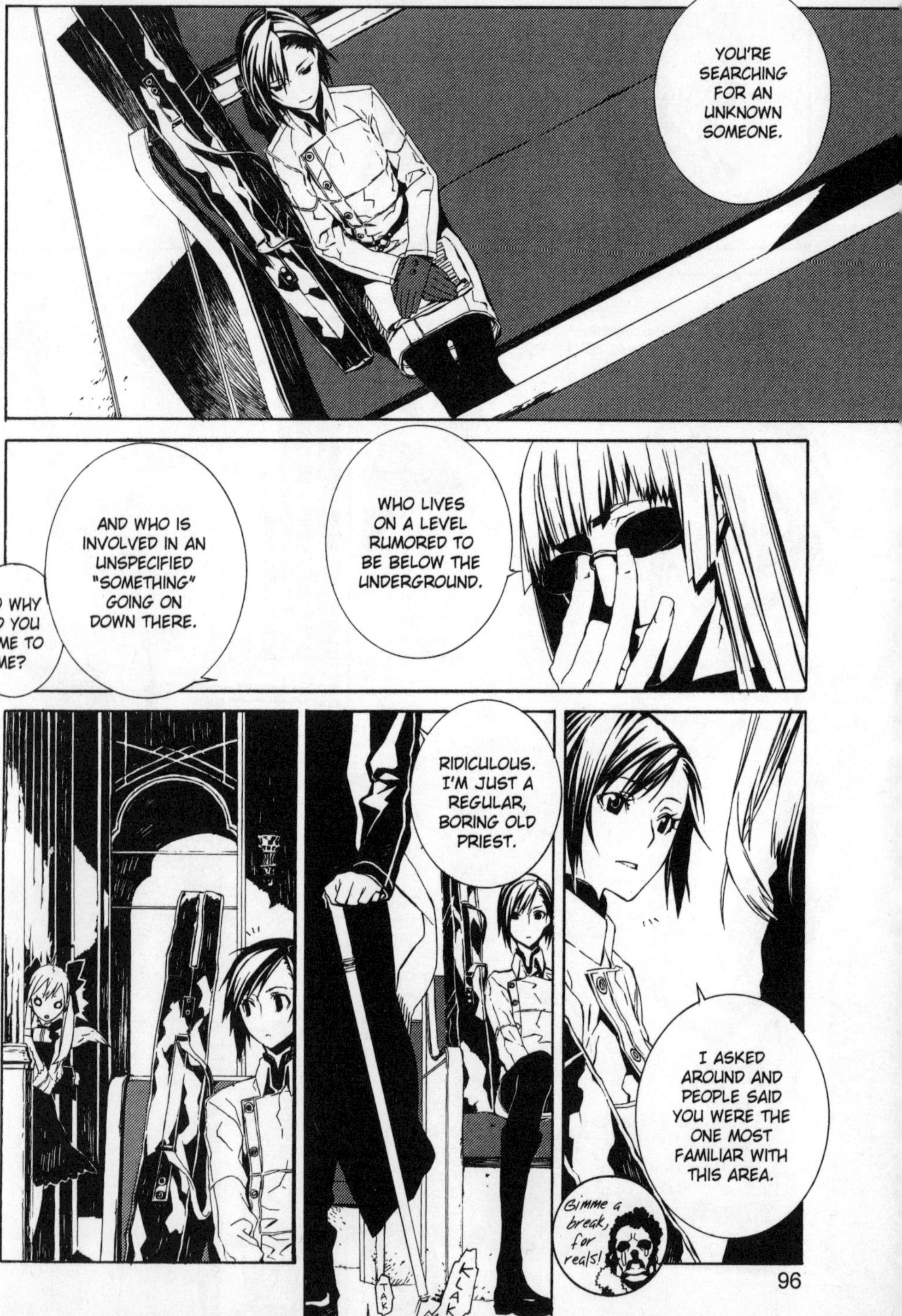
YOU'RE SEARCHING FOR AN UNKNOWN SOMEONE.
WHO LIVES ON A LEVEL RUMORED TO BE BELOW THE UNDERGROUND.
AND WHO IS INVOLVED IN AN UNSPECIFIED "SOMETHING" GOING ON DOWN THERE.
SO WHY DID YOU COME TO ME?
I ASKED AROUND AND PEOPLE SAID YOU WERE THE ONE MOST FAMILIAR WITH THIS AREA.
Gimme a break, for reals!
RIDICULOUS. I'M JUST A REGULAR, BORING OLD PRIEST.
TAK
KLAK

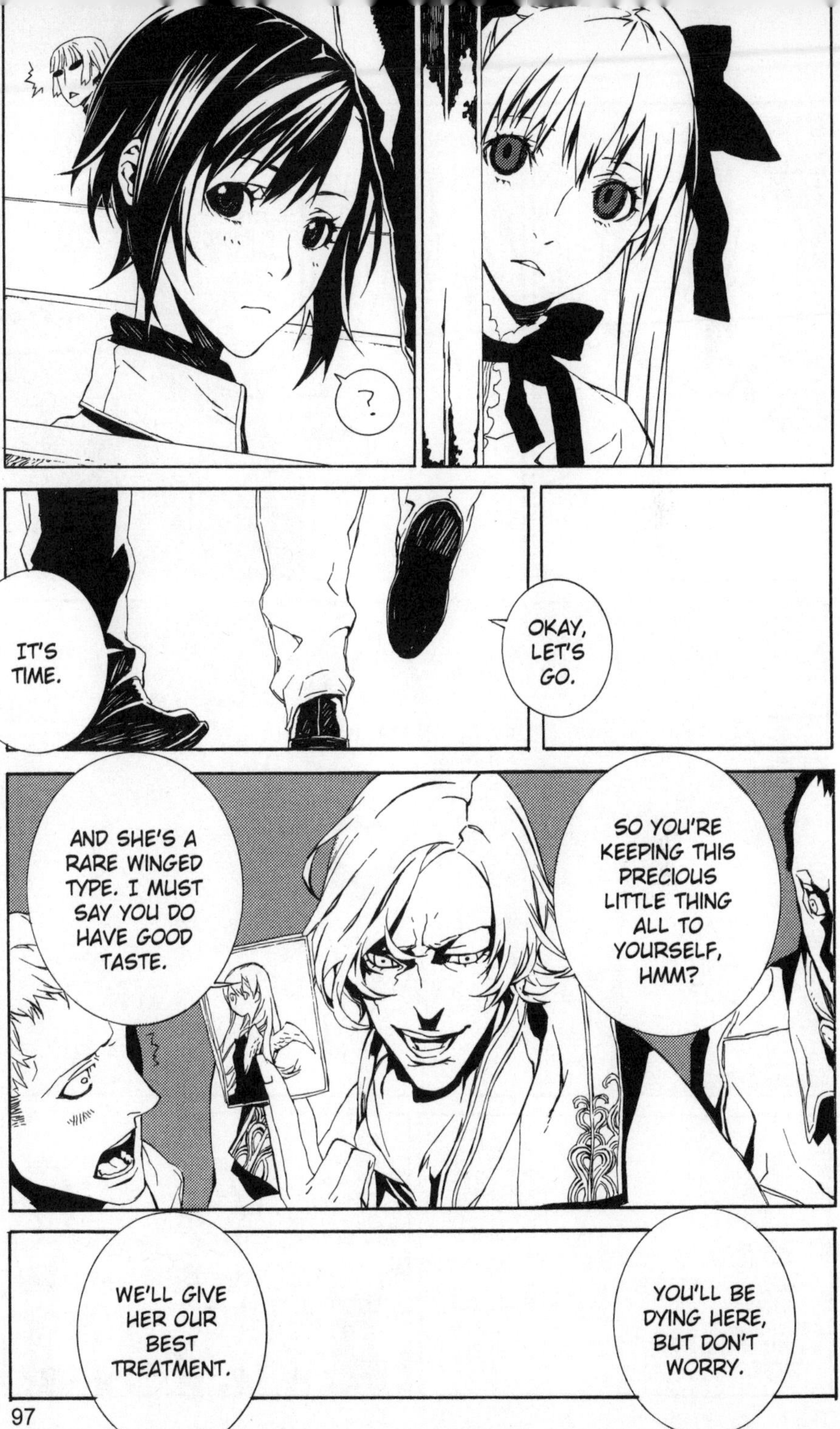
?
OKAY, LET'S GO.
IT'S TIME.
SO YOU'RE KEEPING THIS PRECIOUS LITTLE THING ALL TO YOURSELF, HMM?
AND SHE'S A RARE WINGED TYPE. I MUST SAY YOU DO HAVE GOOD TASTE.
YOU'LL BE DYING HERE, BUT DON'T WORRY.
WE'LL GIVE HER OUR BEST TREATMENT.

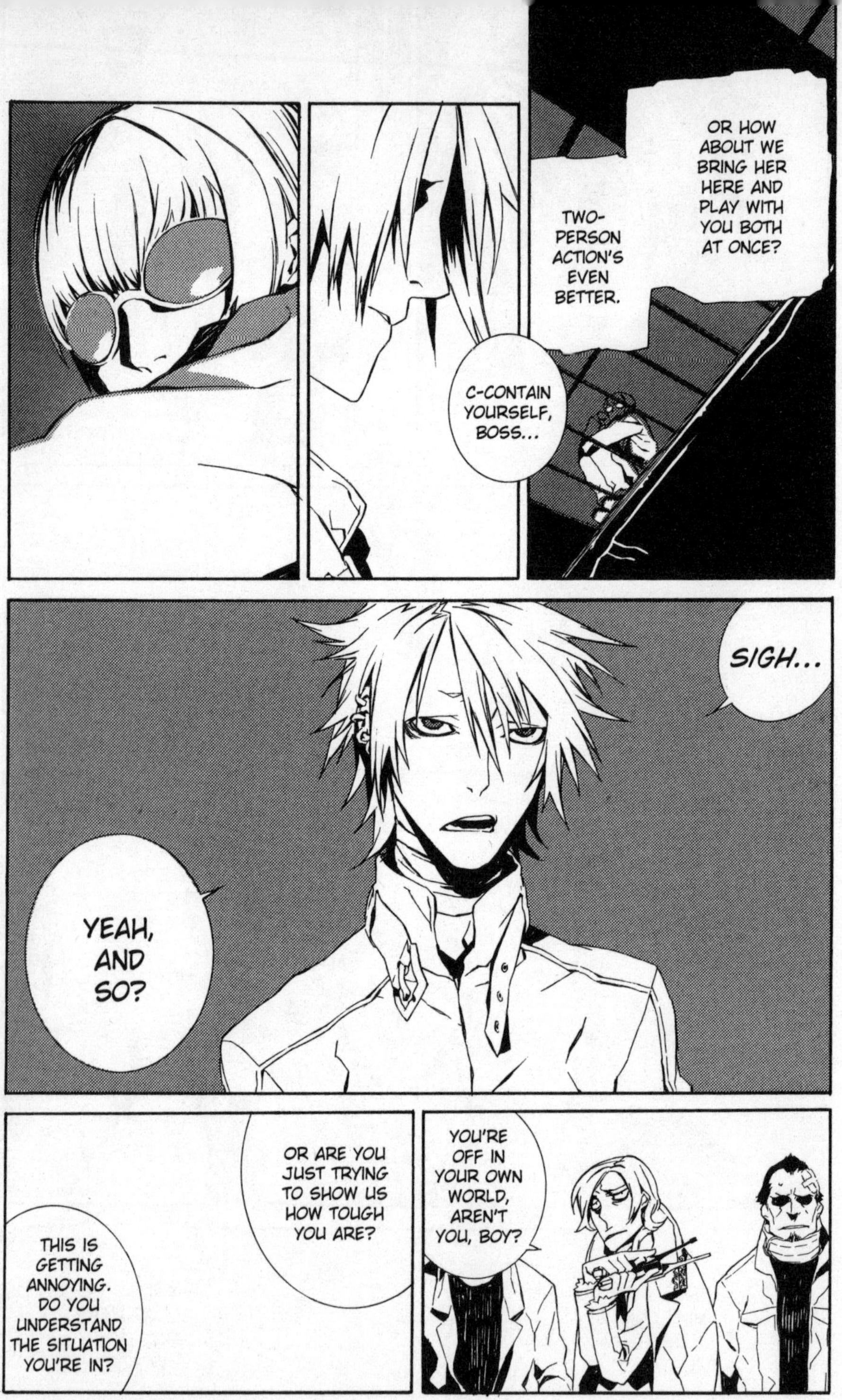
OR HOW ABOUT WE BRING HER HERE AND PLAY WITH YOU BOTH AT ONCE?
TWO-PERSON ACTION'S EVEN BETTER.
C-CONTAIN YOURSELF, BOSS...
SIGH...
YEAH, AND SO?
YOU'RE OFF IN YOUR OWN WORLD, AREN'T YOU, BOY?
OR ARE YOU JUST TRYING TO SHOW US HOW TOUGH YOU ARE?
THIS IS GETTING ANNOYING. DO YOU UNDERSTAND THE SITUATION YOU'RE IN?

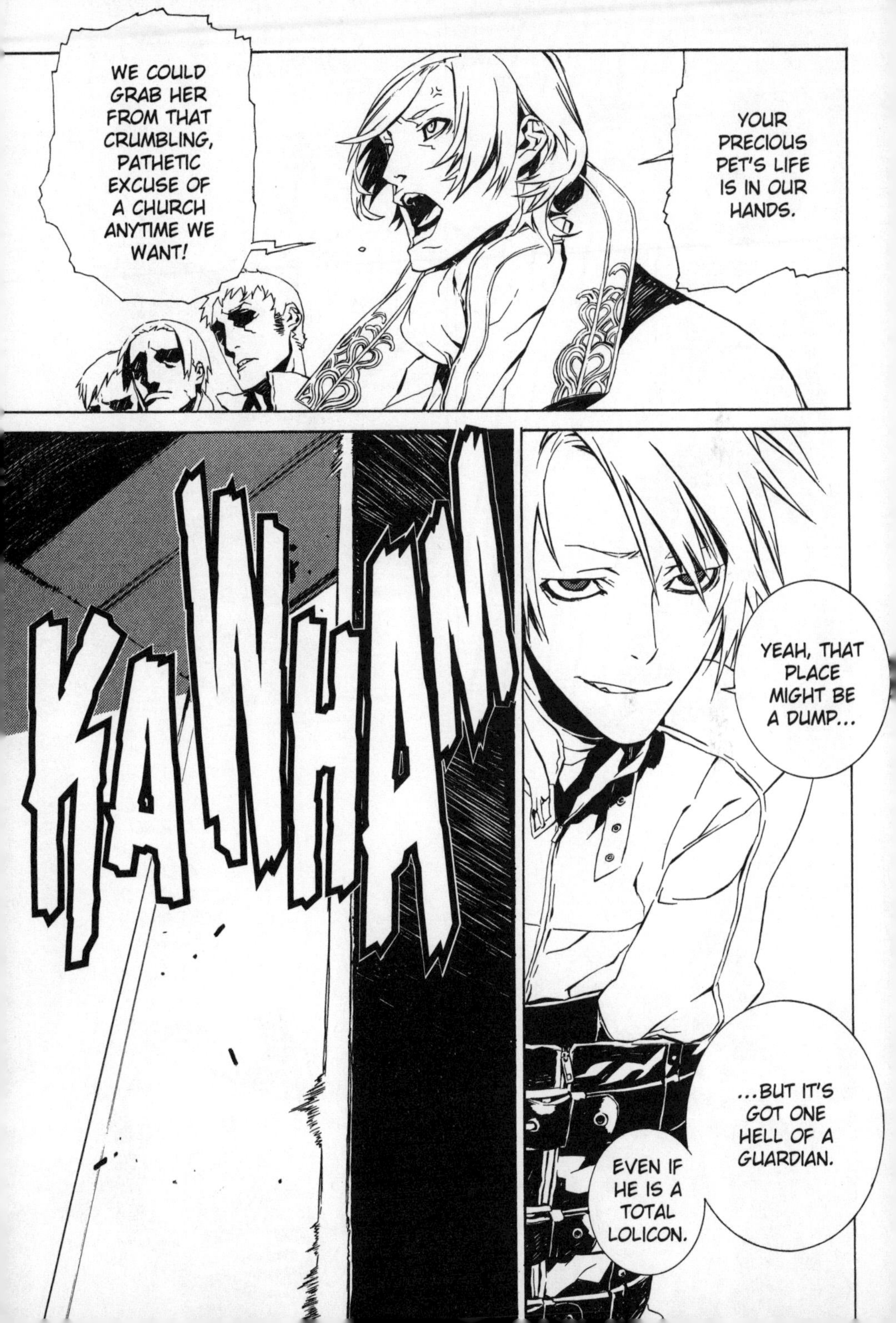
YOUR PRECIOUS PET'S LIFE IS IN OUR HANDS.
WE COULD GRAB HER FROM THAT CRUMBLING, PATHETIC EXCUSE OF A CHURCH ANYTIME WE WANT!
YEAH, THAT PLACE MIGHT BE A DUMP...
...BUT IT'S GOT ONE HELL OF A GUARDIAN.
EVEN IF HE IS A TOTAL LOLICON.
KAWHAM

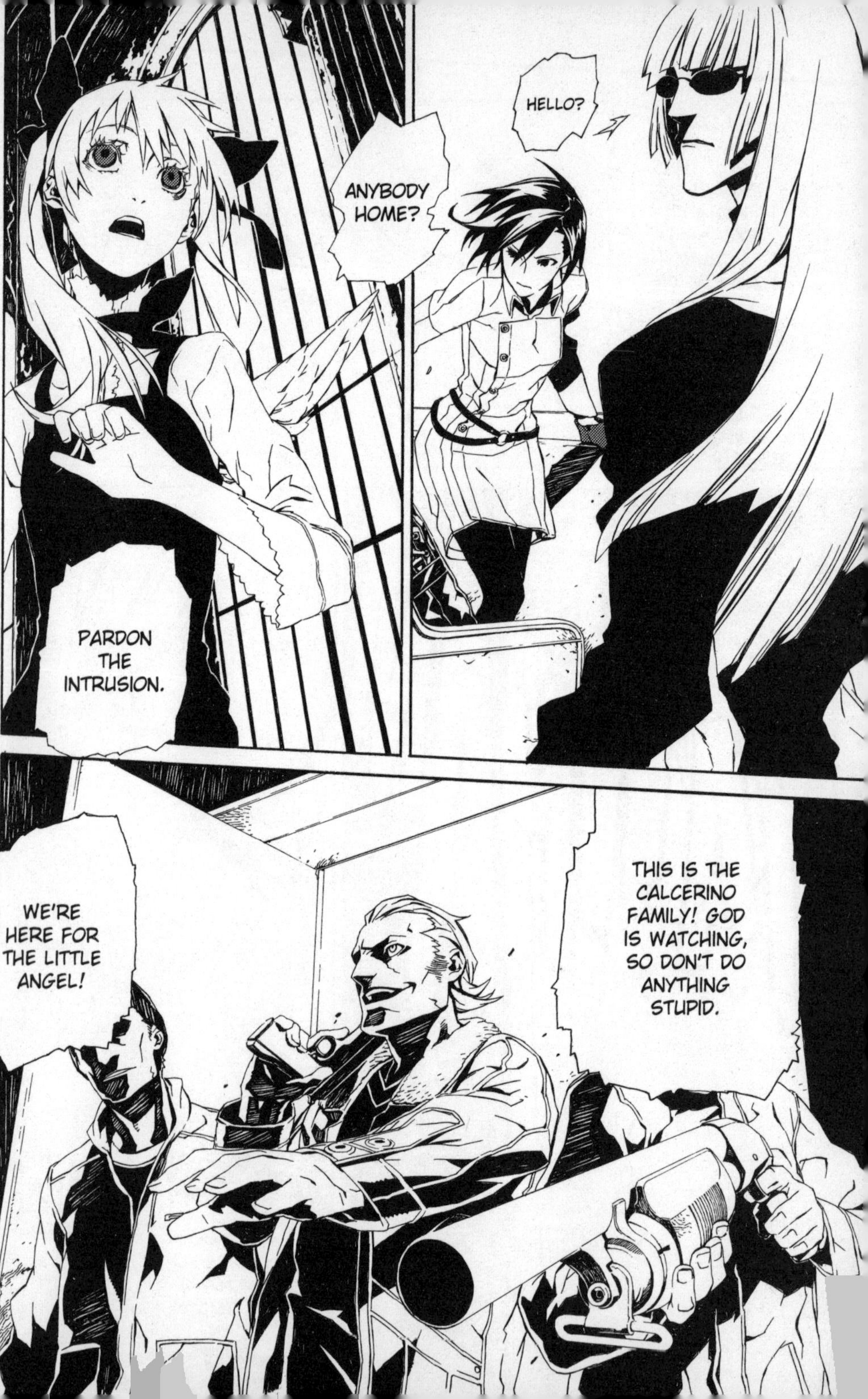
HELLO?
ANYBODY HOME?
PARDON THE INTRUSION.
THIS IS THE CALCERINO FAMILY! GOD IS WATCHING, SO DON'T DO ANYTHING STUPID.
WE'RE HERE FOR THE LITTLE ANGEL!

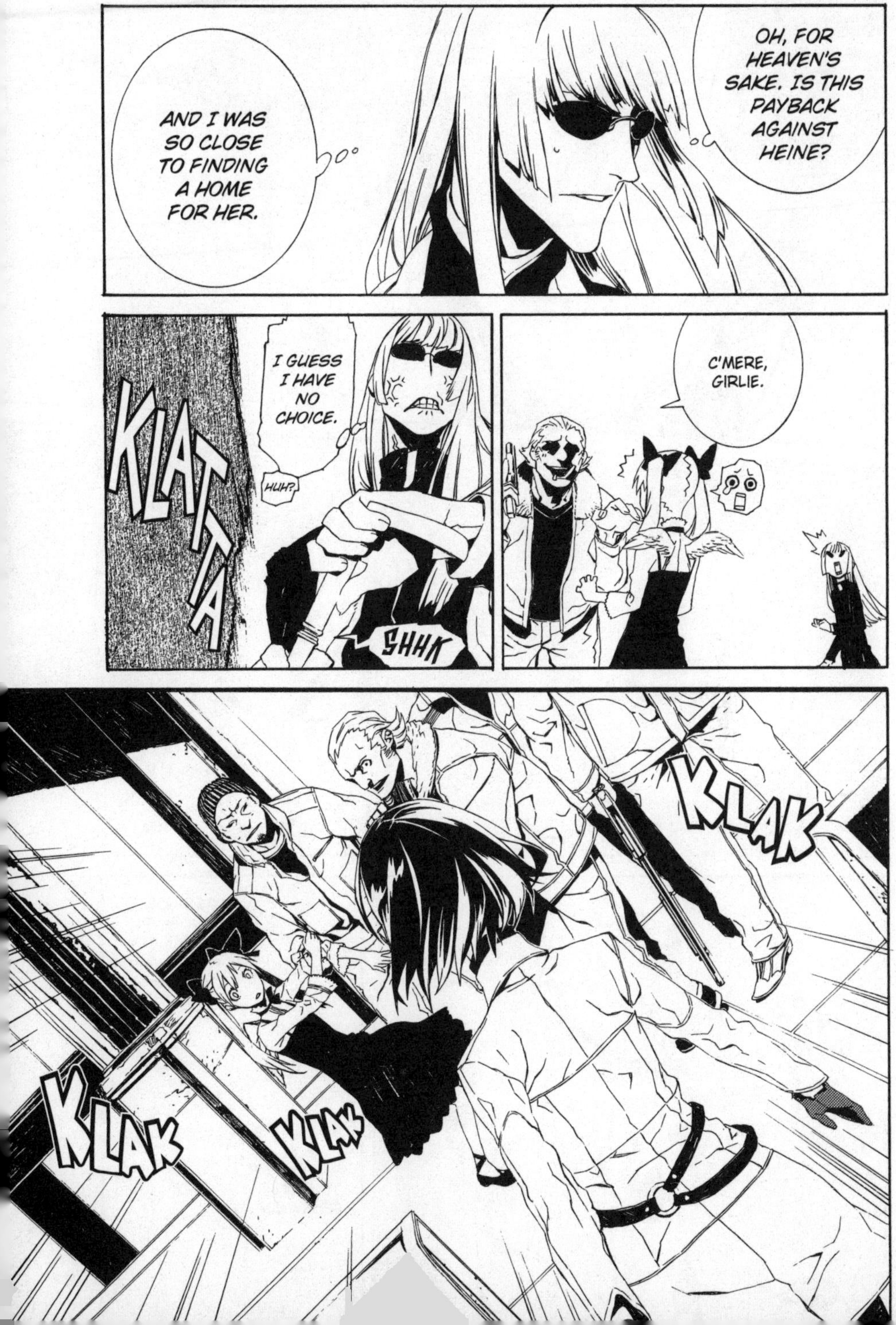
OH, FOR HEAVEN'S SAKE. IS THIS PAYBACK AGAINST HEINE?
AND I WAS SO CLOSE TO FINDING A HOME FOR HER.
C'MERE, GIRLIE.
I GUESS I HAVE NO CHOICE.
HUH?
KLATTA
SHHK
KLAK
KLAK
KLAK

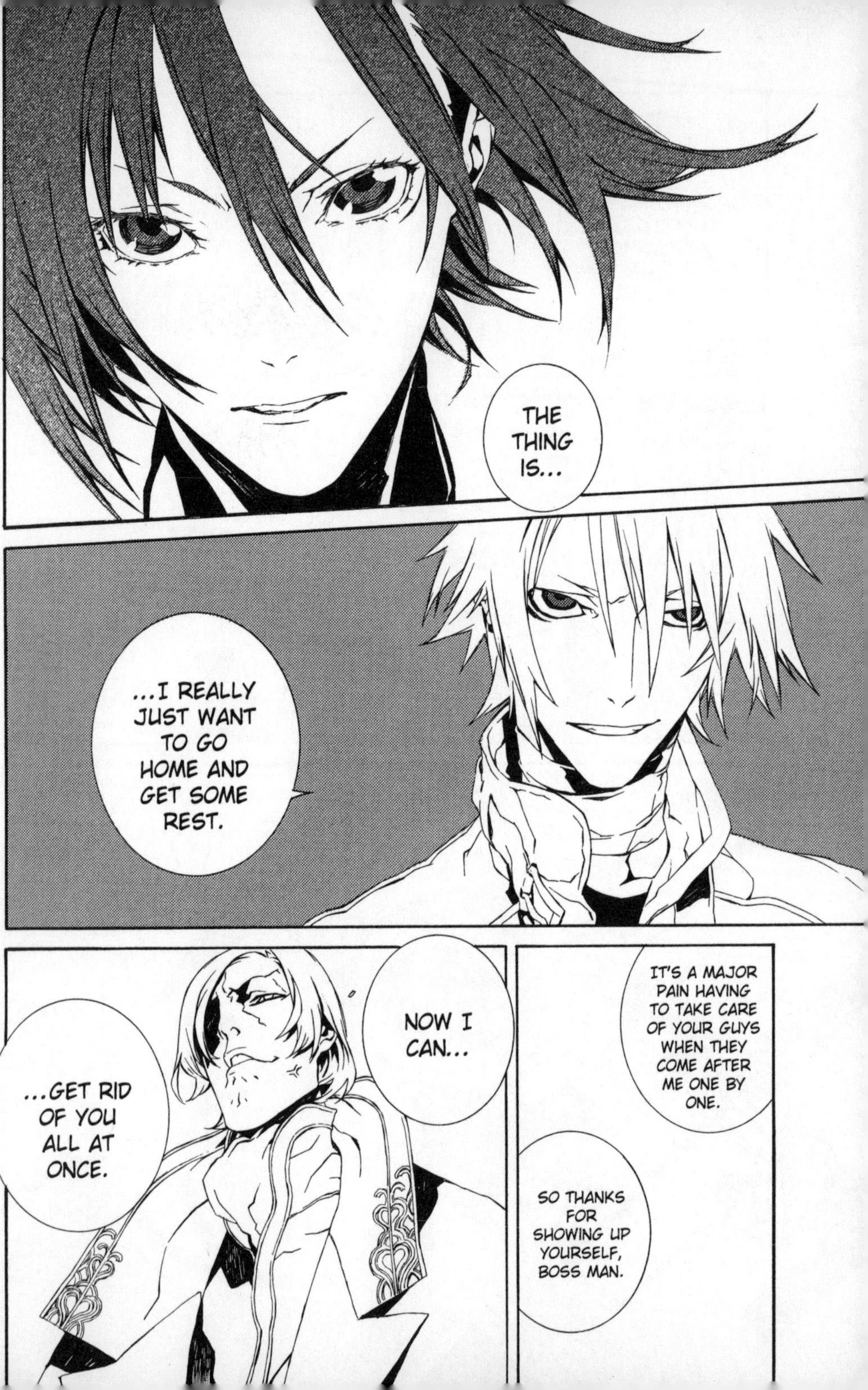
THE THING IS...
...I REALLY JUST WANT TO GO HOME AND GET SOME REST.
IT'S A MAJOR PAIN HAVING TO TAKE CARE OF YOUR GUYS WHEN THEY COME AFTER ME ONE BY ONE.
SO THANKS FOR SHOWING UP YOURSELF, BOSS MAN.
NOW I CAN...
...GET RID OF YOU ALL AT ONCE.

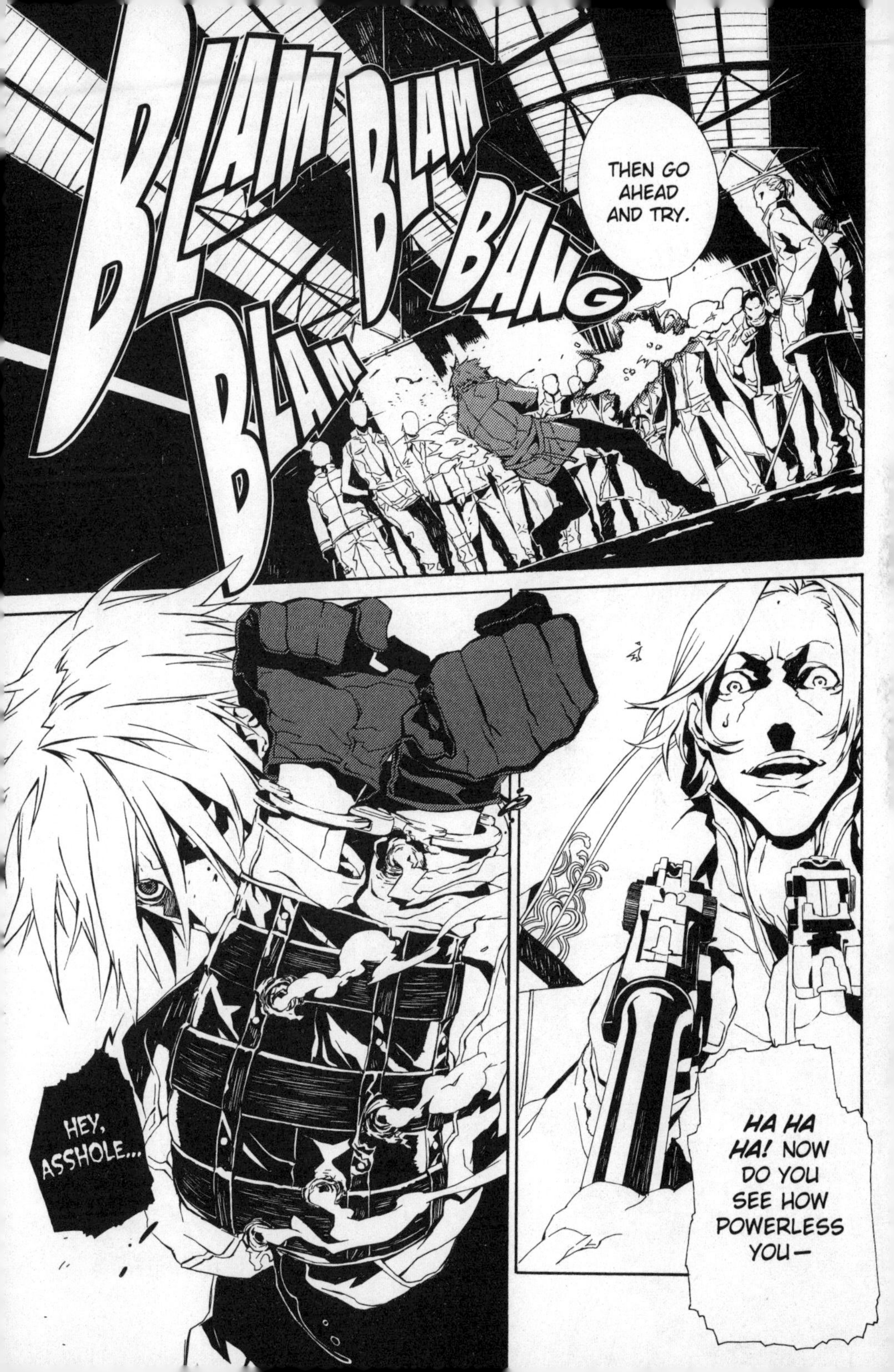
THEN GO AHEAD AND TRY.
BANG
BLAM
BLAM
BLAM
HA HA HA! NOW DO YOU SEE HOW POWERLESS YOU—
HEY, ASSHOLE...

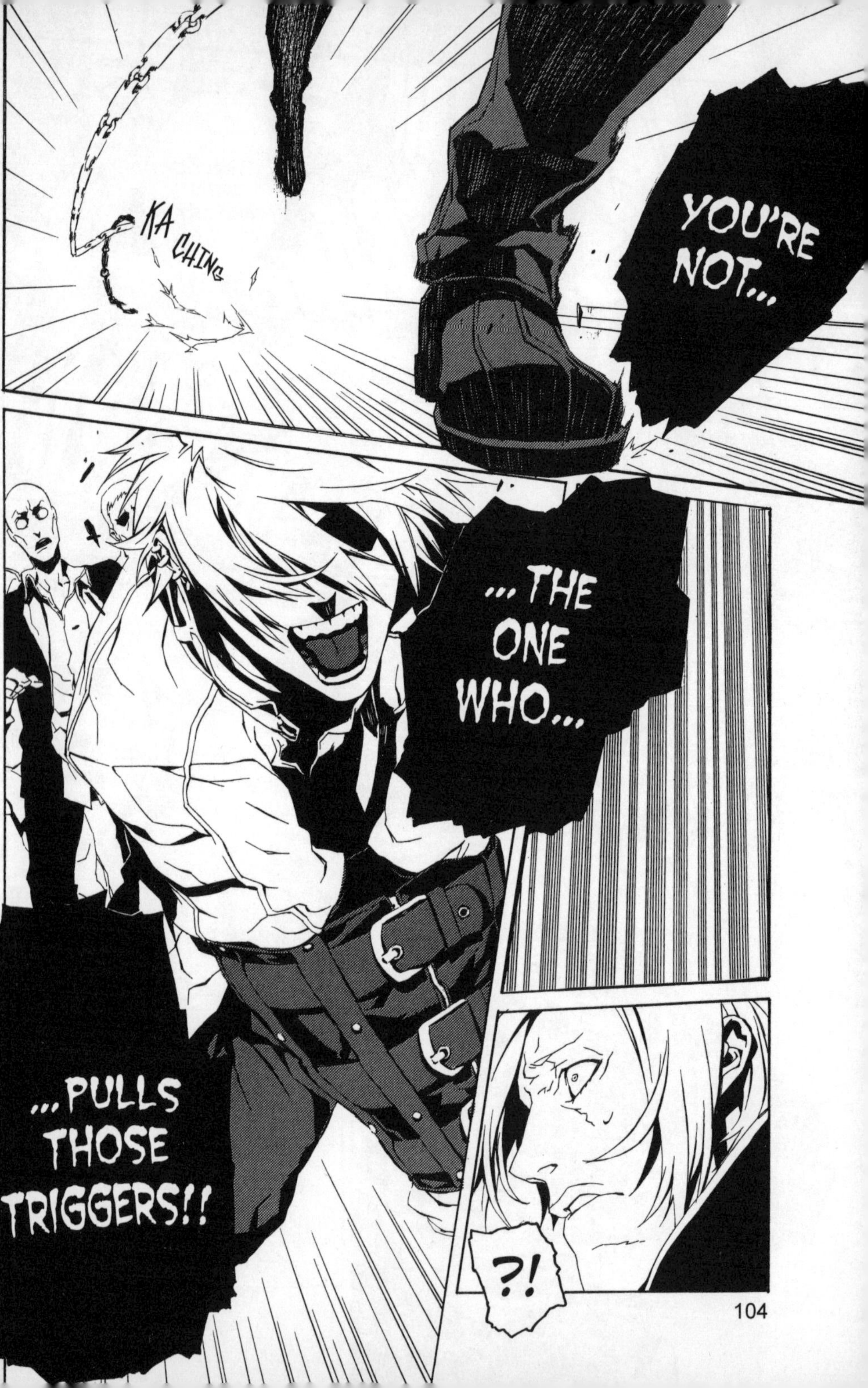
YOU'RE NOT...
KA CHING
...THE ONE WHO...
...PULLS THOSE TRIGGERS!!
?!

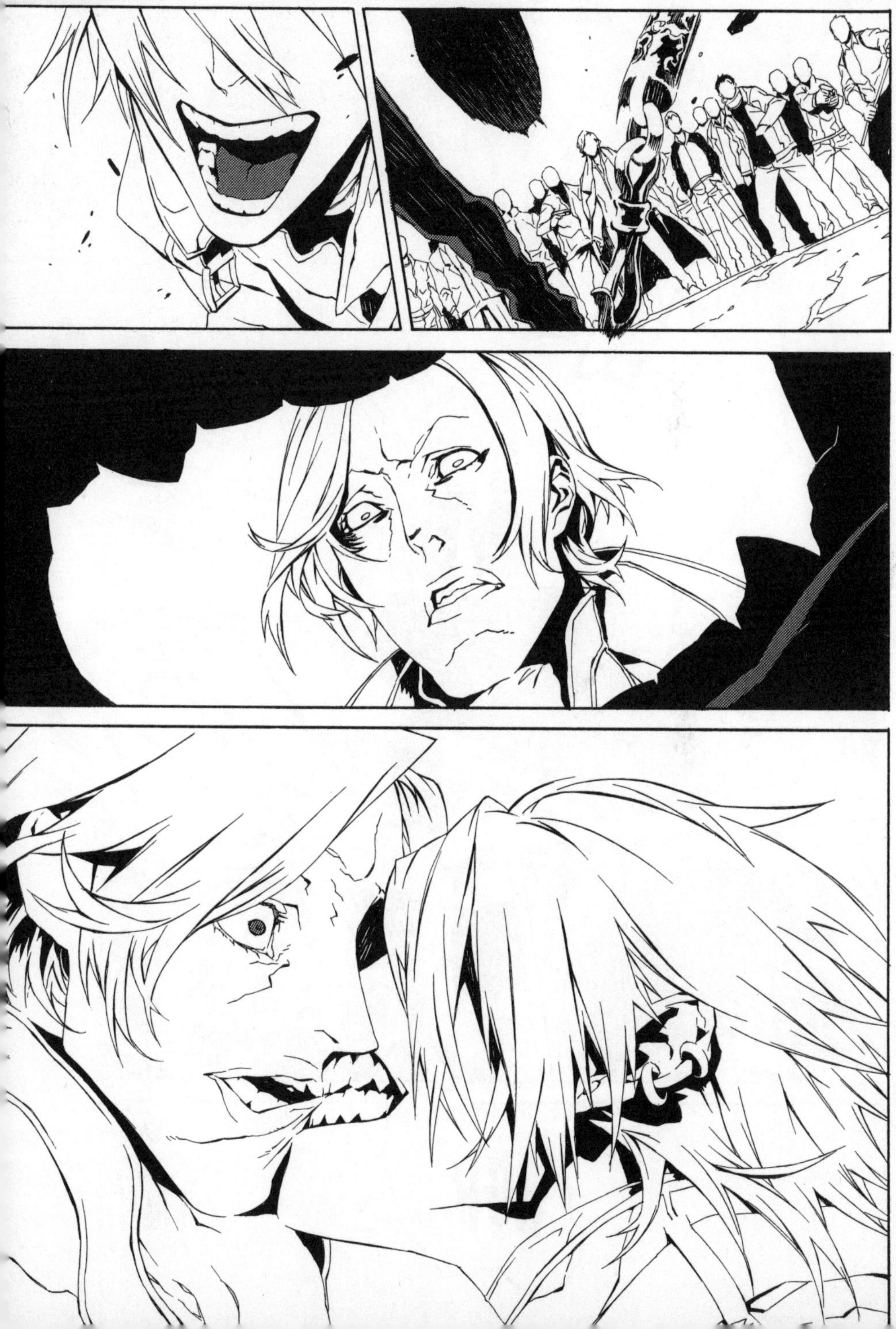

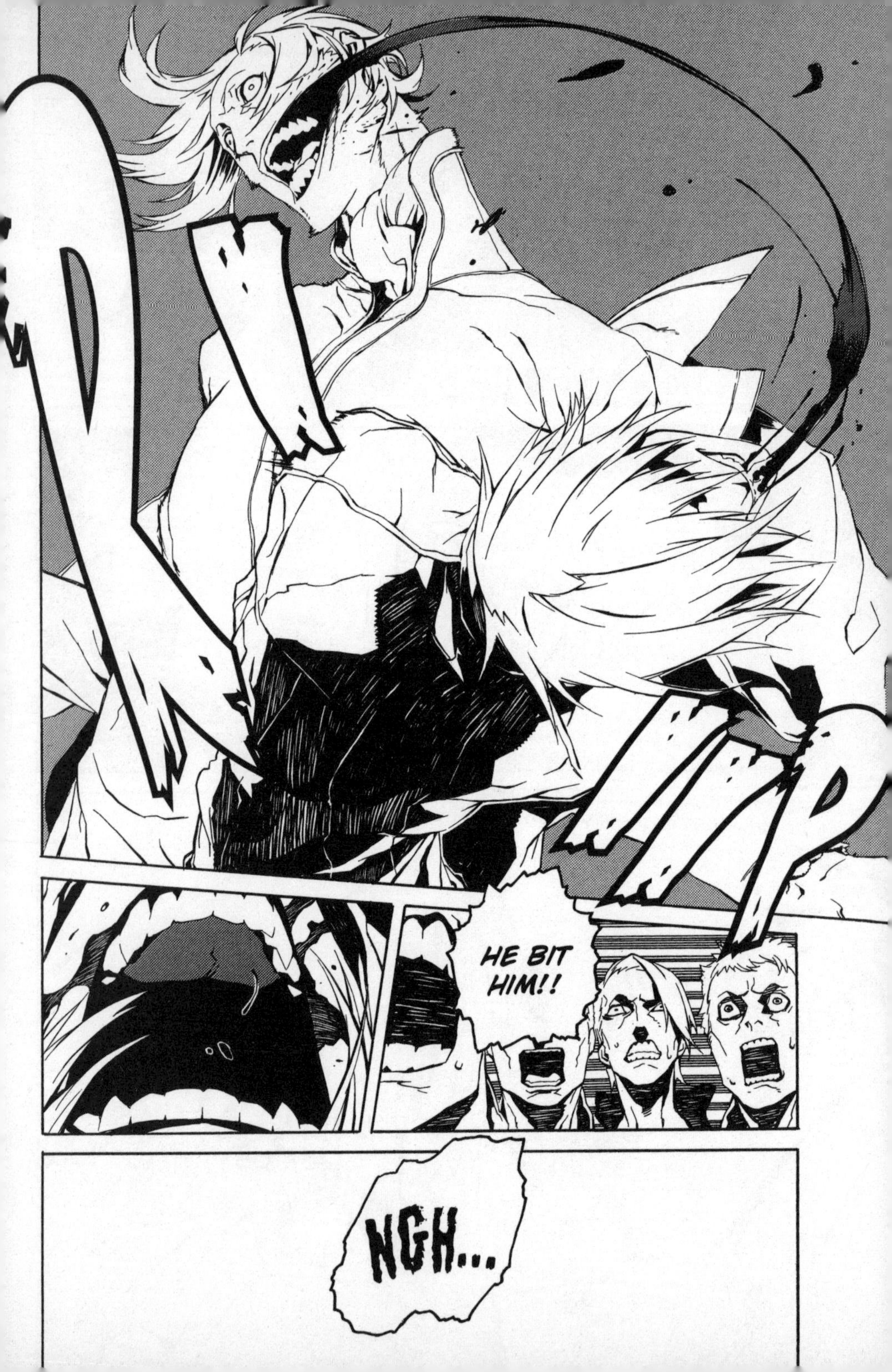
HE BIT HIM!!
NGH...

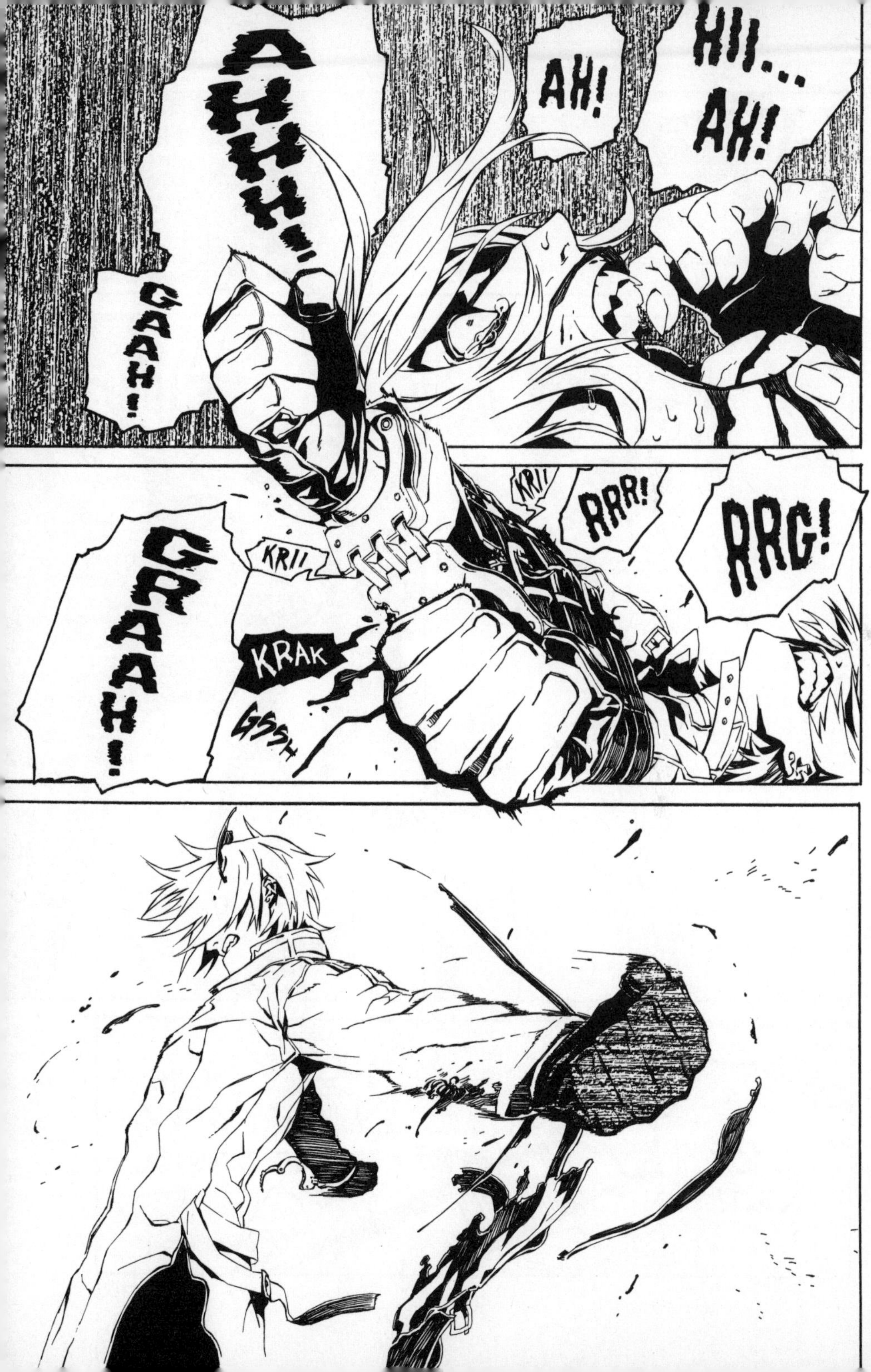
HII... AH!
AH!
AHHH!!
GAAH!!
RRG!
RRR!
KRI!
KRI!
GRAAAH!!
KRAK
GSSH

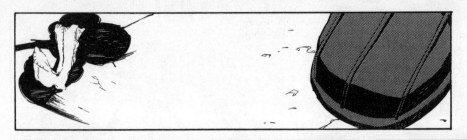

HA HA HA!

THIS GUY'S NUTS!

LOOK OUT!

SHAK

CH CHAK

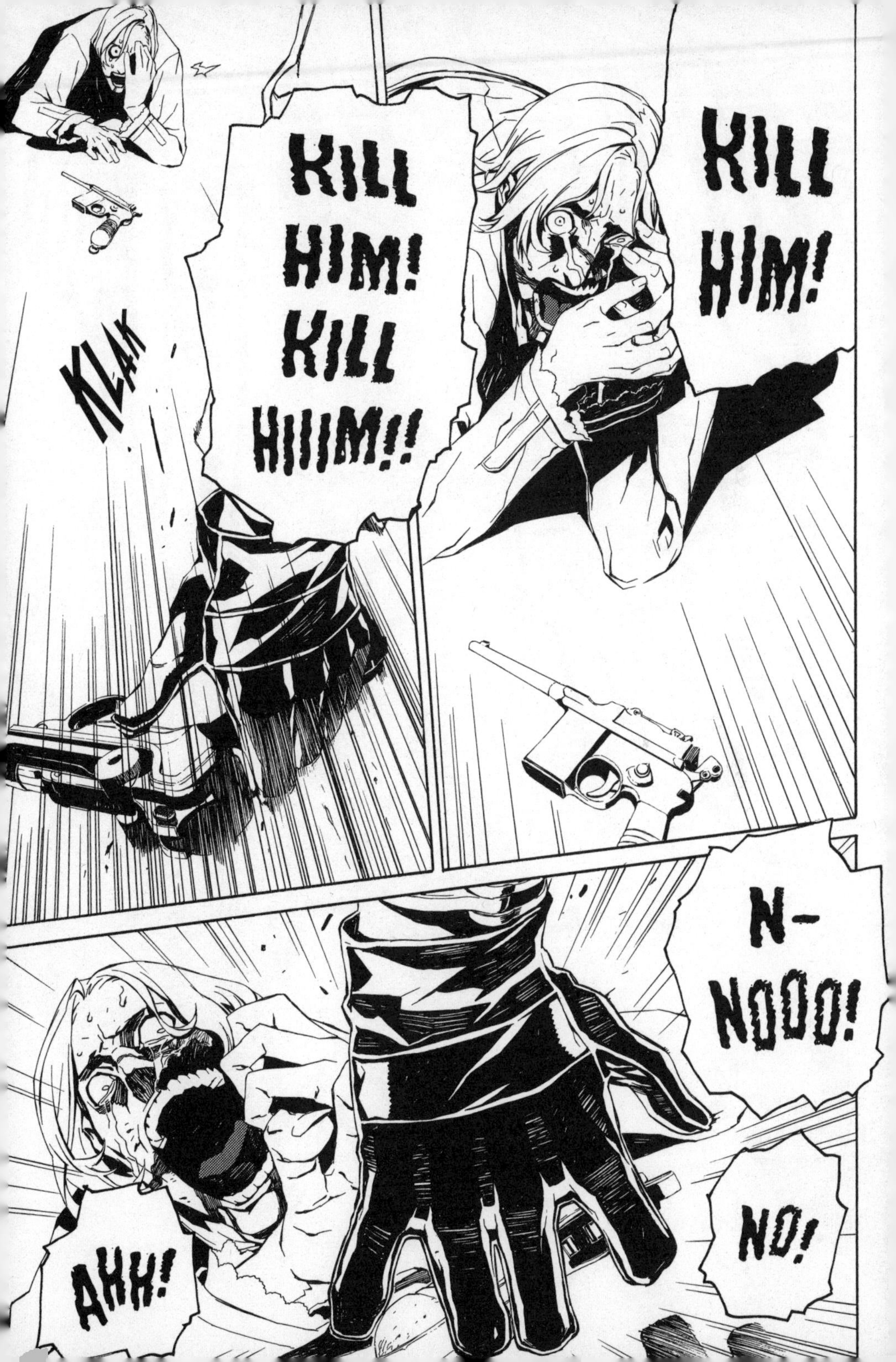
KILL HIM!
KILL HIM! KILL HIIIM!!
KLAK
N- NOOO!
NO!
AHH!

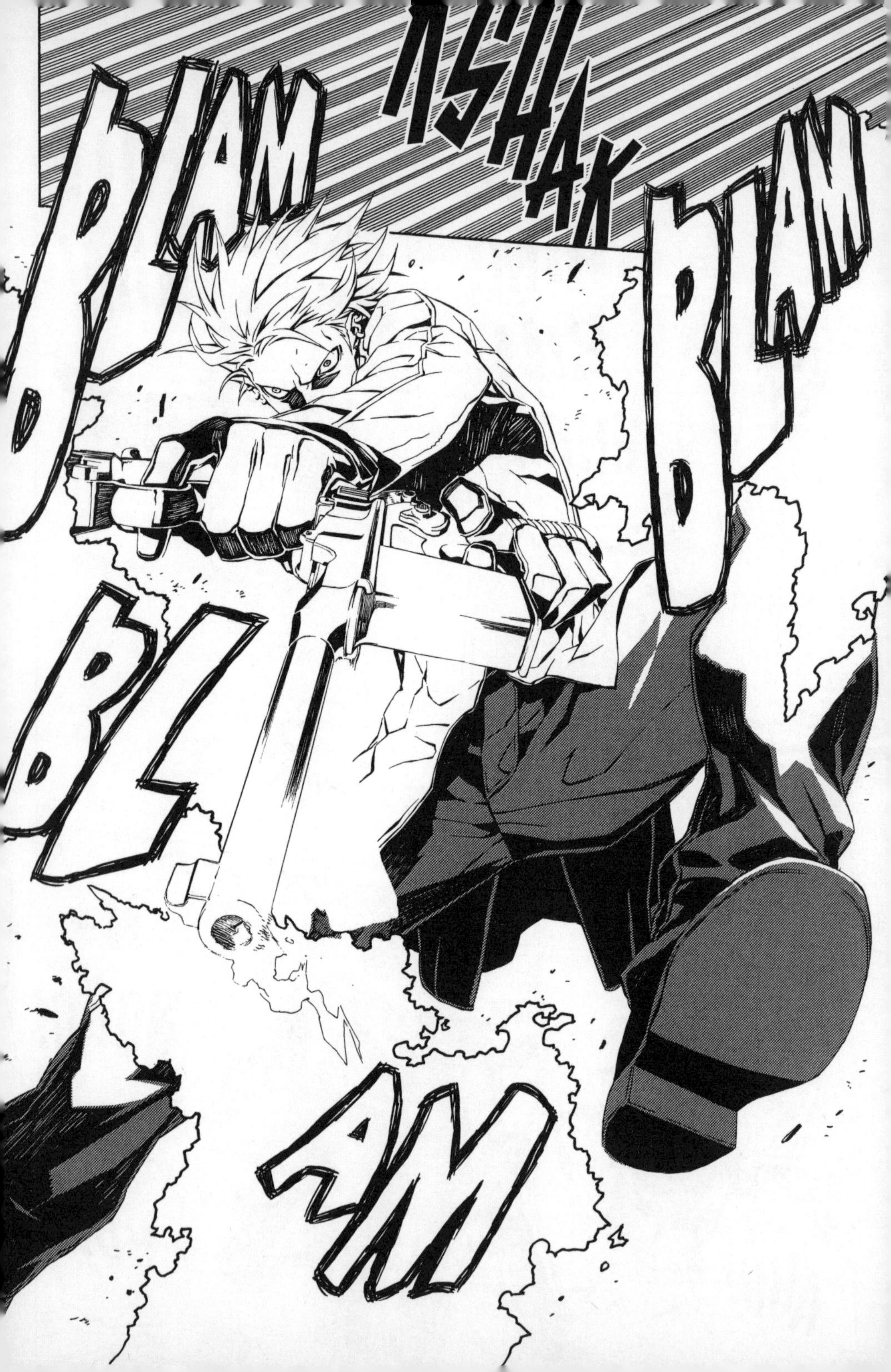
BLAM
KSHAK
BLAM
BLAM

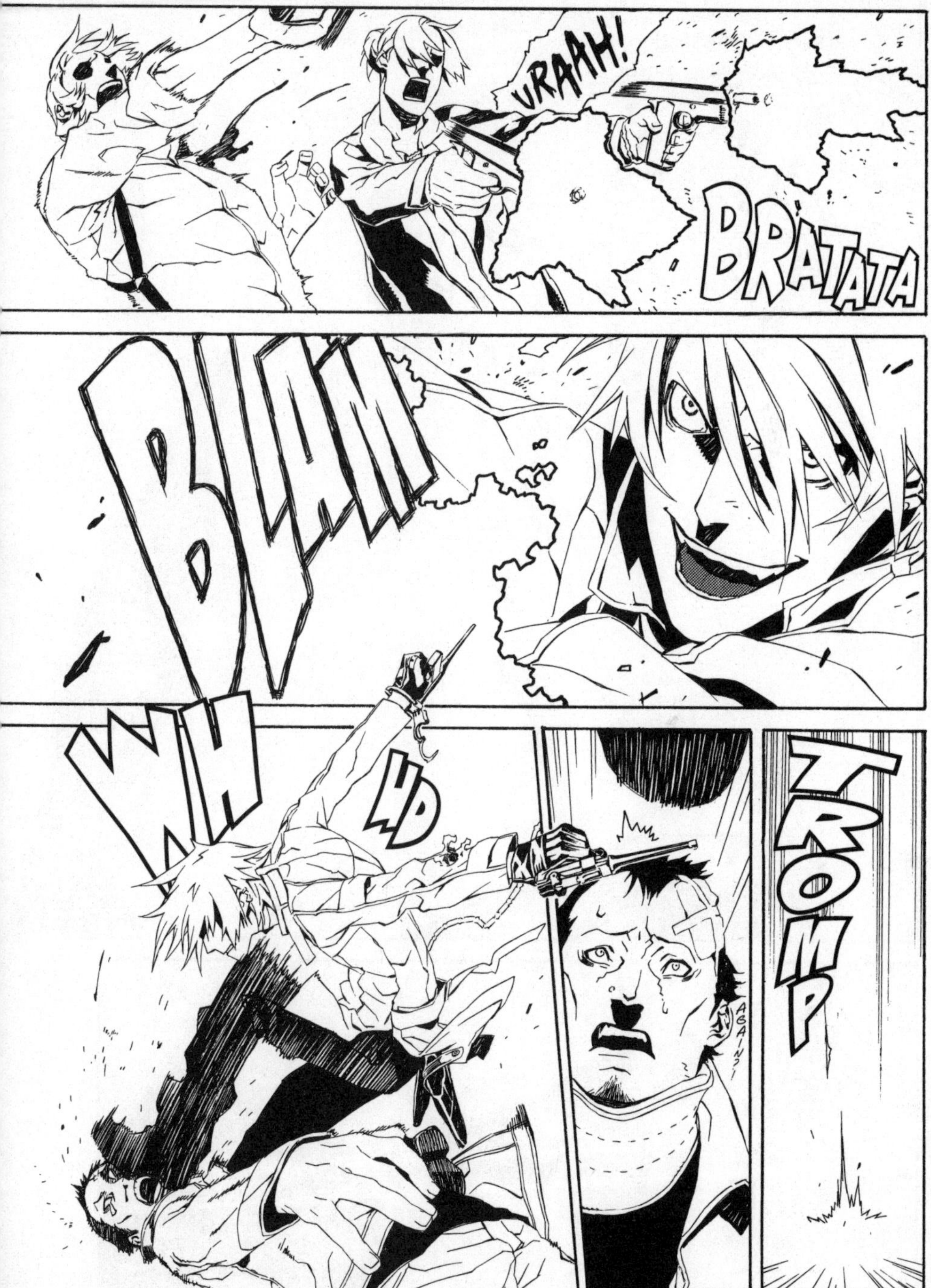
URAAH!
BRATATA
BLAM
TROMP
AGAIN?!
WHUD

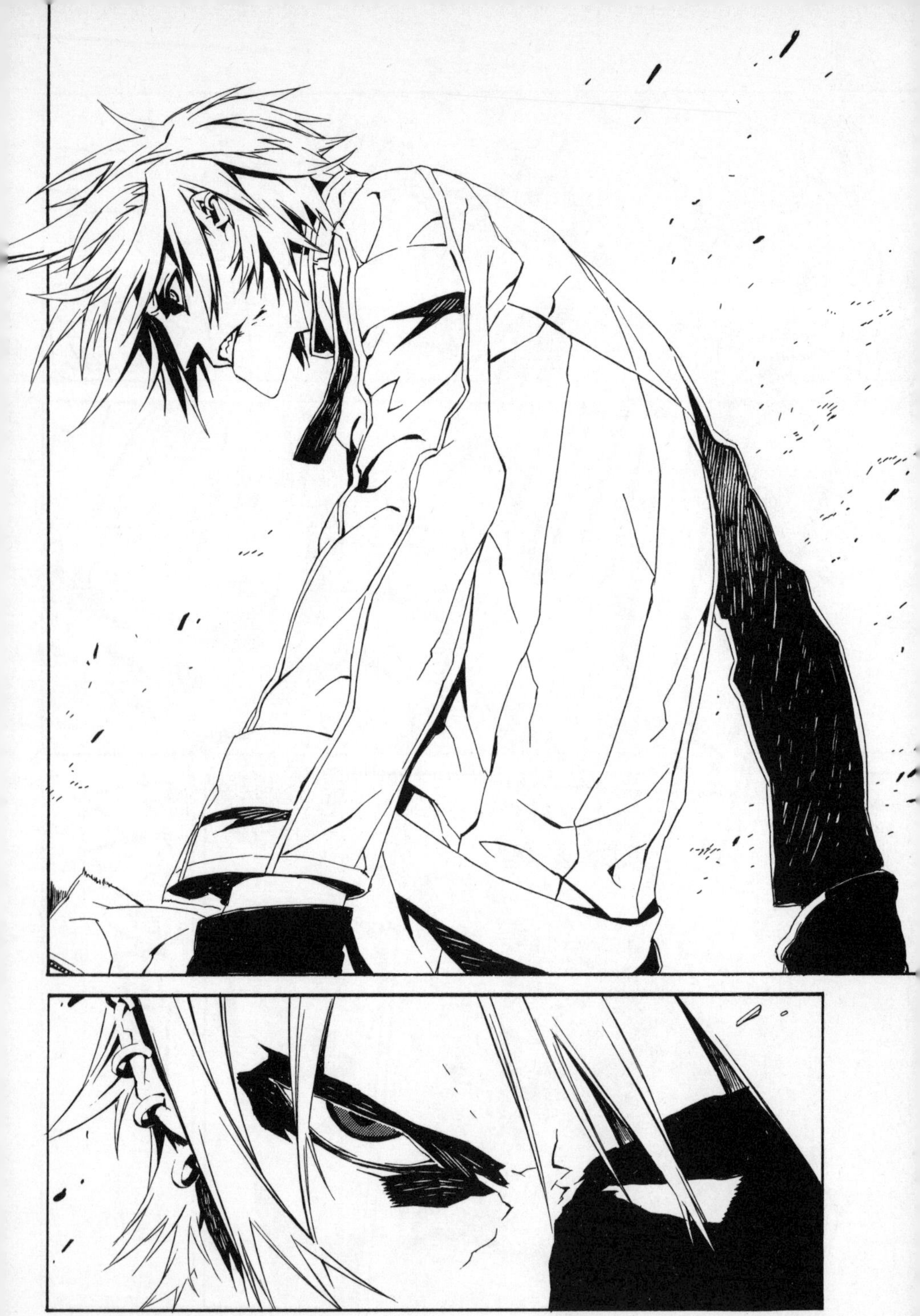

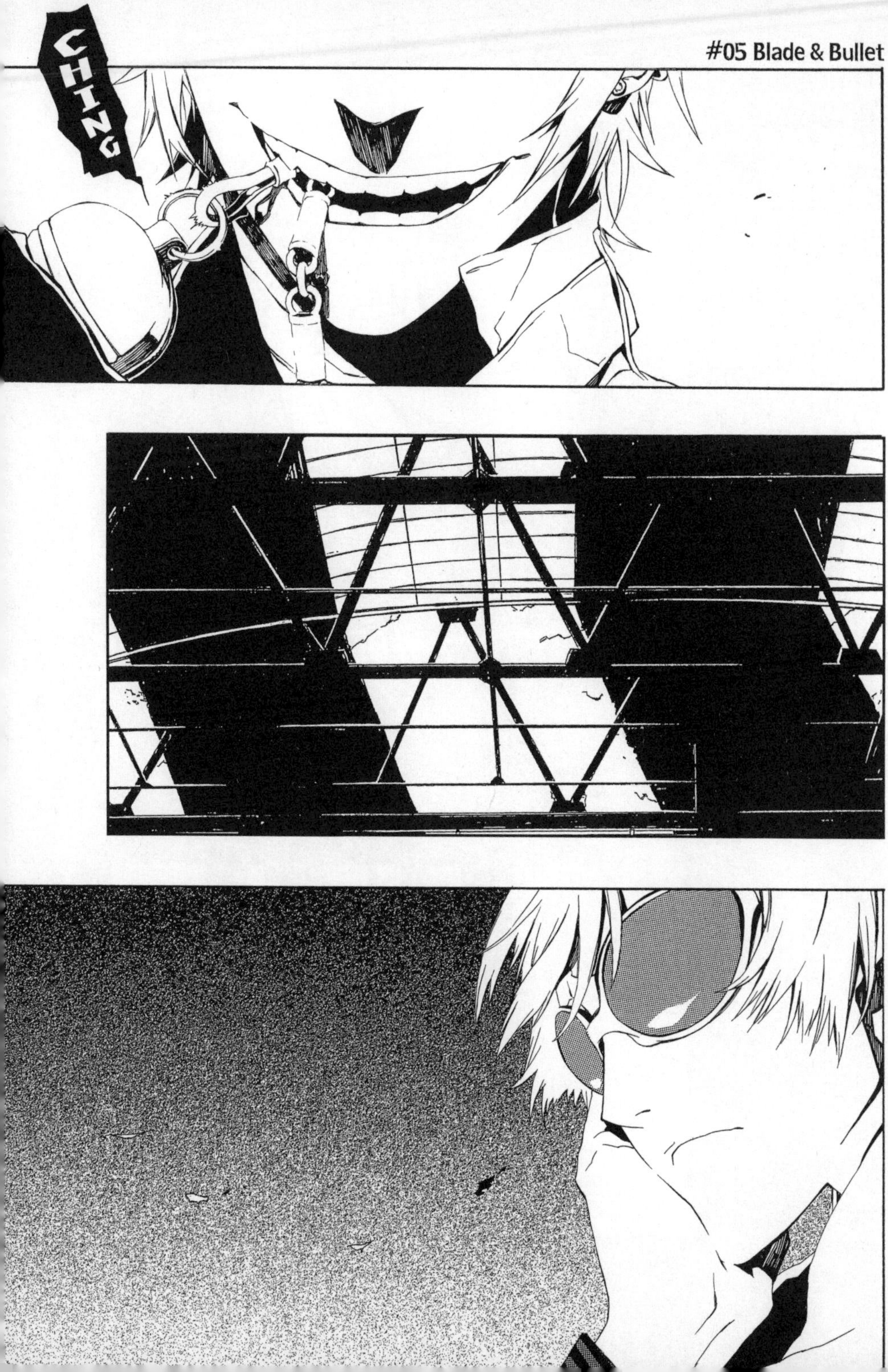
CHING

#05 Blade & Bullet

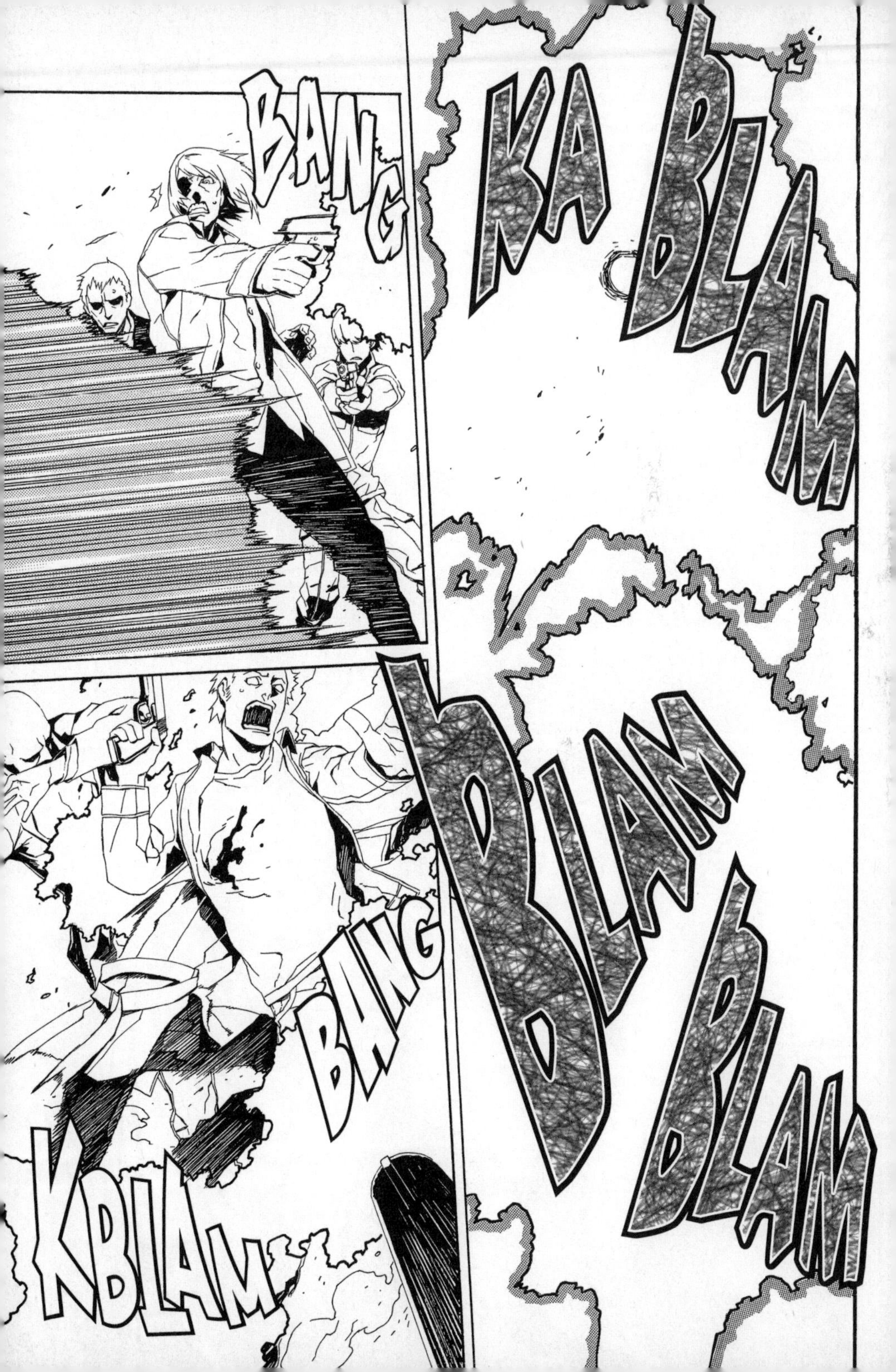
KA BLAM
BLAM
BLAM
BANG
BANG
KBLAM

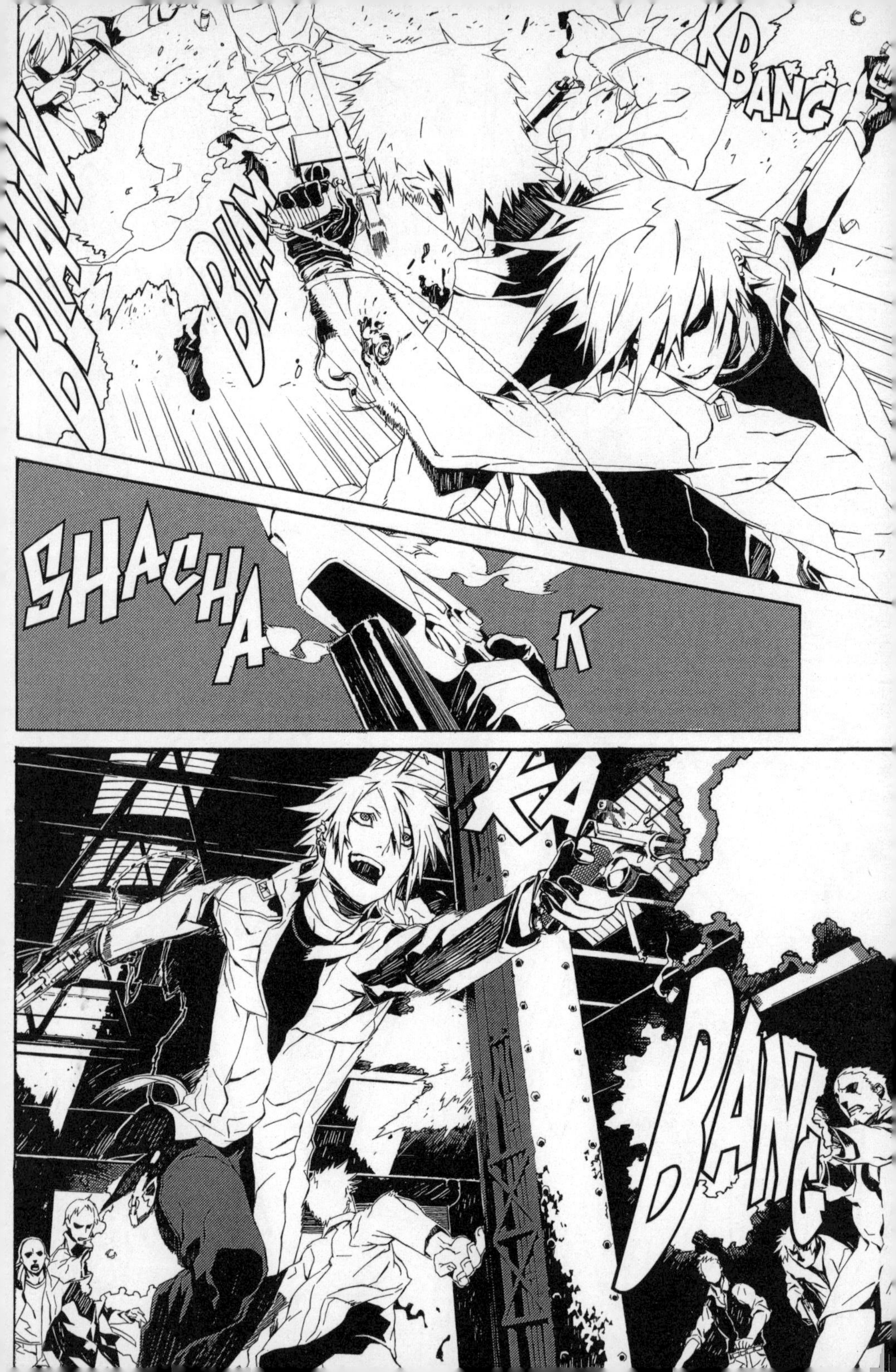
KBANG
BLAM
BLAM
SHACHAK
KA
BANG

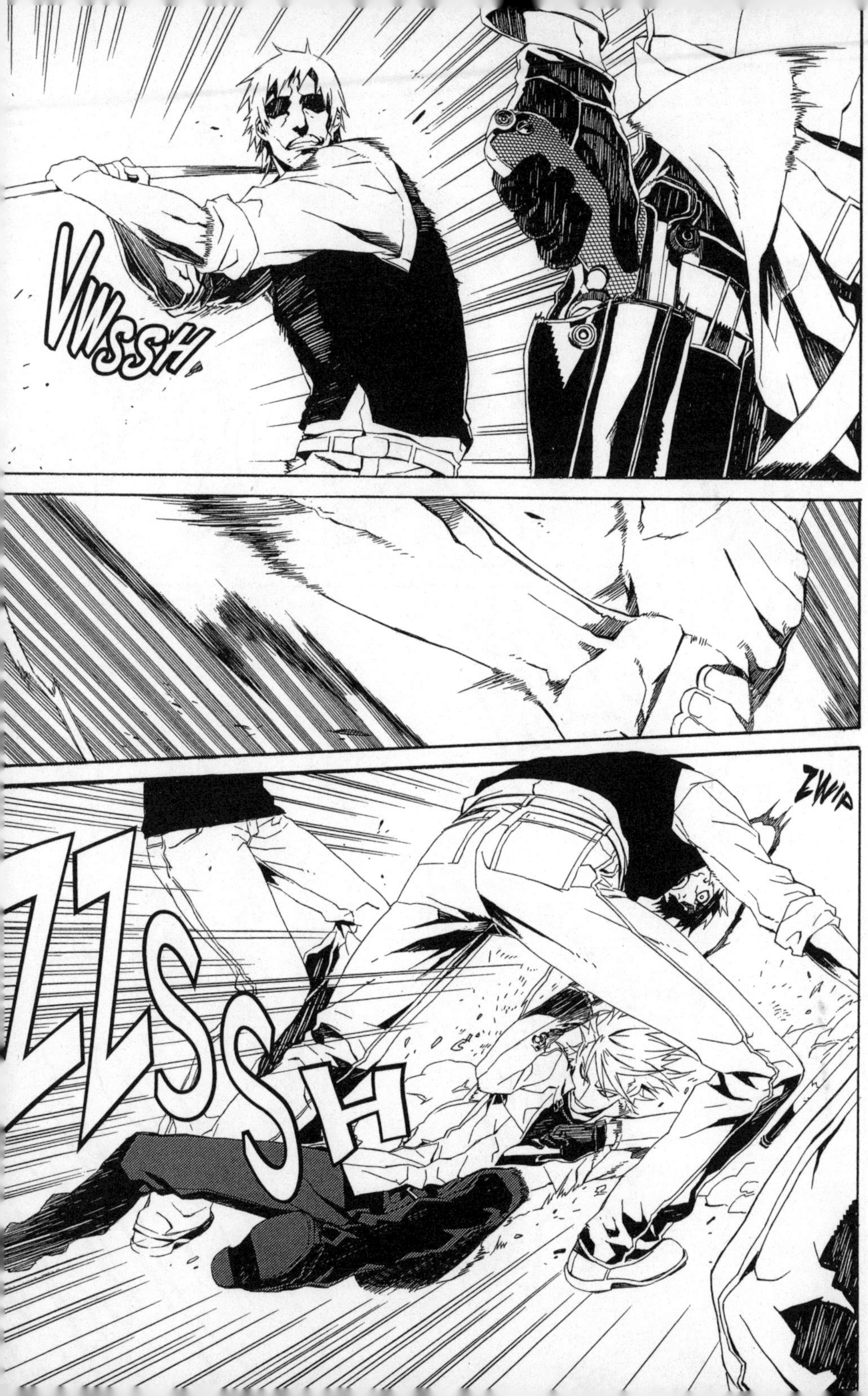
VWSSH
ZWIP
ZZSSSH

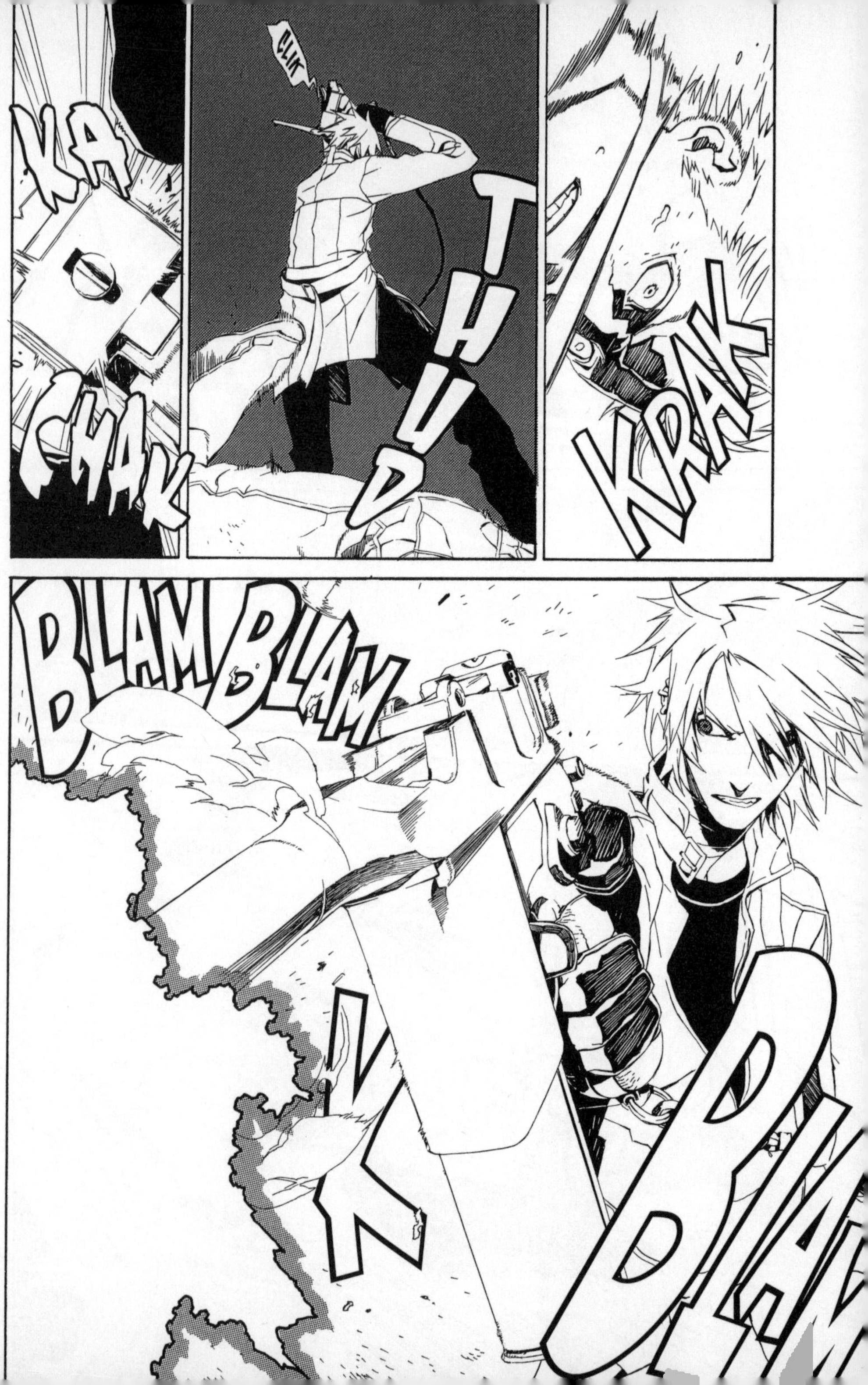
KRAK
CLIK
THUD
KA
CHAK
BLAM BLAM

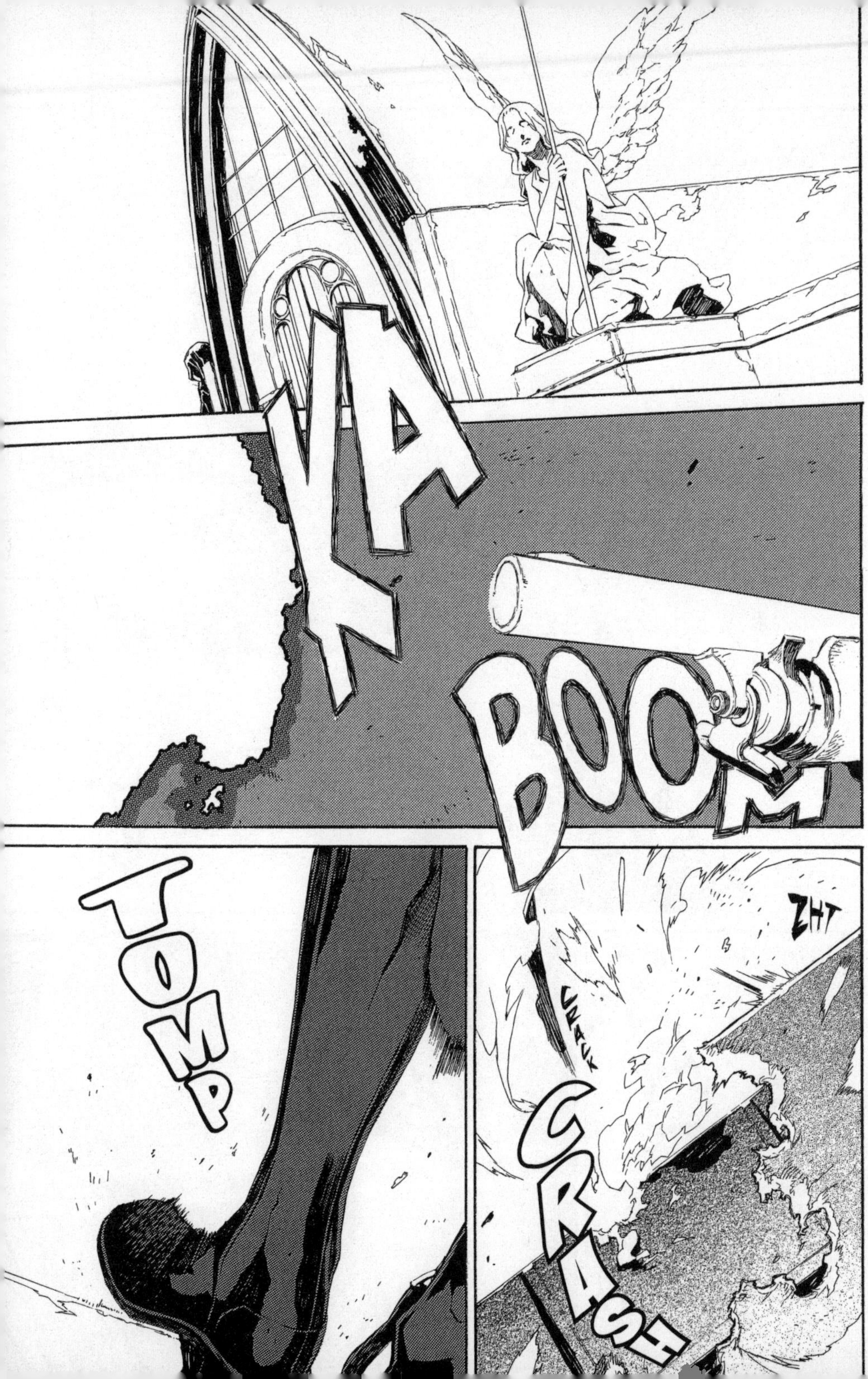
KABOOM
ZHT
CRACK
CRASH
TOMP

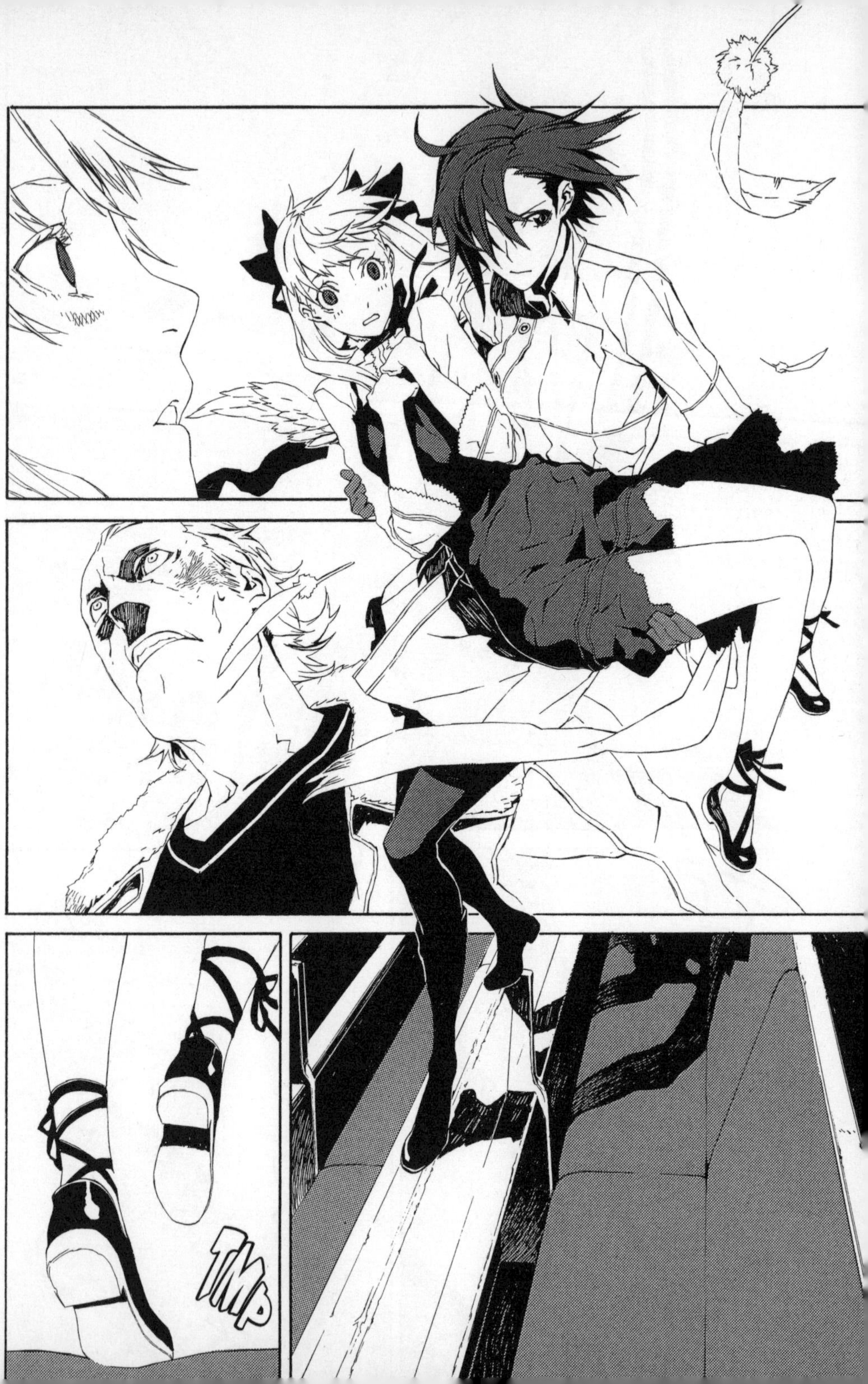
TMP

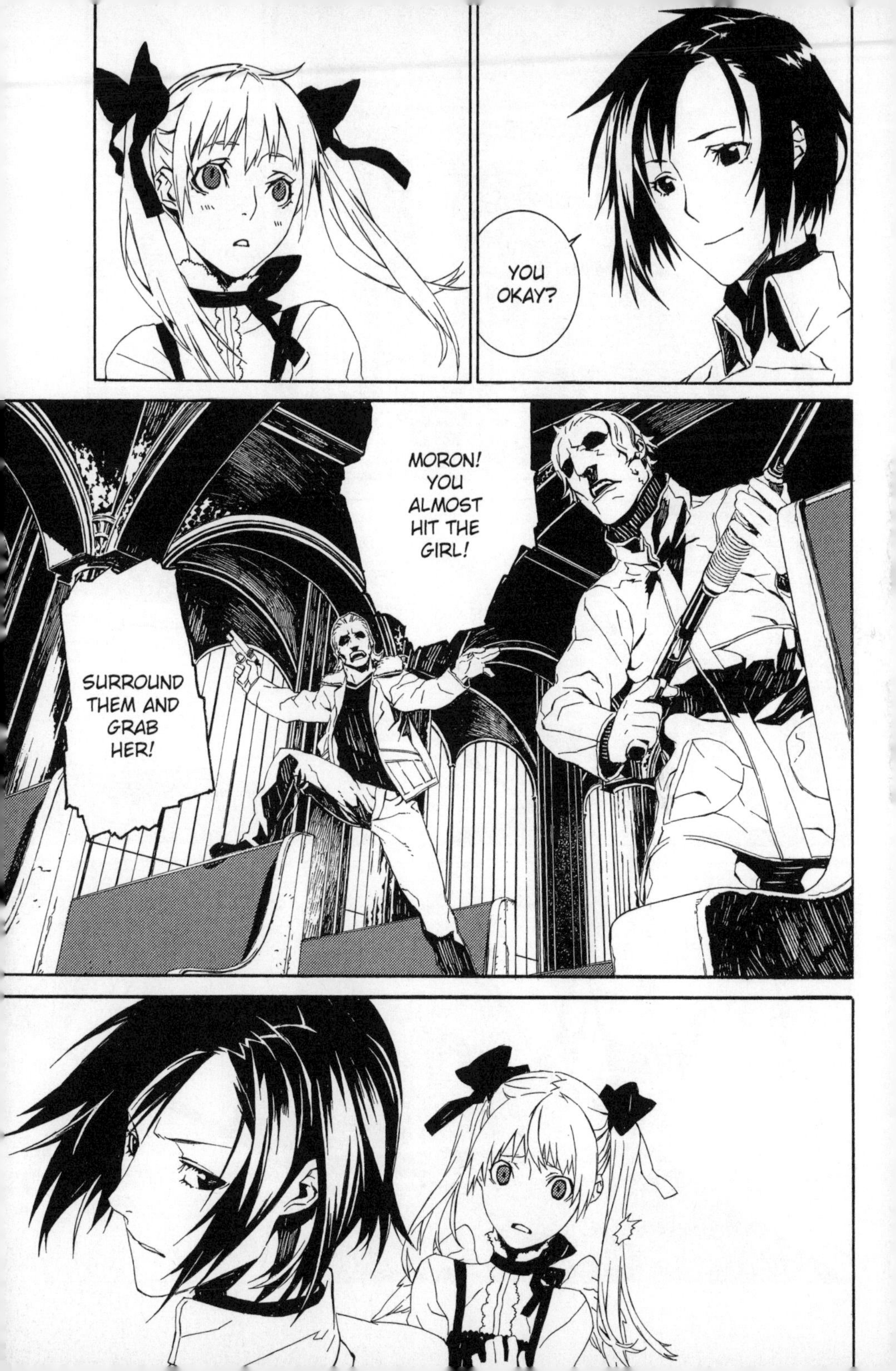
YOU OKAY?
MORON! YOU ALMOST HIT THE GIRL!
SURROUND THEM AND GRAB HER!

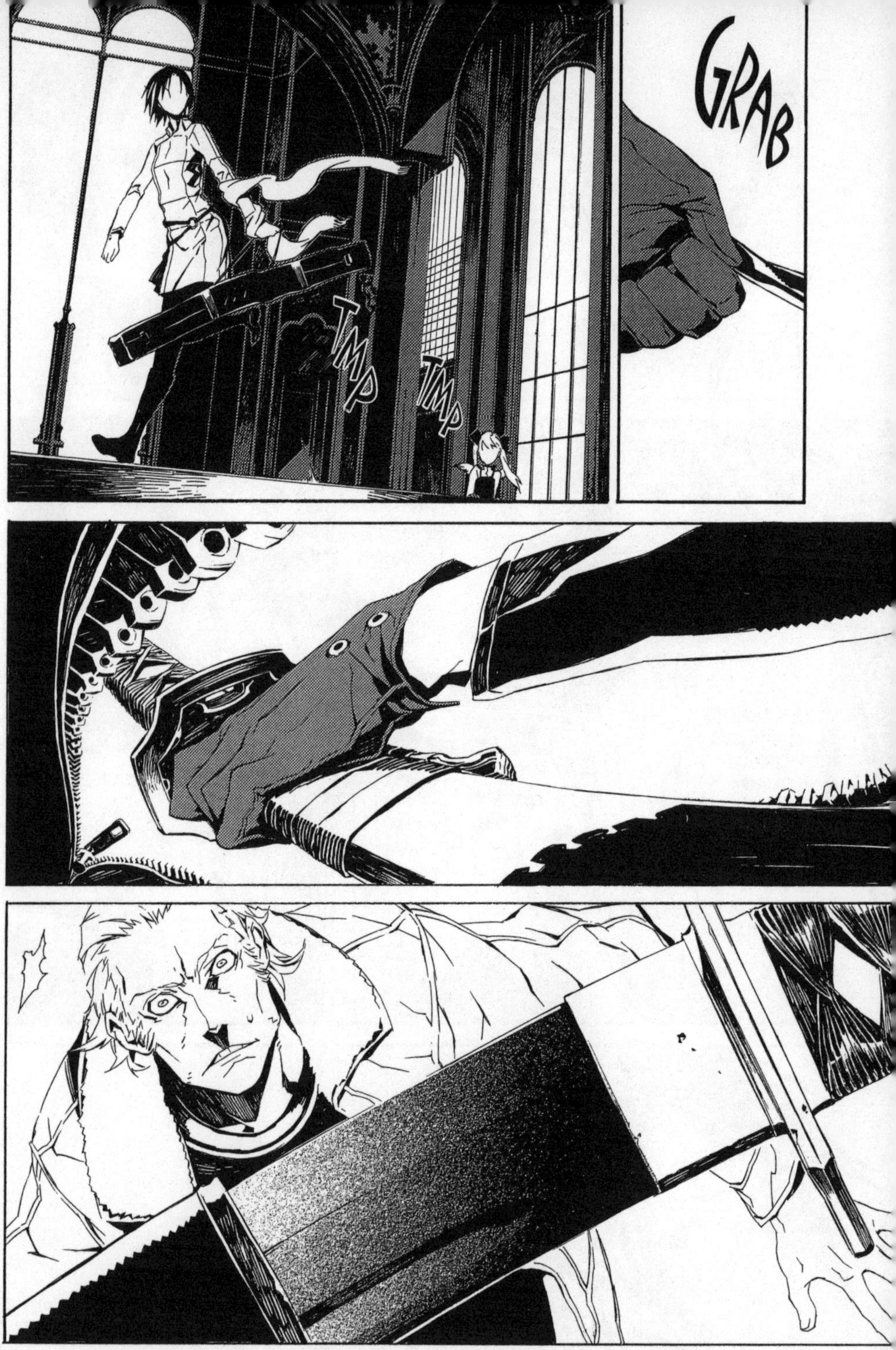
GRAB
TMP
TMP

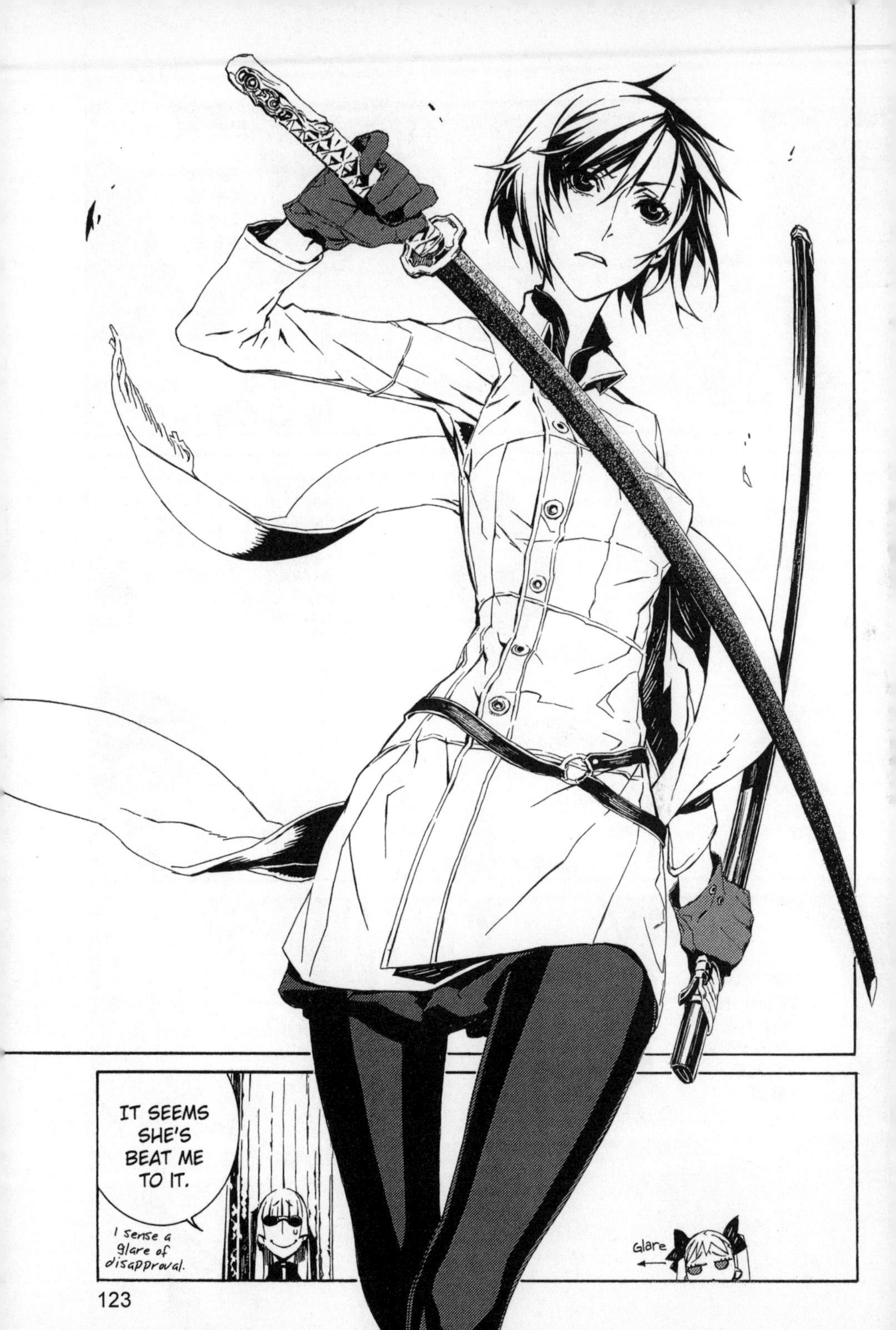
IT SEEMS SHE'S BEAT ME TO IT.
Glare
I sense a glare of disapproval.

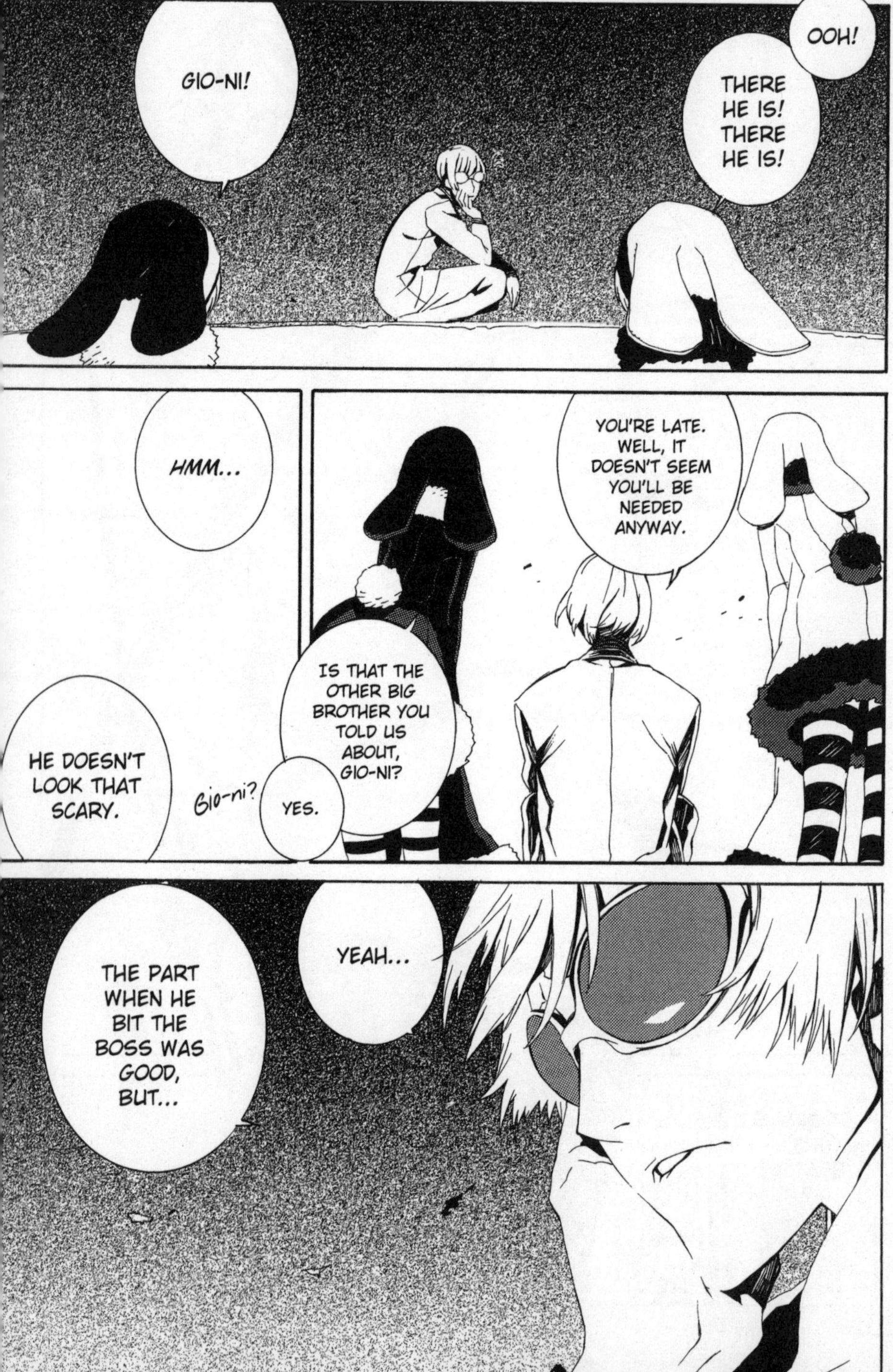
OOH!
THERE HE IS! THERE HE IS!
GIO-NI!
YOU'RE LATE. WELL, IT DOESN'T SEEM YOU'LL BE NEEDED ANYWAY.
IS THAT THE OTHER BIG BROTHER YOU TOLD US ABOUT, GIO-NI?
YES.
HMM...
Gio-ni?
HE DOESN'T LOOK THAT SCARY.
YEAH...
THE PART WHEN HE BIT THE BOSS WAS GOOD, BUT...

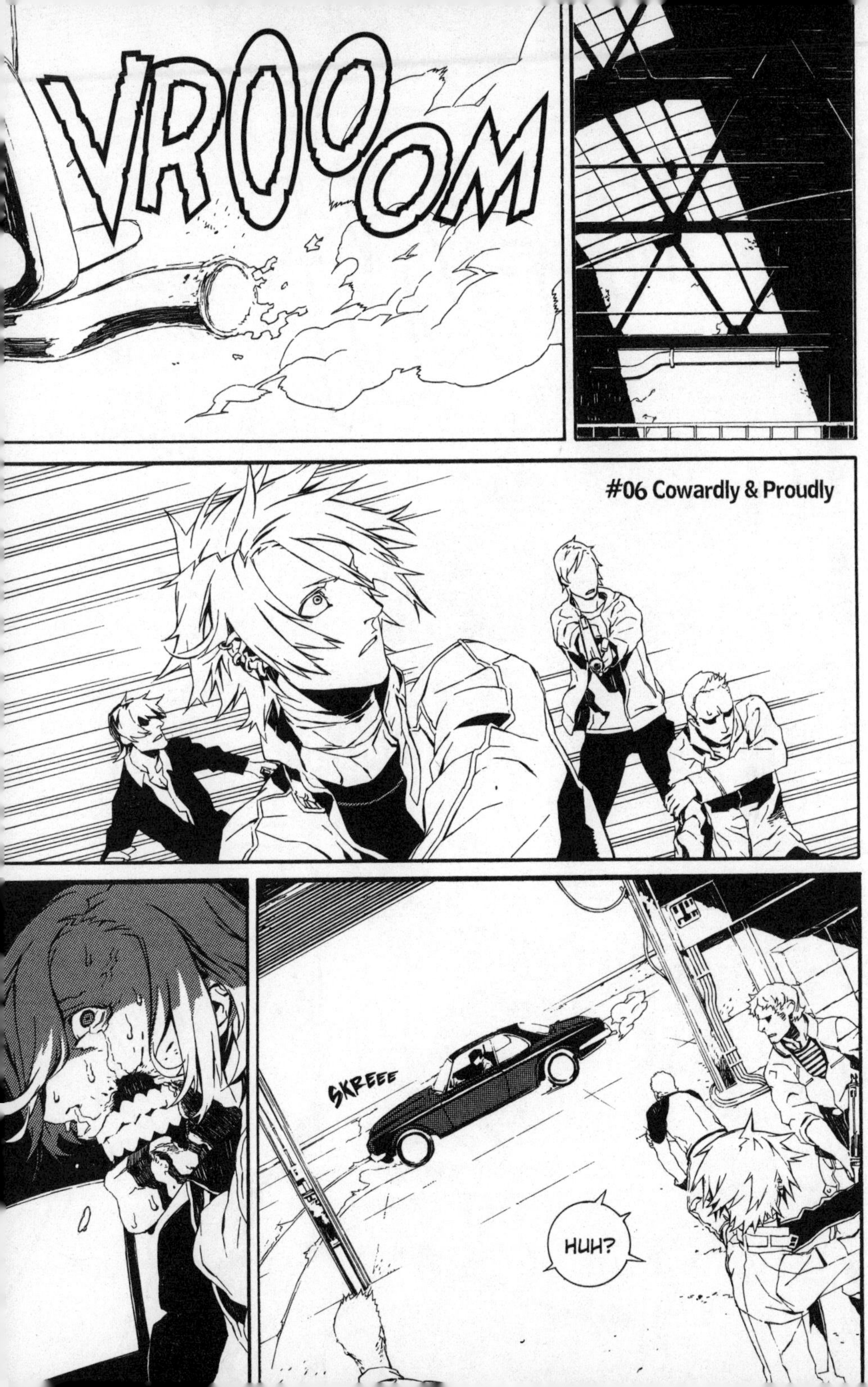
VROOOM
#06 Cowardly & Proudly
SKREEE
HUH?

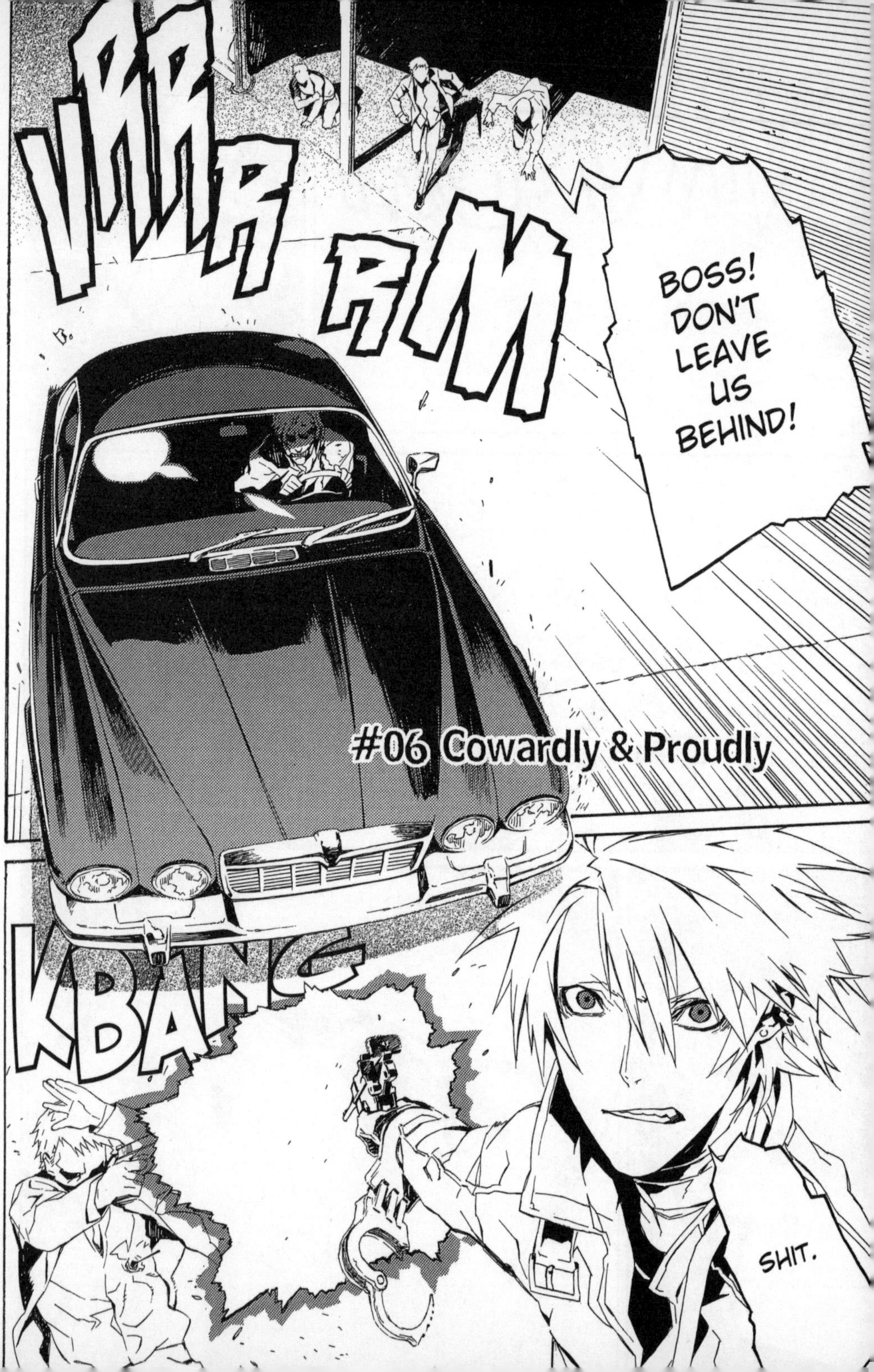
BOSS! DON'T LEAVE US BEHIND!
VRRRRM
#06 Cowardly & Proudly
SHIT.
KBANG

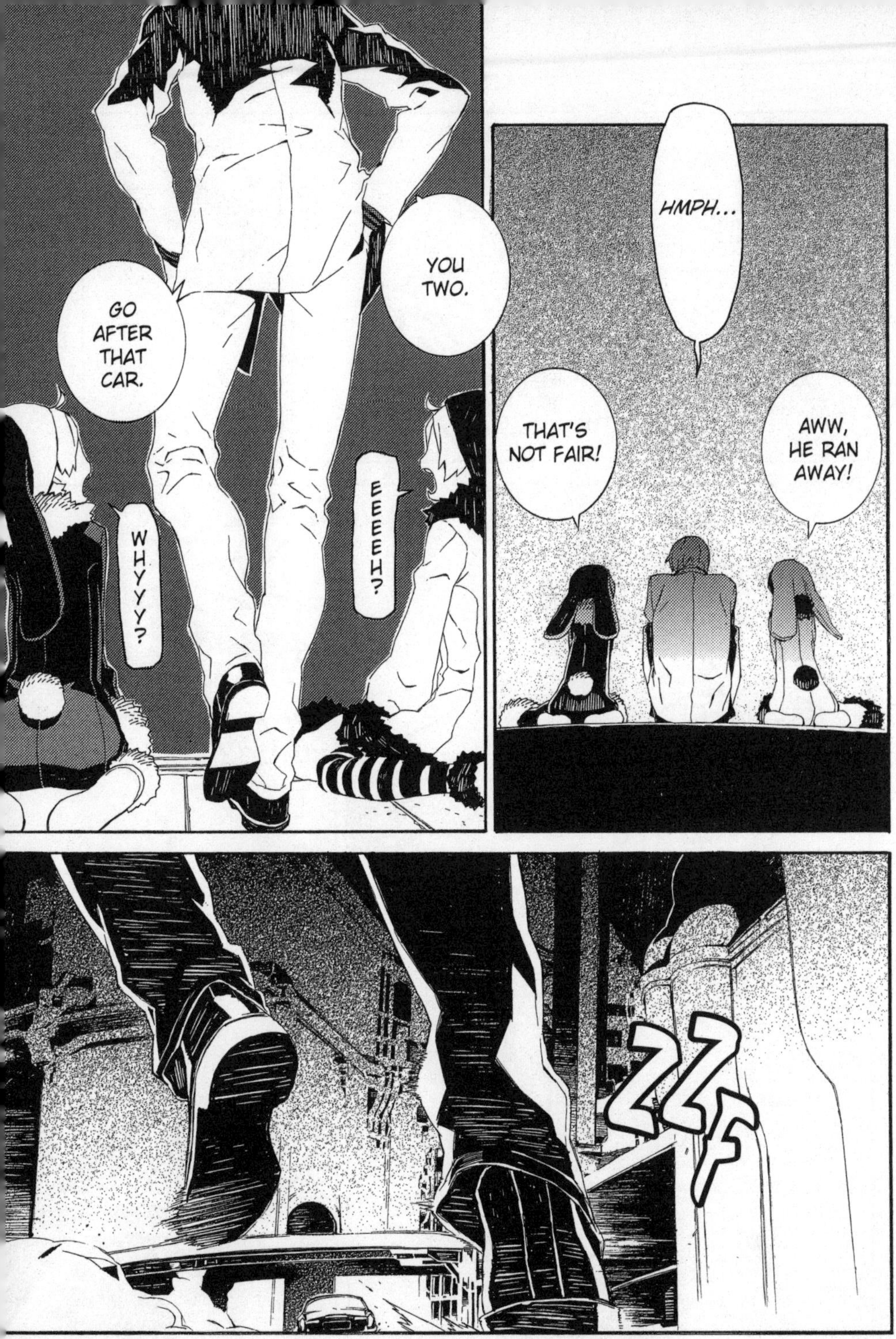

HMPH...
AWW, HE RAN AWAY!
THAT'S NOT FAIR!
YOU TWO.
GO AFTER THAT CAR.
EEEEEH?
WHYYY?
ZZF

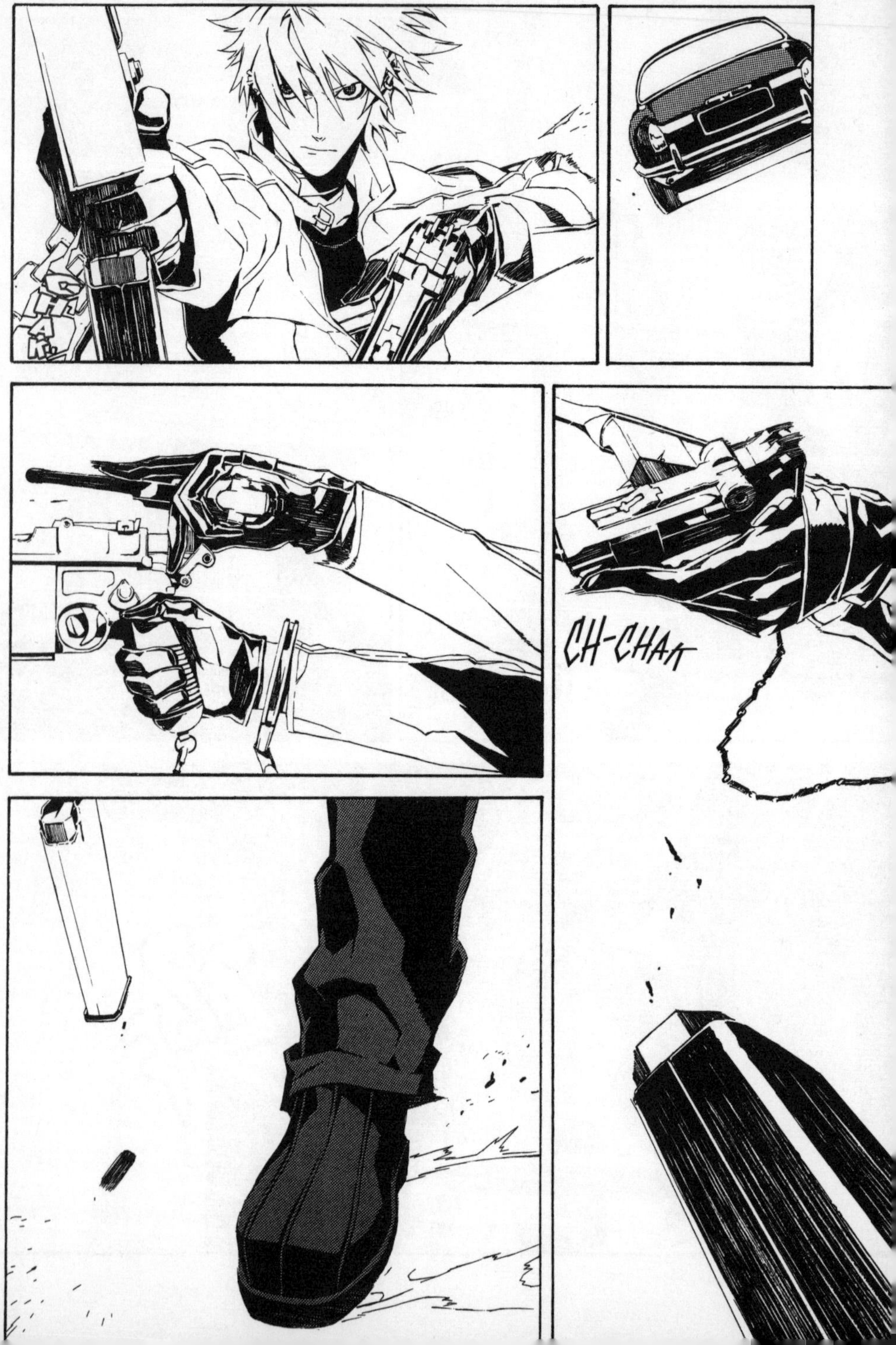
CHAK..
CH-CHAK

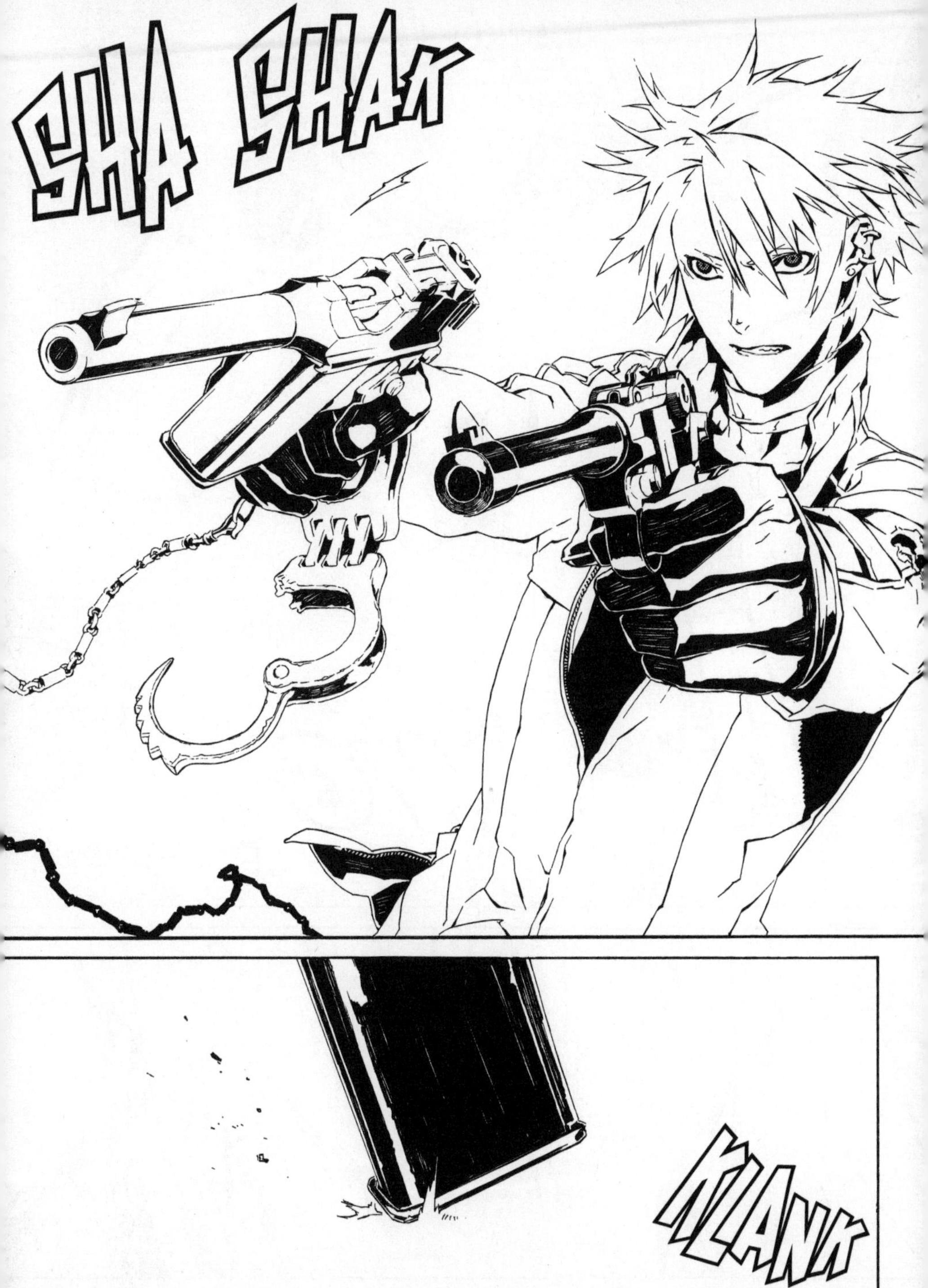
SHA SHAK
KLANK

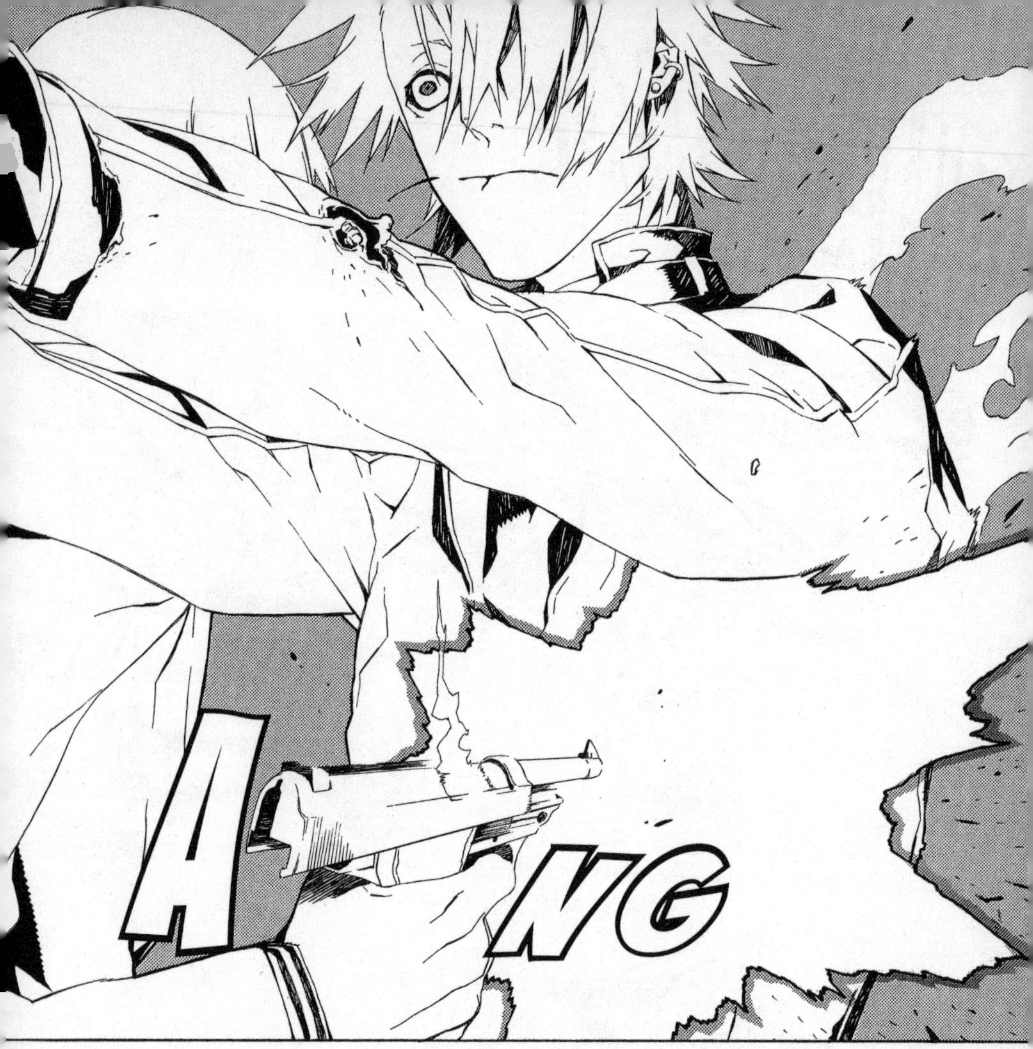
A NG
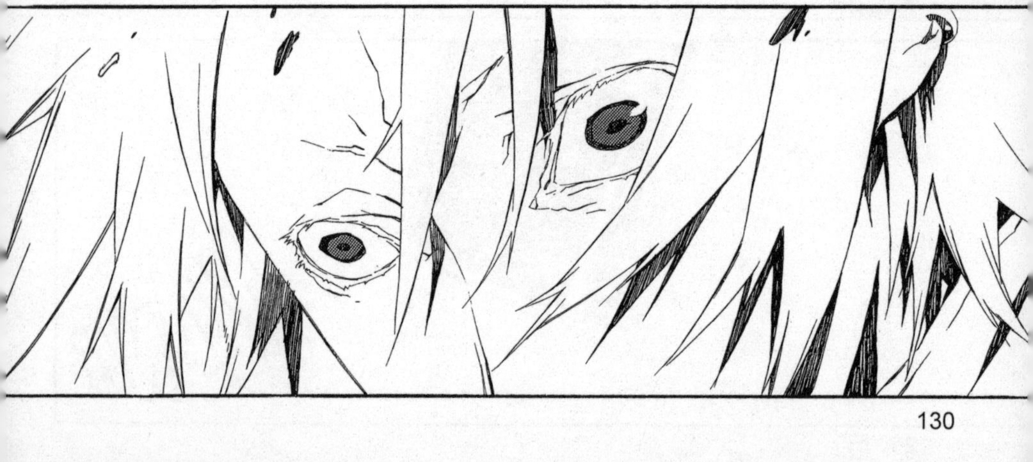

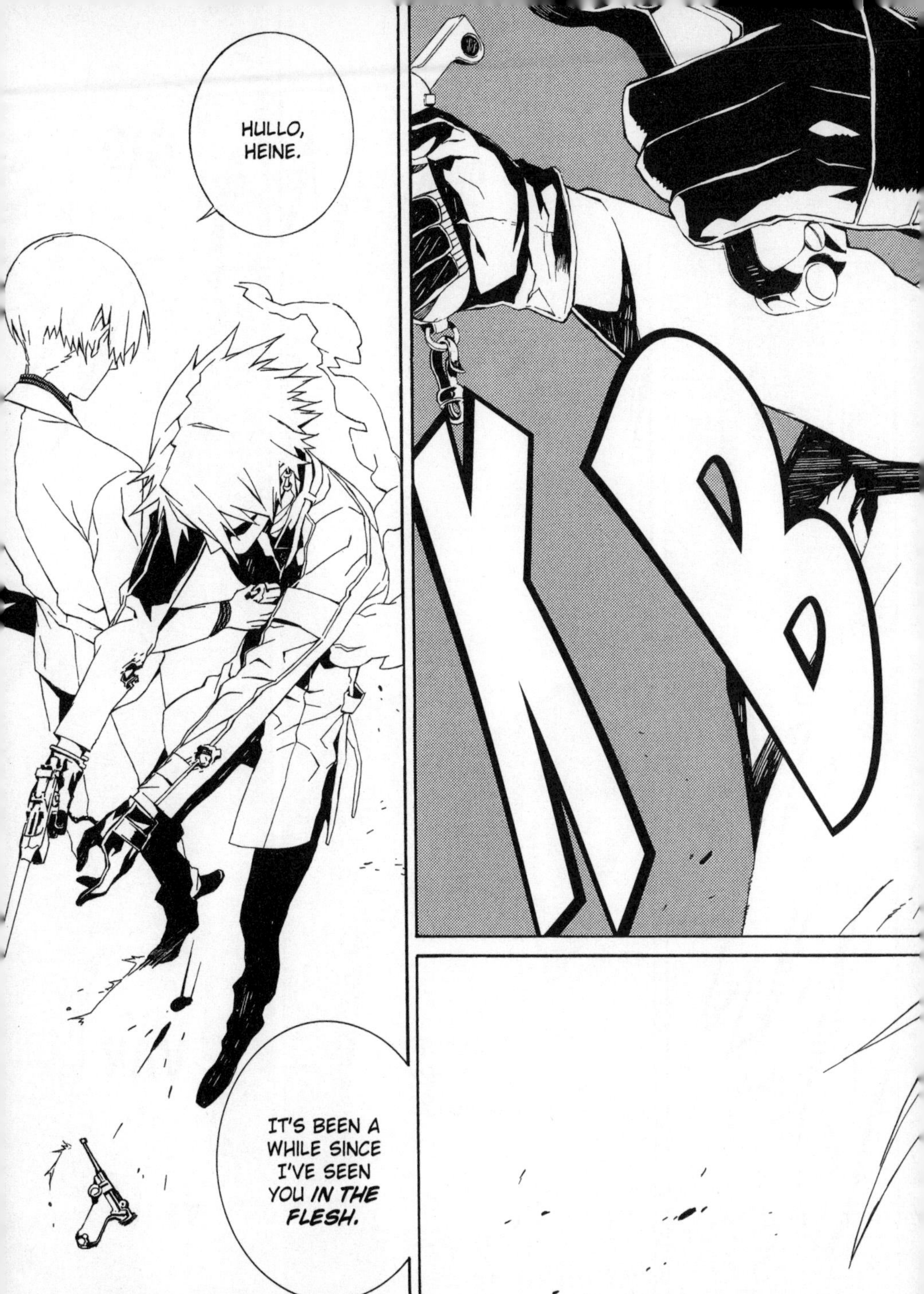
HULLO, HEINE.
IT'S BEEN A WHILE SINCE I'VE SEEN YOU *IN THE FLESH.*

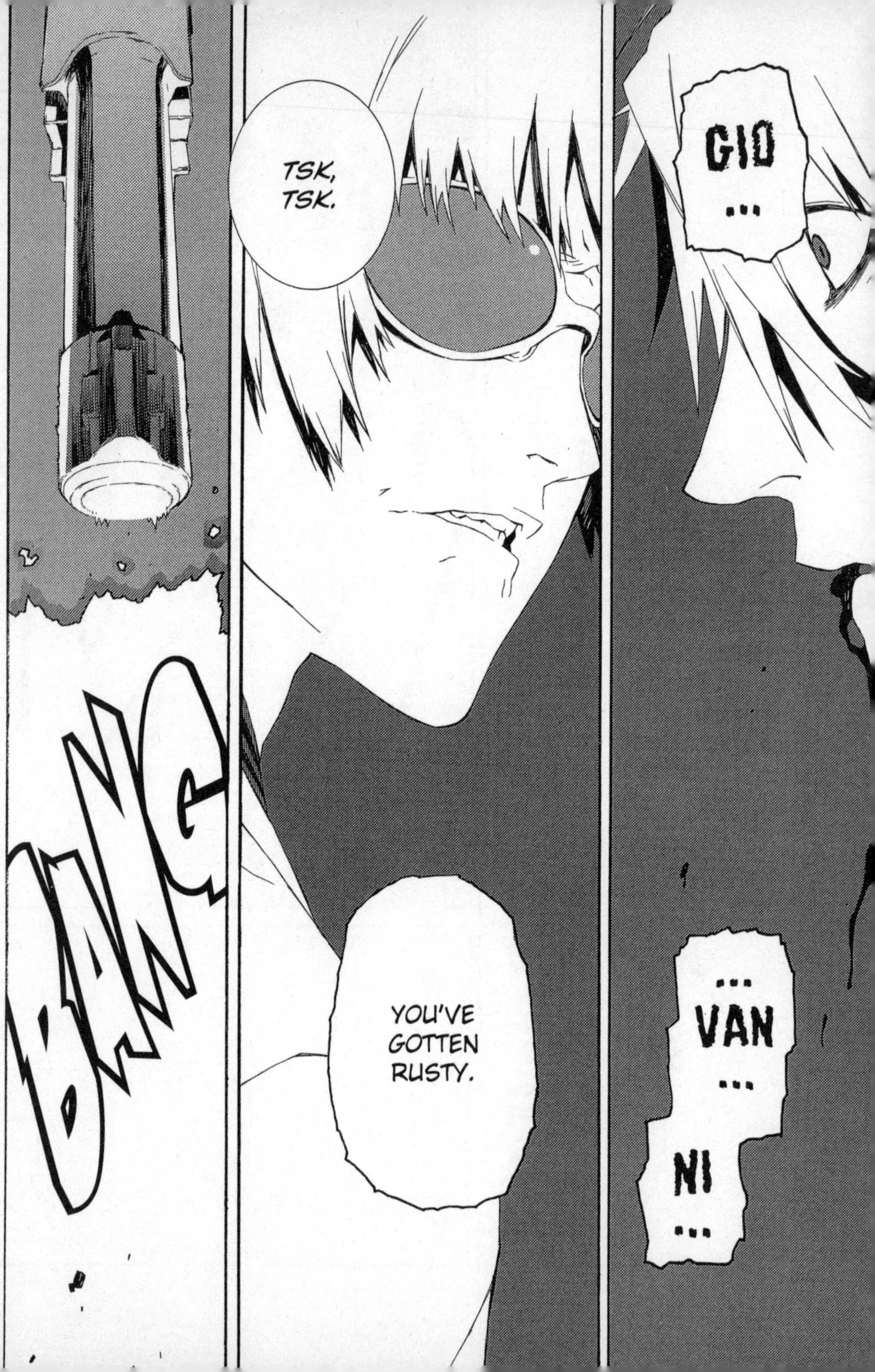
GIO ...
... VAN ... NI ...
TSK, TSK.
YOU'VE GOTTEN RUSTY.
BANG

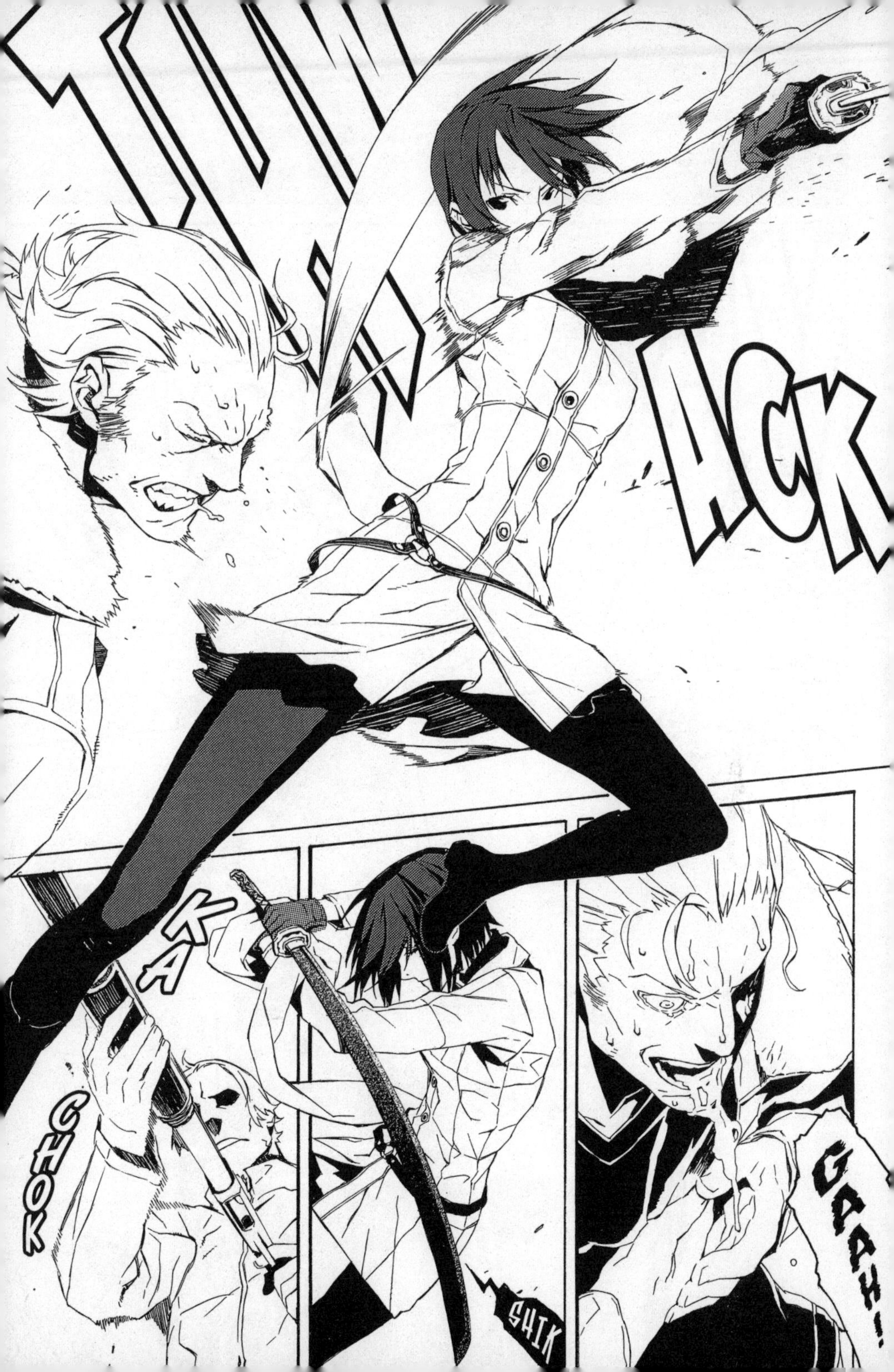
ACK
GAAH!
SHIK
KA
CHOK

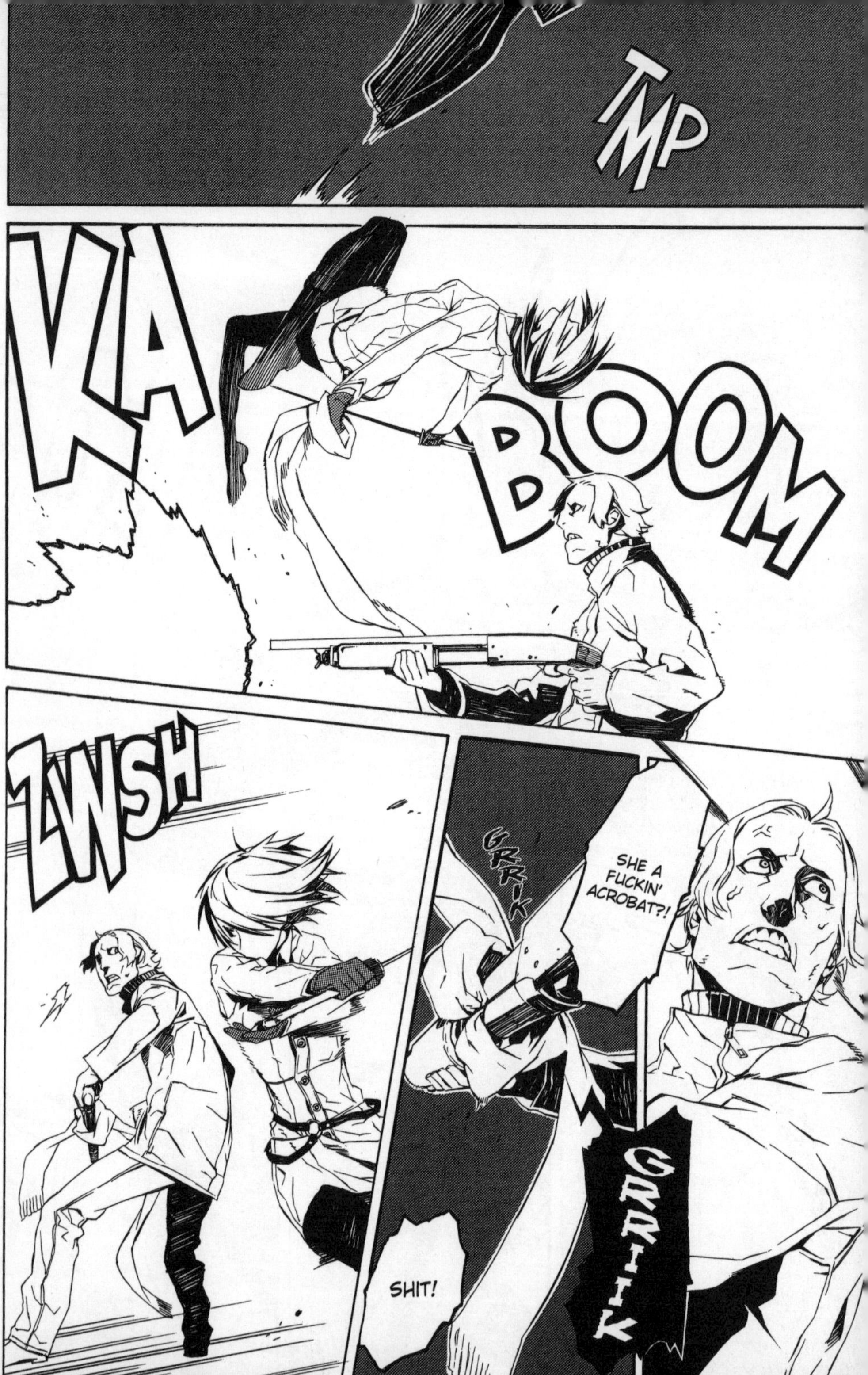
TMP
KA
BOOM
SHE A FUCKIN' ACROBAT?!
GRRIK
GRRIIK
SHIT!
ZWSH

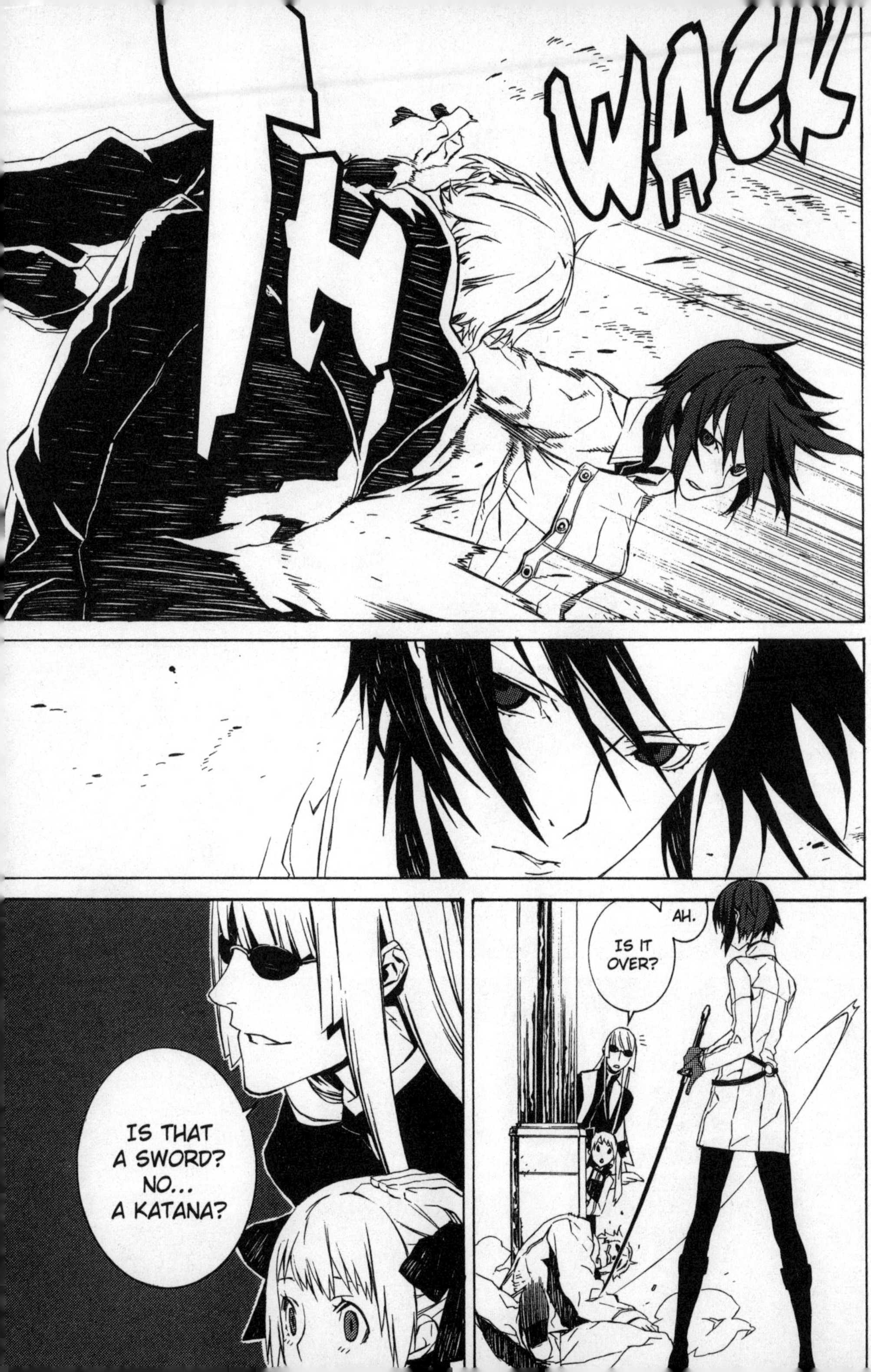
THWACK
AH.
IS IT OVER?
IS THAT A SWORD? NO... A KATANA?

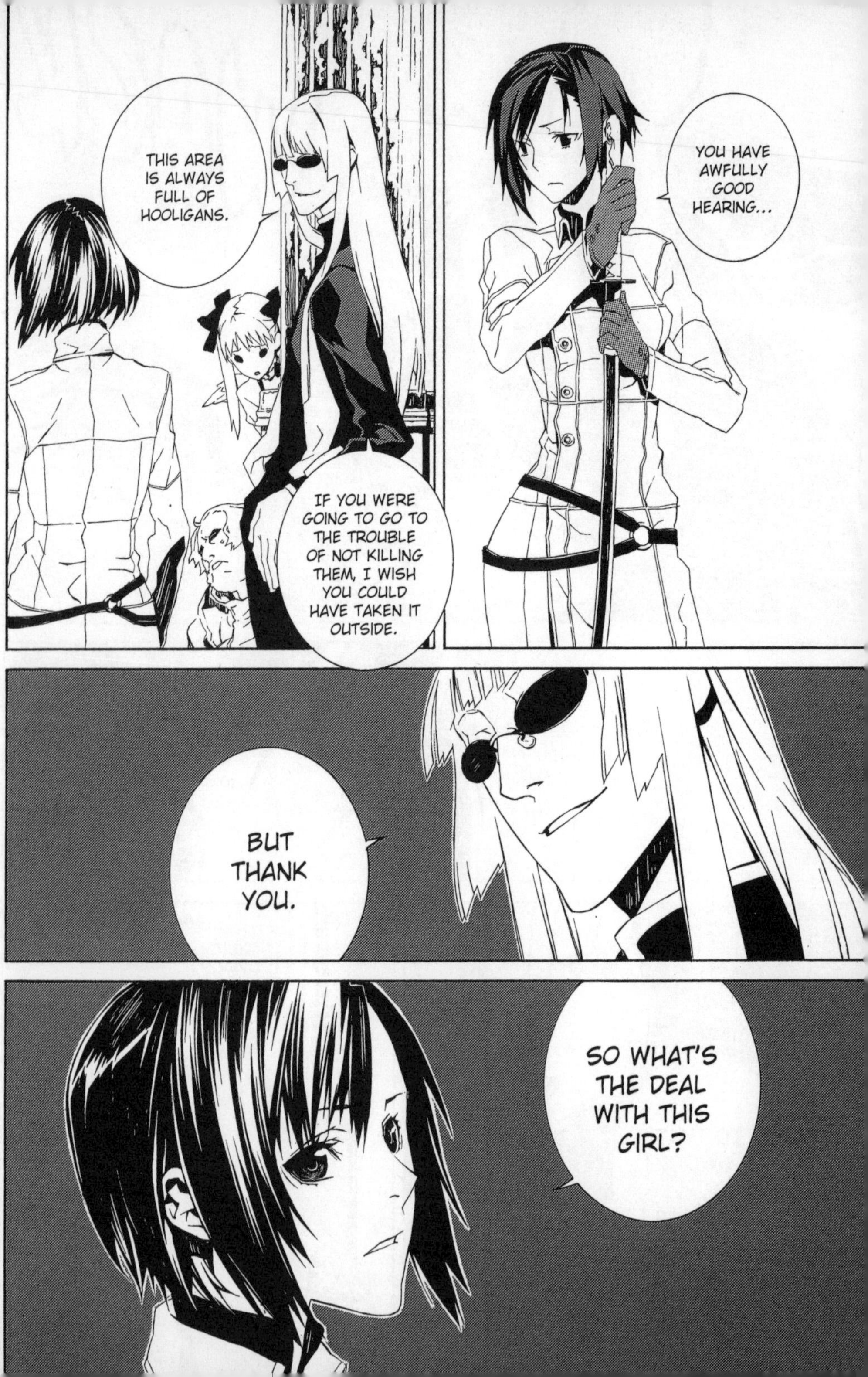
YOU HAVE AWFULLY GOOD HEARING...
THIS AREA IS ALWAYS FULL OF HOOLIGANS.
IF YOU WERE GOING TO GO TO THE TROUBLE OF NOT KILLING THEM, I WISH YOU COULD HAVE TAKEN IT OUTSIDE.
BUT THANK YOU.
SO WHAT'S THE DEAL WITH THIS GIRL?

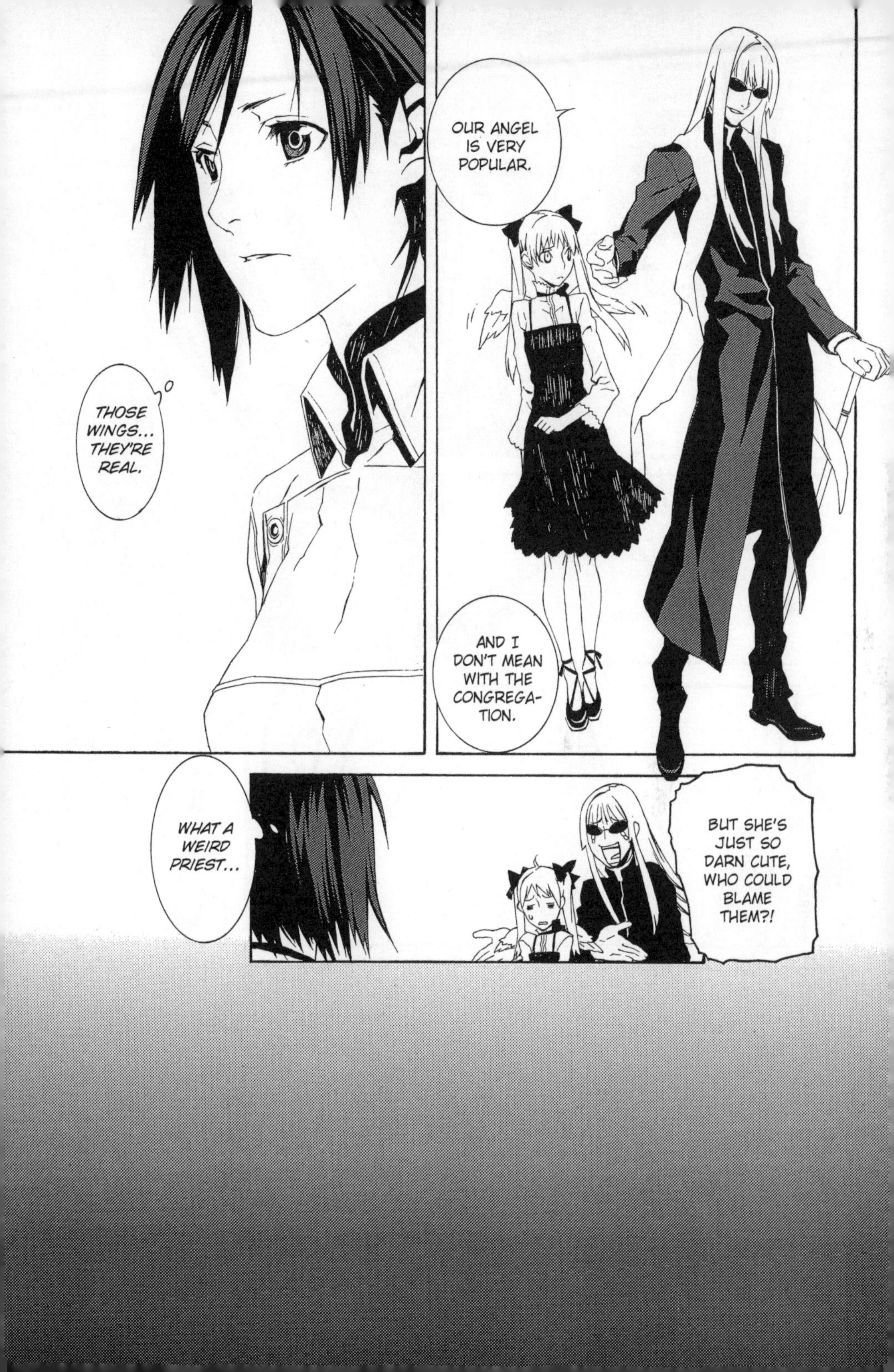
OUR ANGEL IS VERY POPULAR.
AND I DON'T MEAN WITH THE CONGREGATION.
THOSE WINGS... THEY'RE REAL.
BUT SHE'S JUST SO DARN CUTE, WHO COULD BLAME THEM?!
WHAT A WEIRD PRIEST...

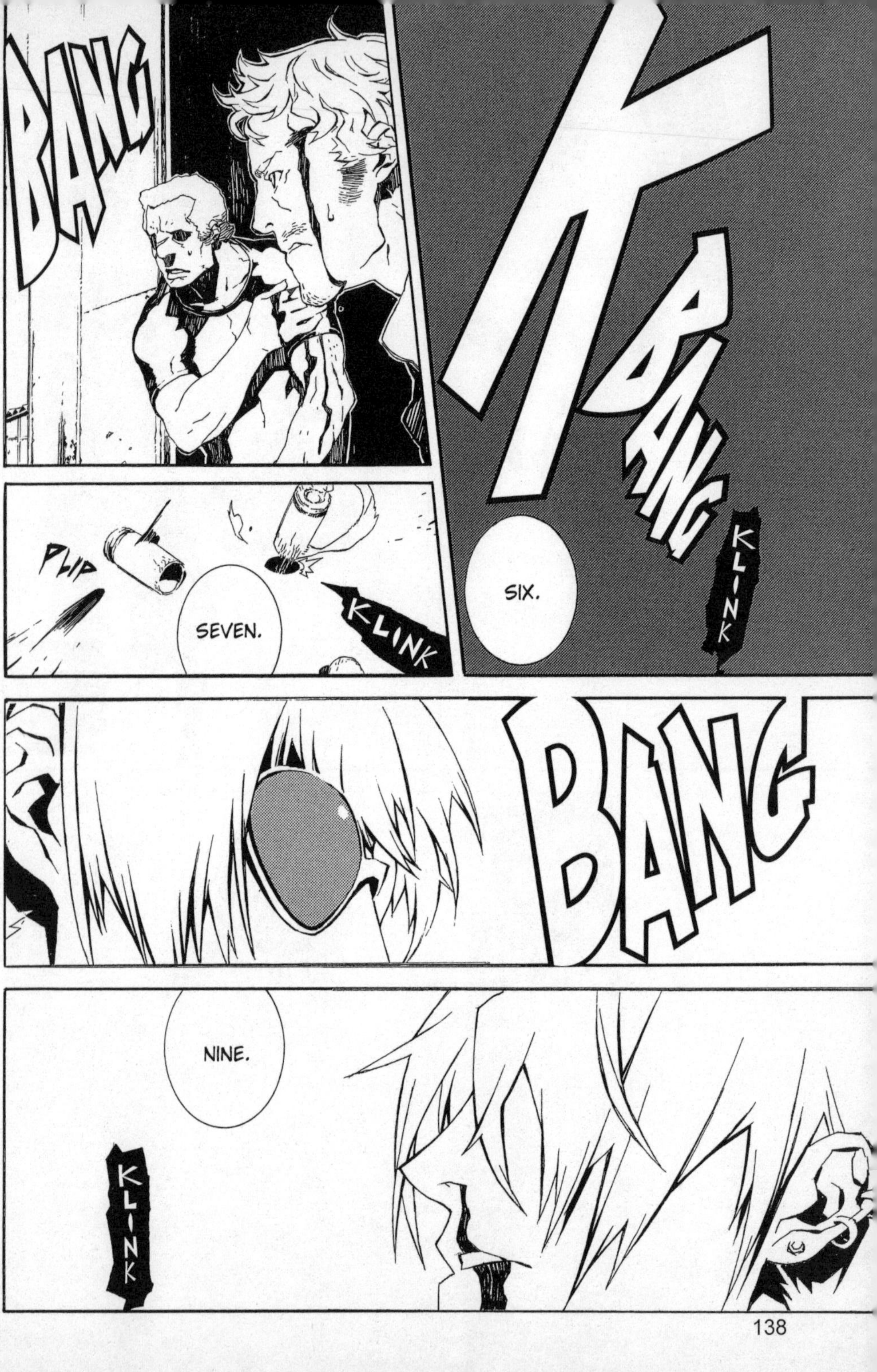
BANG
SIX.
KLINK
BANG
KLINK
SEVEN.
PLIP
BANG
NINE.
KLINK

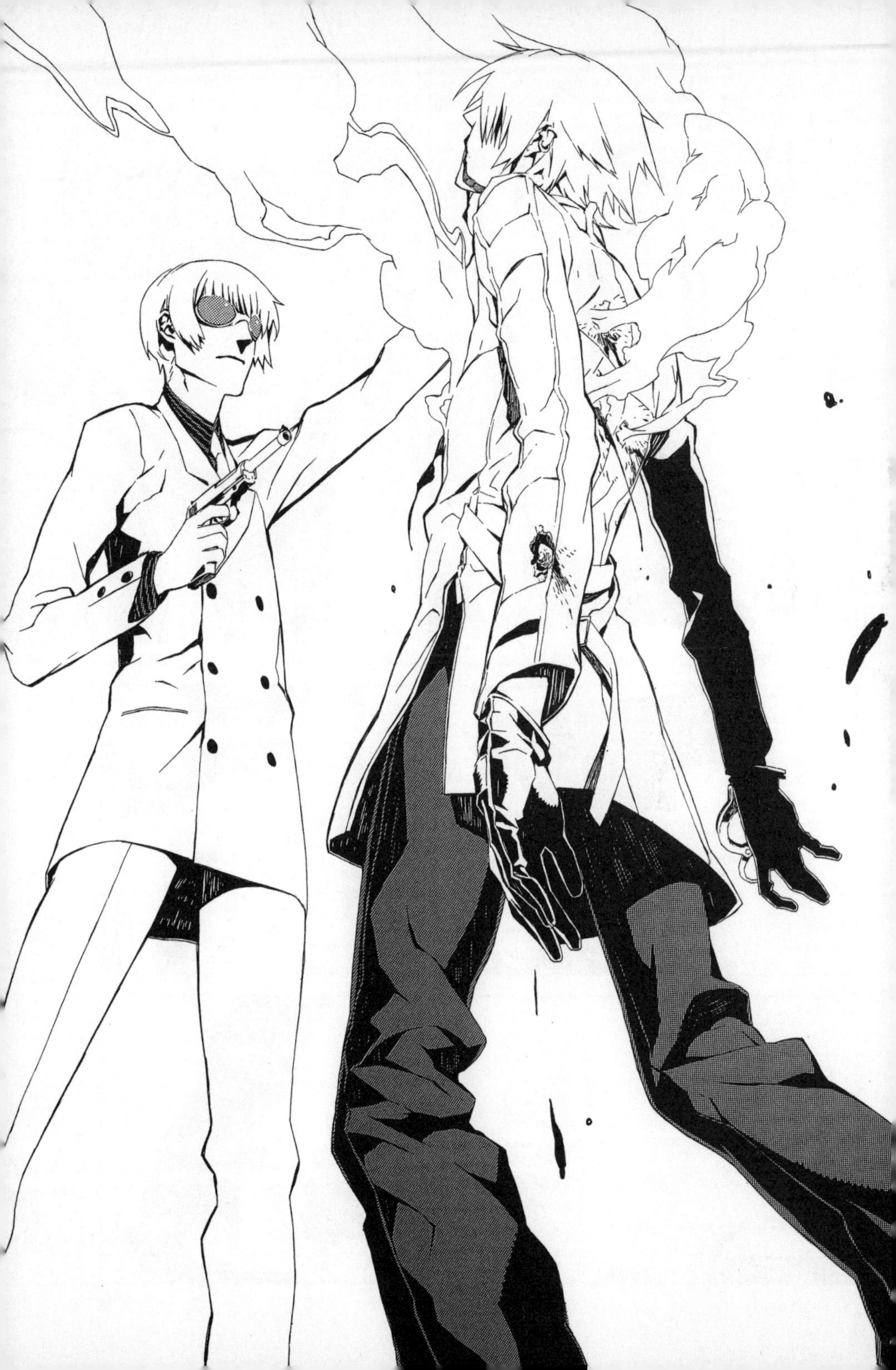

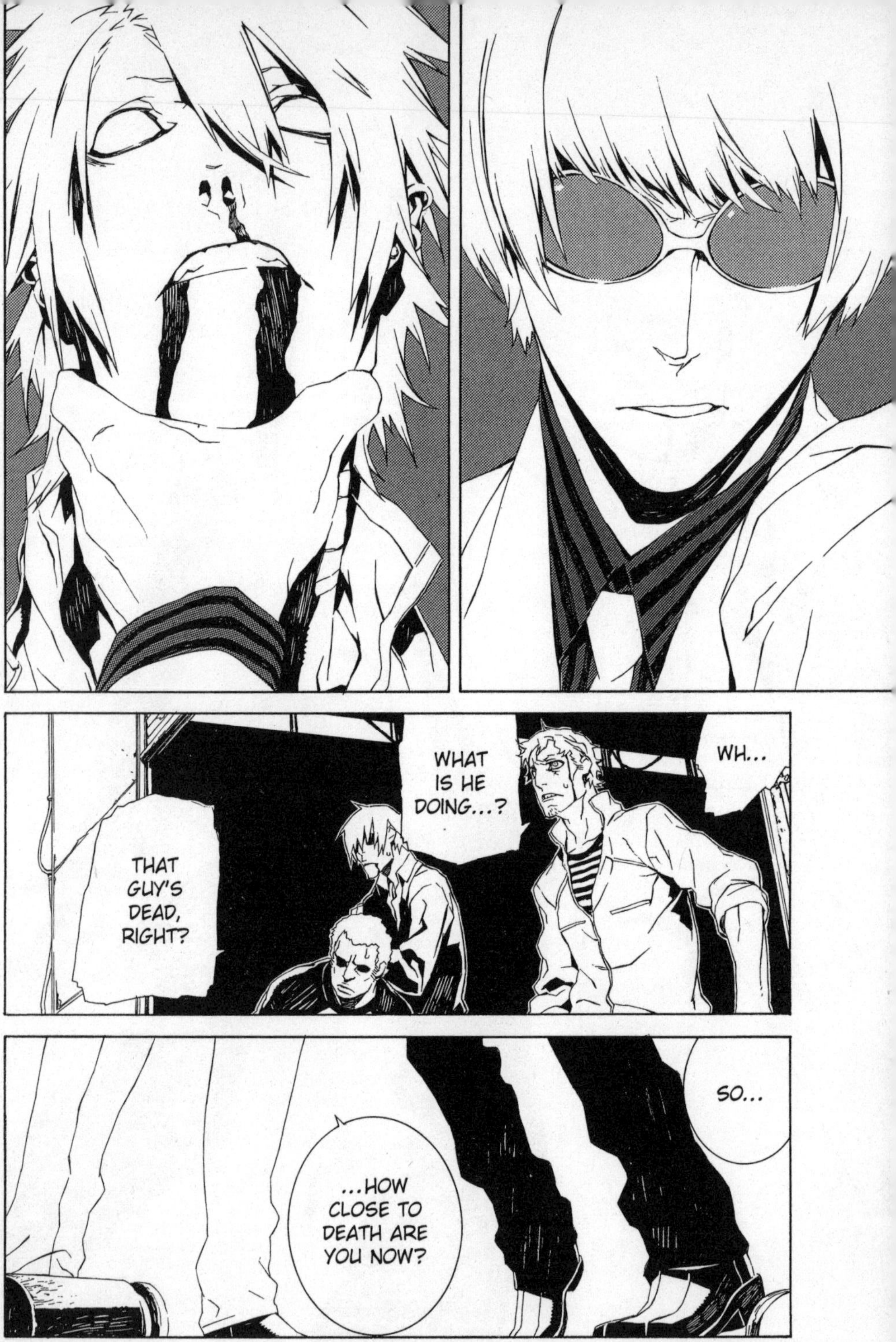
WH...
WHAT IS HE DOING...?
THAT GUY'S DEAD, RIGHT?
SO...
...HOW CLOSE TO DEATH ARE YOU NOW?

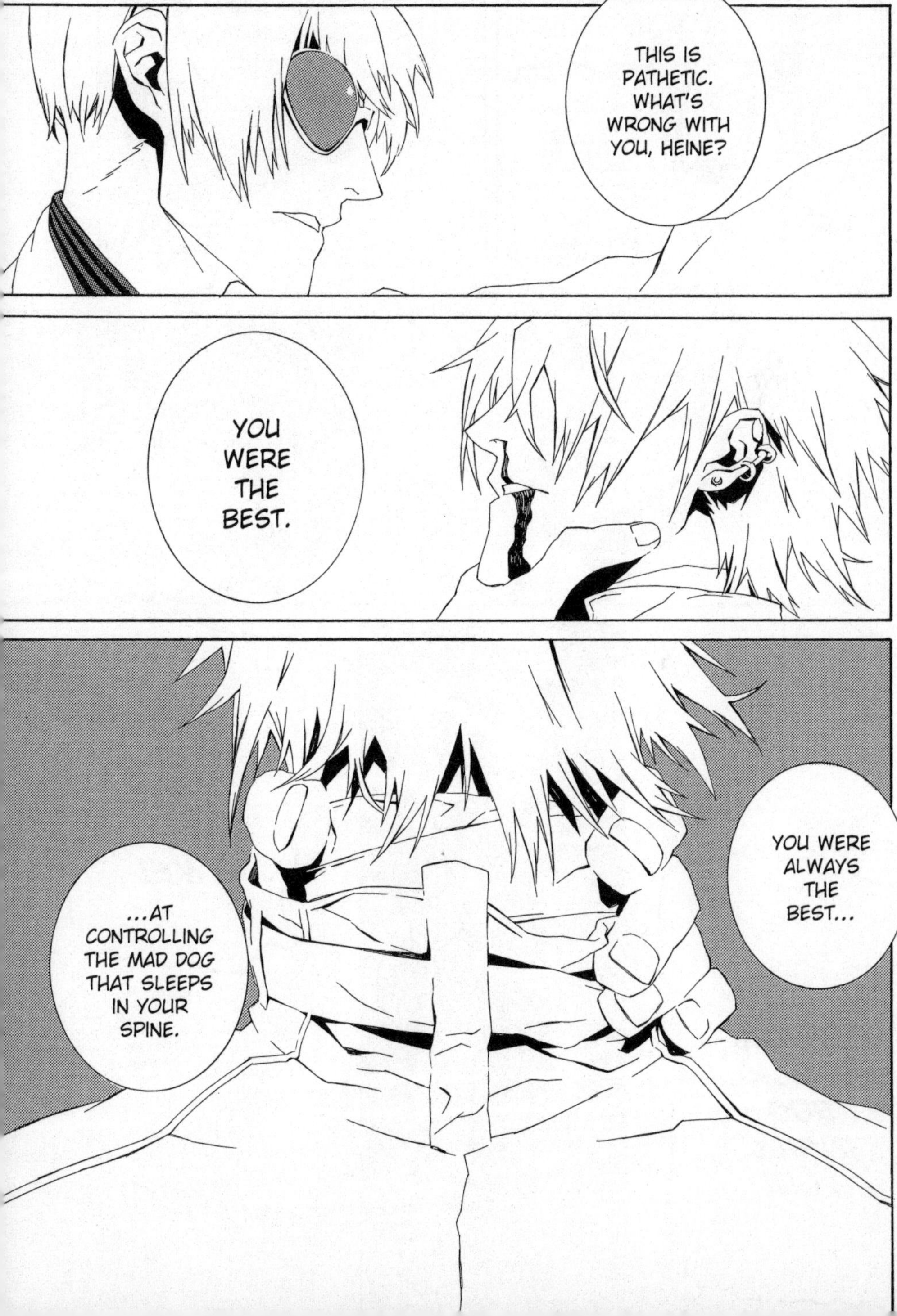
THIS IS PATHETIC. WHAT'S WRONG WITH YOU, HEINE?
YOU WERE THE BEST.
YOU WERE ALWAYS THE BEST...
...AT CONTROLLING THE MAD DOG THAT SLEEPS IN YOUR SPINE.

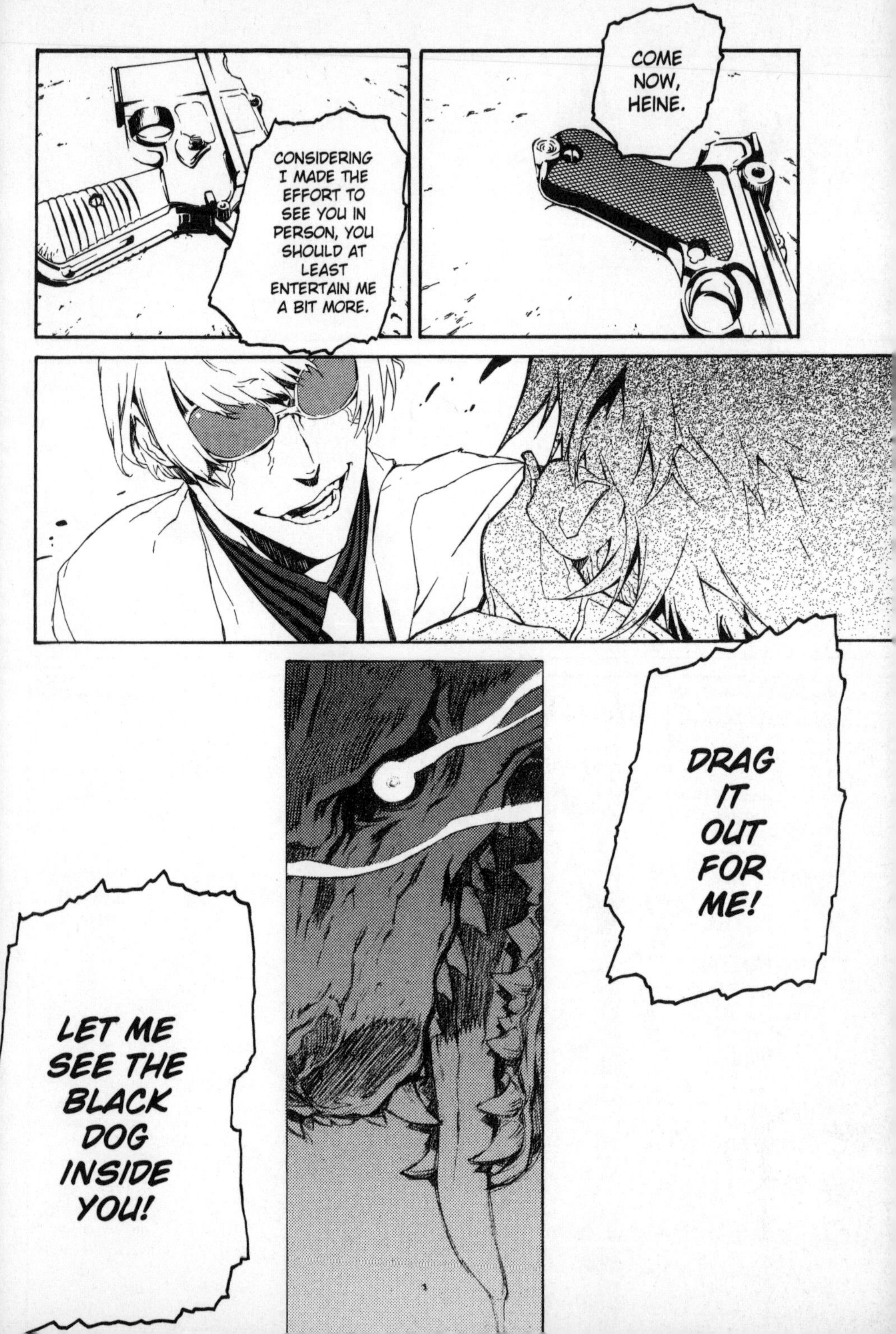
COME NOW, HEINE.
CONSIDERING I MADE THE EFFORT TO SEE YOU IN PERSON, YOU SHOULD AT LEAST ENTERTAIN ME A BIT MORE.
DRAG IT OUT FOR ME!
LET ME SEE THE BLACK DOG INSIDE YOU!

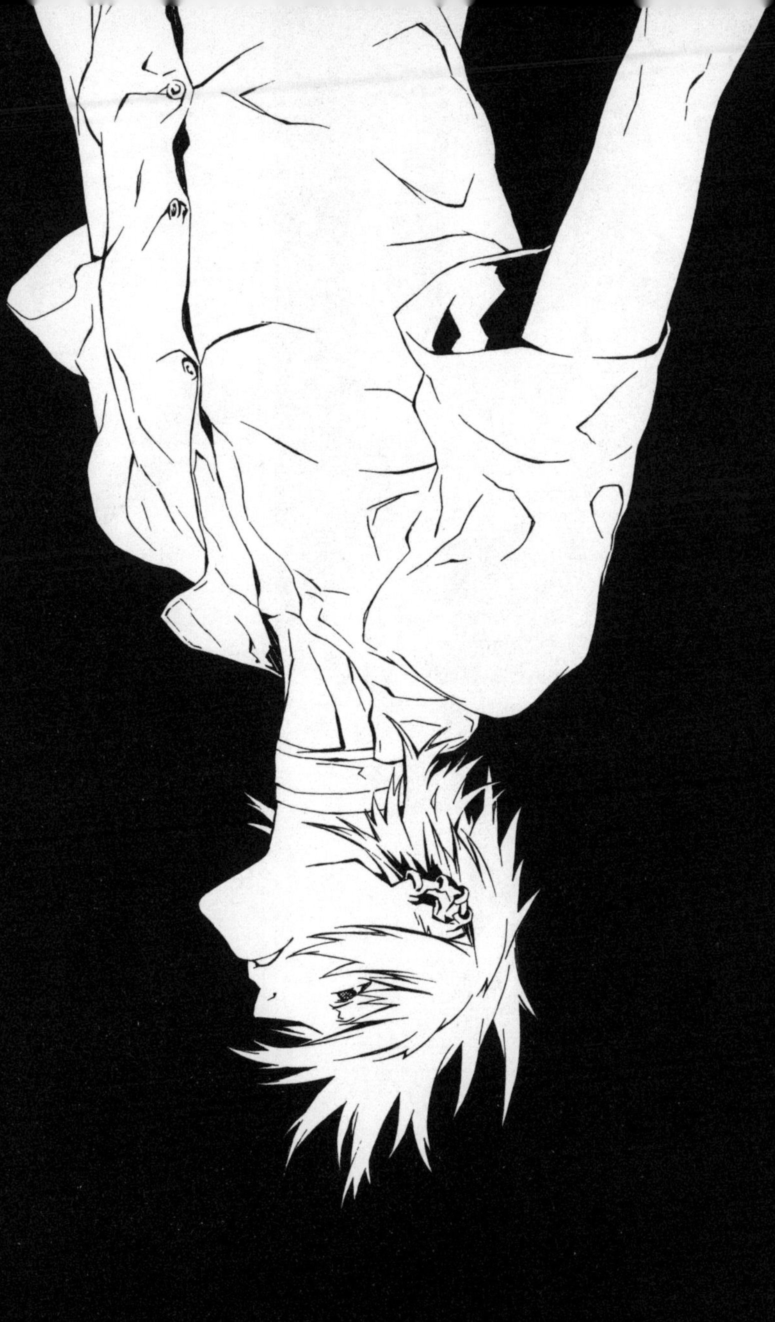

#07 Servant & Strayer I

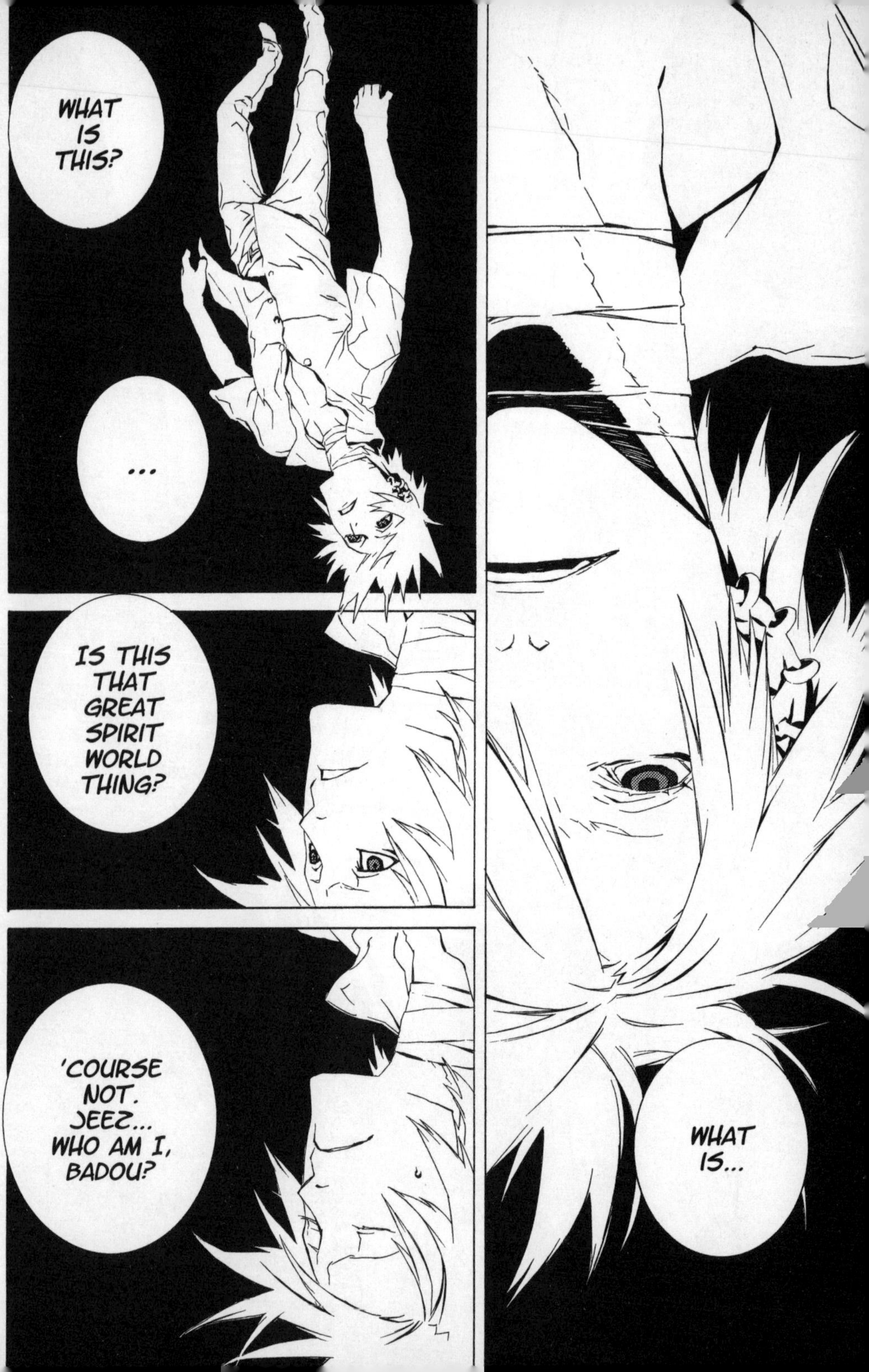
WHAT IS...
WHAT IS THIS?
...
IS THIS THAT GREAT SPIRIT WORLD THING?
'COURSE NOT. JEEZ... WHO AM I, BADOU?

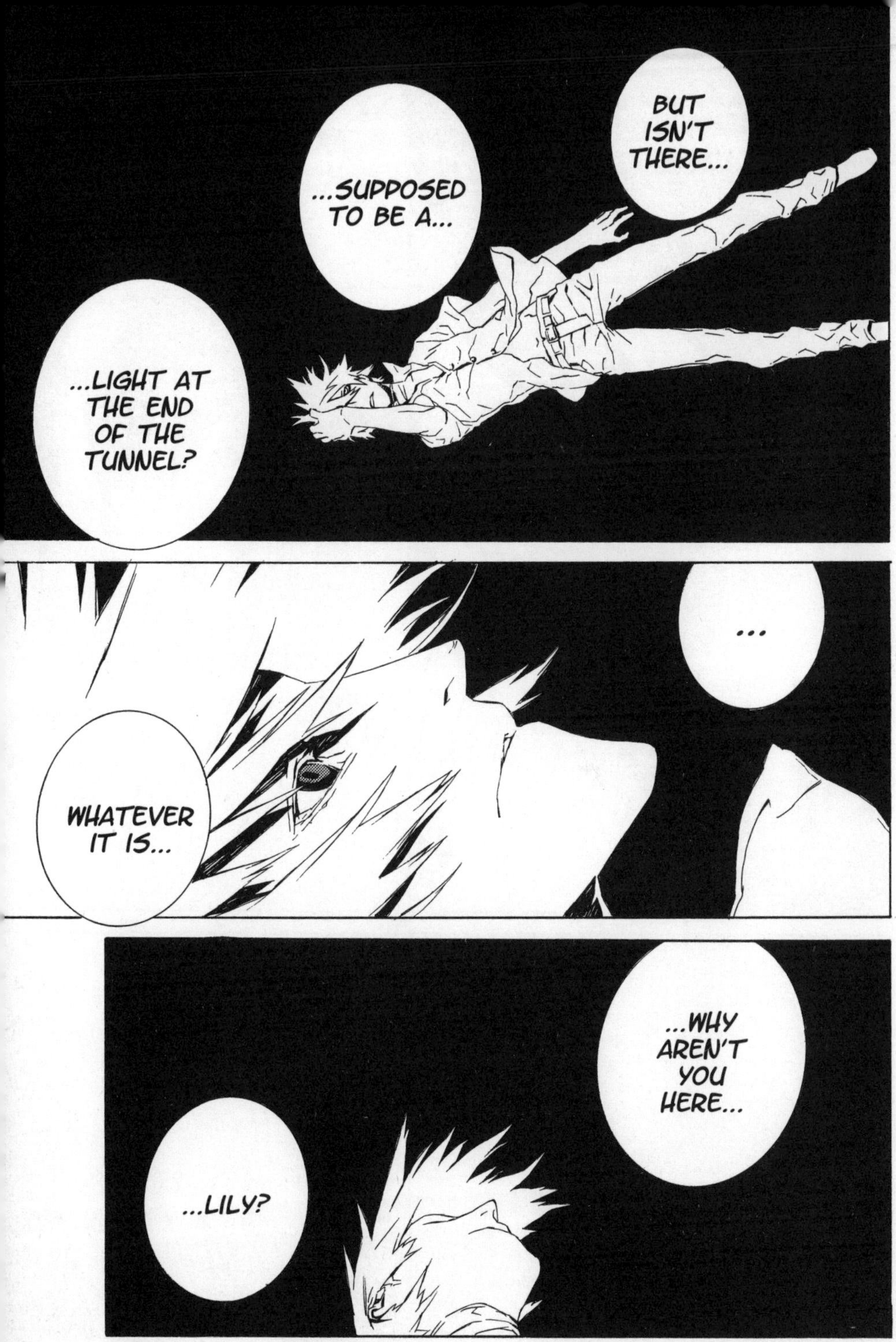
BUT ISN'T THERE...
...SUPPOSED TO BE A...
...LIGHT AT THE END OF THE TUNNEL?
...
WHATEVER IT IS...
...WHY AREN'T YOU HERE...
...LILY?

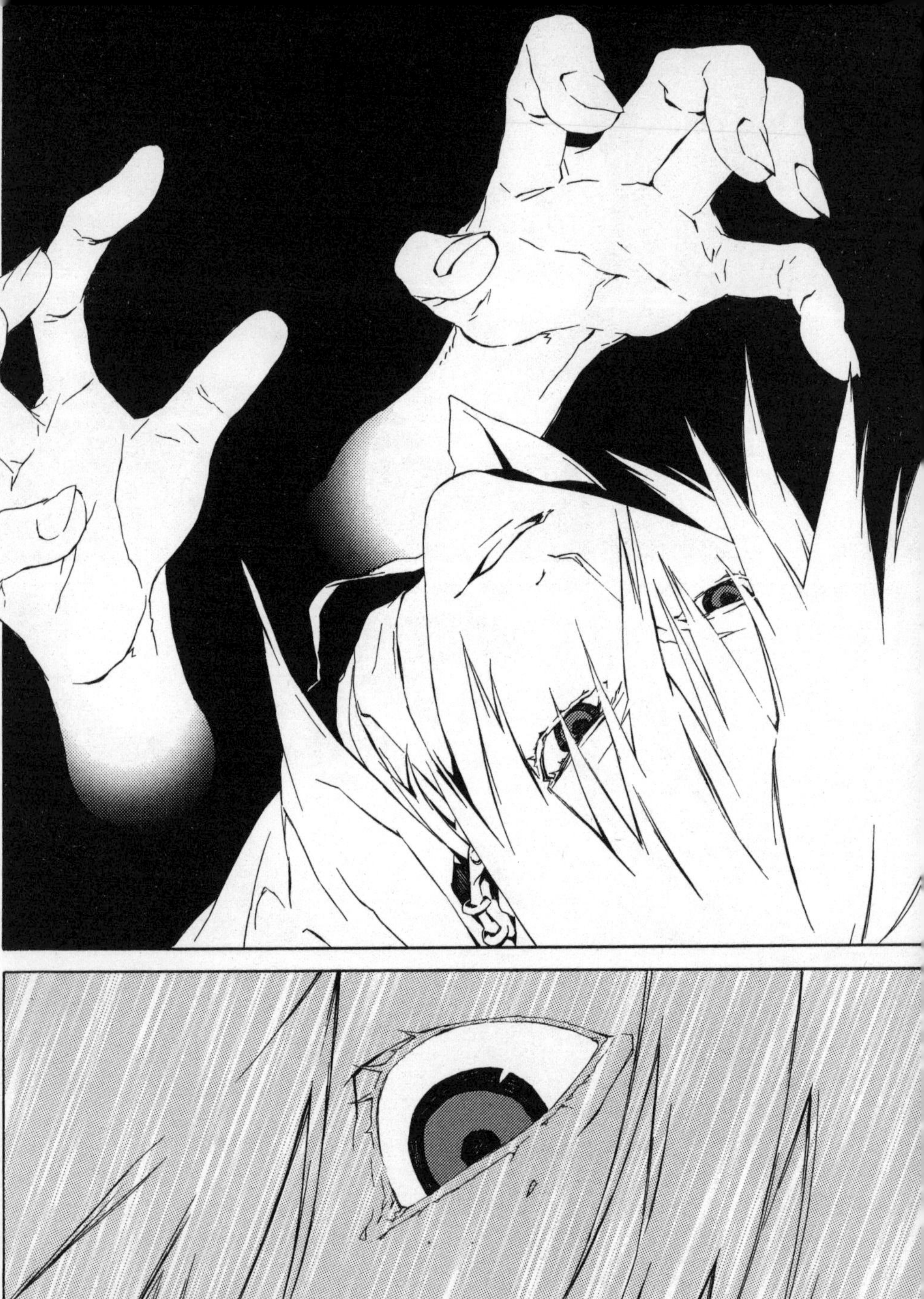

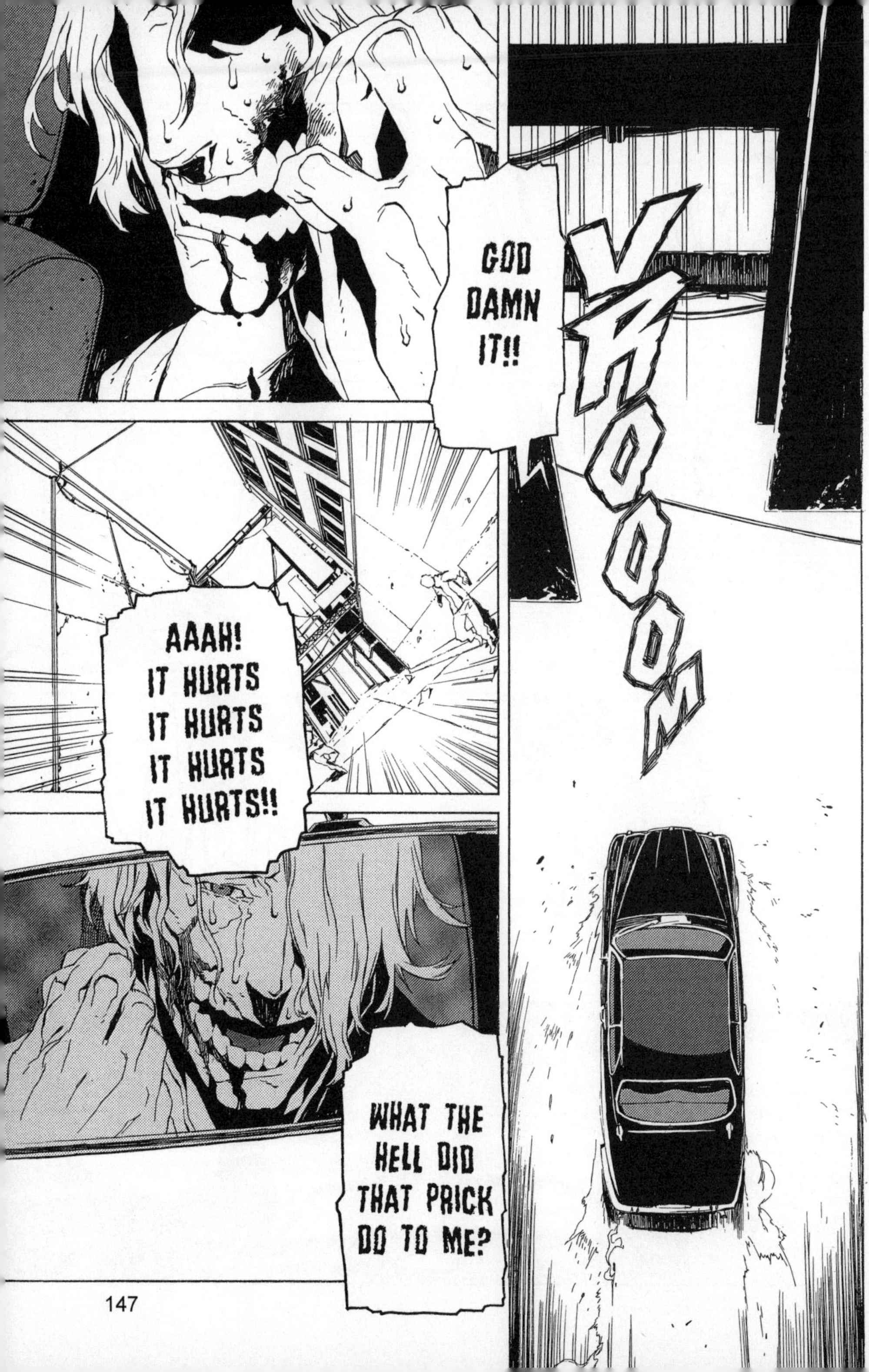
VROOOM
GOD DAMN IT!!
AAAH! IT HURTS IT HURTS IT HURTS IT HURTS!!
WHAT THE HELL DID THAT PRICK DO TO ME?

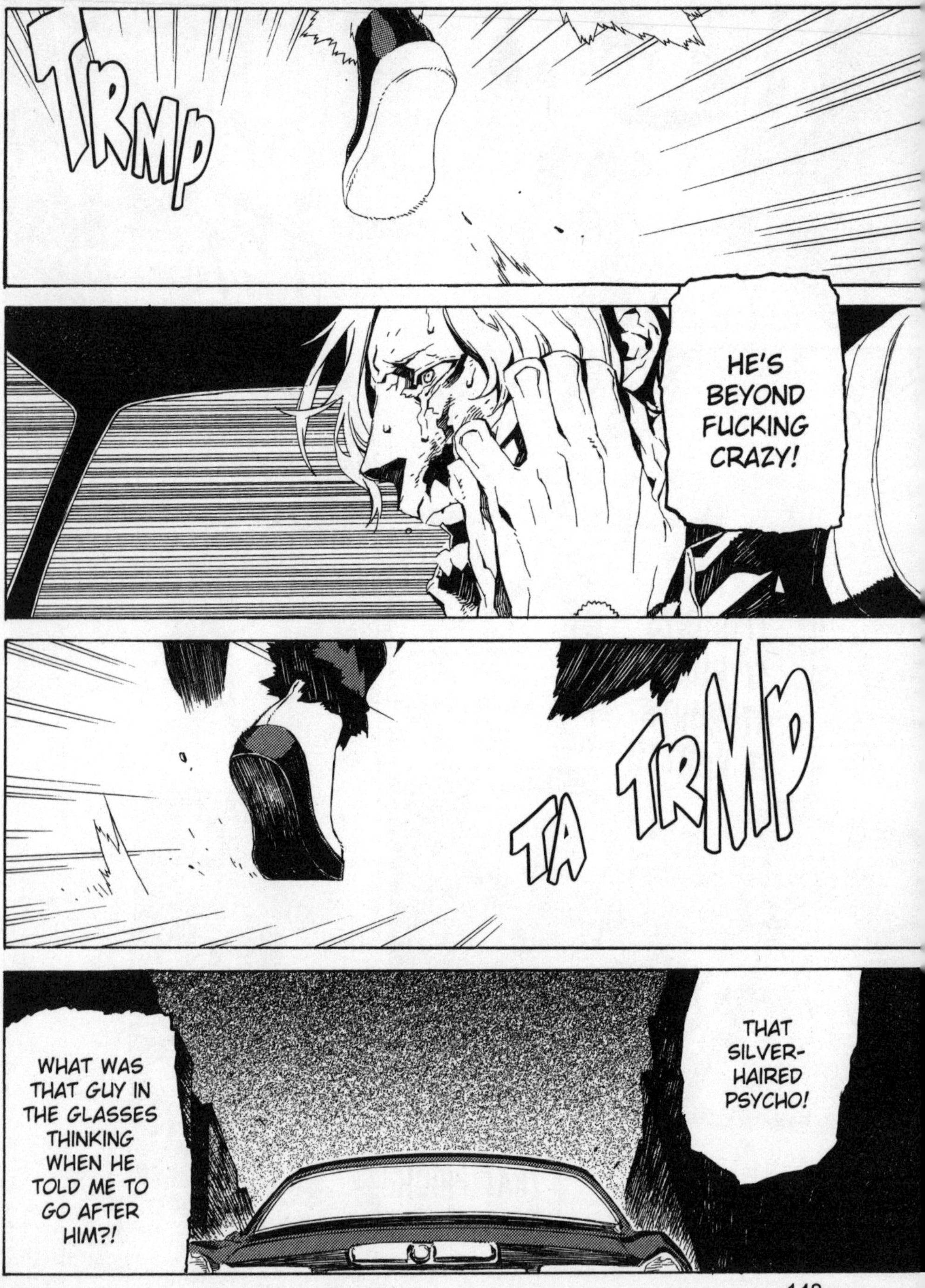
TRMP
HE'S BEYOND FUCKING CRAZY!
TA TRMP
THAT SILVER-HAIRED PSYCHO!
WHAT WAS THAT GUY IN THE GLASSES THINKING WHEN HE TOLD ME TO GO AFTER HIM?!

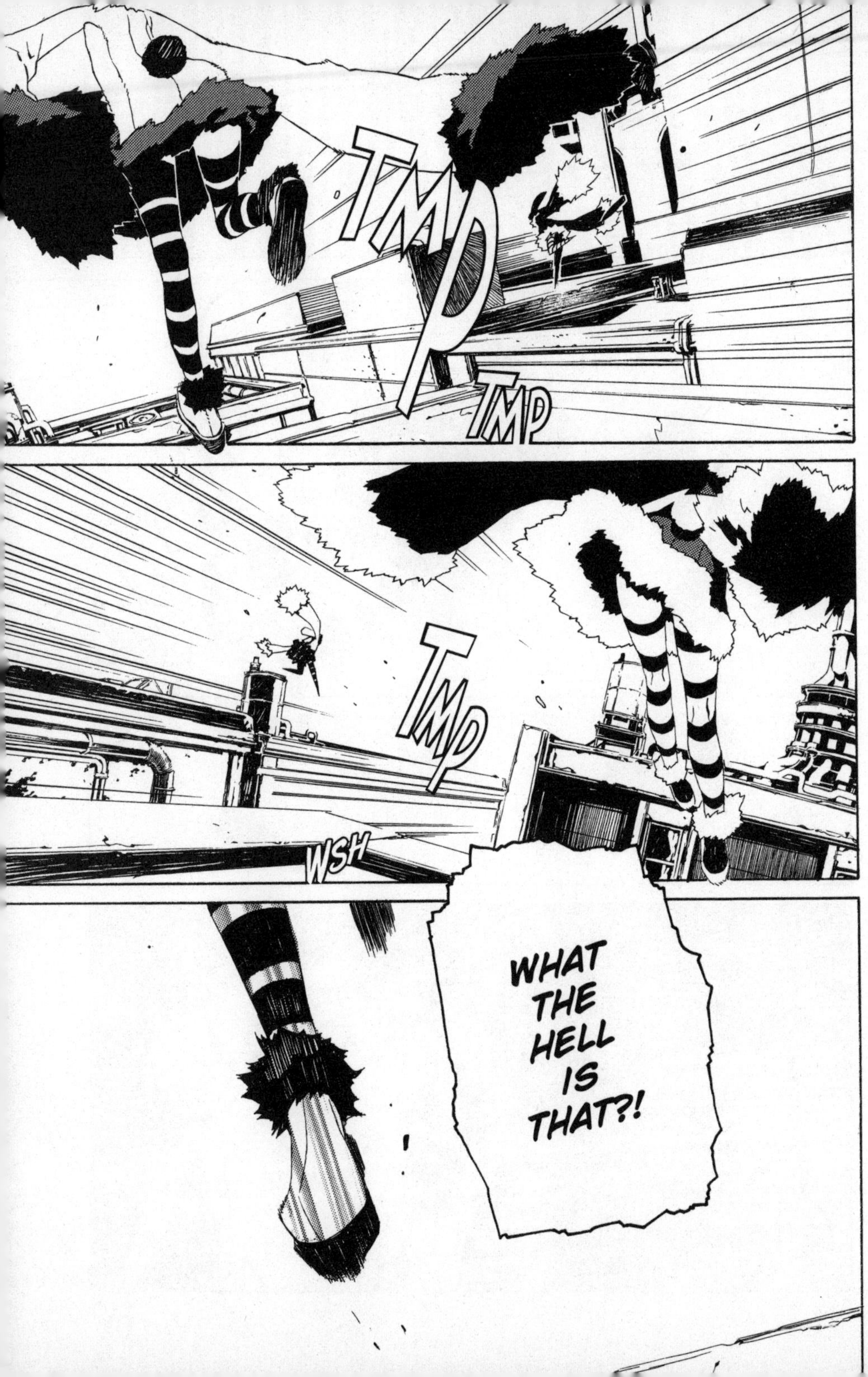
TMP
TMP
TMP
WSH
WHAT THE HELL IS THAT?!

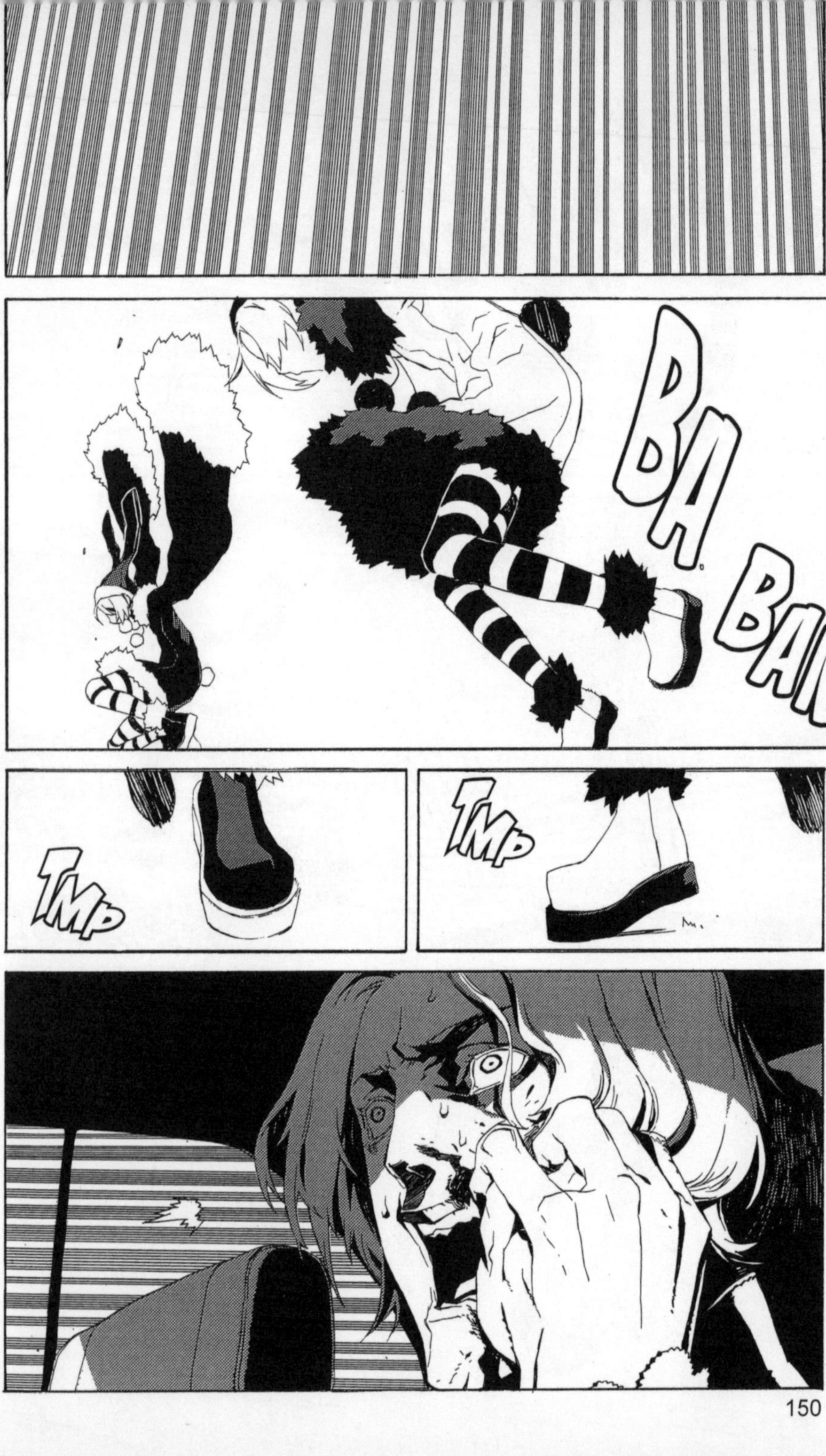
BA BAM
TMP
TMP

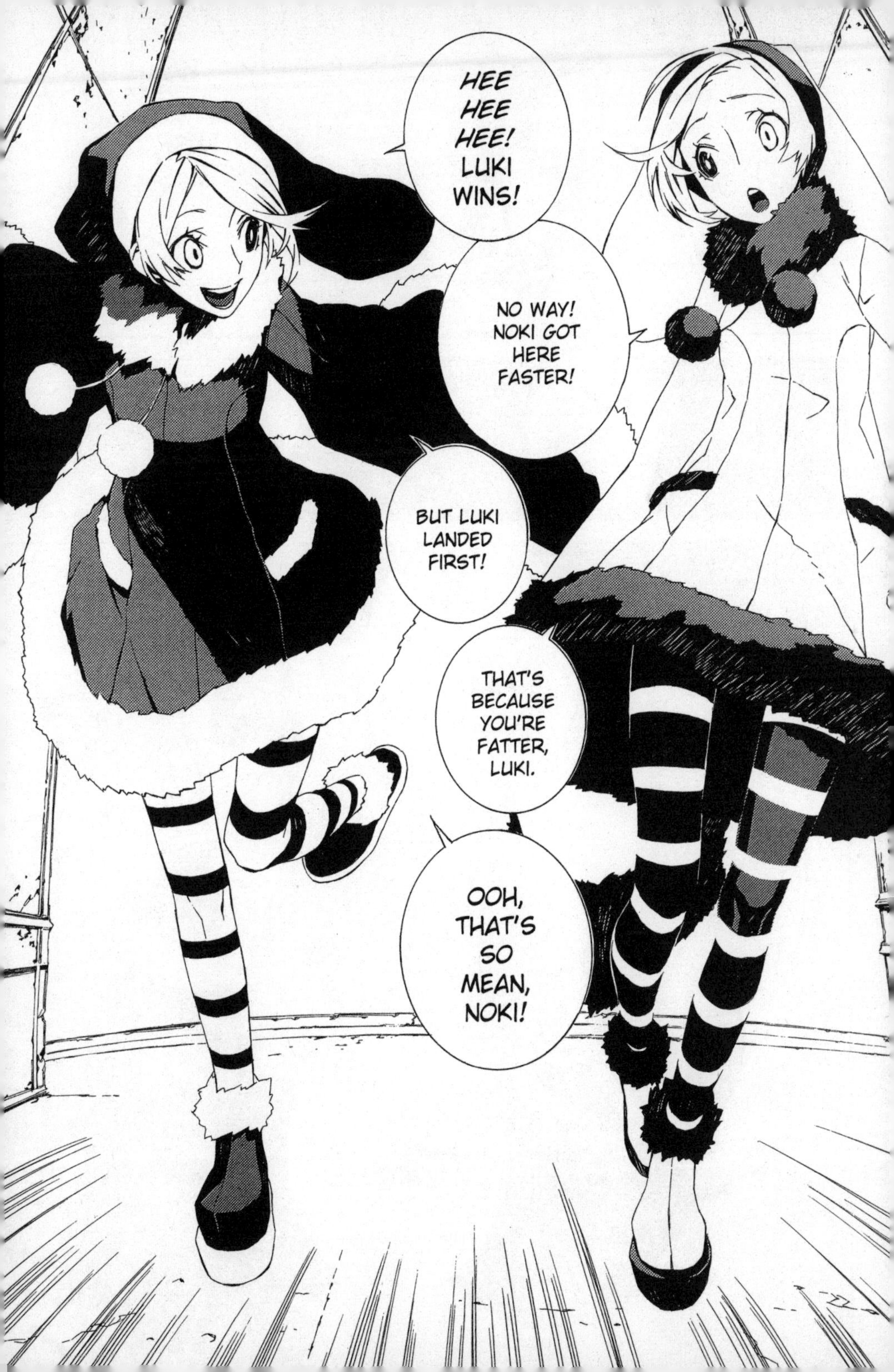
HEE HEE HEE! LUKI WINS!
NO WAY! NOKI GOT HERE FASTER!
BUT LUKI LANDED FIRST!
THAT'S BECAUSE YOU'RE FATTER, LUKI.
OOH, THAT'S SO MEAN, NOKI!

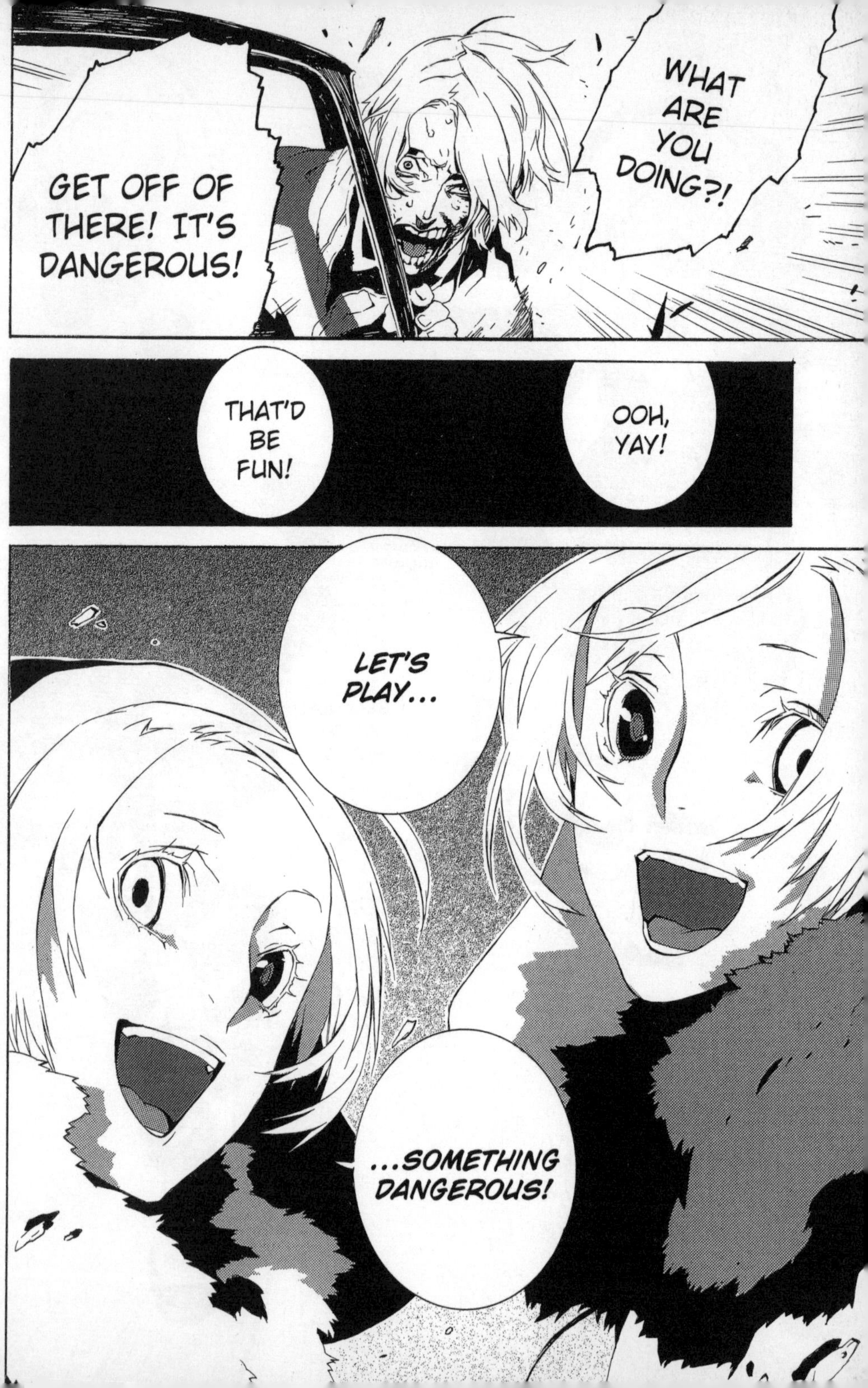
WHAT ARE YOU DOING?!
GET OFF OF THERE! IT'S DANGEROUS!
OOH, YAY!
THAT'D BE FUN!
LET'S PLAY...
...SOMETHING DANGEROUS!

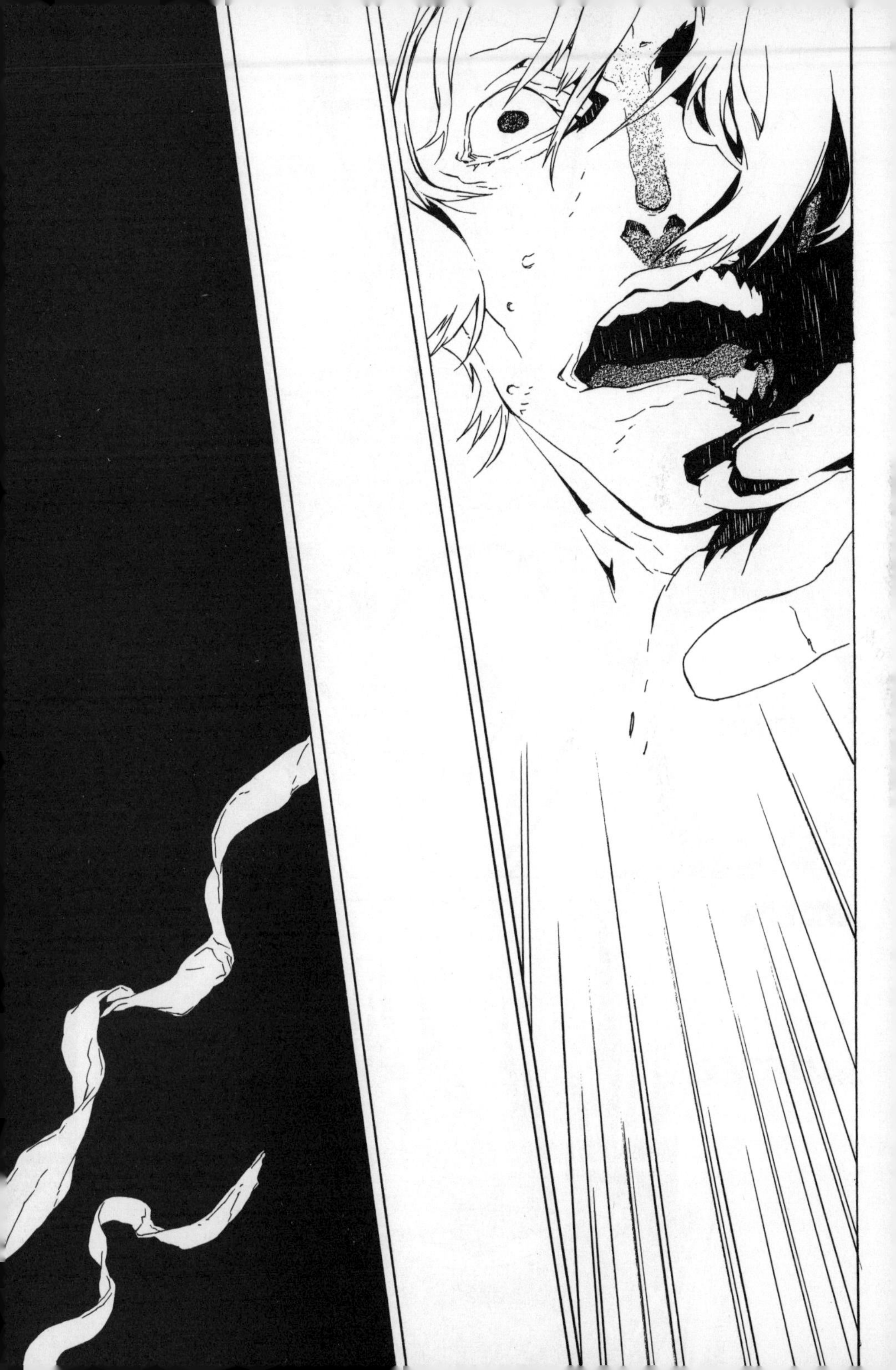

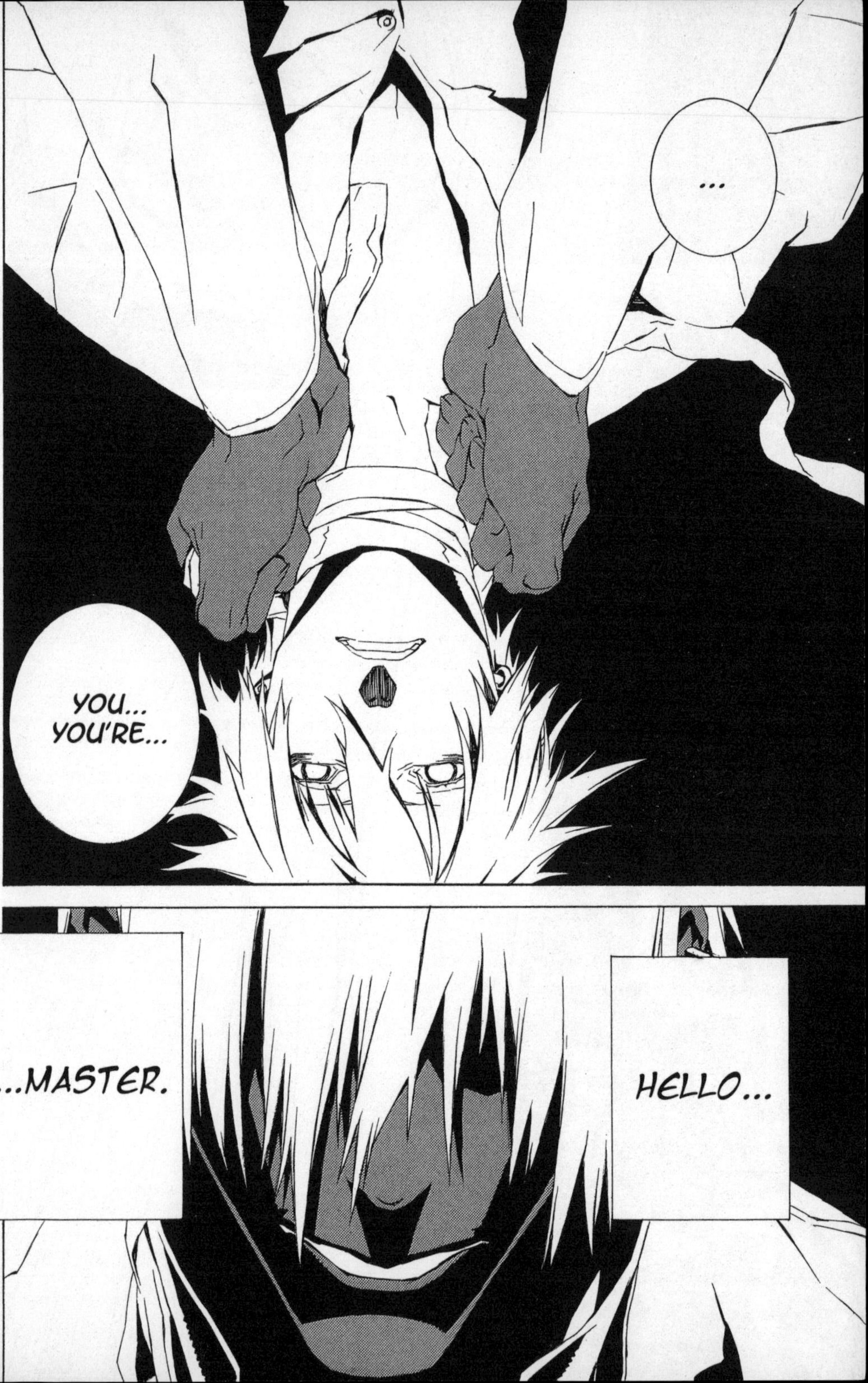
...
YOU... YOU'RE...
HELLO...
...MASTER.

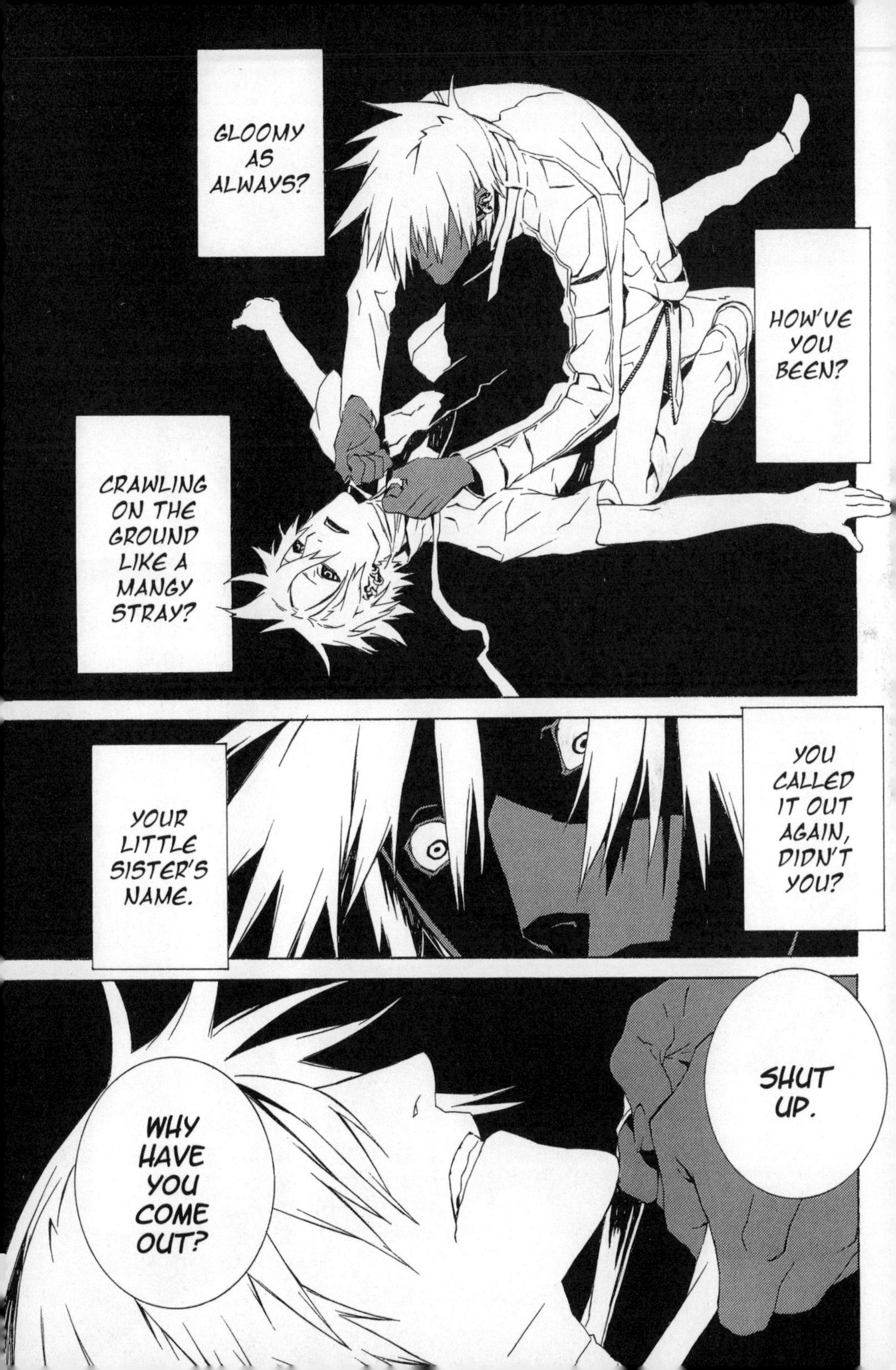
HOW'VE YOU BEEN?
GLOOMY AS ALWAYS?
CRAWLING ON THE GROUND LIKE A MANGY STRAY?
YOU CALLED IT OUT AGAIN, DIDN'T YOU?
YOUR LITTLE SISTER'S NAME.
SHUT UP.
WHY HAVE YOU COME OUT?

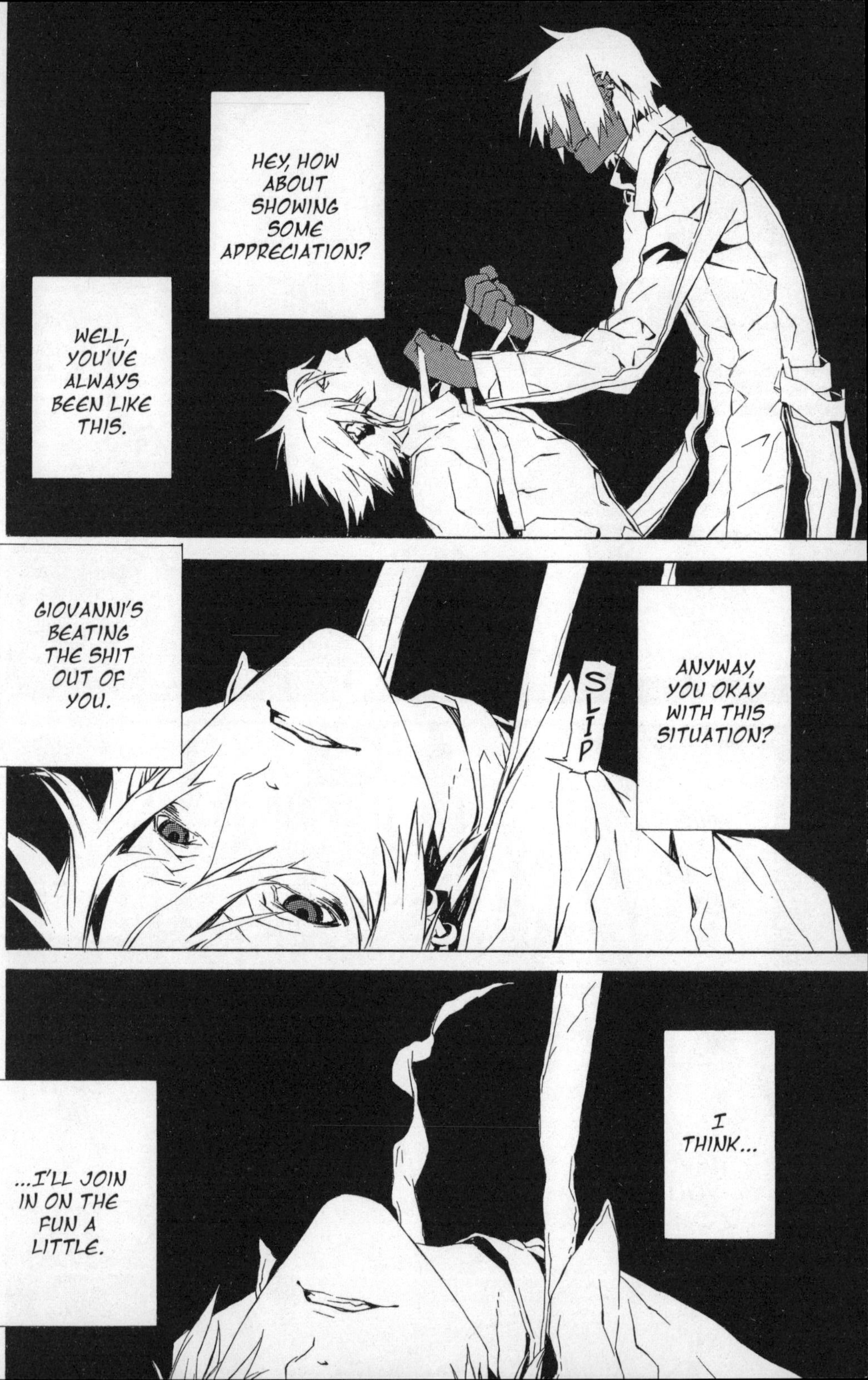
HEY, HOW ABOUT SHOWING SOME APPRECIATION?
WELL, YOU'VE ALWAYS BEEN LIKE THIS.
ANYWAY, YOU OKAY WITH THIS SITUATION?
SLIP
GIOVANNI'S BEATING THE SHIT OUT OF YOU.
I THINK...
...I'LL JOIN IN ON THE FUN A LITTLE.

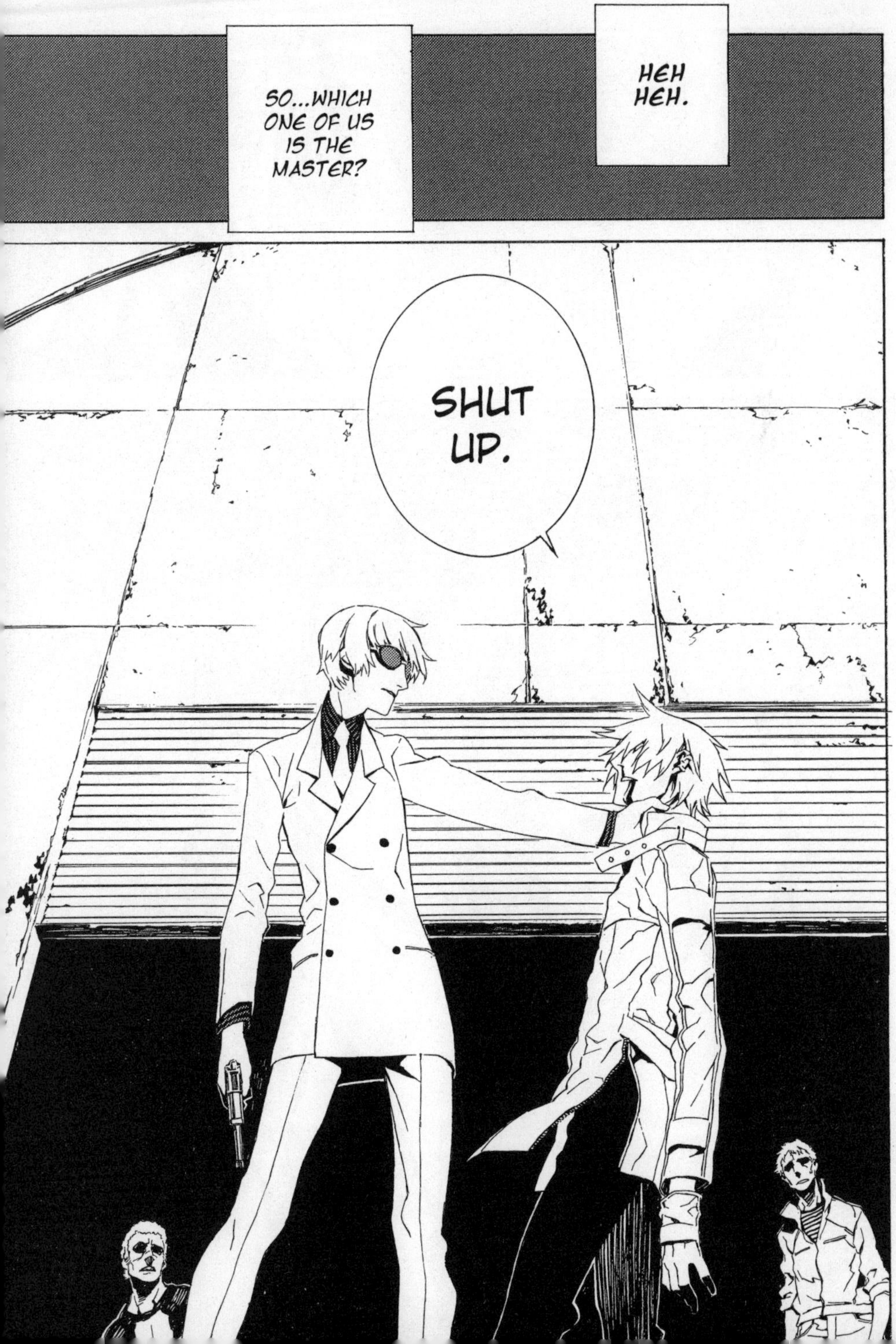
HEH HEH.
SO...WHICH ONE OF US IS THE MASTER?
SHUT UP.

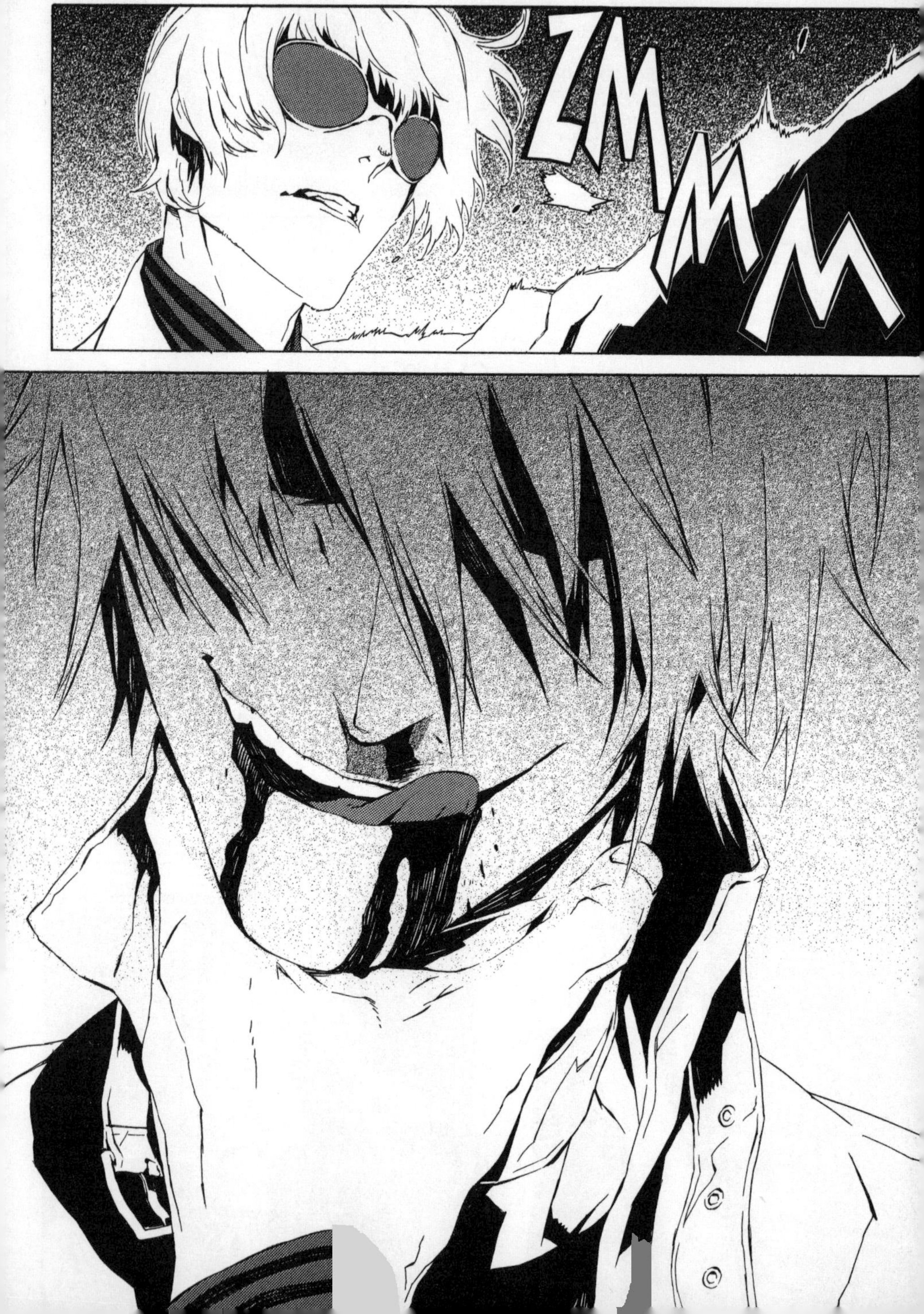
ZMMMM

#08 Servant & Strayer Ⅱ

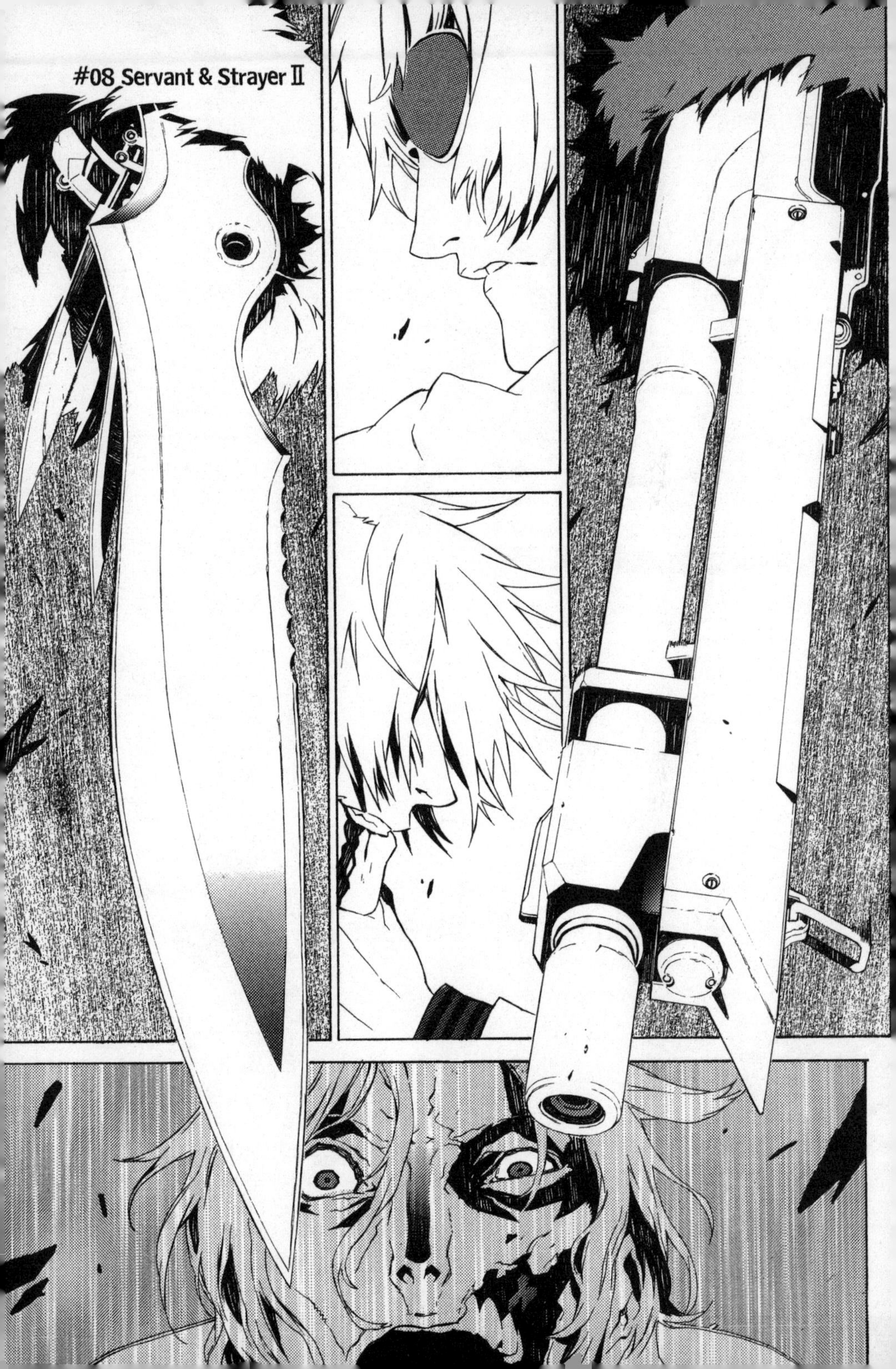

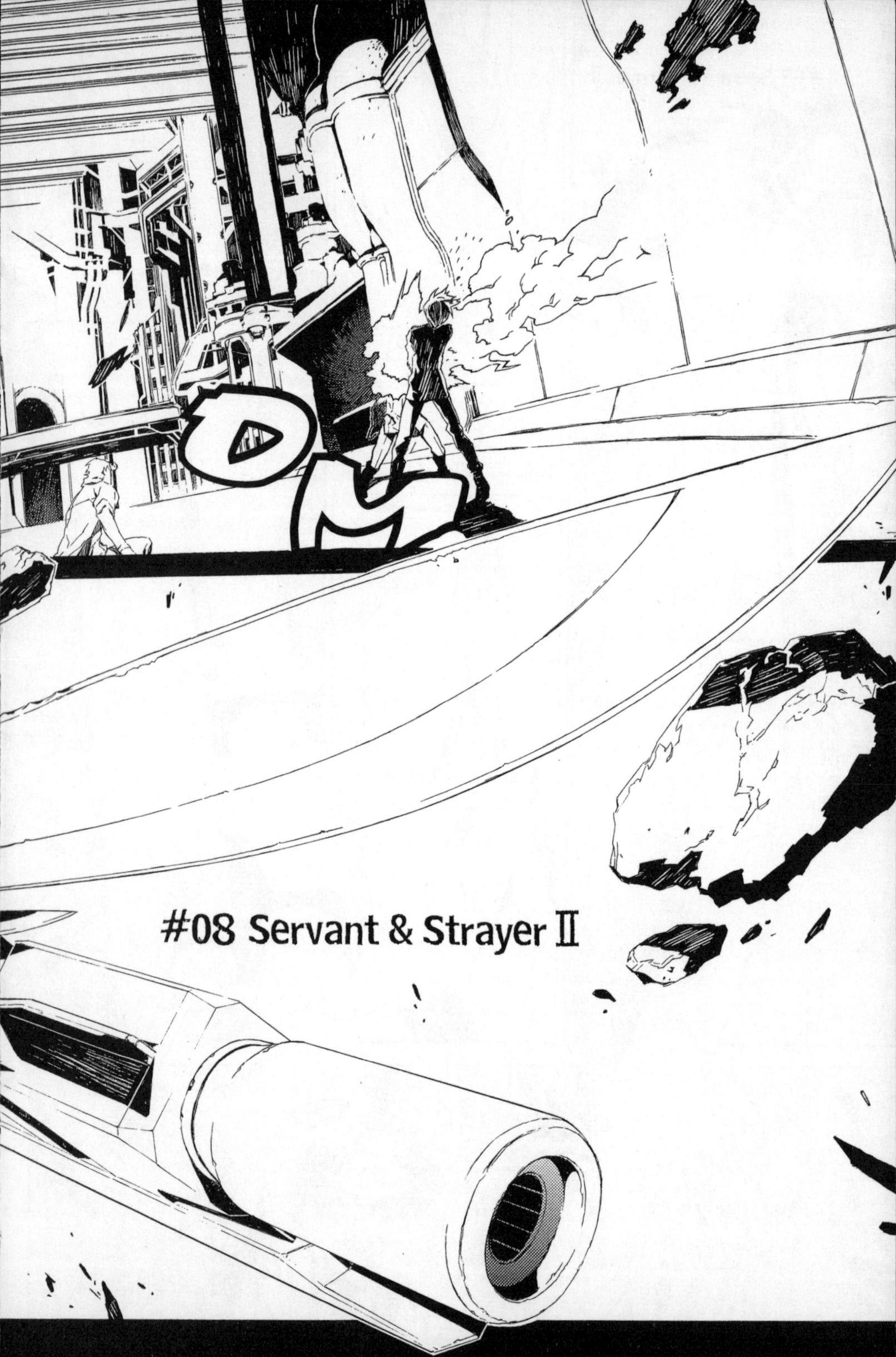
#08 Servant & Strayer II

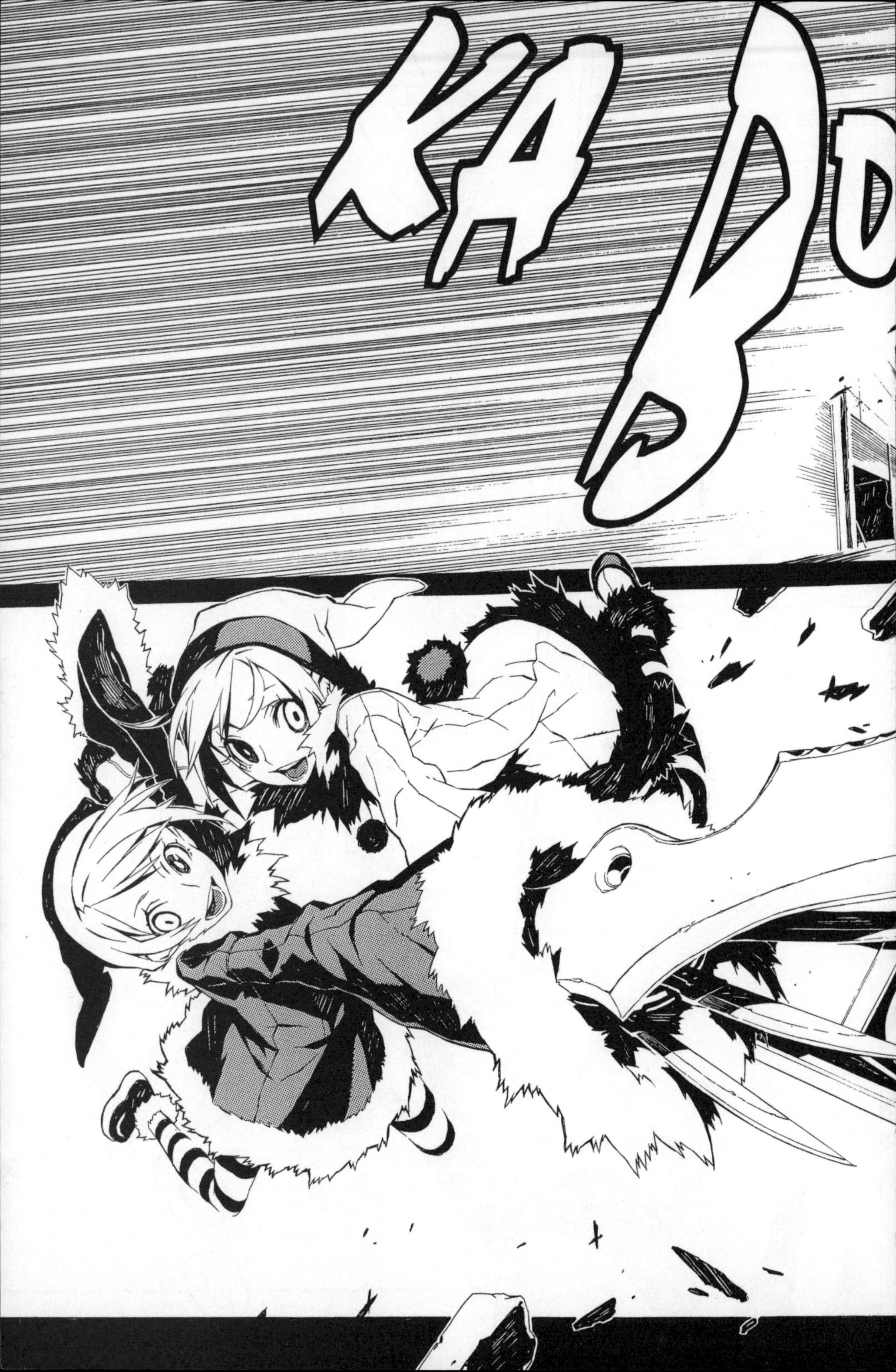
KA D

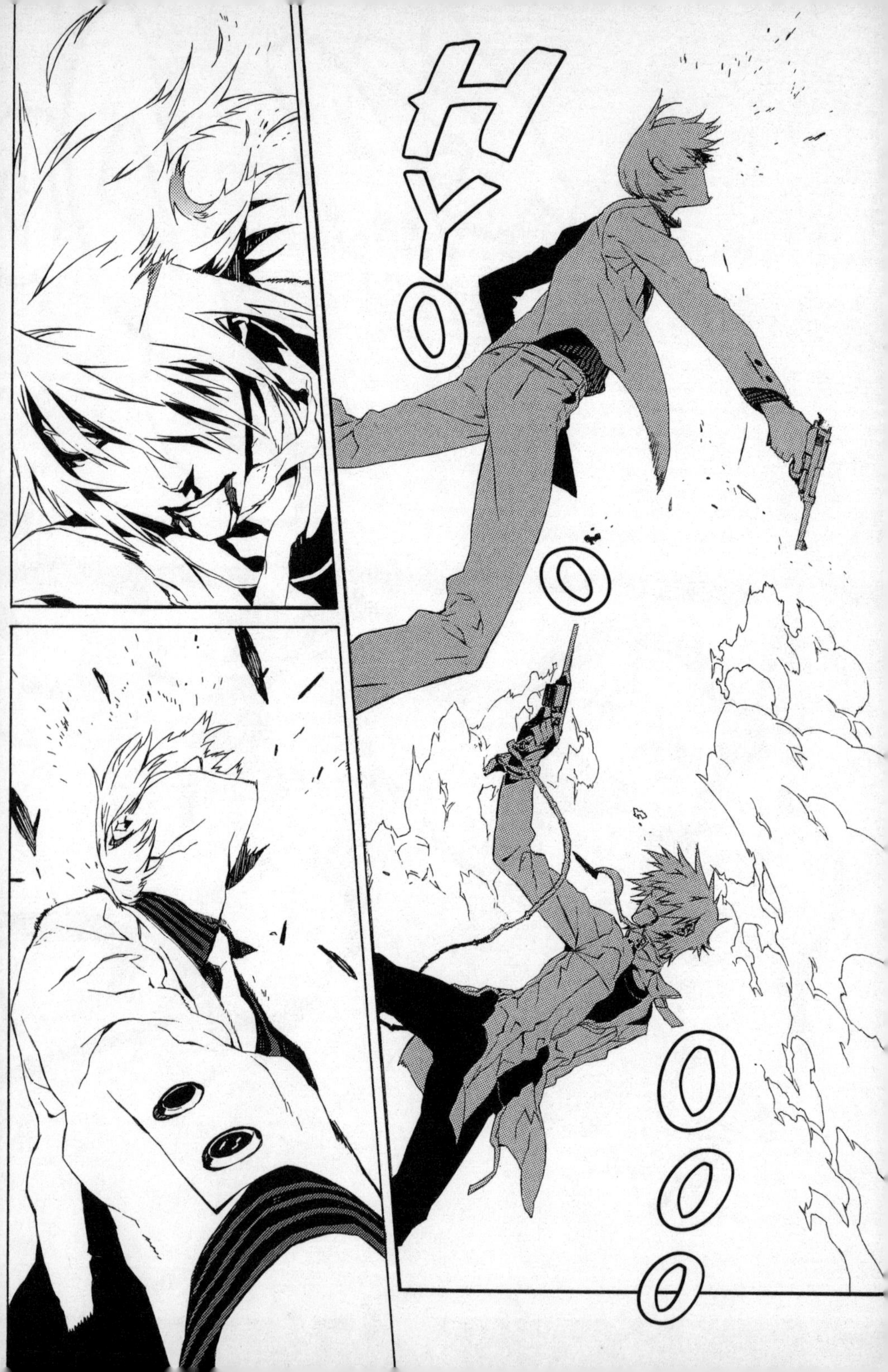
HYOOOOOO

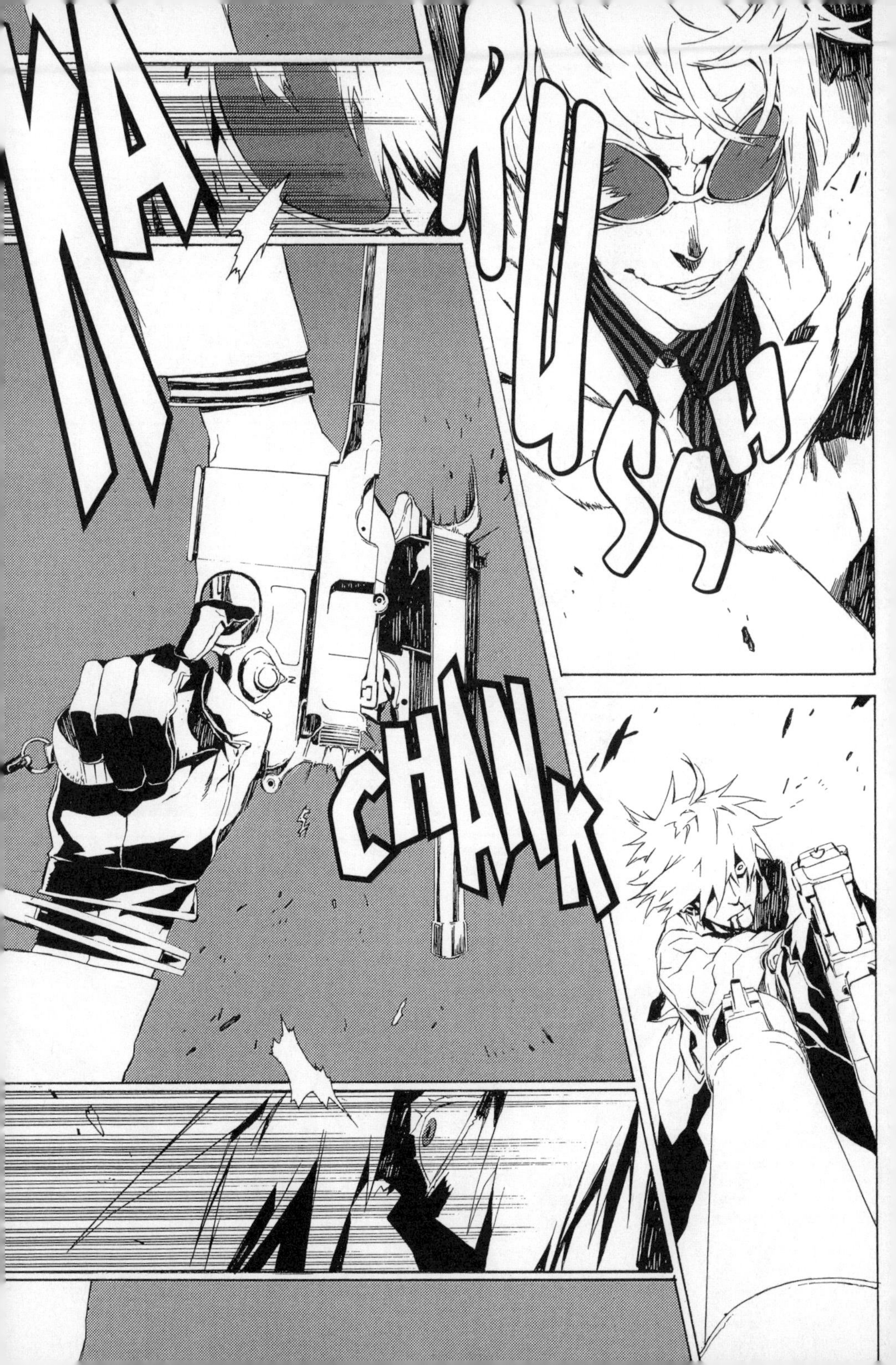
CHANK

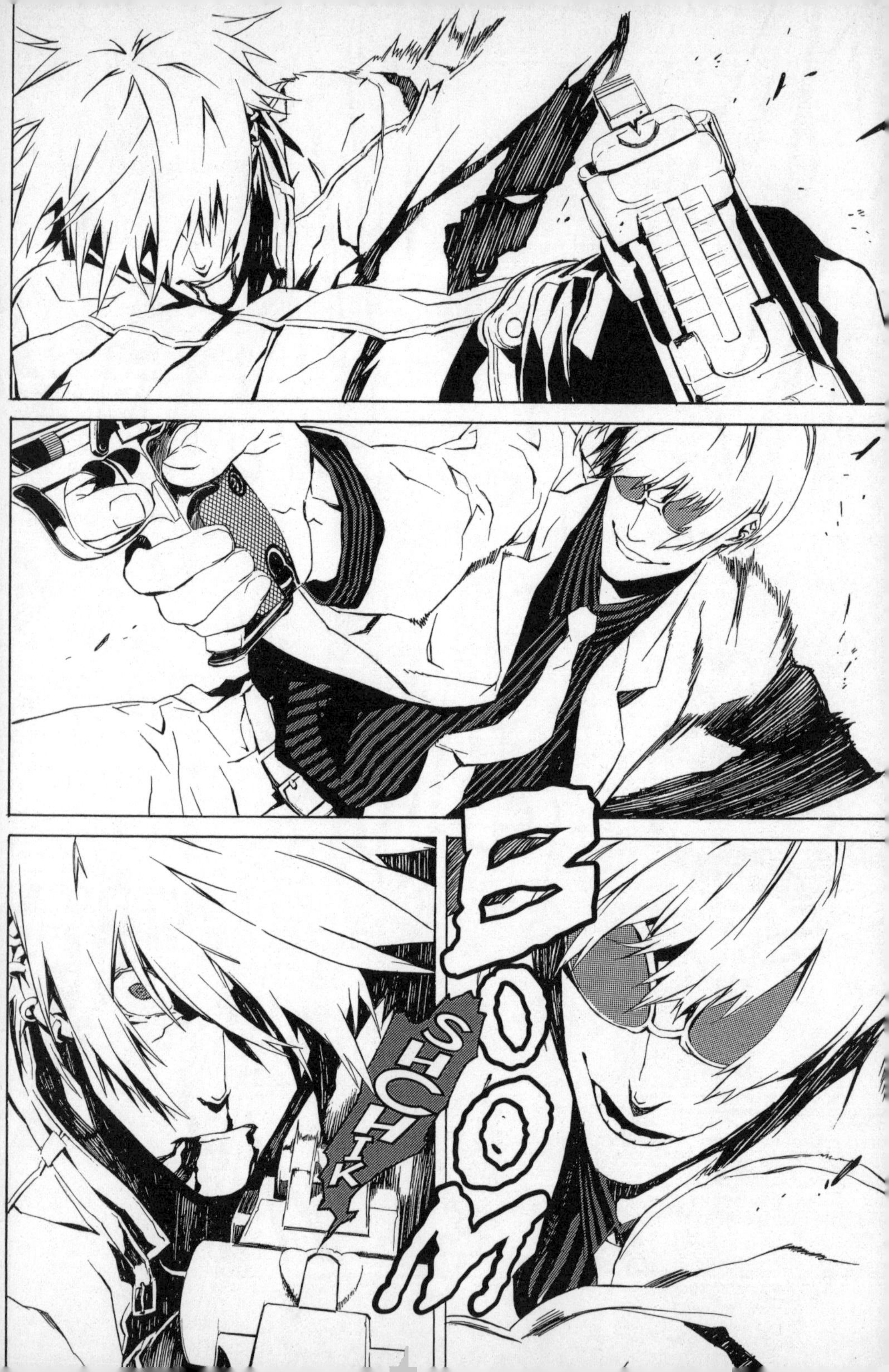
BOOM
SHCHIK

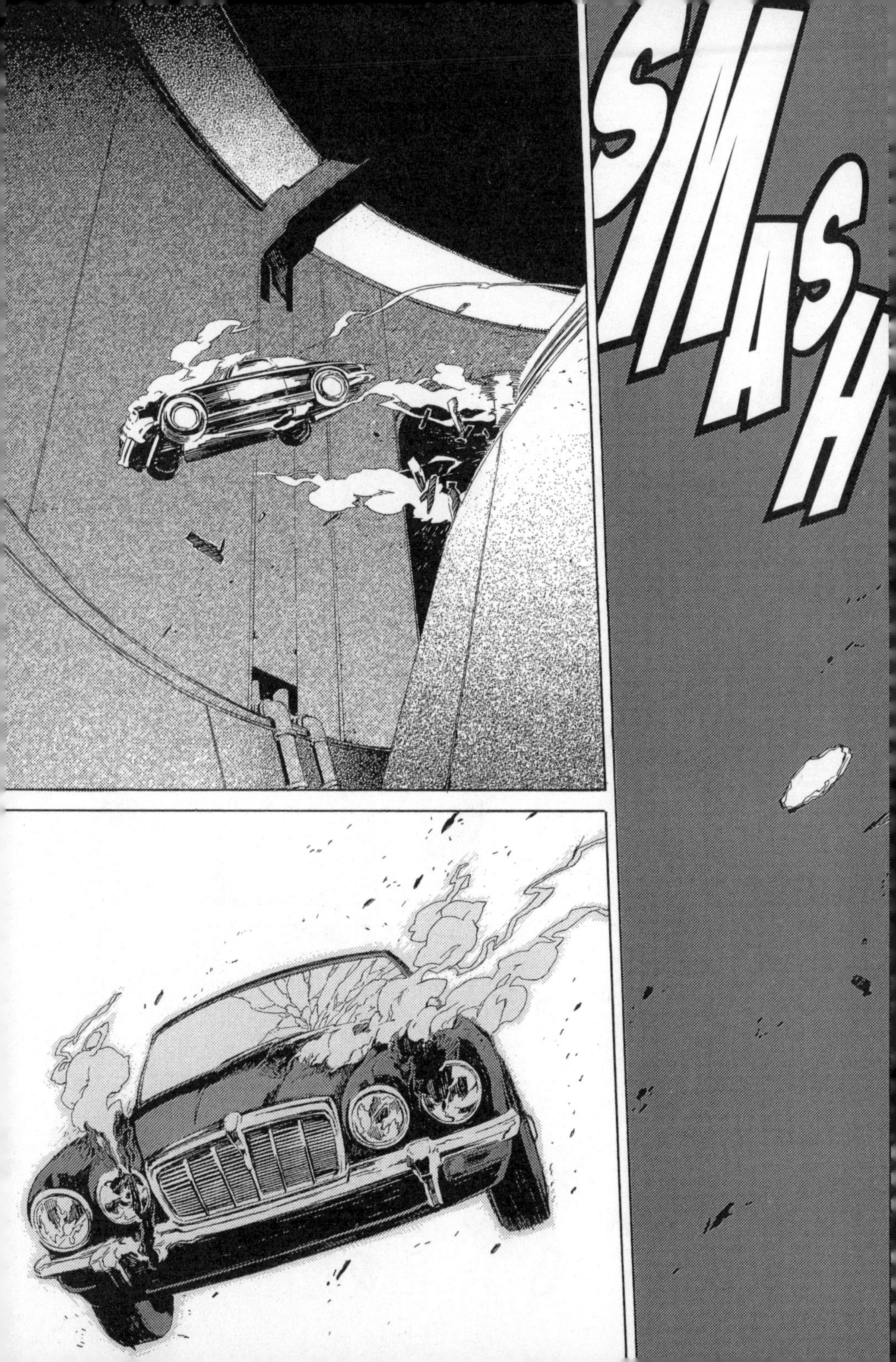
SMASH

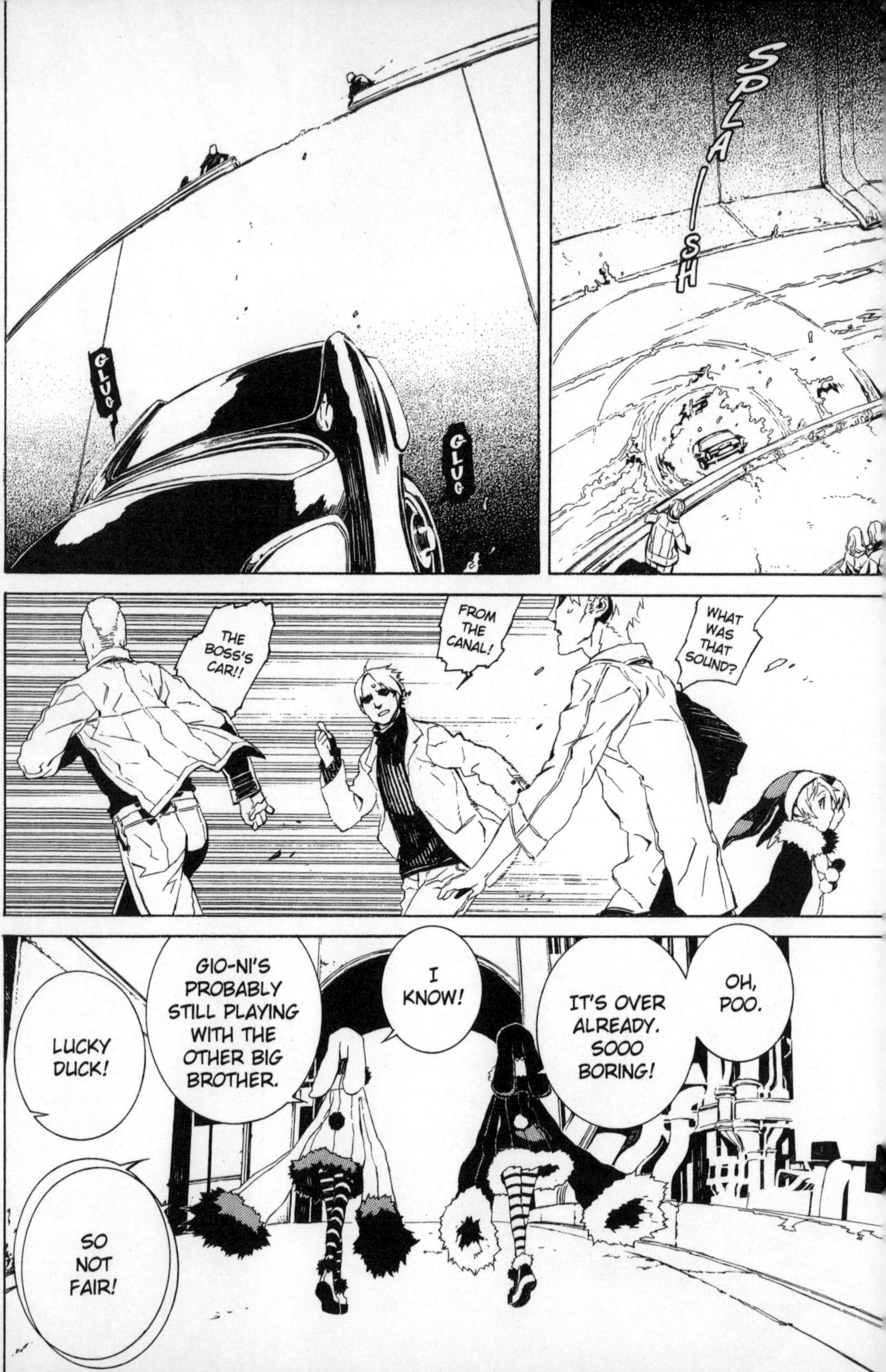
SPLAISH
GLUG
GLUG
WHAT WAS THAT SOUND?
FROM THE CANAL!
THE BOSS'S CAR!!
OH, POO.
IT'S OVER ALREADY. SOOO BORING!
I KNOW!
GIO-NI'S PROBABLY STILL PLAYING WITH THE OTHER BIG BROTHER.
LUCKY DUCK!
SO NOT FAIR!

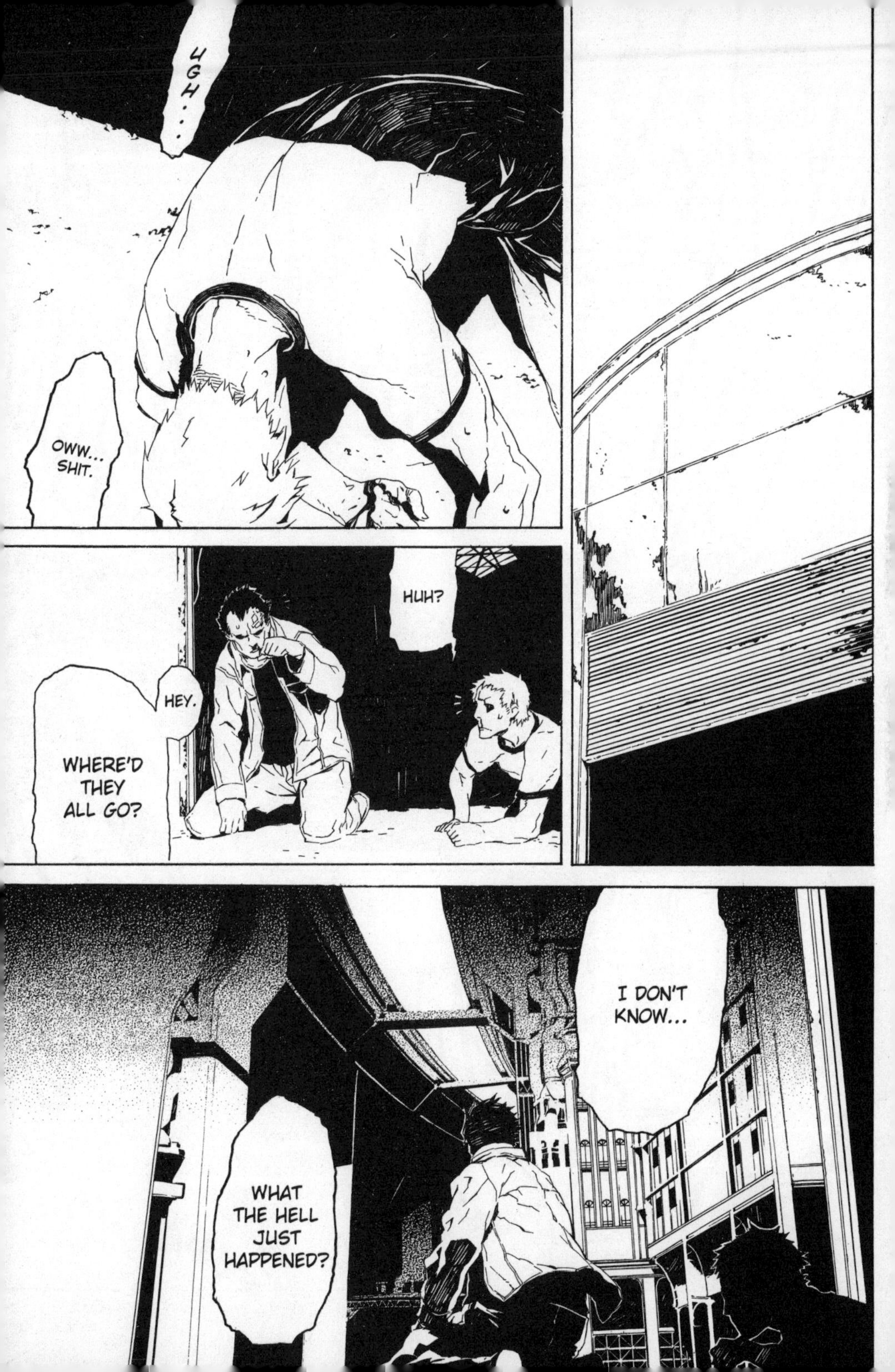
UGH...
OWW... SHIT.
HUH?
HEY.
WHERE'D THEY ALL GO?
I DON'T KNOW...
WHAT THE HELL JUST HAPPENED?

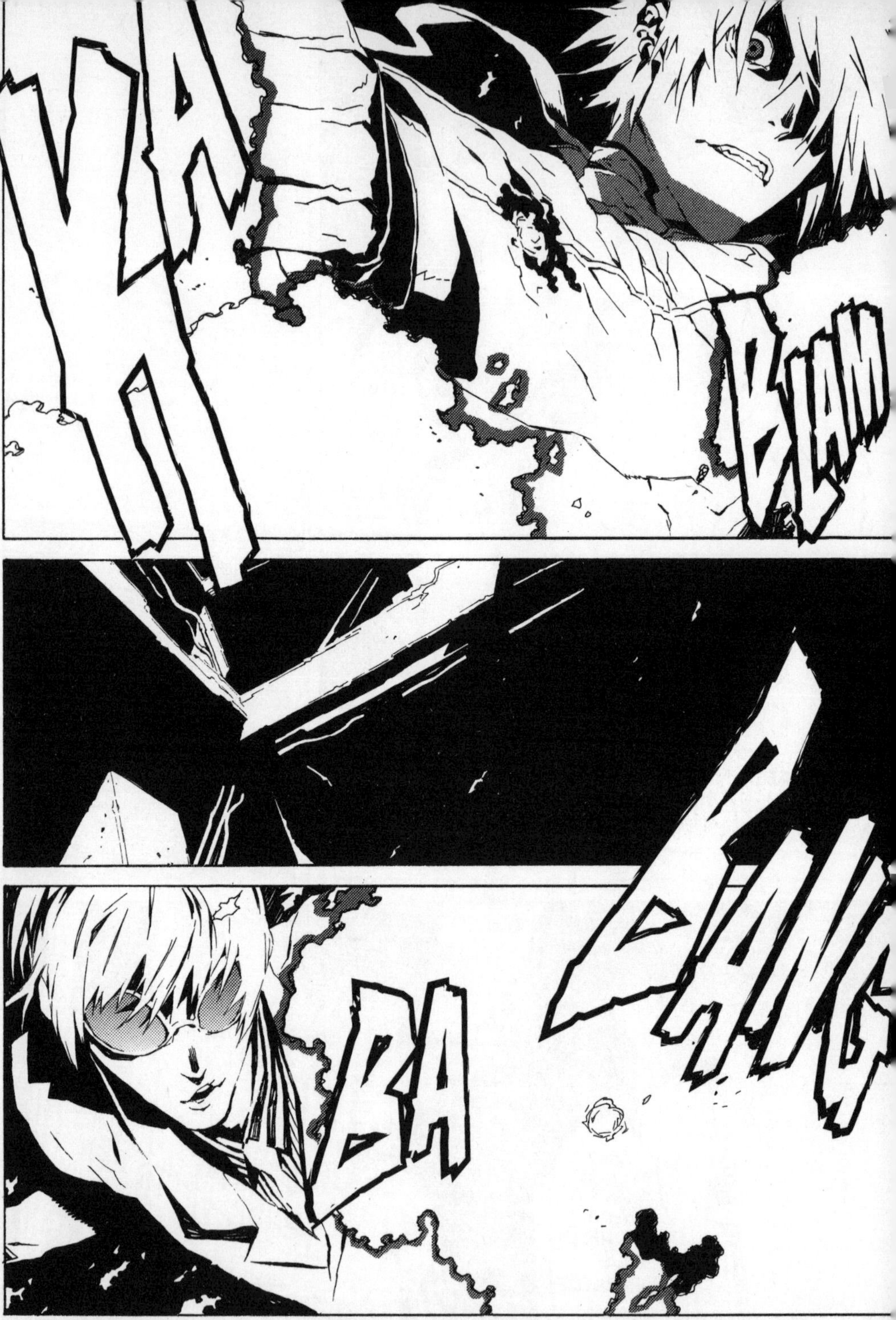
BLAM
KA
BANG
BA

#09 Servant & Strayer III

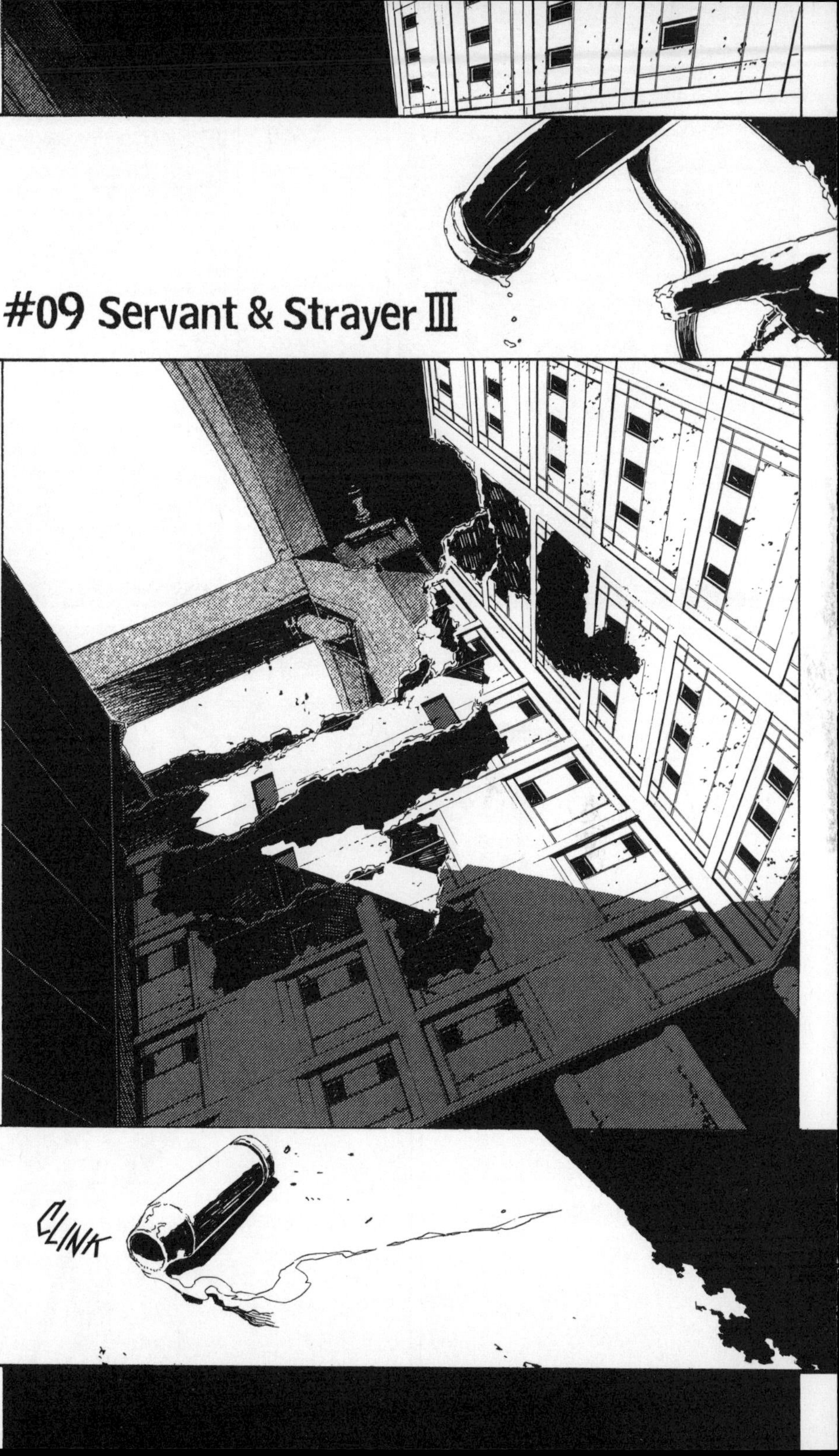
CLINK

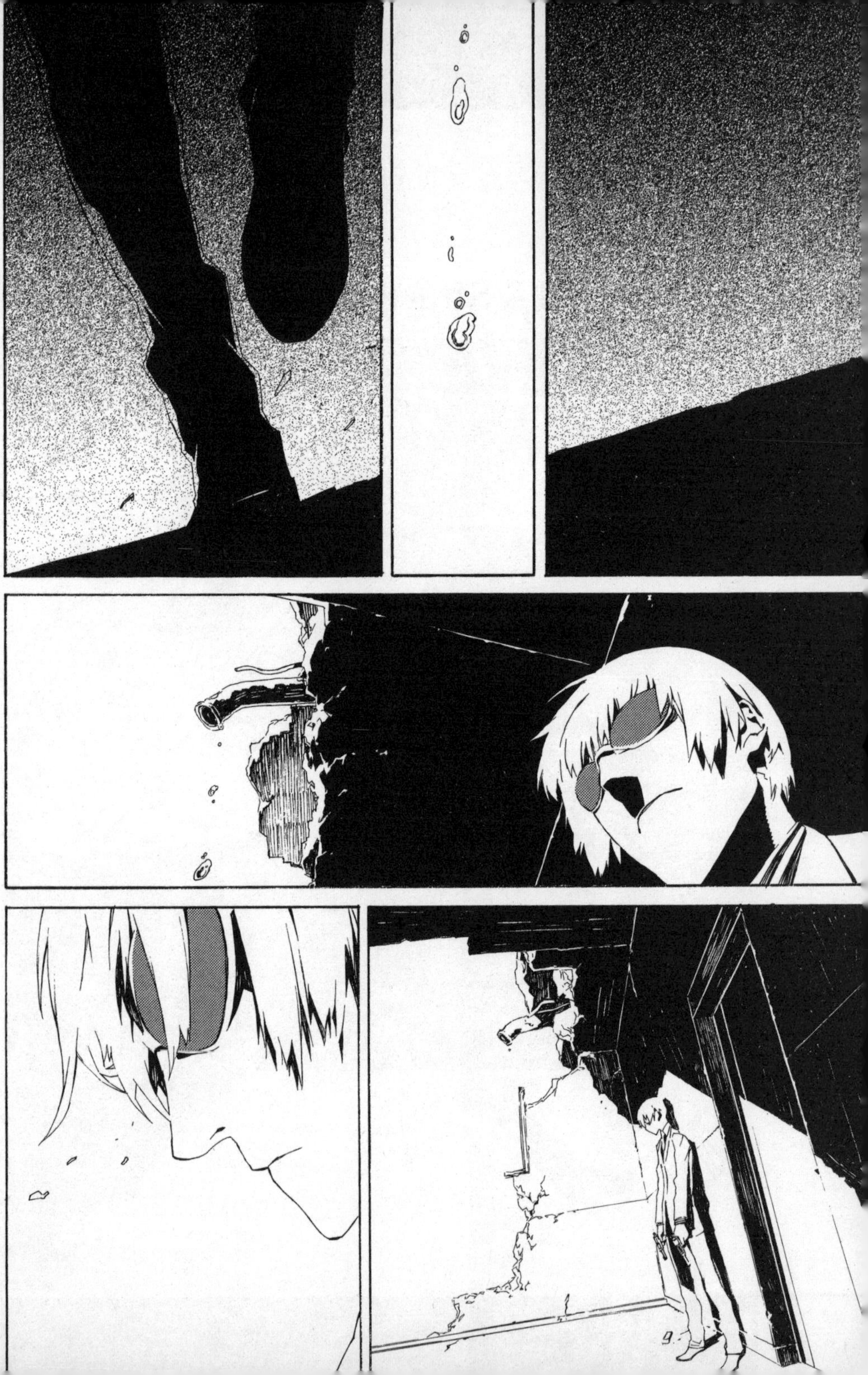

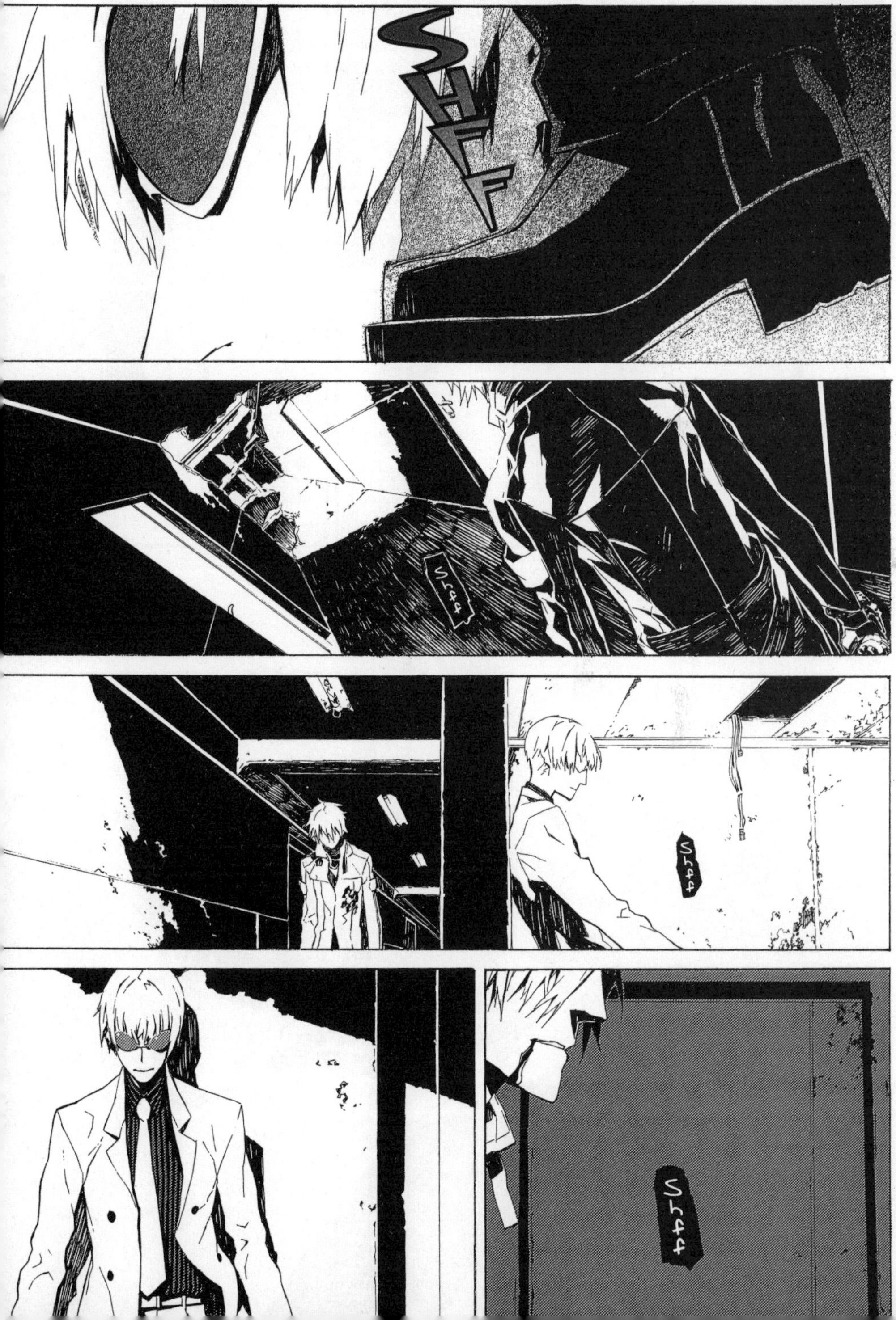
SHFF
Shff
Shff
Shff

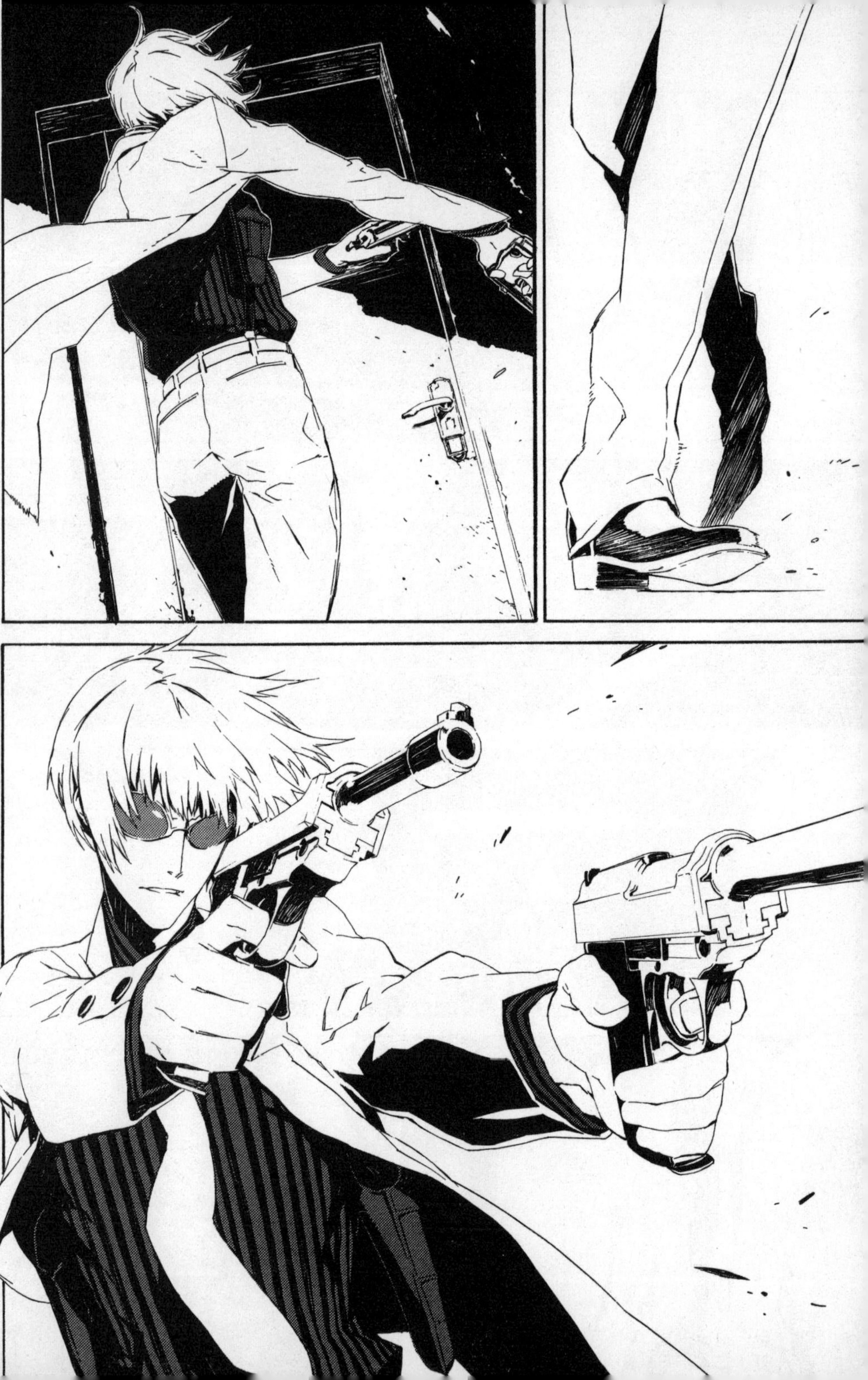

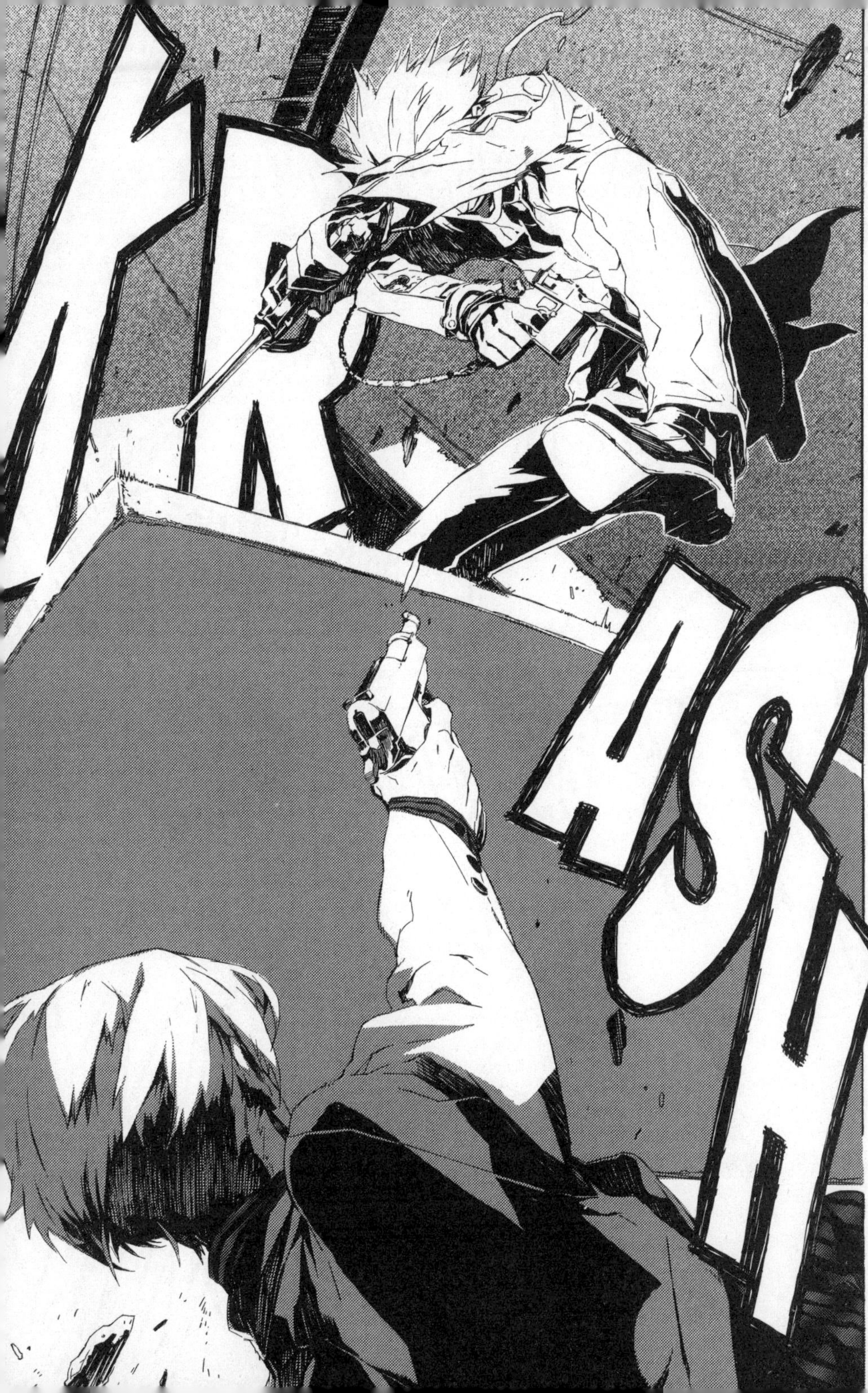

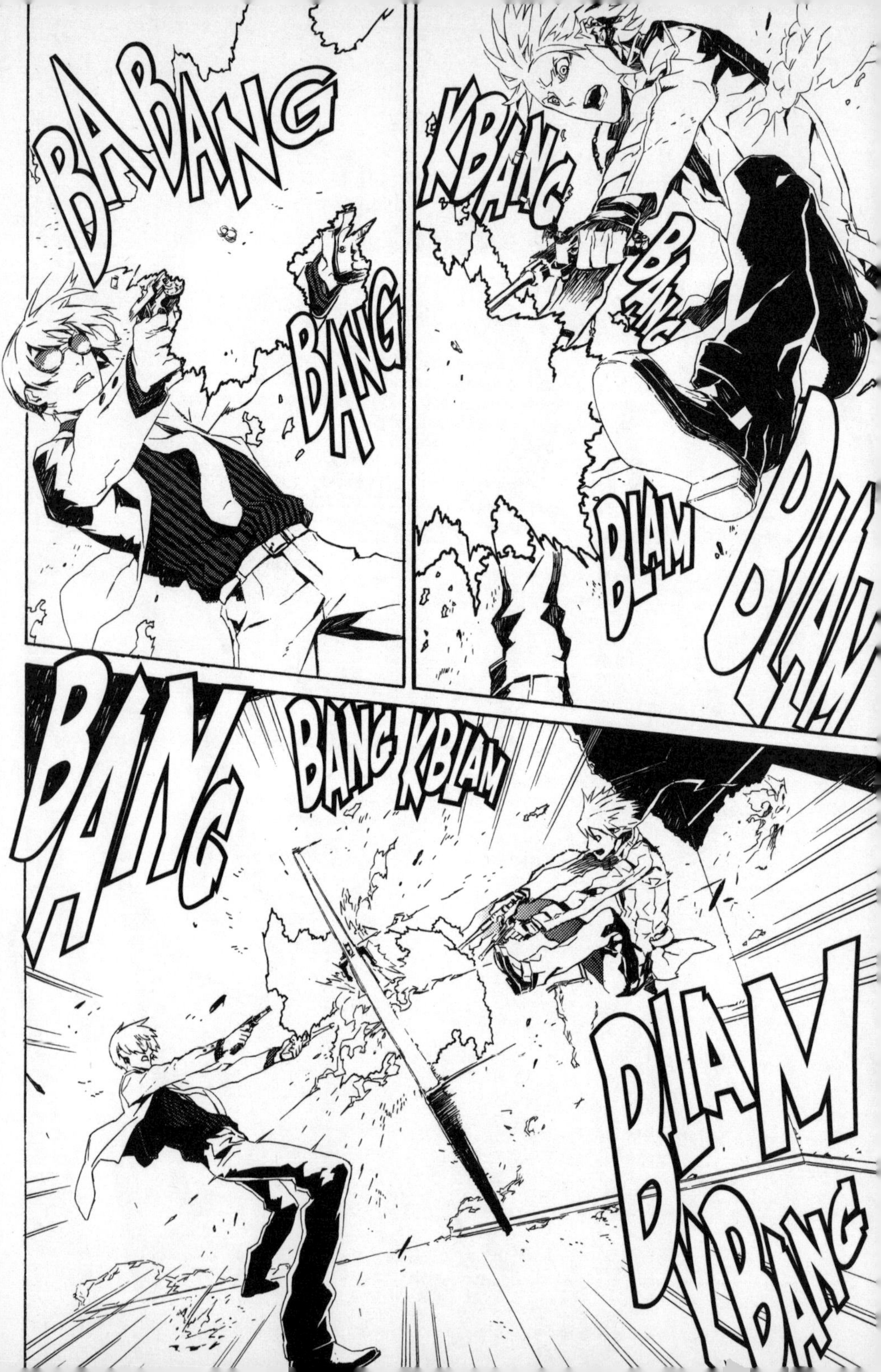

KBANG
BANG
BLAM
BLAM
BABANG
BANG
BLAM
BANG
BANG
KBLAM
BANG

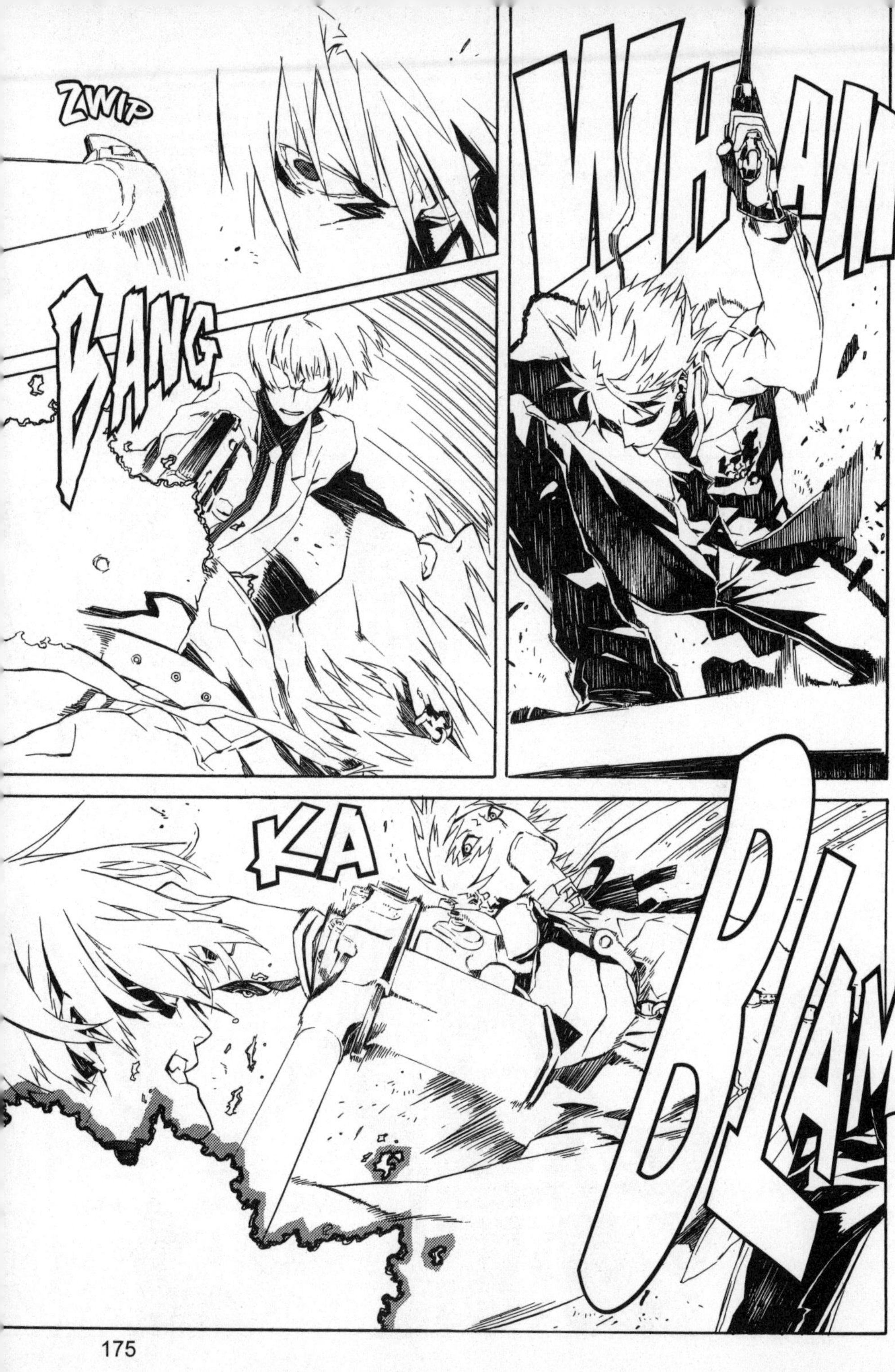
WHAM
ZWIP
BANG
BLAM
KA

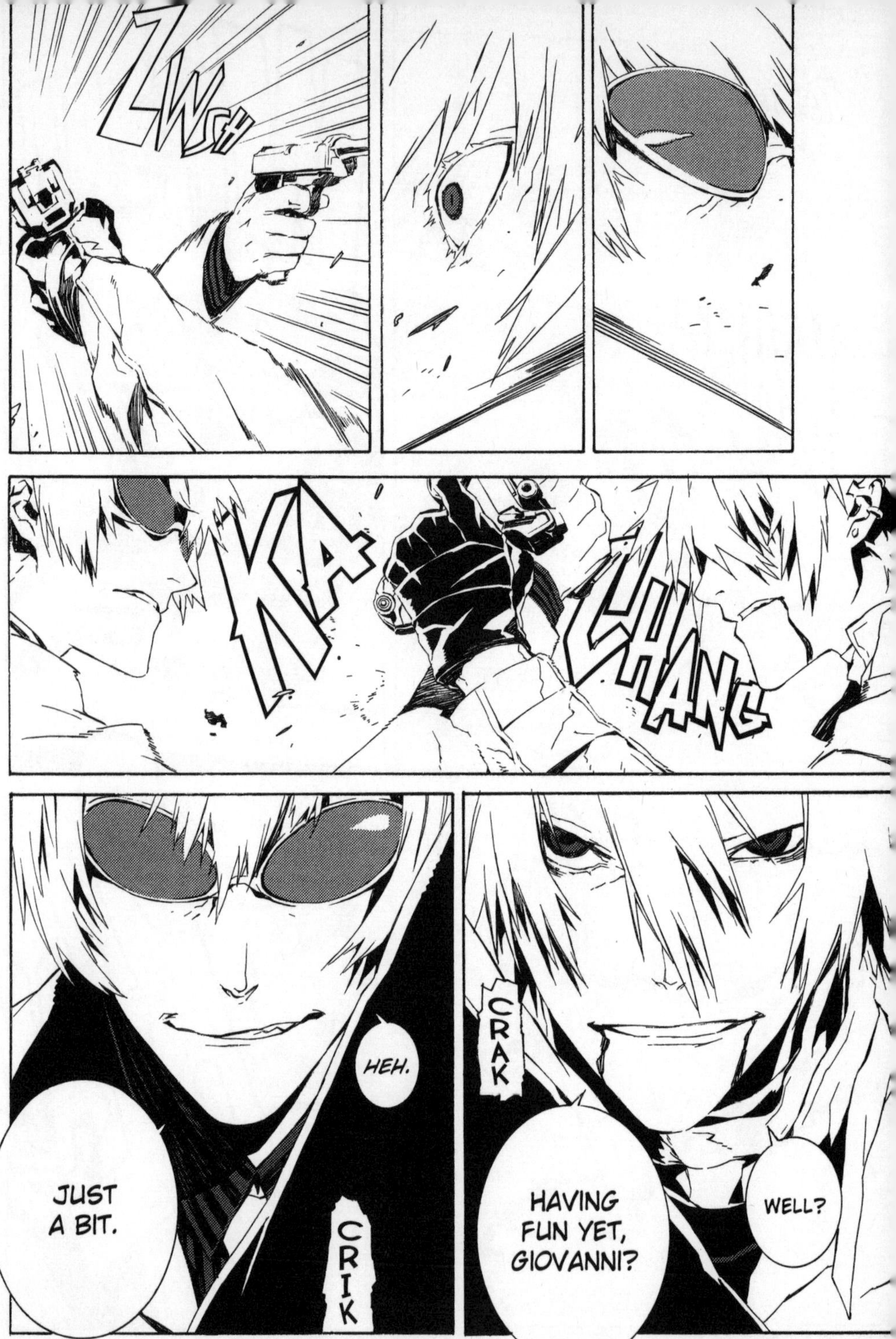

ZWSH
KA
CHANG
CRAK
WELL?
HAVING FUN YET, GIOVANNI?
HEH.
JUST A BIT.
CRIK

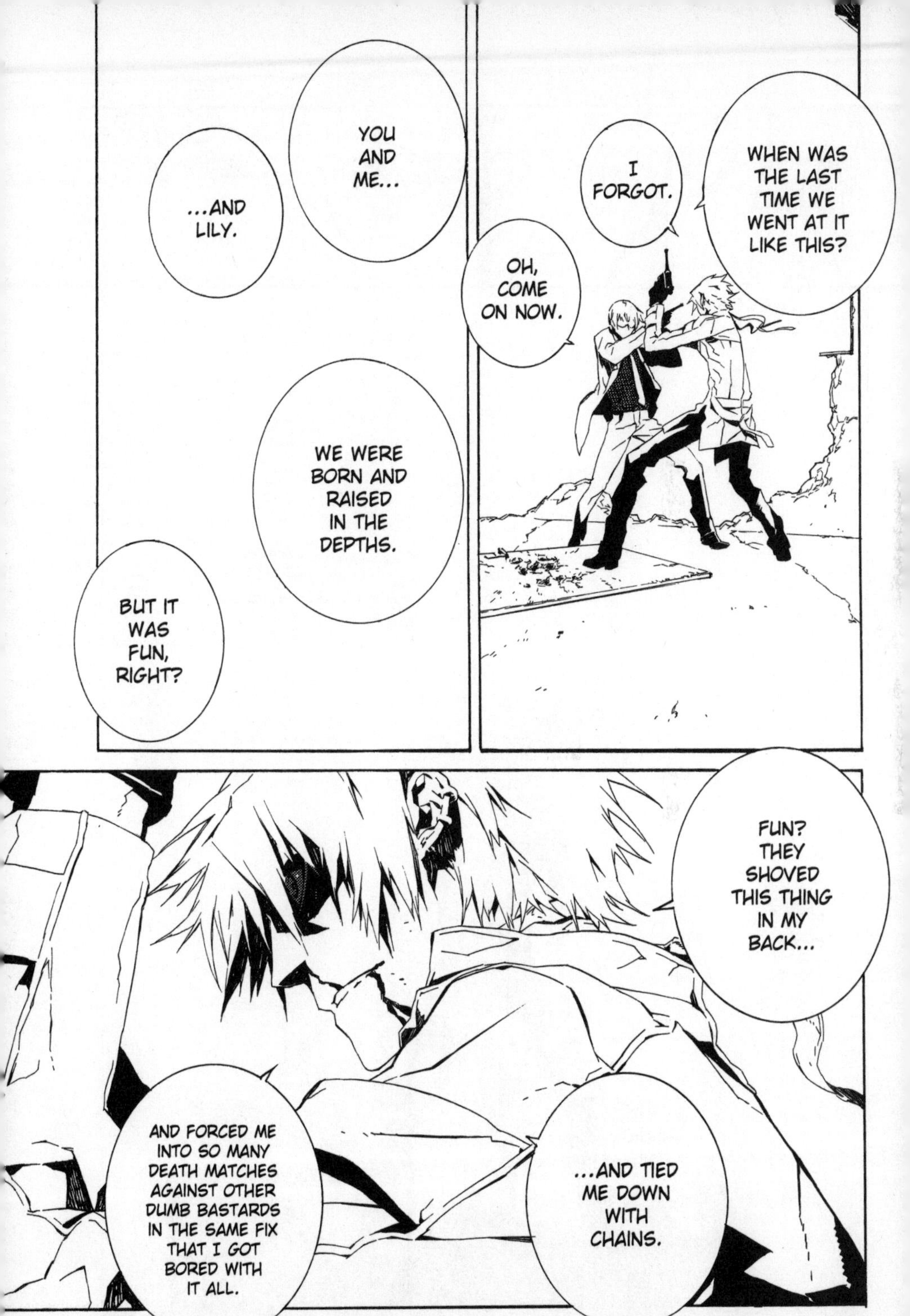
WHEN WAS THE LAST TIME WE WENT AT IT LIKE THIS?
I FORGOT.
OH, COME ON NOW.
YOU AND ME...
...AND LILY.
WE WERE BORN AND RAISED IN THE DEPTHS.
BUT IT WAS FUN, RIGHT?
FUN? THEY SHOVED THIS THING IN MY BACK...
...AND TIED ME DOWN WITH CHAINS.
AND FORCED ME INTO SO MANY DEATH MATCHES AGAINST OTHER DUMB BASTARDS IN THE SAME FIX THAT I GOT BORED WITH IT ALL.

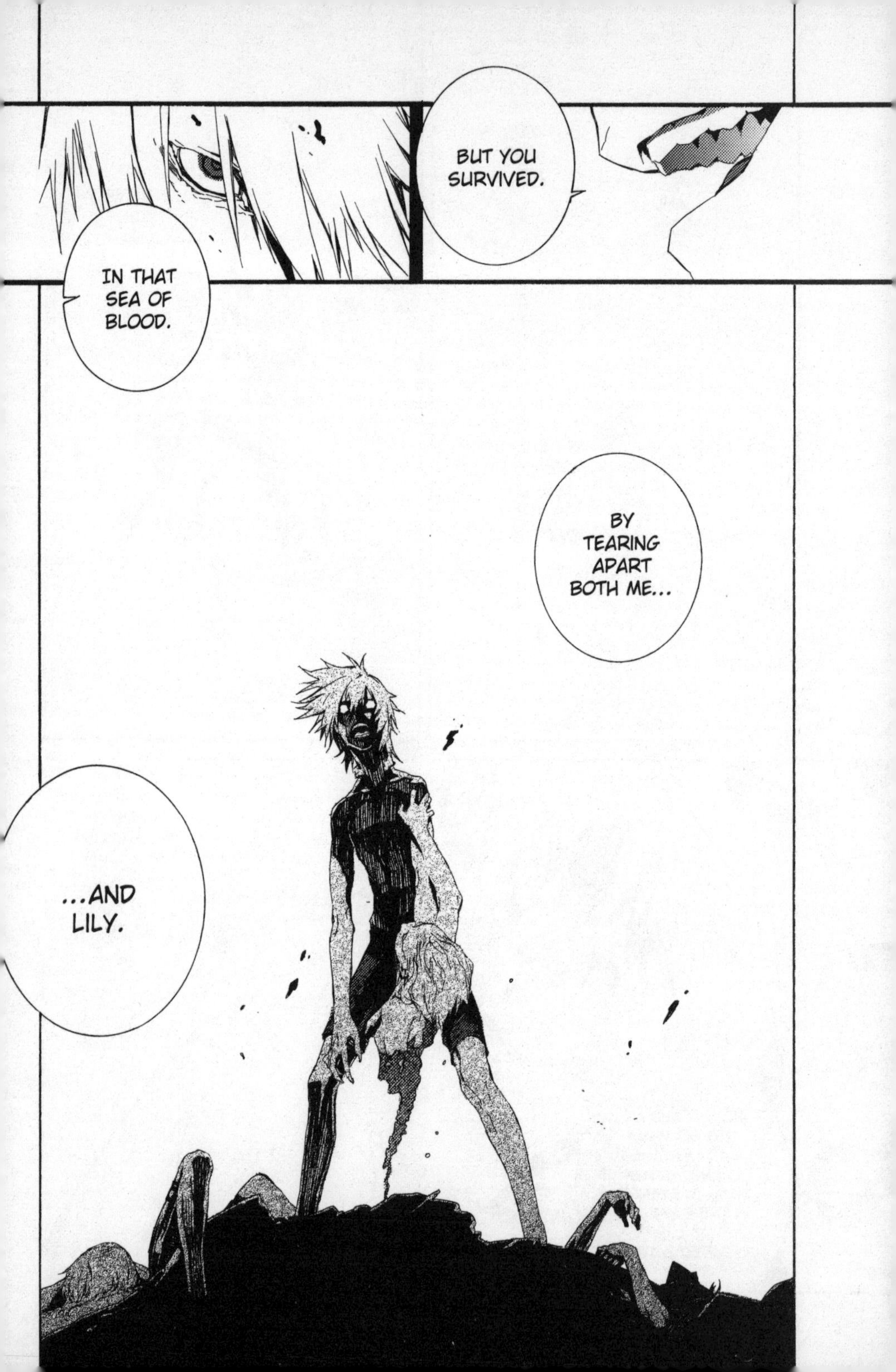
BUT YOU SURVIVED.
IN THAT SEA OF BLOOD.
BY TEARING APART BOTH ME...
...AND LILY.

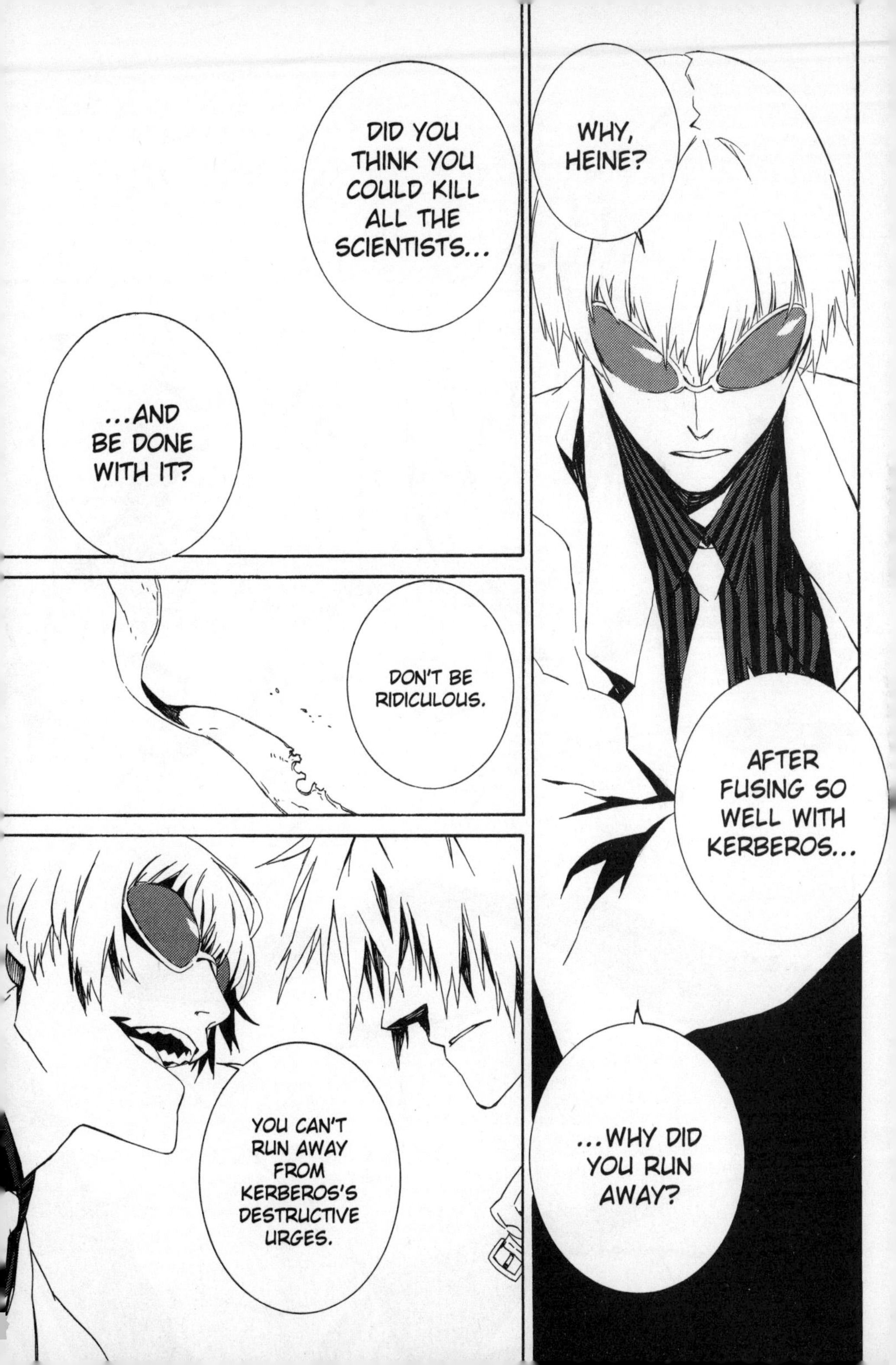
WHY, HEINE?
AFTER FUSING SO WELL WITH KERBEROS...
...WHY DID YOU RUN AWAY?
DID YOU THINK YOU COULD KILL ALL THE SCIENTISTS...
...AND BE DONE WITH IT?
DON'T BE RIDICULOUS.
YOU CAN'T RUN AWAY FROM KERBEROS'S DESTRUCTIVE URGES.

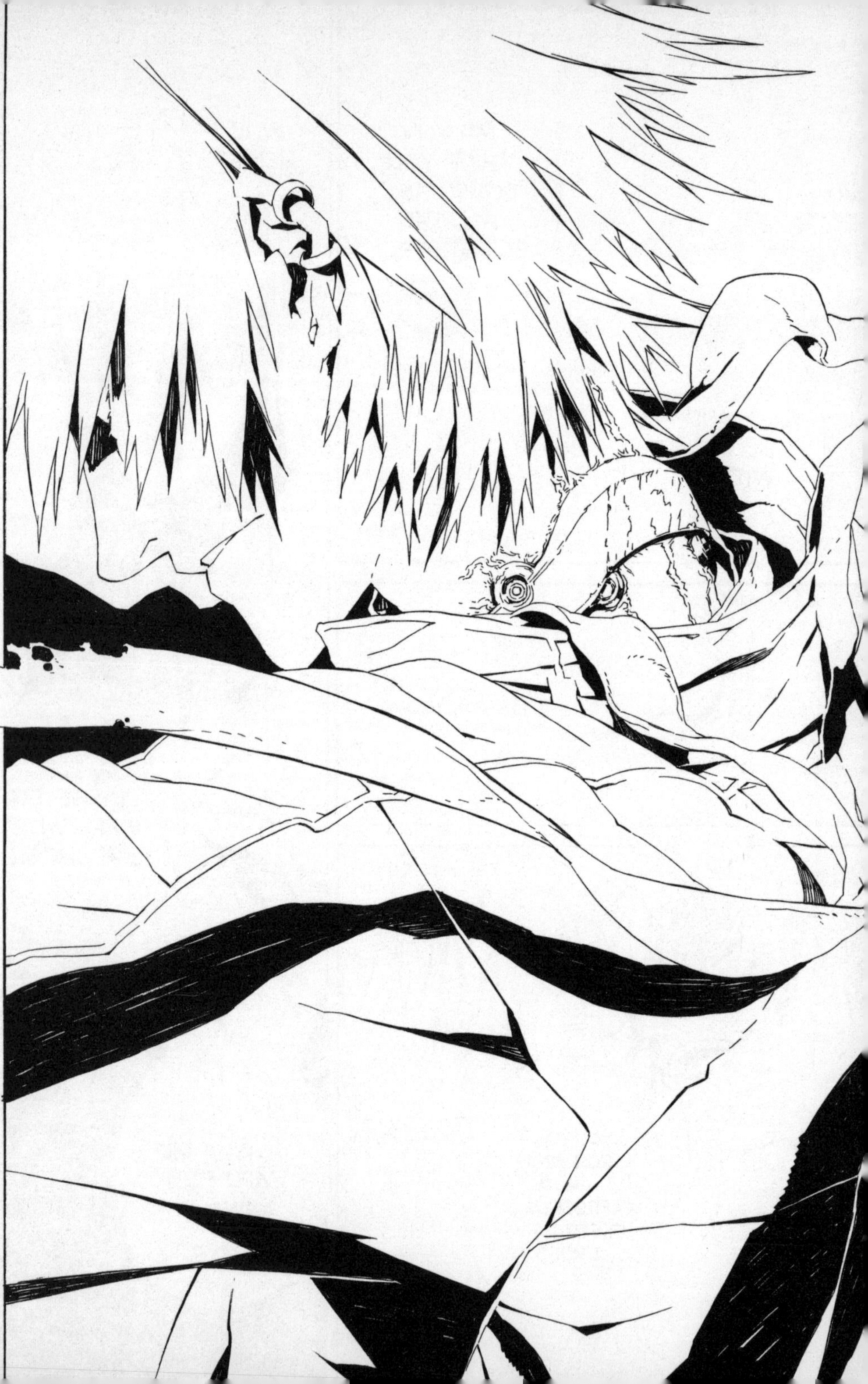

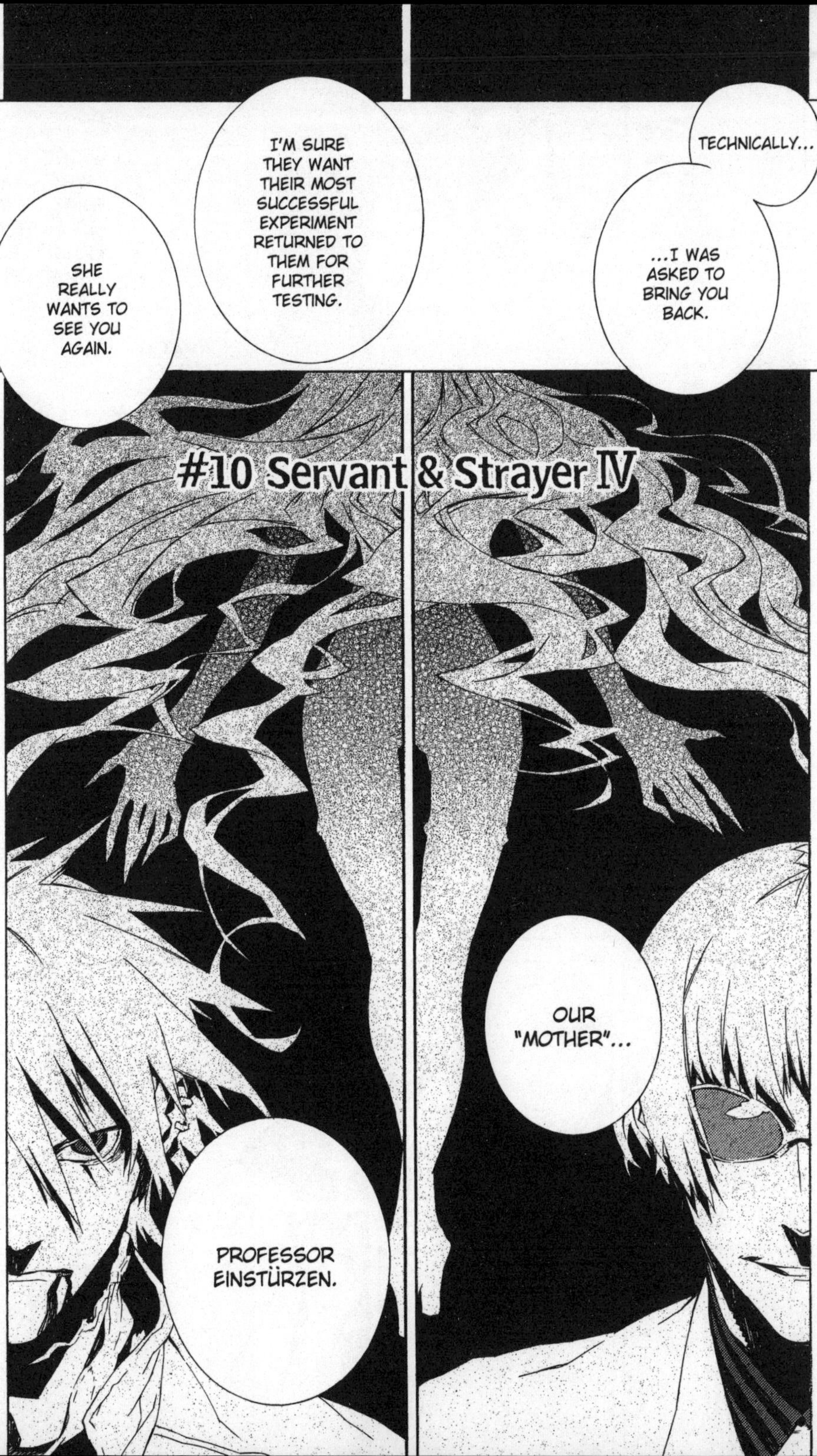
TECHNICALLY...
...I WAS ASKED TO BRING YOU BACK.
I'M SURE THEY WANT THEIR MOST SUCCESSFUL EXPERIMENT RETURNED TO THEM FOR FURTHER TESTING.
SHE REALLY WANTS TO SEE YOU AGAIN.
#10 Servant & Strayer IV
OUR "MOTHER"...
PROFESSOR EINSTÜRZEN.

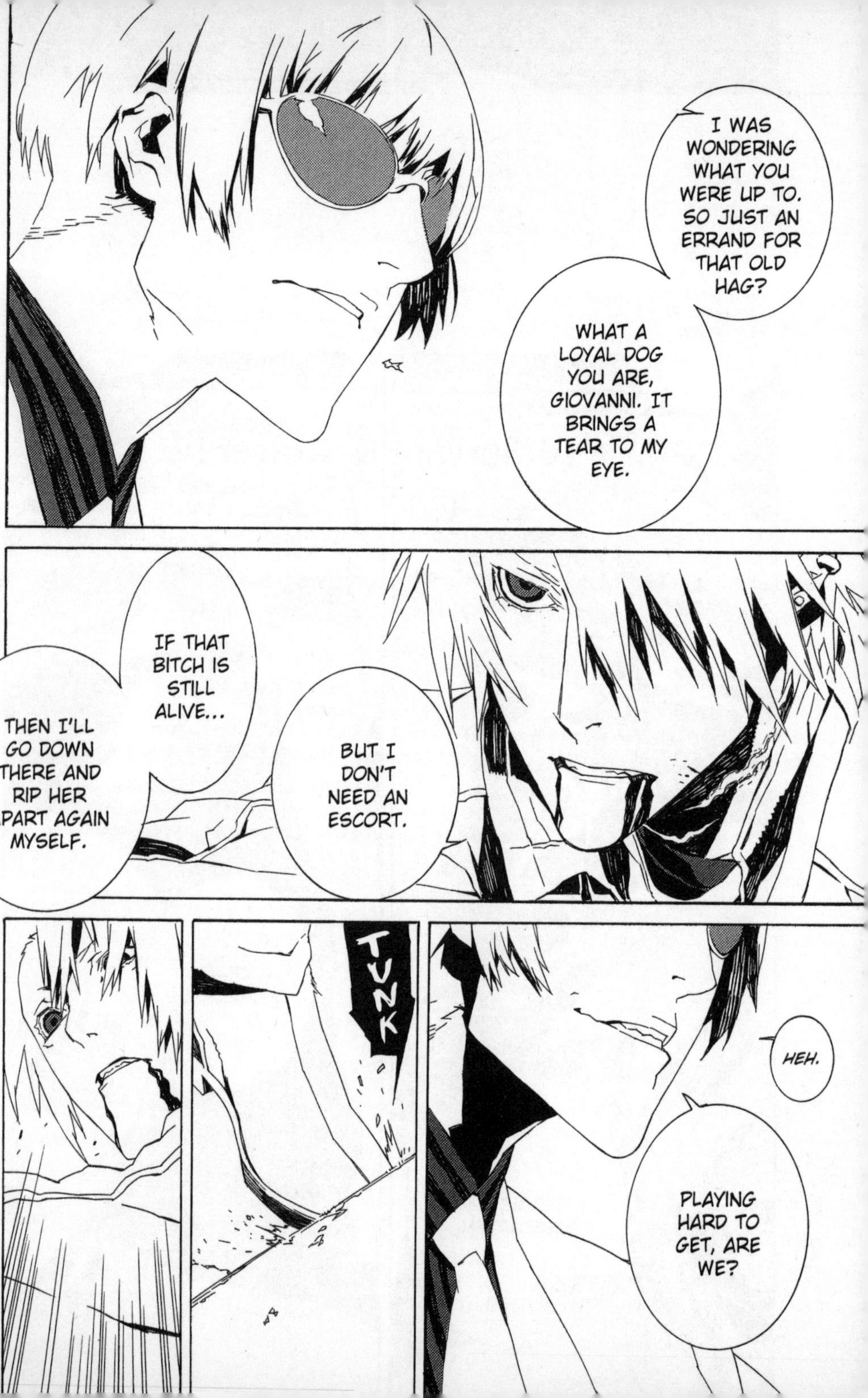
I WAS WONDERING WHAT YOU WERE UP TO. SO JUST AN ERRAND FOR THAT OLD HAG?
WHAT A LOYAL DOG YOU ARE, GIOVANNI. IT BRINGS A TEAR TO MY EYE.
BUT I DON'T NEED AN ESCORT.
IF THAT BITCH IS STILL ALIVE...
THEN I'LL GO DOWN THERE AND RIP HER APART AGAIN MYSELF.
HEH.
PLAYING HARD TO GET, ARE WE?
TUNK

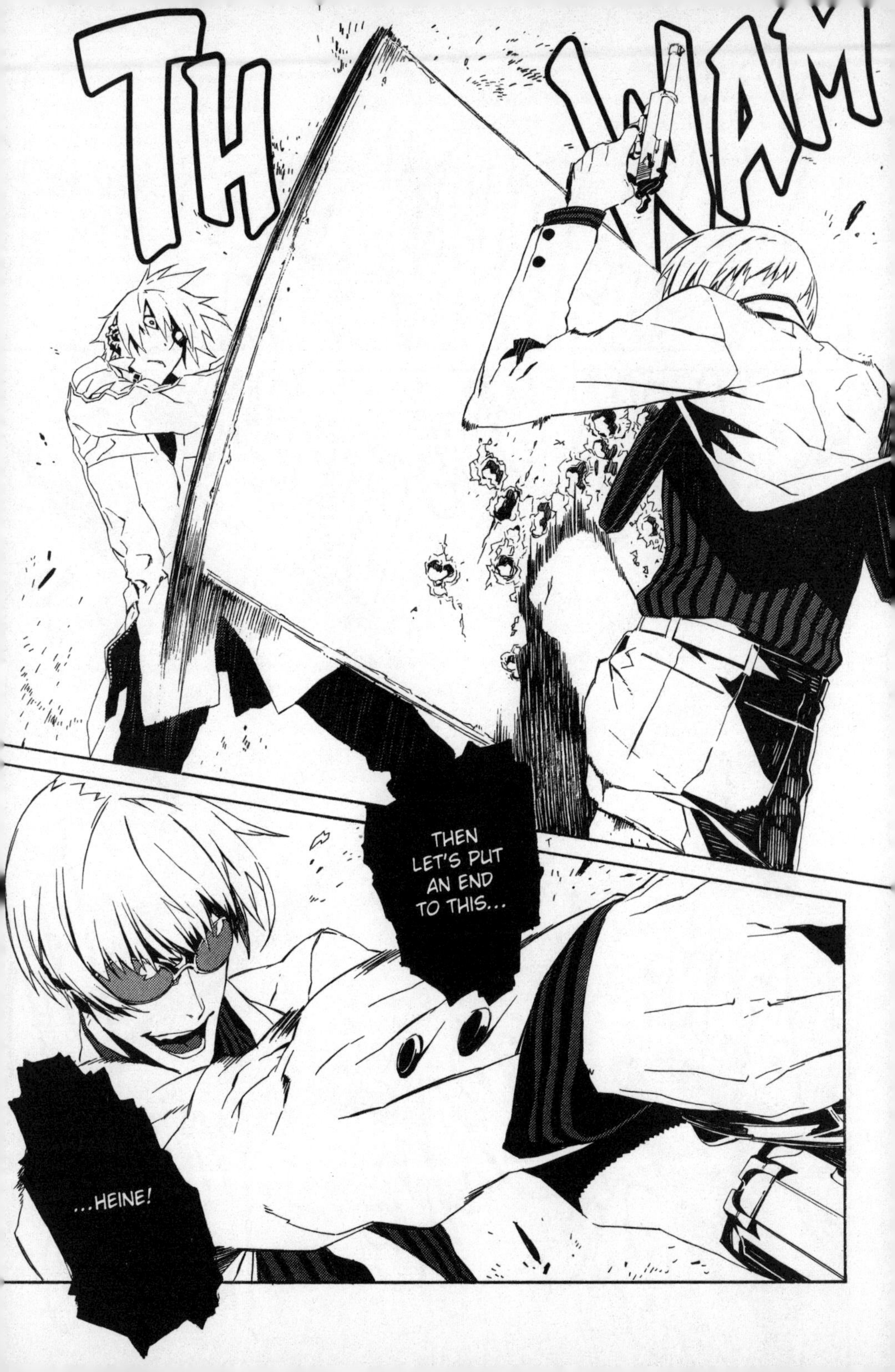
THWAM
THEN LET'S PUT AN END TO THIS...
...HEINE!

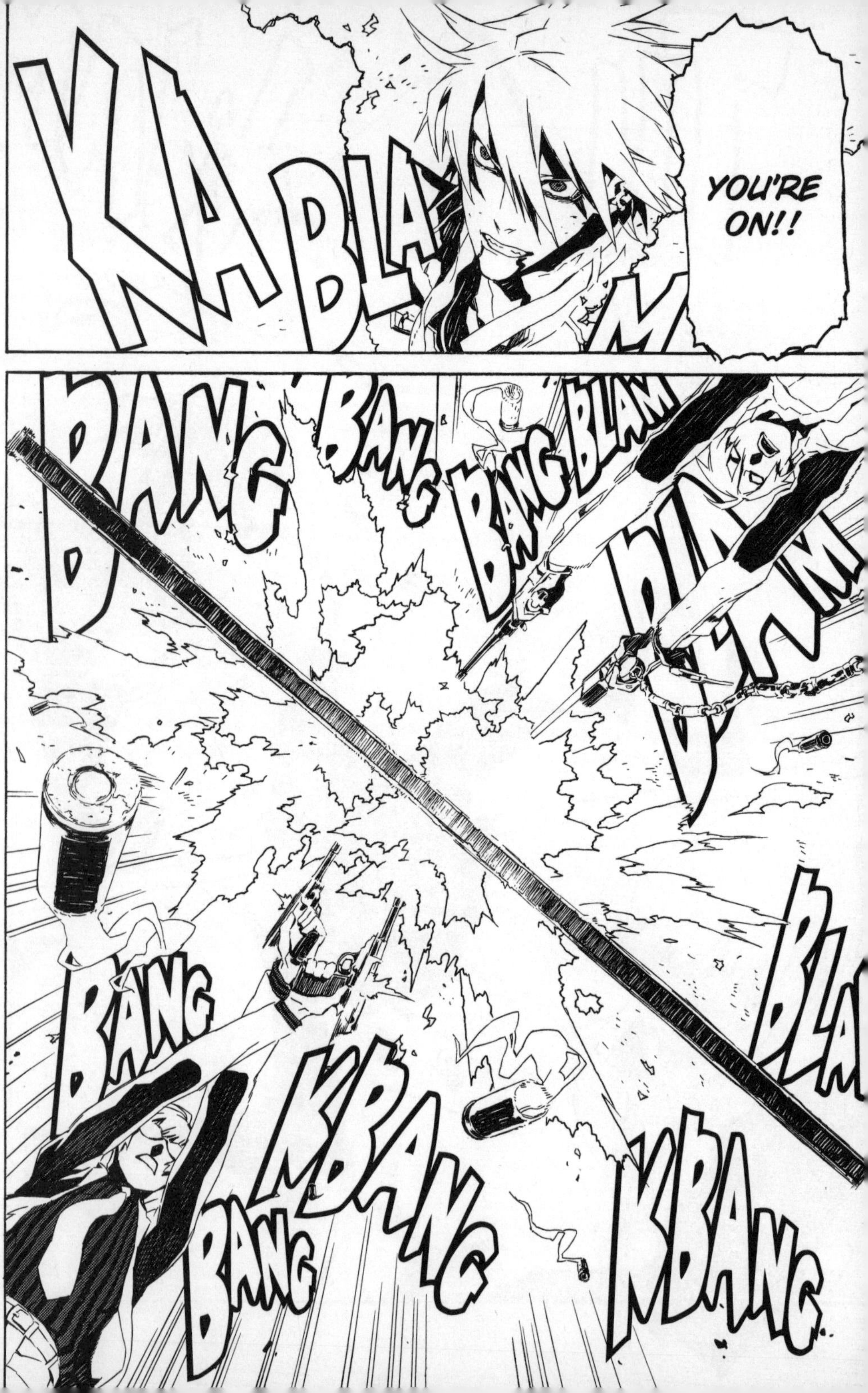
YOU'RE ON!!
KA BLAM
BANG BLAM
BLAM
BANG
BANG
BLAM
KBANG
KBANG
BANG
BANG

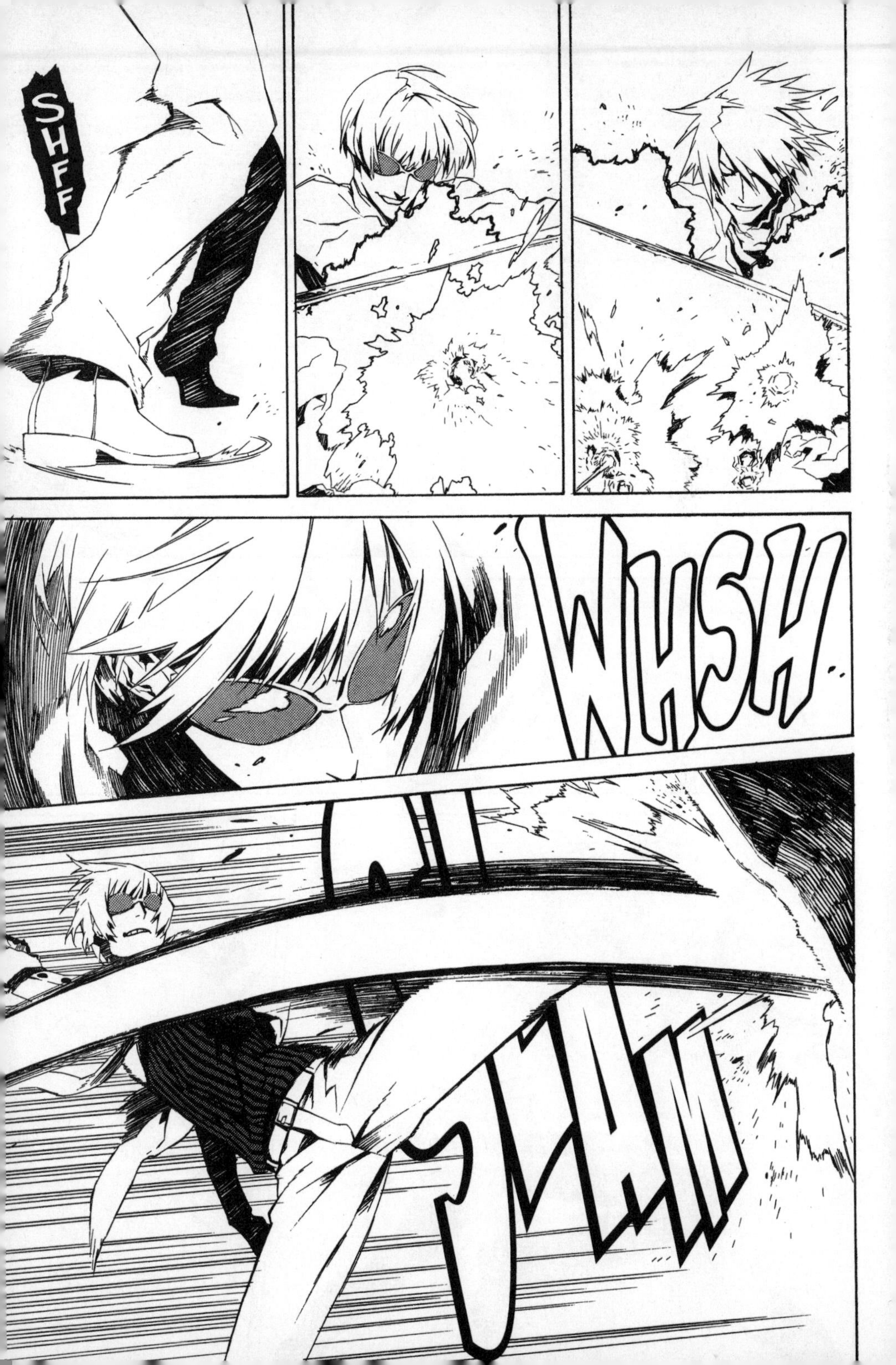
SHFF
WHSH
THAM

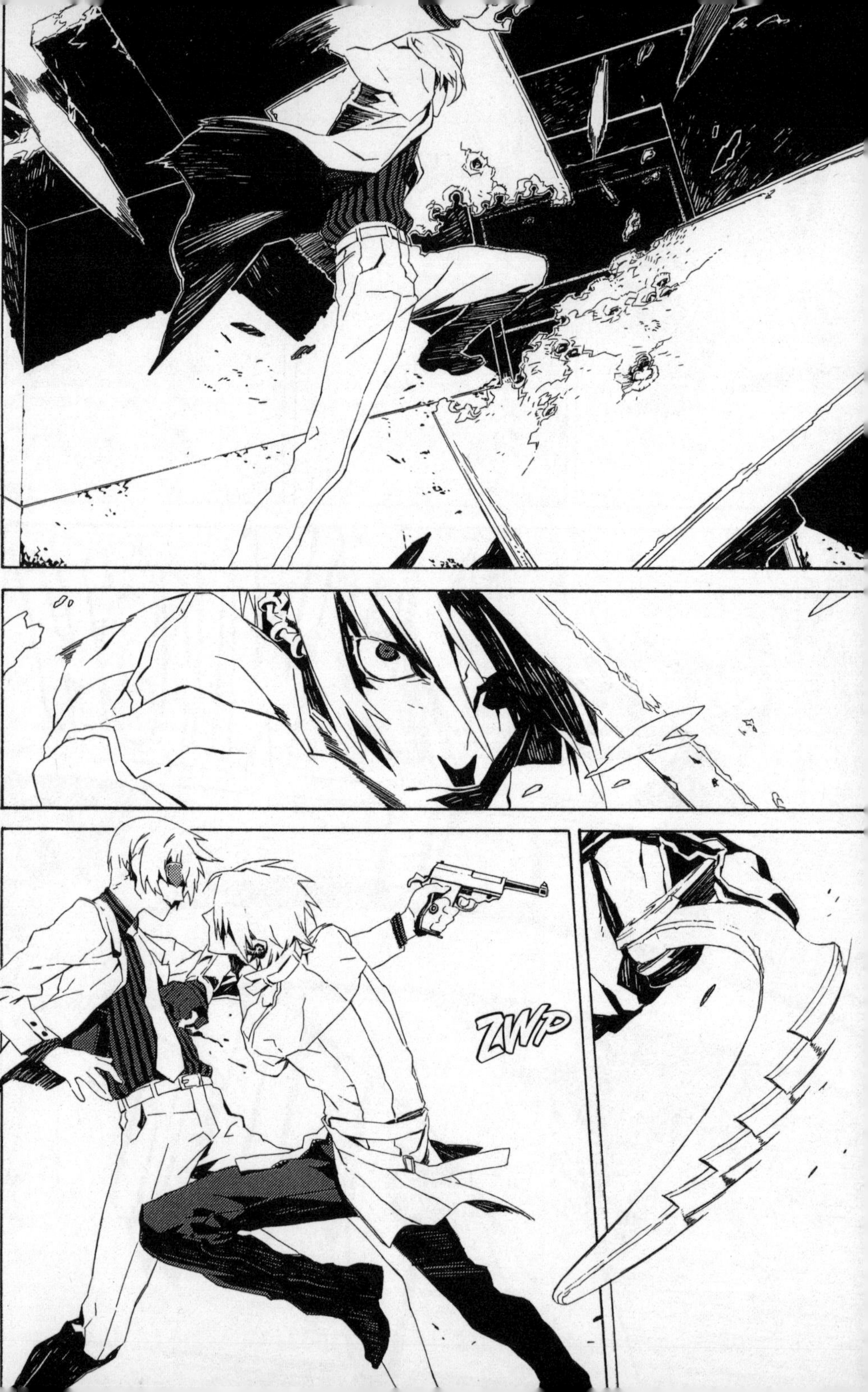
ZWIP

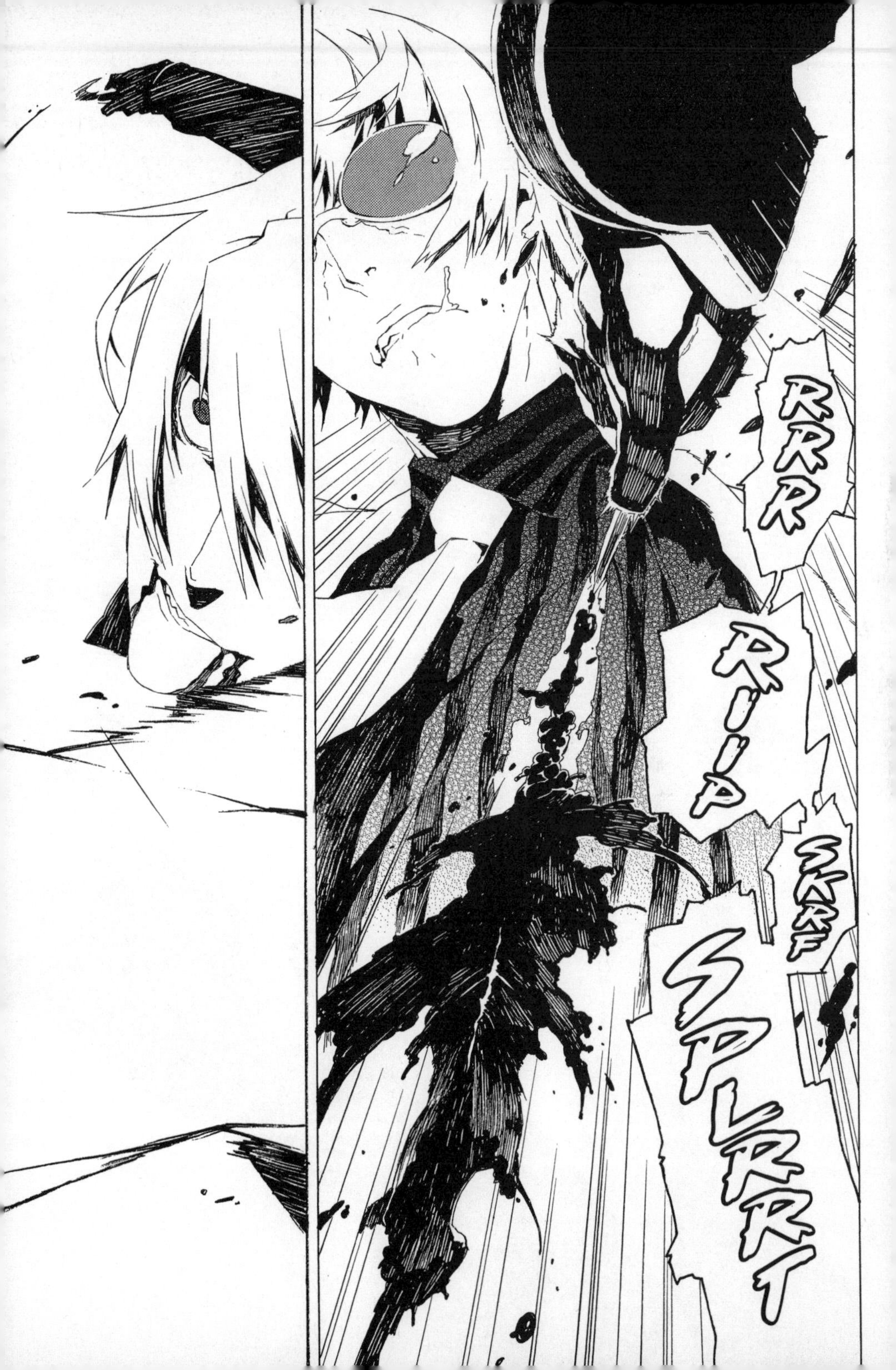
RRRR
RIIP
SKRF
SPLRRT

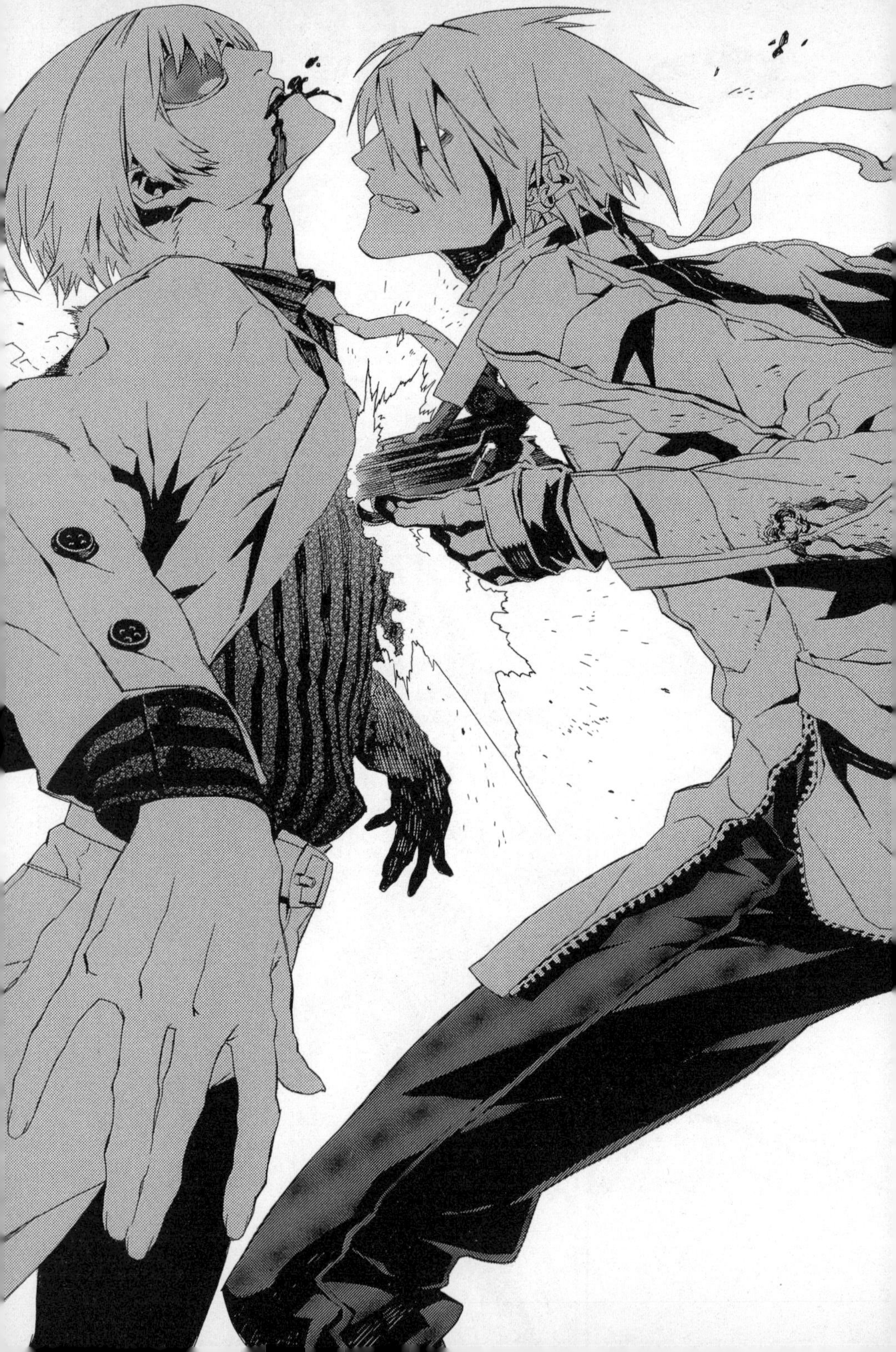

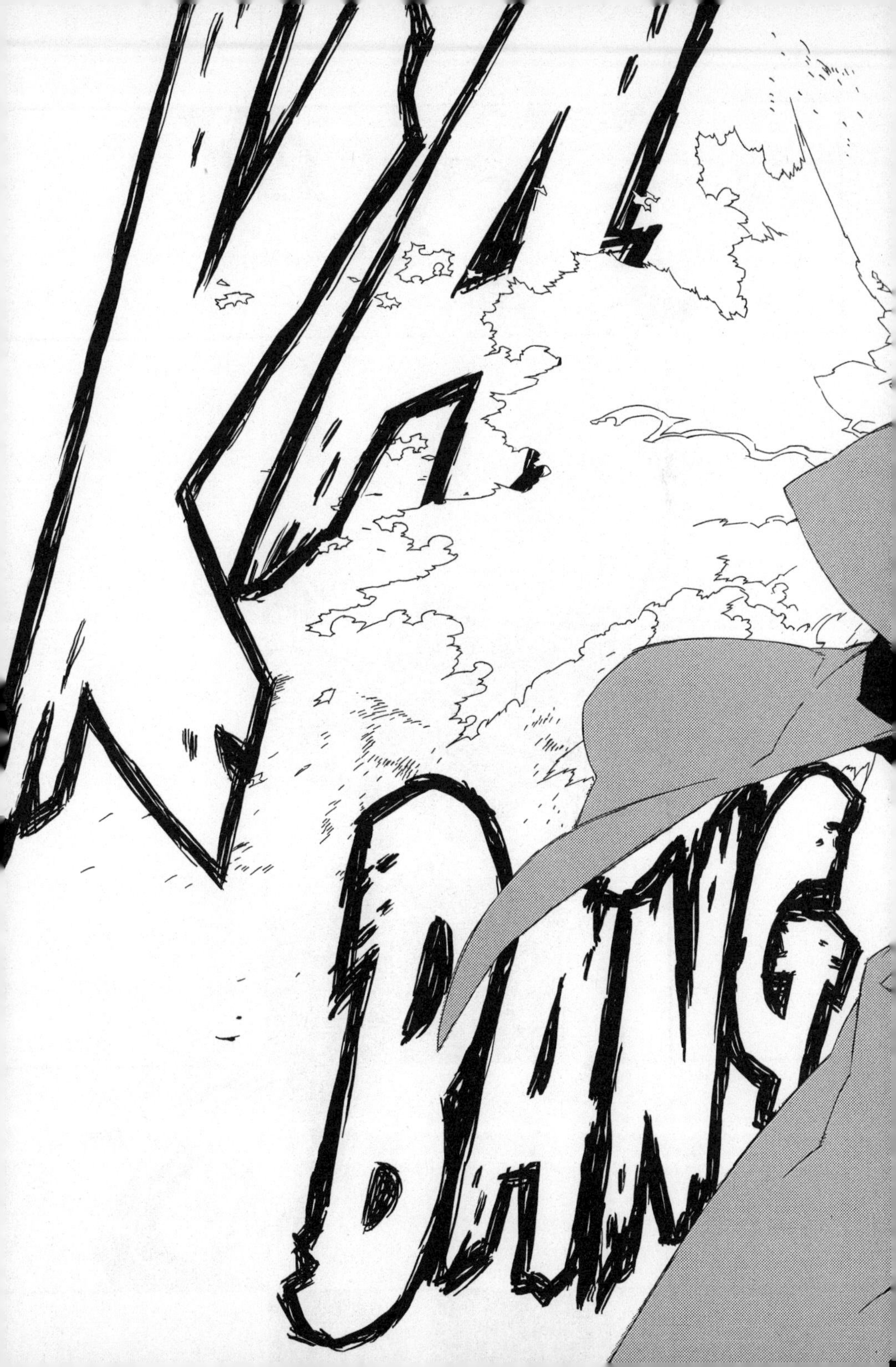

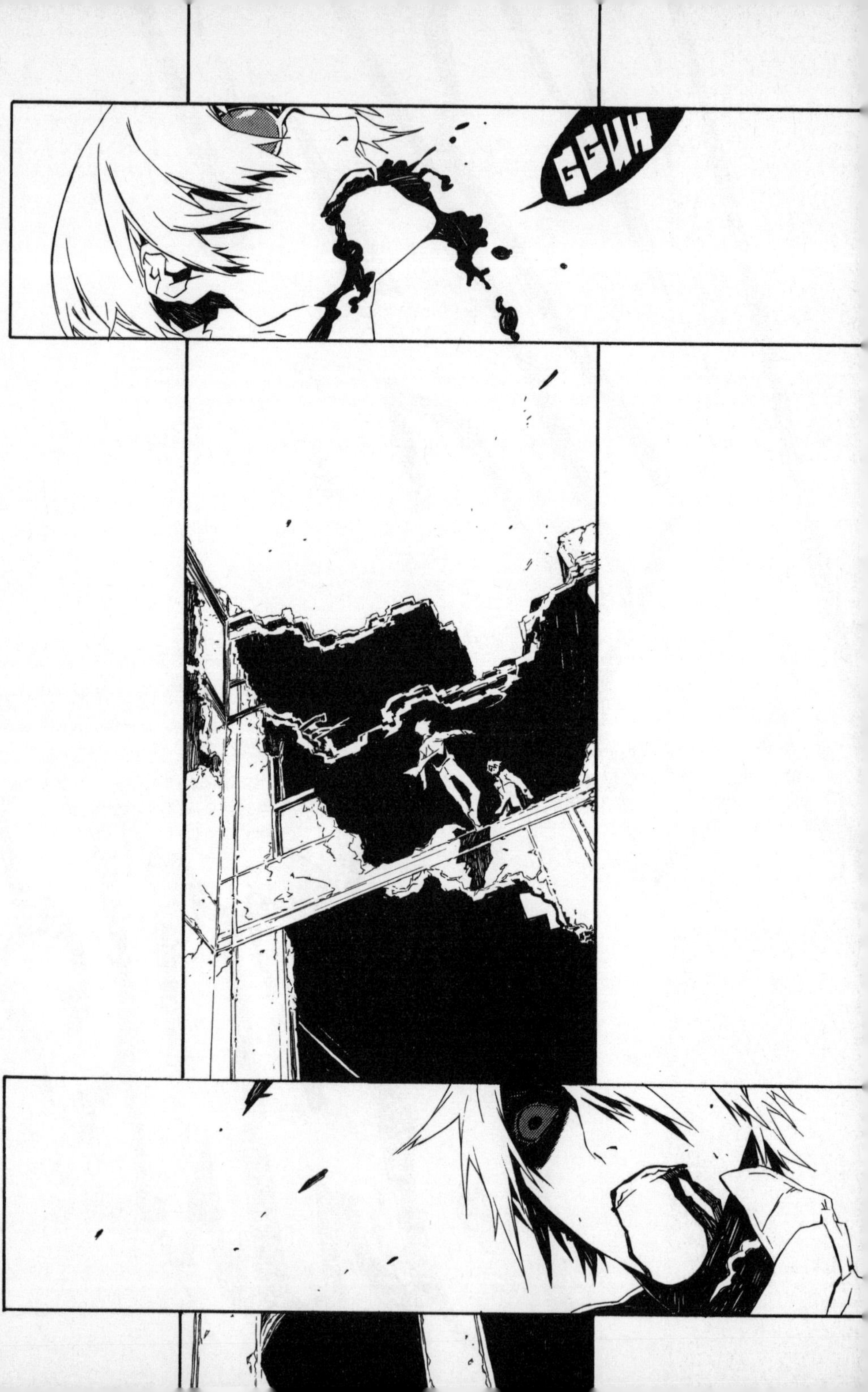
GGUH

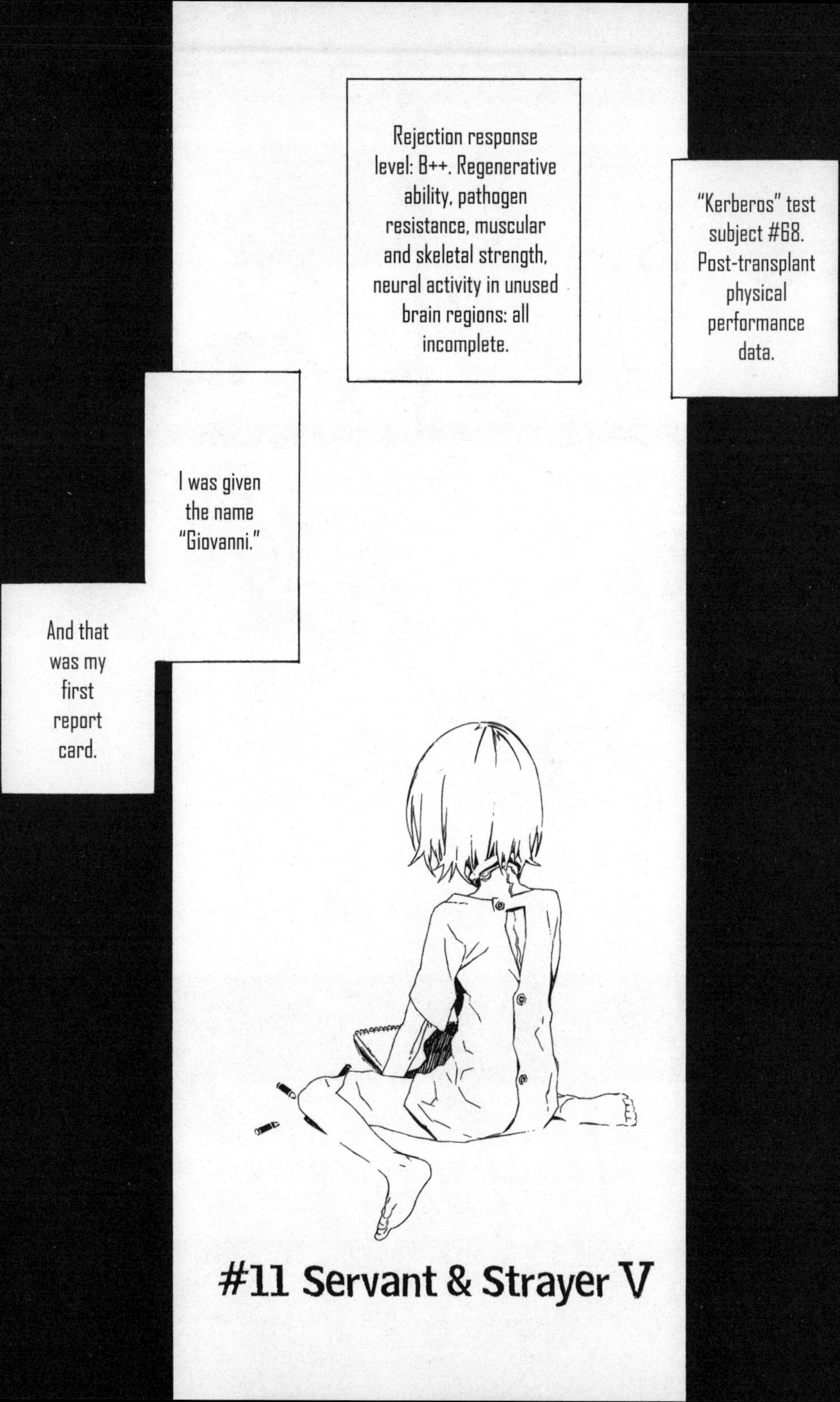

"Kerberos" test subject #68. Post-transplant physical performance data.
Rejection response level: B++. Regenerative ability, pathogen resistance, muscular and skeletal strength, neural activity in unused brain regions: all incomplete.
I was given the name "Giovanni."
And that was my first report card.
#11 Servant & Strayer V

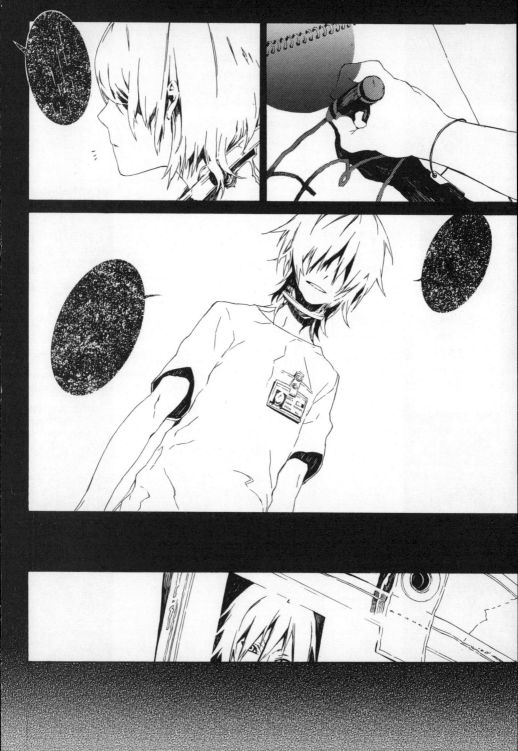

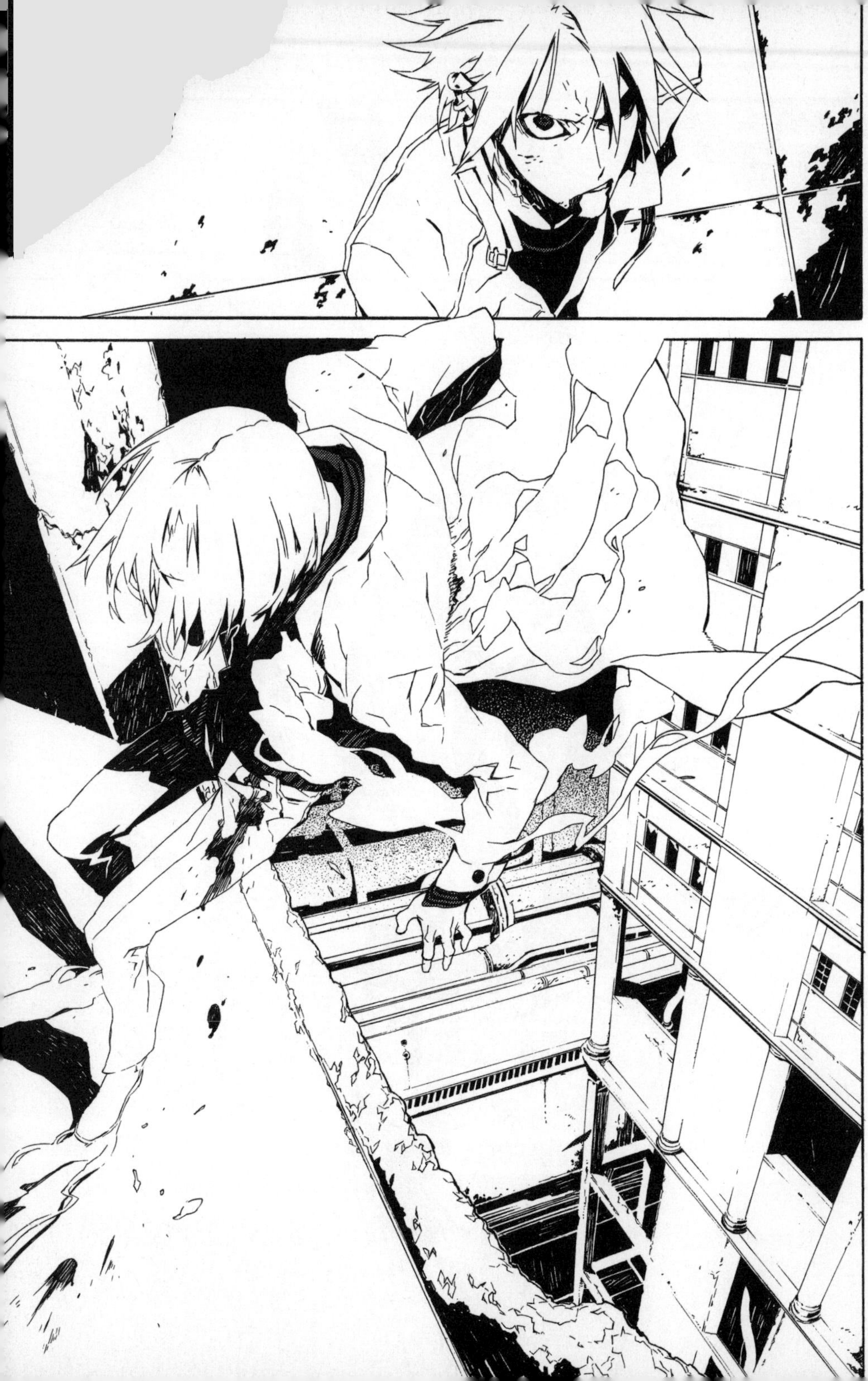

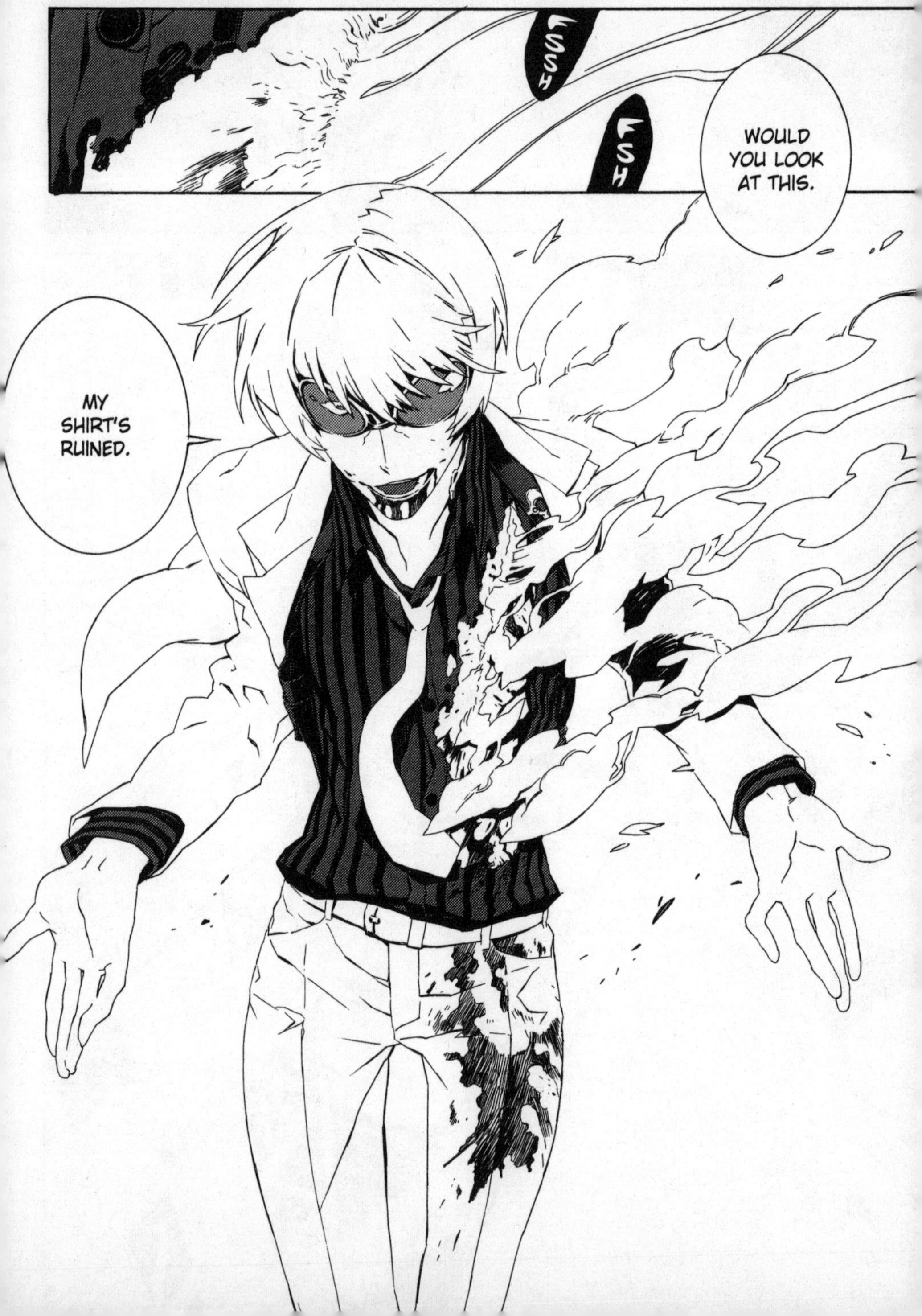
FSSH
FSH
WOULD YOU LOOK AT THIS.
MY SHIRT'S RUINED.

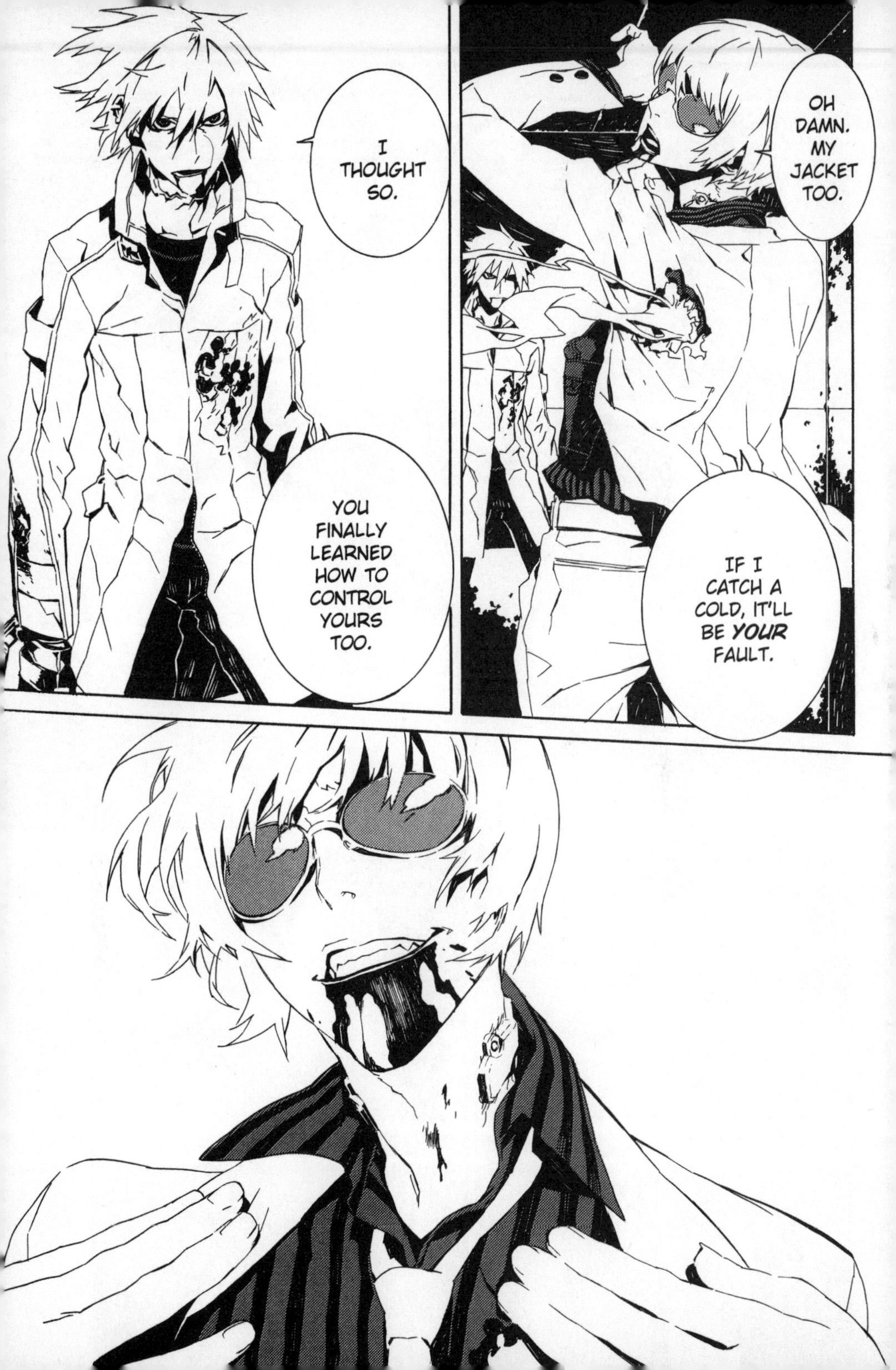
OH DAMN. MY JACKET TOO.
IF I CATCH A COLD, IT'LL BE ***YOUR*** FAULT.
I THOUGHT SO.
YOU FINALLY LEARNED HOW TO CONTROL YOURS TOO.

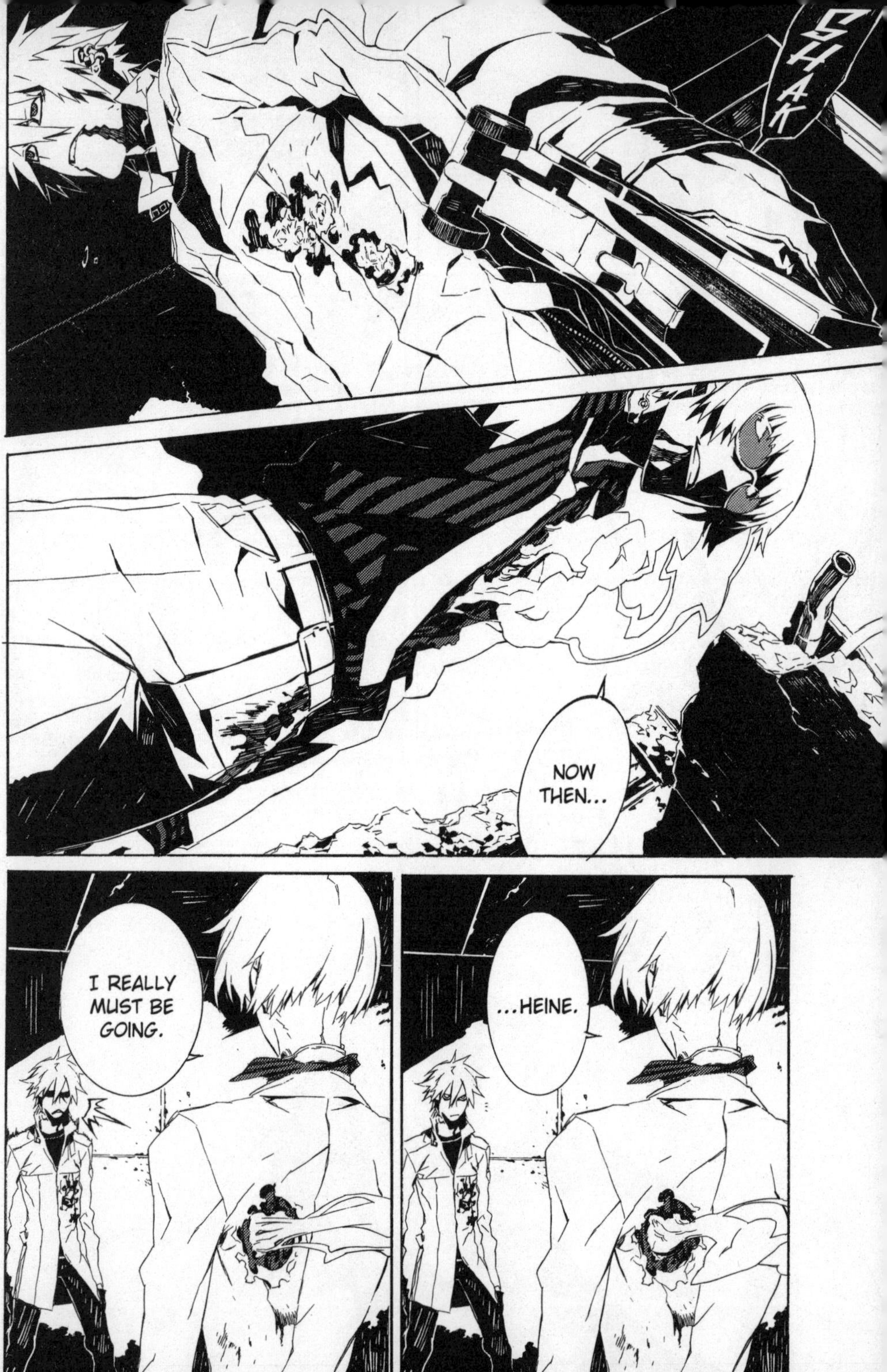
SHAK
NOW THEN...
...HEINE.
I REALLY MUST BE GOING.

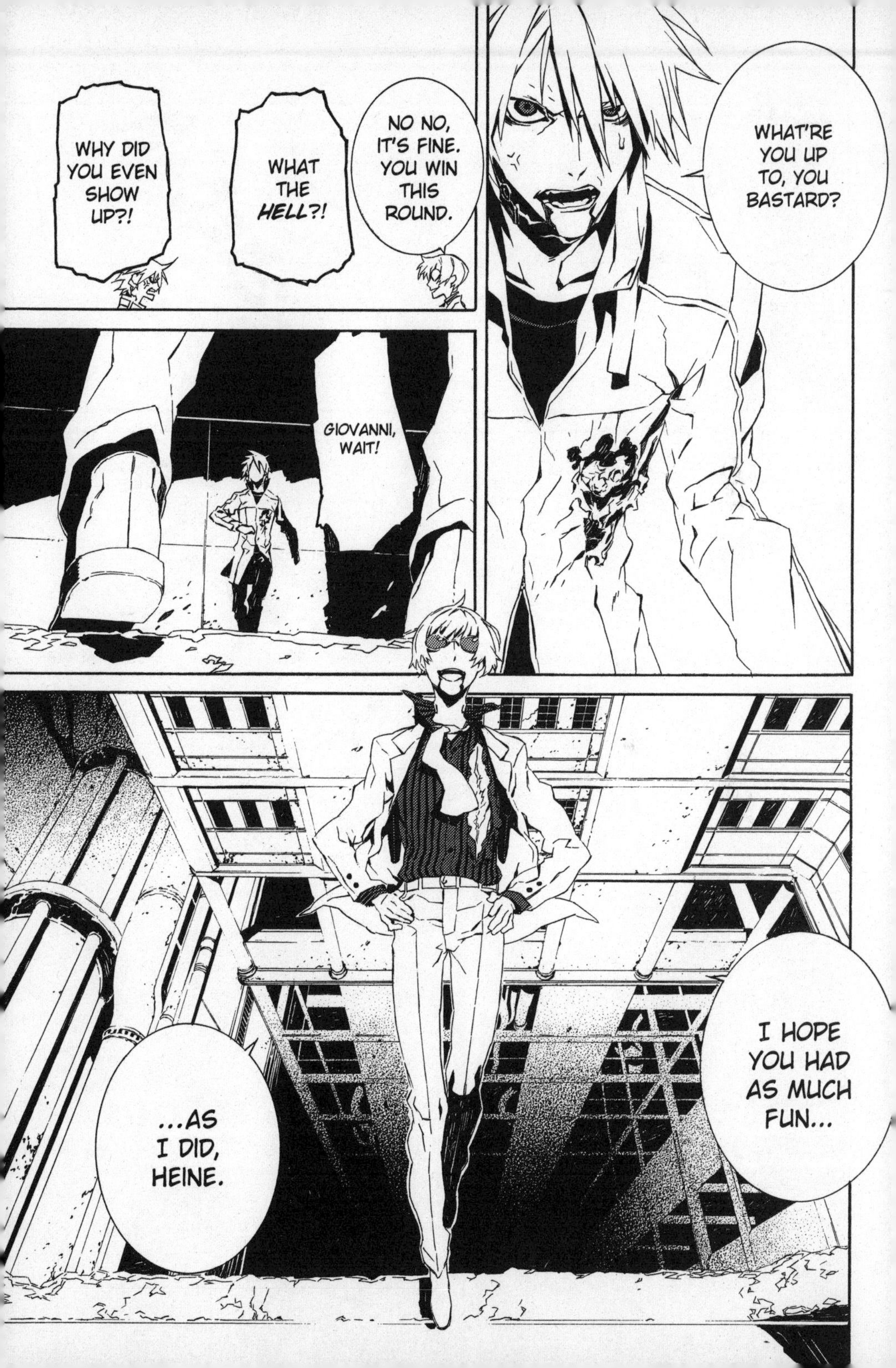
WHAT'RE YOU UP TO, YOU BASTARD?
NO NO, IT'S FINE. YOU WIN THIS ROUND.
WHAT THE *HELL*?!
WHY DID YOU EVEN SHOW UP?!
GIOVANNI, WAIT!
I HOPE YOU HAD AS MUCH FUN...
...AS I DID, HEINE.

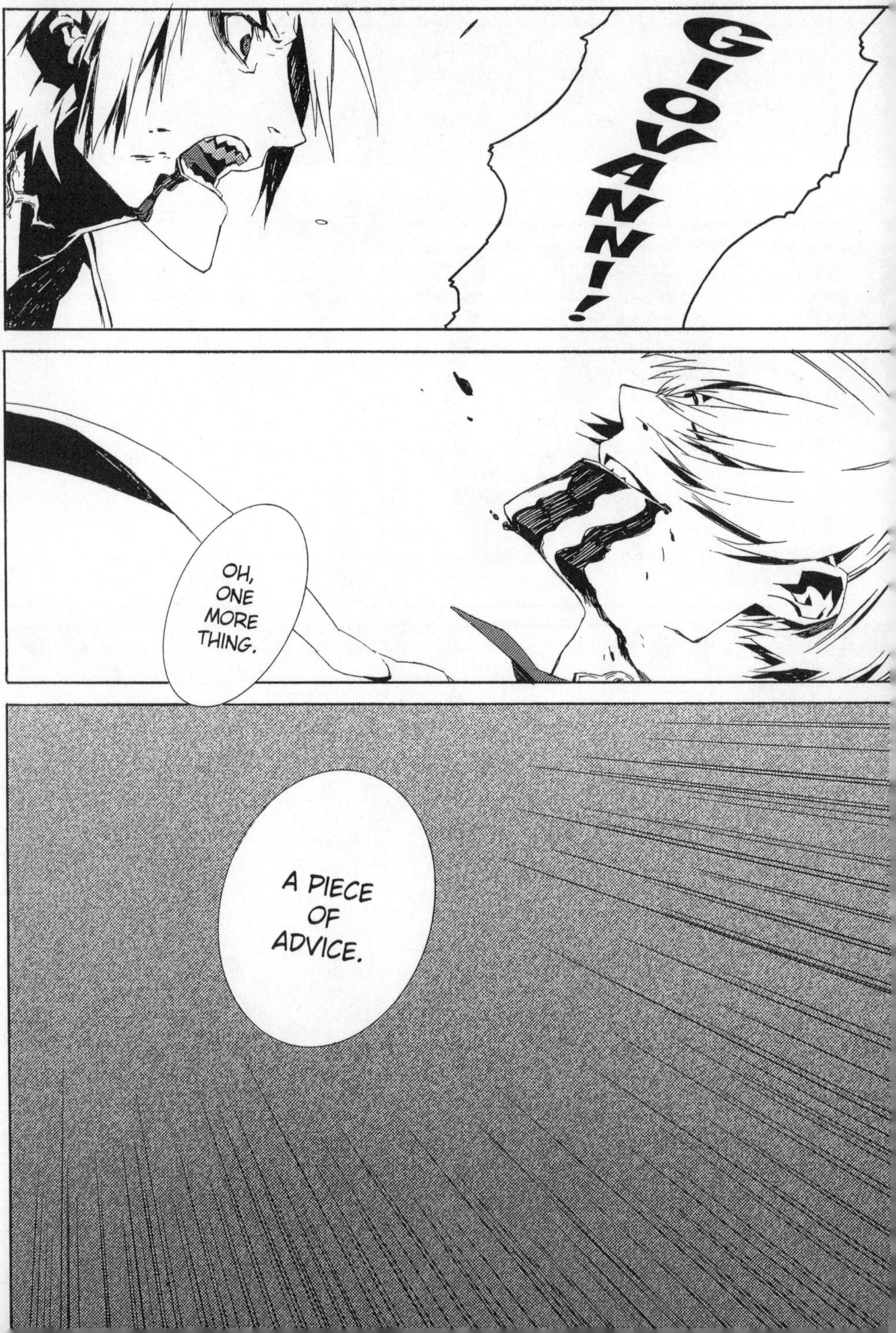
GIOVANNI!
OH, ONE MORE THING.
A PIECE OF ADVICE.

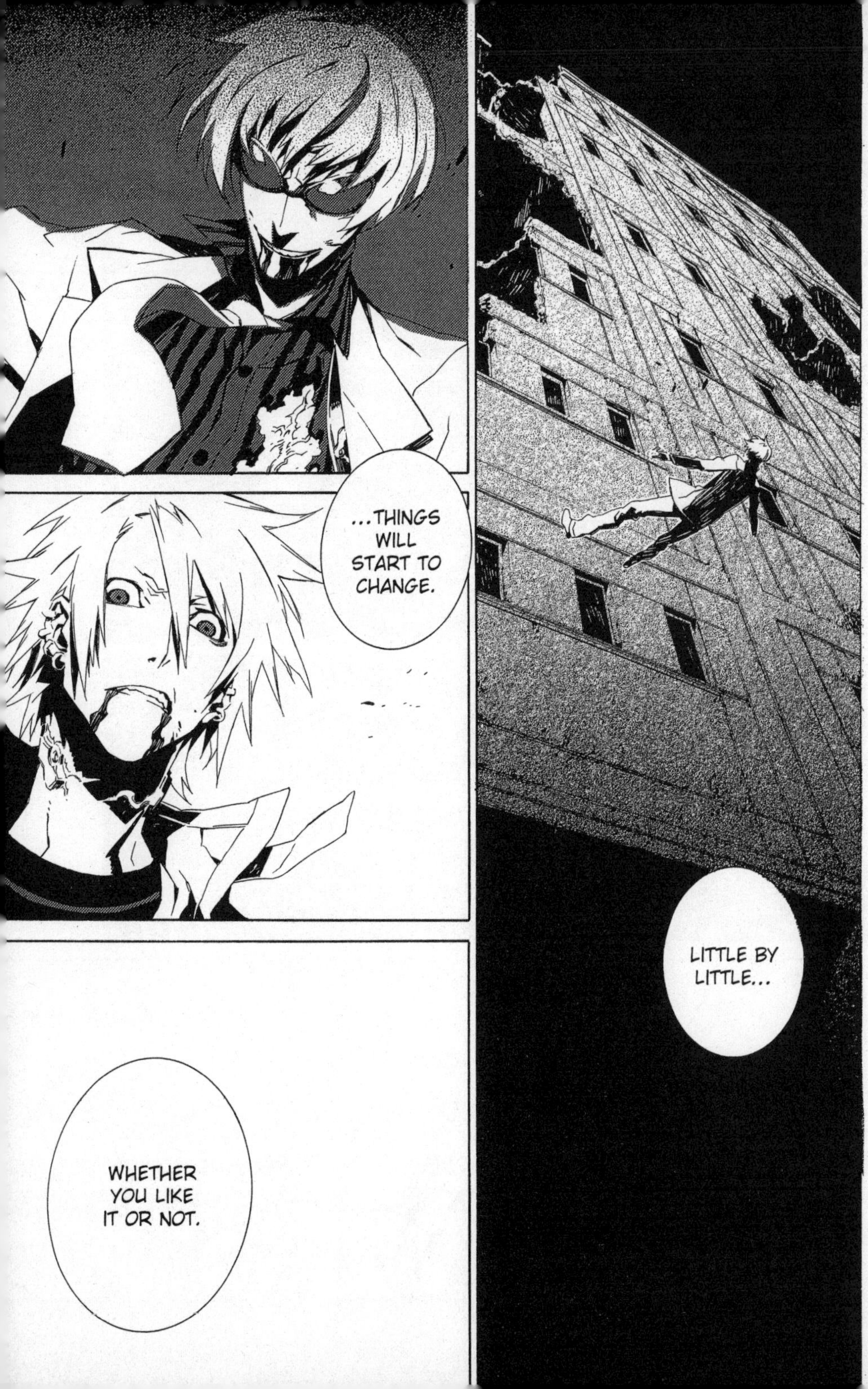
LITTLE BY LITTLE...
...THINGS WILL START TO CHANGE.
WHETHER YOU LIKE IT OR NOT.

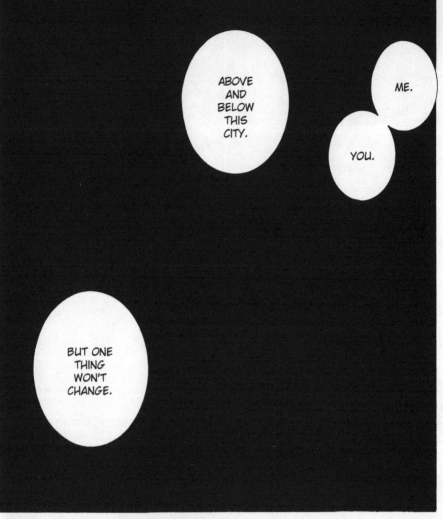

ABOVE AND BELOW THIS CITY.

ME.

YOU.

BUT ONE THING WON'T CHANGE.

NO MATTER WHERE WE ARE, AS LONG AS WE HAVE THESE COLLARS, WE'RE "DOGS."

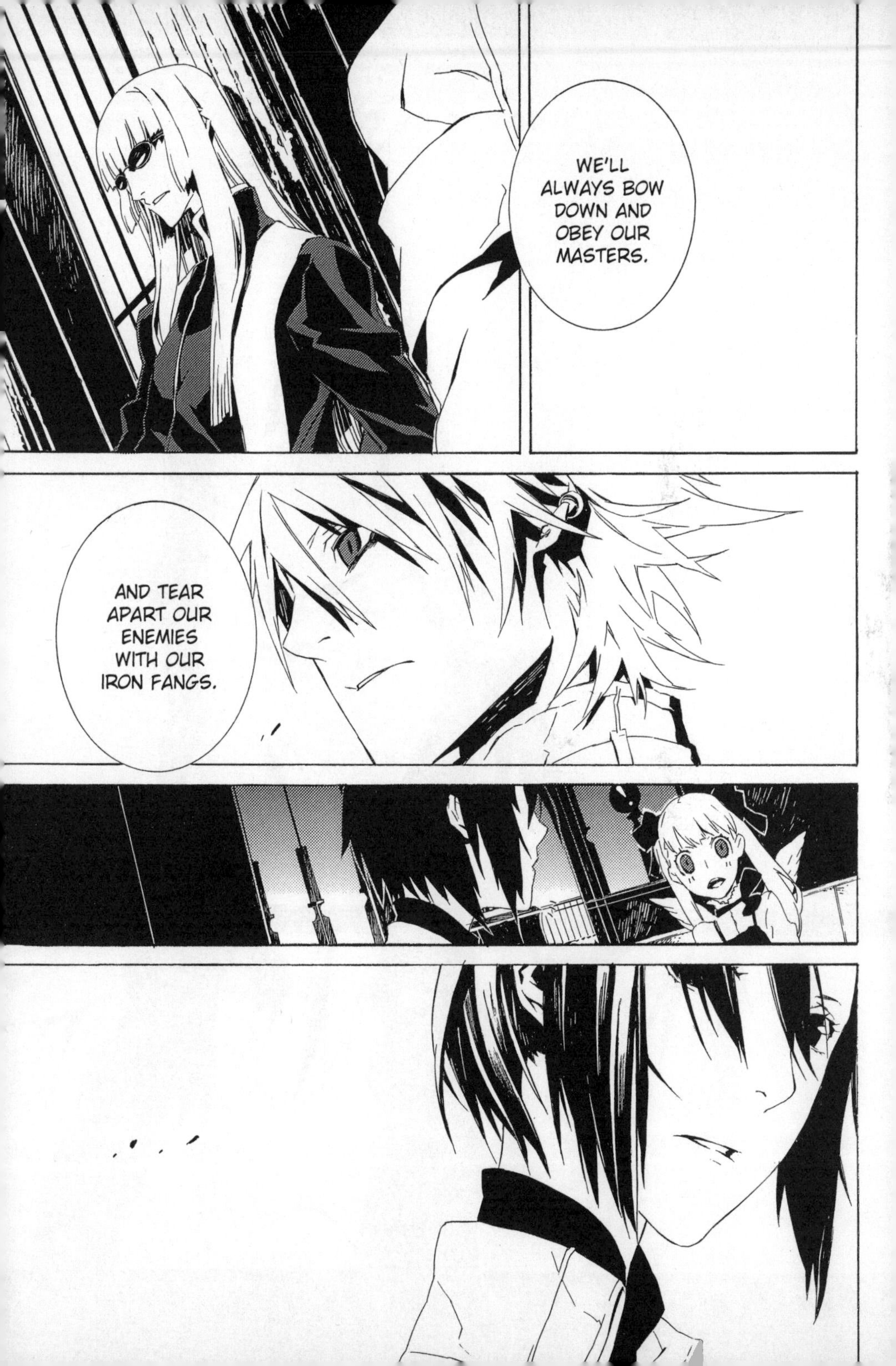
WE'LL ALWAYS BOW DOWN AND OBEY OUR MASTERS.
AND TEAR APART OUR ENEMIES WITH OUR IRON FANGS.

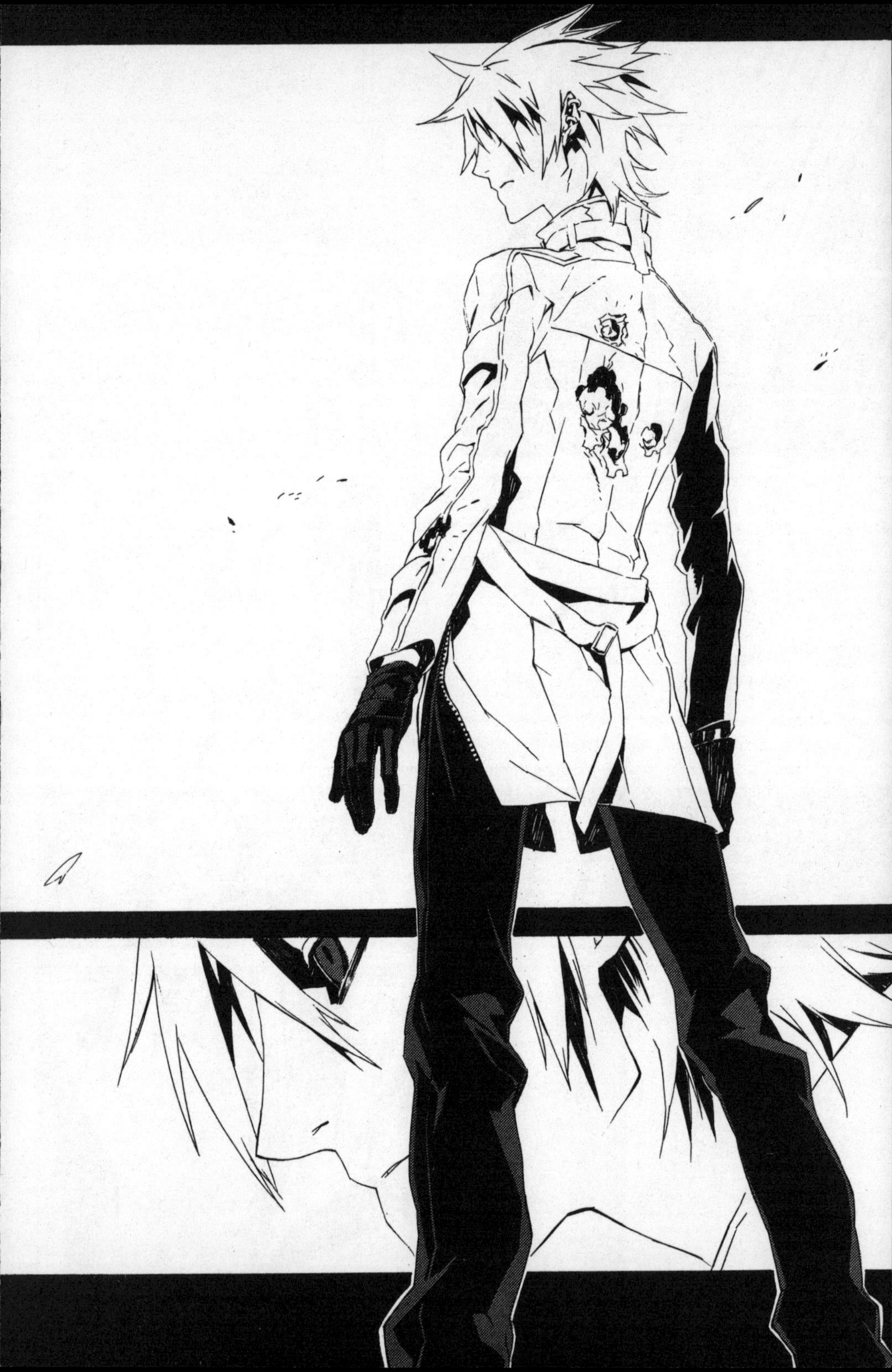

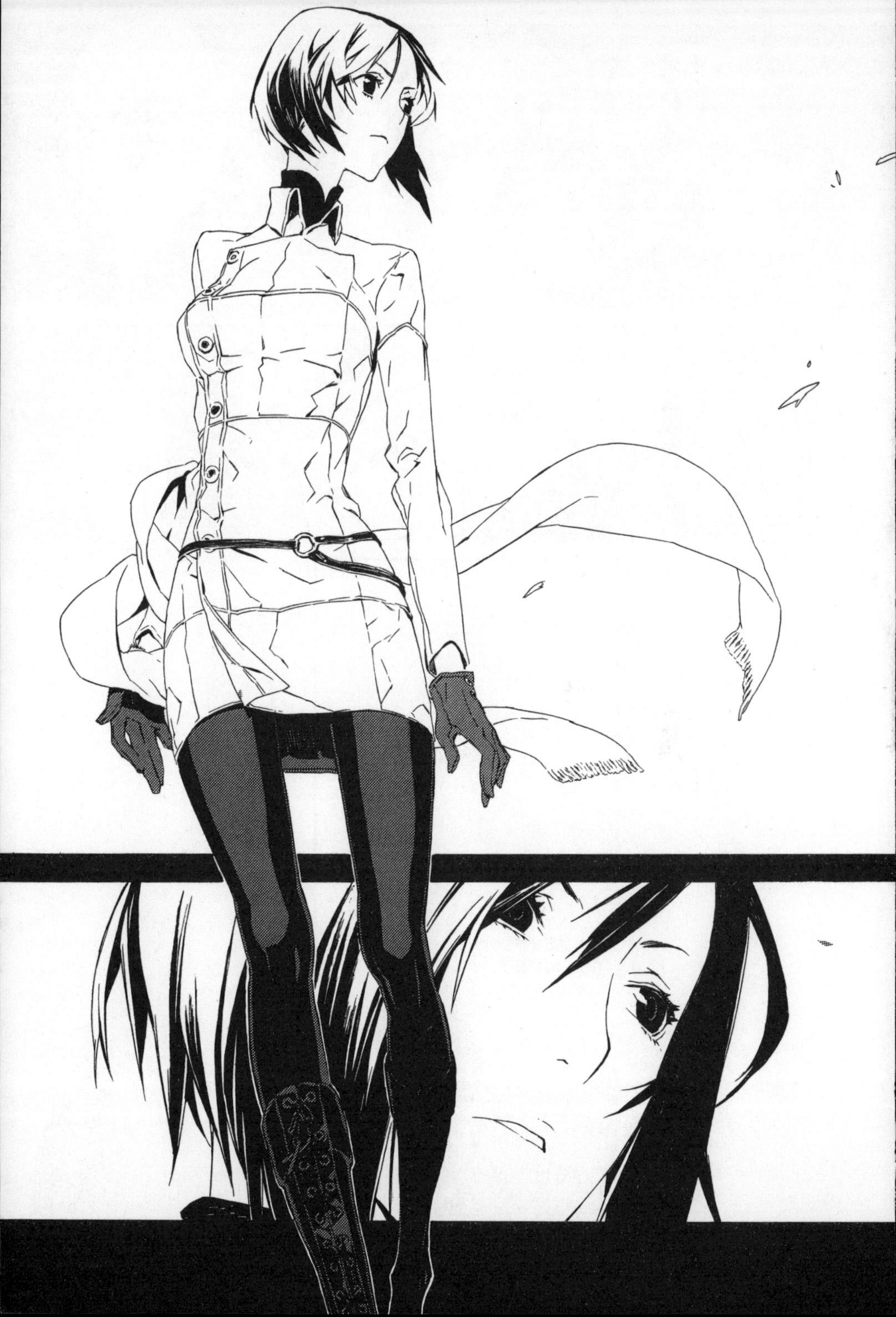

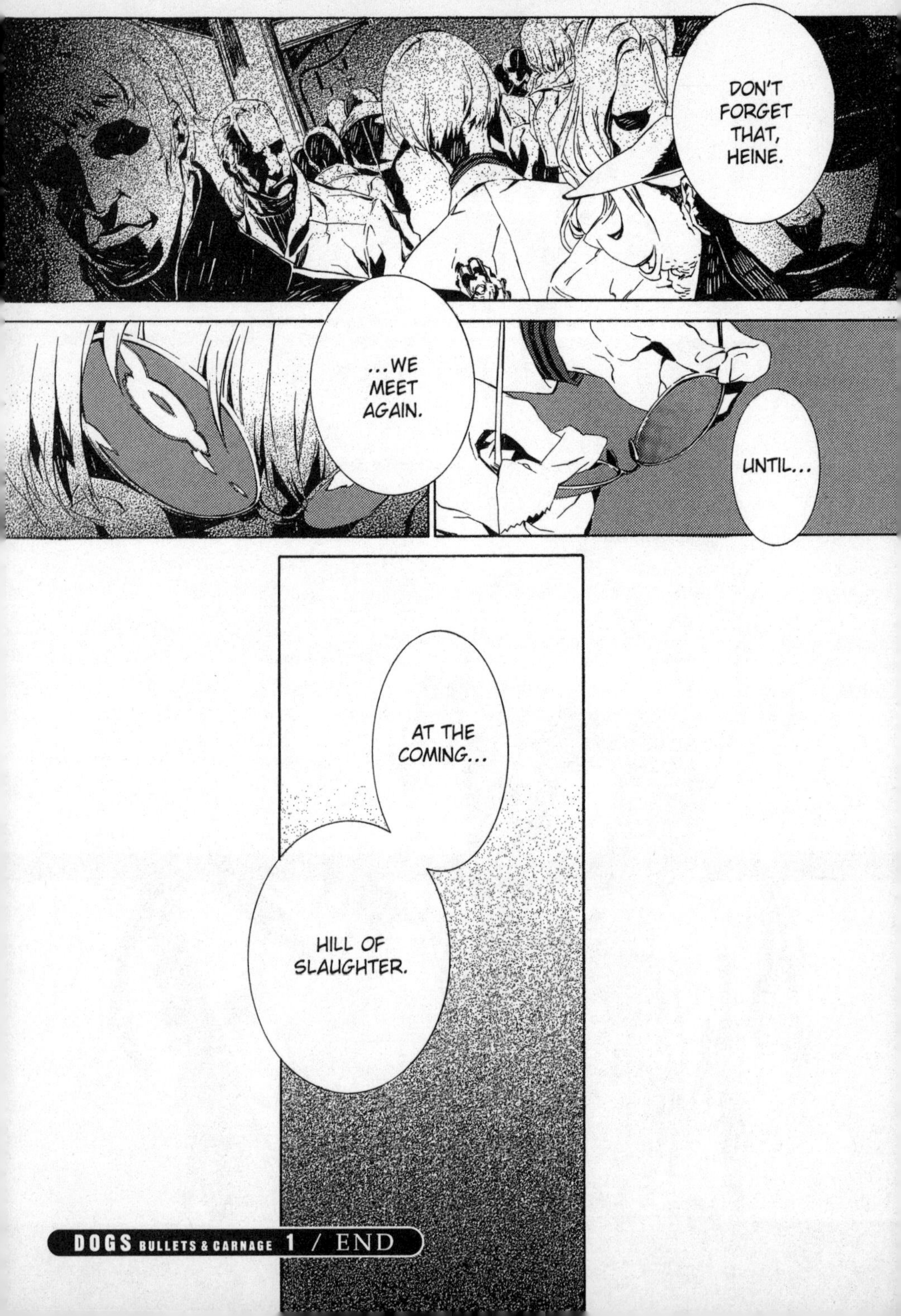
DON'T FORGET THAT, HEINE.
UNTIL...
...WE MEET AGAIN.
AT THE COMING...
HILL OF SLAUGHTER.
DOGS BULLETS & CARNAGE 1 / END

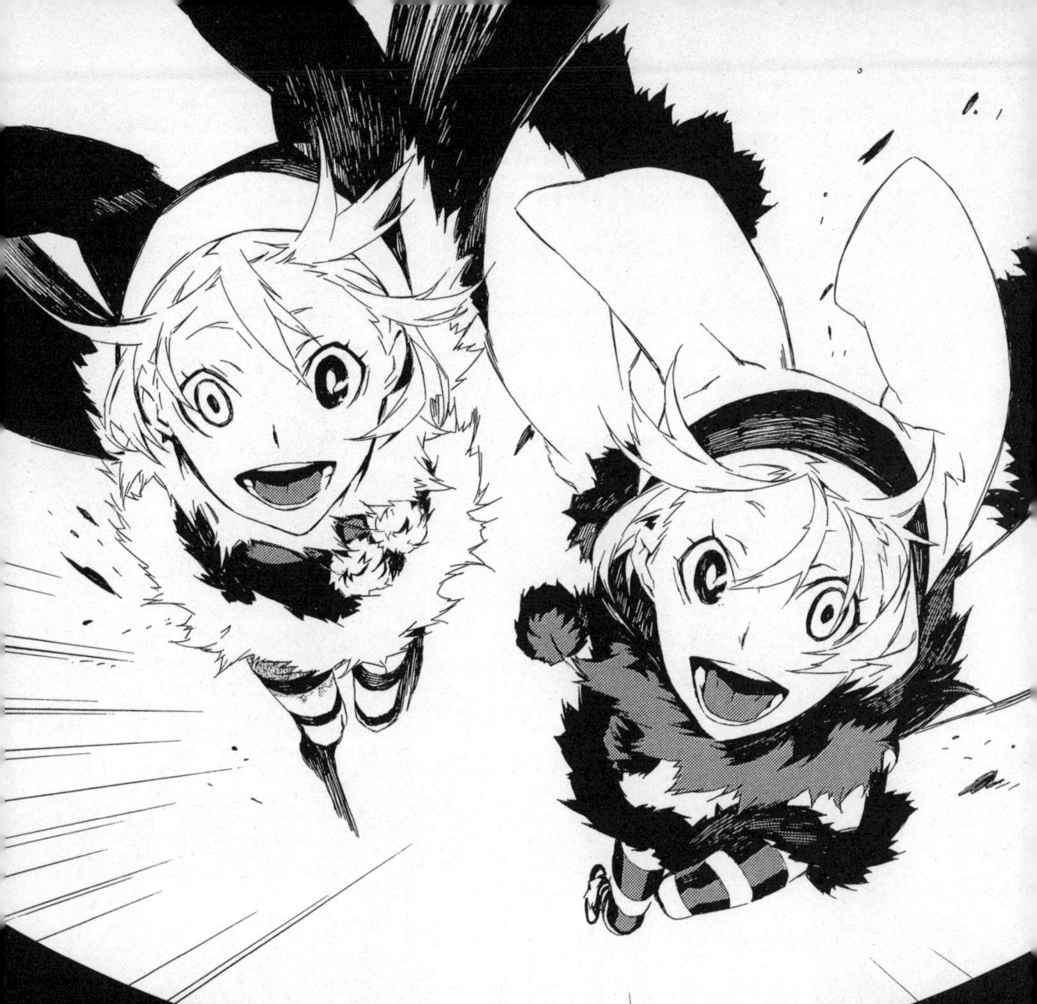

IN THE NEXT VOLUME

In her search for the assassin who "stole her past," Naoto follows Heine and Badou to go see the head of one of the Underground's gangs. But what starts out as a simple quest for information ends up as a rampageous firefight. And just when it seems it couldn't get worse, the Hardcore Twins, Luki and Noki, show up to "play." Which is when things really get interesting...

Available Now

A NOTE ON NAMES AND GUNS

The "Eisen" in the chapter title "Maiden & Eisen" is the German word for "iron," referring to Naoto's sword.

Prof. Angelika Einstürzen's last name is in honor of the equally fierce music of the German industrial band Einstürzende Neubauten.

Luki and Noki's nickname for Giovanni is a contraction of his name and *nii*, the Japanese word for "older brother." *Nii* can also be used to address a boy or young man older than the speaker, even if he's not related.

And the weapons that Giovanni/Gio-ni loves tormenting Heine with so much are based on Walther P-38s.

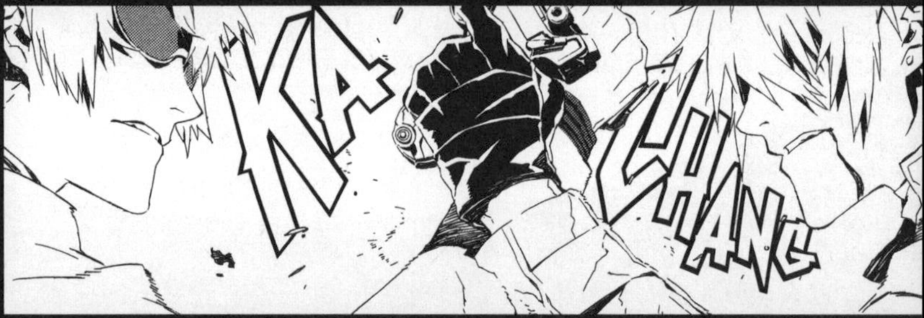
KA
CHANG

SPECIAL THANKS
Kotarou Mori
Kousuke Kurose
Iko Sasagawa
Kuroame
TOMO

SERIES EDITOR
Youichi Hasegawa

BOOK EDITOR
Rie Endou

ORIGINAL DESIGN
LIGHTNING

 ## ABOUT THE AUTHOR

Shirow Miwa debuted in *UltraJump* magazine in 1999 with the short series *Black Mind*. His next series, *Dogs*, published in the magazine from 2000 to 2001, instantly became a popular success. He returned in 2005 with *Dogs: Bullets & Carnage*, which is currently running in *UltraJump*. Miwa also creates illustrations for books, music videos and magazines, and produces doujinshi (independent comics) under the circle name m.m.m.WORKS. His website is http://mmm-gee.net.

DOGS: BULLETS & CARNAGE
Volume 1

VIZ Signature Edition

Story & Art by
SHIROW MIWA

Translation & Adaptation/Alexis Kirsch
Touch-up Art & Lettering/Eric Erbes
Cover & Graphic Design/Sam Elzway
Editor/Leyla Aker

Printed in the U.S.A.

Published by VIZ Media, LLC
P.O. Box 77010
San Francisco, CA 94107

10 9 8 7 6
First printing, August 2009
Sixth printing, September 2014

RATED M FOR MATURE

PARENTAL ADVISORY
DOGS is rated M for Mature and is recommended for mature readers. This volume contains graphic violence and mature themes.

ratings.viz.com

VIZ media
www.viz.com

VIZ SIGNATURE
www.vizsignature.com

IKIGAMI
THE ULTIMATE LIMIT

Dear Citizen,

Congratulations! As part
of its ongoing program
to help combat apathy and
laziness, the government has
randomly selected you to die
within 24 hours.

Thank you for your continued
attention and cooperation.

To participate in future experiments,
get *Ikigami: The Ultimate Limit*
manga—on sale now!

By Motoro Mase

On sale at store.viz.com
Also available at your local
bookstore or comic store.

IKIGAMI © Motoro MASE/Shogakukan Inc.

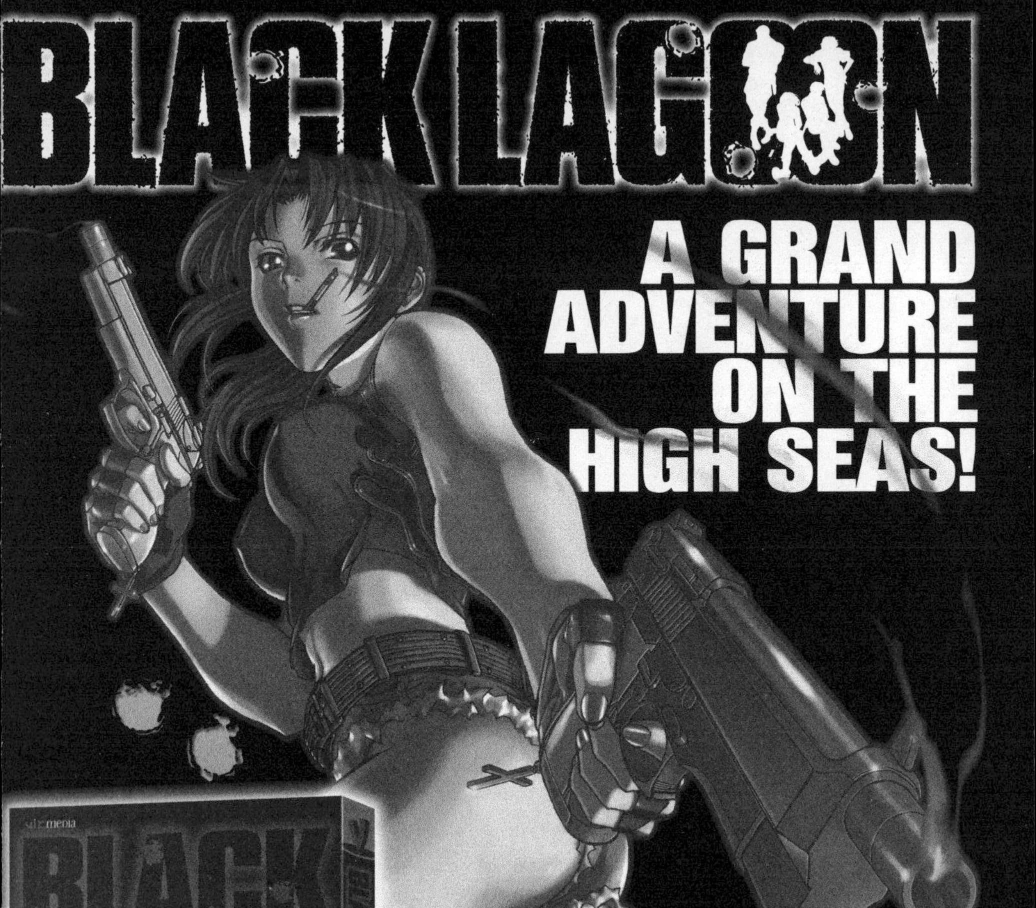
BLACK LAGOON
A GRAND ADVENTURE ON THE HIGH SEAS!
viz media
BLACK LAGOON
001
REI HIROE
PARENTAL ADVISORY EXPLICIT CONTENT

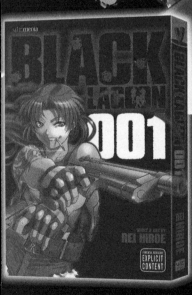

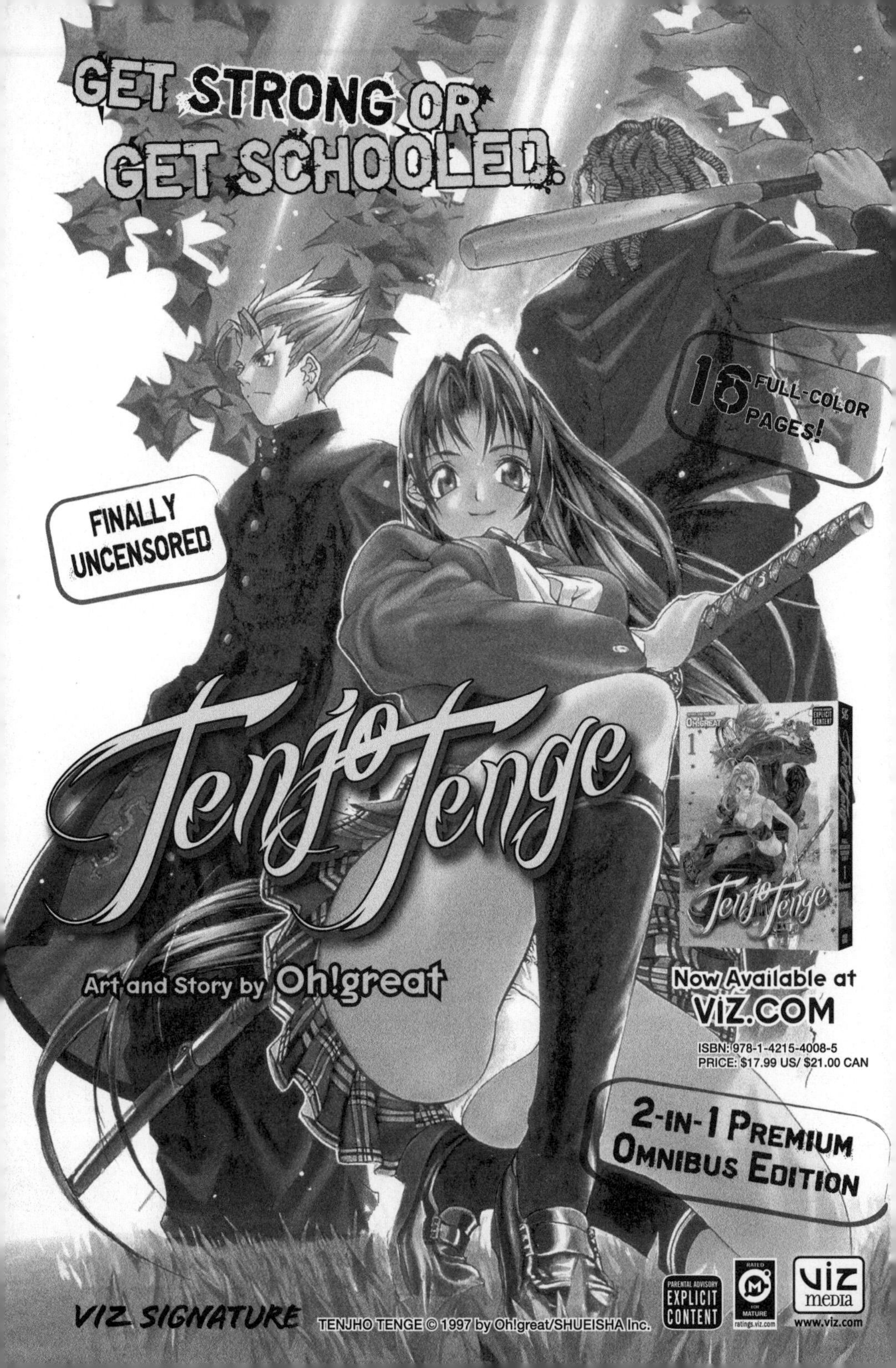

Hey, you're reading the wrong way.

Badou's right—this is actually the end of the book.

To properly enjoy this VIZ graphic novel, please turn it over and begin reading the pages from right to left, starting at the upper right corner of each page and ending at the lower left.

This book has been printed in the Japanese format (right to left) instead of the English format (left to right) in order to preserve the original orientation of the artwork and stay true to the artist's intent. So please flip it over—and have fun.